Lecture Notes in Computer Science 9769

Commenced Publication in 1973
Founding and Former Series Editors:
Gerhard Goos, Juris Hartmanis, and Jan van Leeuwen

More information about this series at http://www.springer.com/series/7412

Lucio Tommaso De Paolis · Antonio Mongelli (Eds.)

Augmented Reality, Virtual Reality, and Computer Graphics

Third International Conference, AVR 2016
Lecce, Italy, June 15–18, 2016
Proceedings, Part II

 Springer

Editors
Lucio Tommaso De Paolis
University of Salento
Lecce
Italy

Antonio Mongelli
University of Salento
Lecce
Italy

ISSN 0302-9743   ISSN 1611-3349 (electronic)
Lecture Notes in Computer Science
ISBN 978-3-319-40650-3   ISBN 978-3-319-40651-0 (eBook)
DOI 10.1007/978-3-319-40651-0

Library of Congress Control Number: 2016941288

LNCS Sublibrary: SL6 – Image Processing, Computer Vision, Pattern Recognition, and Graphics

Printed on acid-free paper

This Springer imprint is published by Springer Nature
The registered company is Springer International Publishing AG Switzerland

Preface

This book contains the contributions to the Third International Conference on Augmented Reality, Virtual Reality and Computer Graphics (SALENTO AVR 2016) that has held in Otranto (Italy) during June 15-18, 2016. We cordially invite you to visit the SALENTO AVR website (http://www.salentoavr.it) where you can find all relevant information about this event.

SALENTO AVR 2016 intended to bring together researchers, scientists, and practitioners to discuss key issues, approaches, ideas, open problems, innovative applications, and trends on virtual and augmented reality, 3D visualization, and computer graphics in the areas of medicine, cultural heritage, arts, education, entertainment, and the industrial and military sectors.

We are very grateful to Patrick Bourdot, co-chair of the conference, as well as the Program Committee and local Organizing Committee members for their support and for reviewing and discussing the submitted papers in a timely and professional manner. We would like to sincerely thank the keynote and tutorial speakers who willingly accepted our invitation and shared their expertise through illuminating talks, helping us to fully meet the conference objectives.

In this edition of SALENTO AVR we were honored to have the following keynote speakers:

- Antonio Emmanuele Uva - Polytechnic Institute of Bari, Italy
- Leo Joskowicz - University of Jerusalem, Israel
- Matteo Dellepiane - ISTI-CNR, Pisa, Italy
- Stefano Baldassi - Meta Company, California, USA

We extend our thanks to the University of Salento and the Department of Engineering for Innovation for the enthusiastic acceptance to sponsor the conference and to provide support in the organization of the event.

SALENTO AVR attracted high-quality paper submissions from many countries. We would like to thank the authors of all accepted papers for submitting and presenting their works at the conference and all the conference attendees for making SALENTO AVR an excellent forum on virtual and augmented reality, facilitating the exchange of ideas, fostering new collaborations, and shaping the future of this exciting research field.

For greater readability of the two volumes, the papers are classified into five main parts that include contributions on: Virtual Reality, Augmented and Mixed Reality, Human–Computer Interaction, Applications of VR/AR in Medicine, and Applications of VR/AR in Cultural Heritage.

We hope the readers will find in these pages interesting material and fruitful ideas for their future work.

June 2016

Lucio Tommaso De Paolis
Antonio Mongelli

Organization

Conference Chair

Lucio Tommaso De Paolis   University of Salento, Italy

Conference Co-chair

Patrick Bourdot   CNRS/LIMSI, University of Paris-Sud, France

Honorary Chair

Giovanni Aloisio   University of Salento, Italy

Scientific Program Committee

Andrea Abate	University of Salerno, Italy
Selim Balcisoy	Sabancı University, Turkey
Vitoantonio Bevilacqua	Polytechnic of Bari, Italy
Monica Bordegoni	Politecnico di Milano, Italy
Davide Borra	NoReal.it, Turin, Italy
Andrea Bottino	Politecnico di Torino, Italy
Pierre Boulanger	University of Alberta, Canada
Andres Bustillo	University of Burgos, Spain
Massimo Cafaro	University of Salento, Italy
Sergio Casciaro	IFC-CNR, Italy
Bruno Carpentieri	University of Salerno, Italy
Marcello Carrozzino	Scuola Superiore Sant'Anna, Italy
Mario Ciampi	ICAR/CNR, Italy
Pietro Cipresso	IRCCS Istituto Auxologico Italiano, Italy
Lucio Colizzi	CETMA, Italy
Jean-Marc Cieutat	ESTIA Recherche, France
Arnis Cirulis	Vidzeme University of Applied Sciences, Latvia
Yuri Dekhtyar	Riga Technical University, Latvia
Matteo Dellepiane	National Research Council (CNR), Italy
Giorgio De Nunzio	University of Salento, Italy
Francisco José Domínguez Mayo	University of Seville, Spain
Aldo Franco Dragoni	Università Politecnica delle Marche, Italy
Italo Epicoco	University of Salento, Italy
María José Escalona Cuaresma	University of Seville, Spain

Krzysztof Walczak   Poznan University, Poland
Anthony Whitehead   Carleton University, Canada

Organizing Committee

Ilenia Paladini   University of Salento, Italy
Valerio De Luca   University of Salento, Italy
Antonio Meo   University of Salento, Italy
Pietro Vecchio   University of Salento, Italy

Contents – Part II

Applications of VR/AR in Cultural Heritage

Human-Computer Interaction

Contents – Part I

Augmented and Mixed Reality

Applications of VR/AR in Medicine

A Novel Tabletop and Tablet-Based Display System to Support Learner-Centric Ophthalmic Anatomy Education

R. Codd-Downey[1], R. Shewaga[2], A. Uribe-Quevedo[2,3,4],
B. Kapralos[2,5]([⊠]), K. Kanev[1,2,5], and M. Jenkin[1,5]

[1] Electrical Engineering and Computer Science, York University, Toronto, Canada
{robert,jenkin}@cse.yorku.ca
[2] Faculty of Business and Information Technology,
University of Ontario Institute of Technology, Oshawa, Canada
{rob.shewaga,bill.kapralos}@uoit.ca
[3] Industrial Engineering, Nueva Granada Mil. University, Bogota, Colombia
alvaro.j.uribe@ieee.org
[4] The Games Institute, University of Waterloo, Waterloo, Canada
[5] Research Institute of Electronics, Shizuoka University, Hamamatsu, Japan
kanev@rie.shizuoka.ac.jp

Abstract. This work couples the use of augmented and virtual reality, a tabletop display, and mobile devices (tablets and smartphones) to develop an innovative, system to support learner-centric anatomy education and training. The system provides a common tabletop interaction surface where a global view of an anatomical model is provided. This global view is available to all of the users (instructor and trainees) whom can interact with the model using the touch-sensitive tabletop display surface. In addition to this global view, each of the trainees has access to the model through a mobile device that is synchronized with the global view and provides each trainee with an individualized (local) view of the scene and interaction mechanisms. This paper outlines our integrated tabletop computer-tablet display and its use to facilitate virtual-based eye anatomy training.

Keywords: Tabletop computer · Mobile device · Anatomy education · Individualized education · Virtual reality · Augmented reality

1 Introduction

Human anatomy is an integral component of medical education that helps prepare the medical undergraduate trainee for their training in clinical specialties [3]. Human anatomy training also provides trainees with a first "impression" regarding the structure which forms the basis for understanding both pathologic and clinical problems [11], and is vital to ensure safe and efficient medical practice [12]. Human anatomy training often occurs in the laboratory with the

L.T. De Paolis and A. Mongelli (Eds.): AVR 2016, Part II, LNCS 9769, pp. 3–12, 2016.
DOI: 10.1007/978-3-319-40651-0_1

instructor and the trainees around a cadaver table with a cadaver (or dummy cadaver/manakin) placed on top of it. Such a scenario lends itself nicely to a tabletop display platform whereby the cadaver table and the cadaver are replaced with a tabletop display and three-dimensional rendering of the cadaver respectively. This allows the instructor and the trainees to interact actively with the rendered model (e.g., remove anatomical layers), as a group, similar to the traditional setting. Such an approach eliminates the use of a cadaver (at least during the early stages of anatomy training), and the complications associated with real cadavers (e.g., storage, acquisition and disposal, potential risk for pathogen transfer, and cost). Furthermore, it allows for numerous learning opportunities not available when working with a cadaver. For example, labels can overlay the anatomical structures to provide the trainees with information regarding the name and function of the structures. Although useful, the tabletop display and the supported interactions follow a "one size fits all" approach that does not facilitate learner-centric education whereby the instruction is tailored to each individual trainee to account for their prior knowledge level, background, and learning styles. How can one exploit the advantages of a shared tabletop display experience while providing personalized information and interaction to individual participants?

Taking advantage of the inherent collaborative nature of tabletop displays, we have recently begun developing a novel display system that couples a tabletop display, and mobile display technologies (e.g., tablets and smartphones) provided to each trainee, to overcome the "one size fits all" approach inherent when using a tabletop display on its own. Our display system provides a physical infrastructure for promoting learner-centered medical education whereby the information presented to each trainee's mobile device is customized for them to specifically account for their level of learning (e.g., beginner, intermediate, advanced). Rather than multiplexing the main tabletop display as described by Smith and Piekarski [13], our novel infrastructure allows for the seamless interaction between the tabletop display and individual mobile devices.

Each trainee makes use of a mobile display and interaction device (e.g., a tablet or a smartphone) that is synchronized and localized within the global tabletop display, thus providing them with an individualized (local) and interactable view of the scene. This allows the trainees to share a common public workspace (i.e., the tabletop display), while having access to their own private workspace (i.e., mobile device). For example, a novice trainee may choose to view a labeling layer to augment the global view by providing labels to key components of the anatomical model being displayed, while a more advanced trainee may choose to view further anatomical information that includes more specific features than those presented in the global view intended for all of the trainees. Furthermore, the coupling of the tabletop display with the mobile devices enables those trainees who cannot interact with the global view directly (e.g., in a larger classroom setting where it is not feasible for each trainee to be placed around the tabletop display), to take advantage of what the others are doing through remote viewing on their mobile device. More specifically, trainees standing close to the tabletop display can obtain a first-person "hands-on" experience while others lacking a direct line of sight may use their mobile device to keep track of what is happening thus allowing them to follow what others are doing on the tabletop display. This essentially extends the collaborative nature of the tabletop display to everyone in the room and beyond (e.g., those participating remotely), and not only to the limited number of trainees around it.

Although the infrastructure developed has a general purpose application structure, currently we are focusing on its application in eye anatomy education for medical trainees and technicians since the discrete anatomy of the eye's intricate oculomotor system is conceptually difficult for many novice trainees to grasp. Such training is difficult but clinically important given that the eye's oculomotor system is one of the most common sites of clinical intervention in the treatment of a variety of eye disorders [1]. For example, with respect to the ocular ultrasound procedure (a procedure that uses high-frequency sound waves to produce and measure detailed images of the eye), it is important to know where the resultant ultrasound beam is being placed according to the probe position and the eye structures being examined. The most challenging aspect of the ocular ultrasound procedure is the conversion of the two-dimensional slice of an image displayed on a conventional two-dimensional display into three-dimensional interpretations [8]. Despite the presence of simulators that allow for three-dimensional viewing, the majority of existing ophthalmic simulators demonstrate the equipment setup and three-dimensional image perception within a two-dimensional viewing environment but do not simulate the three-dimensional nature of the eye and its structure. This leads to problems for the trainee with respect to depth perception and spatial awareness, both of which are crucial given that the manipulation of instruments within the eye involves distances that are microscopic [8]. Virtual reality-based technologies can be used to facilitate the three-dimensional interpretation of two-dimensional image slices (e.g., using changes in perspective to allow the trainee to view different slices or a combination of slices), in a cost-effective and safe manner. Finally, it has been suggested that future ophthalmic surgeons can develop their hand-eye coordination and become accustomed to the small dimensions of the eye using virtual reality-based tools and technologies [16].

2   Background

Although use of tabletop displays in medical education is limited at present, there are several applications of tabletop displays intended to facilitate medical education and training. For example, the Anatomage Table resembles a typical operating table or hospital bed and the content obtained from real patients (e.g., data are from real patient scans or cadavers), perfectly illustrate the anatomical realism of a living human. The table is capable of displaying "true human gross anatomy in real life size" [2, 4]. Another example is the ongoing work of Dubrowski et al. [5] that is seeing the development of a strategy-based, learner-centric virtual learning environment (VLE) to facilitate interprofessional education in pediatric critical care. The system employs a tabletop display in conjunction with novel image-based sensing and positioning technologies to enable multiple trainees (each taking on the role of one of the critical care team members), to work together in order to stabilize a pediatric patient.

Specific to ophthalmology, we are not aware of any training applications that employ tabletop displays although several virtual simulations and computer-based training systems are currently available. For example, Allen et al. [1] developed an interactive, three-dimensional (3D) virtual model of the muscles and cranial nerves of the oculomotor system within the eye for eye-based anatomy education. The EON EyeSim Virtual Reality ophthalmic training simulator includes realistic three-dimensional ocular anatomy with interactive features, and allows trainees to explore the intricate structures of the eye including pupillary, ocular motility, and cranial nerve dysfunctions in a virtual patient [6].

3   Ophthalmoscope Training

The test environment described here is intended to simulate and facilitate ophthalmoscope training (an ophthalmoscope is a diagnostic clinical device that allows for observing the eye on the inside from the retina). Initial stages of ophthalmoscope training involve reviewing the structures of the eye followed by training in the use of the ophthalmoscope itself. In this test application we utilize the tabletop-mobile device display in two different modes. In the first mode, (*anatomical mode*), the trainees learn the necessary anatomical aspects of the eye while in the second mode (*inspection mode*), the trainees learn to use the ophthalmoscope. In the inspection mode, the mobile device takes on the role of the ophthalmoscope and simulates the ophthalmoscope's function (see [7]).

3.1   Infrastructure

An overview of the integrated display/interaction system is provided in Fig. 1. There has been substantive work in the research and industrial communities on the integration of multiple hand-held devices with a common shared display, and this earlier work is leveraged here. For example, Nacenta et al. [9] examined the application of perspective to address issues associated with multi-display environments where the displays are at different locations and orientations to the trainee and developed a perspective-aware environment (E-conic) that supports dynamic perspective correction of graphical user interface (GUI) objects [9]. In the work presented here the displays and interaction surfaces of the mobile devices are rendered using the Unity game engine [10], and individual mobile devices are integrated through a common communication and 3D model infrastructure. A standard AR/VR marker-based localization system (described in Sect. 3.3) is employed to place the tabletop display and mobile devices within a common rendering 3D space and a communications infrastructure is used to ensure a common rendering model/interaction across all of the display devices.

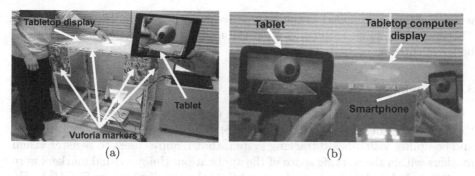

(a)   (b)

Fig. 1. System overview. The tabletop display (anatomical mode) and individualized views as seen from the trainee's viewpoint and displayed on their mobile device (inspection mode). (a) Vuforia markers placed around the tabletop display and single mobile (tablet) device. (b) Multiple mobile devices (tablet and smartphone).

Models, anatomy databases, tracker marker data and the code-base itself are pre-deployed to all devices so that intra-device communication is limited to common state information.

3.2 3D Eye Model

To obtain a suitable digital eye model, anatomical references where considered from traditional sources of study such as photographs, illustrations, and computer tomography scans by researchers and medical experts at the Mil. Nueva Granada University in Bogota, Colombia. This information allowed us to define the forms, the relations, and the textures of each of the eye's parts. The 3D eye model is comprised of several layers and consists of 447, 584 vertices and spherical mapped textures to provide realism (see Fig. 2). To allow content exploration, the model is comprised of several layers, each layer describing different anatomical structures of the eye. The anatomical model is rendered on the tabletop display and on each of the individual mobile devices running clients of the application. Trainees are able to augment the anatomical model on their devices as needed (e.g., a novice trainee can choose to label components of the anatomical model),

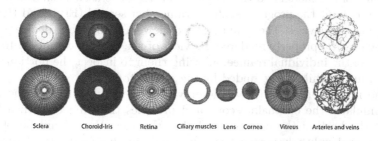

Sclera   Choroid-Iris   Retina   Ciliary muscles Lens Cornea   Vitreus   Arteries and veins

Fig. 2. Decomposed 3D eye model with textures and edge views.

while remaining grounded in the common view of the shared tabletop display. There are no explicit requirements on the model being used so any model can be substituted as necessary.

3.3 Tracking

Tracking the position and orientation of the mobile devices is accomplished using the Vuforia augmented reality platform [15]. The Vuforia platform is a marker- and computer vision-based tracking system that requires users to register visual markers within the working space of the application. Unique visual markers were printed and placed on top of and around the tabletop display (see Fig. 1(a)). By locating (and tracking) these markers, the position and orientation of the camera (on each mobile device) relative to these physical markers can be determined at interactive rates. Surrounding the tabletop display with visual markers allows for the mobile devices to synchronize (and communicate) with the tabletop display irrespective of their position. For proper operation, at least one of the markers must be visible to a mobile device.

3.4 The User Interface

As previously described, the tabletop display user interface is comprised of two modes: (i) *anatomical mode*, and (ii) *inspection mode*. The anatomical mode (see Fig. 3(a)), provides the trainees with an anatomical view of the eye and mechanisms to choose which aspects to display and whether they should be labelled in specific views. An orthographic view of the eye is rendered on the tabletop display (and to each individual mobile device), which trainees can manipulate (e.g., separate the components of the eye, toggle the visibility of the eye's components, and zoom in/out). The anatomical mode interface consists of a main menu, camera menu, object menu, layers menu, and debug menu toggle. The main menu is used to switch to the inspection mode and to reset the program, whereas the camera menu is used to manipulate the camera in 3D space around the model (pan, zoom, rotate, and center). The object menu is used to select specific components of the model in 3D space in order to highlight them (with a red glow around the object), and present a menu with additional detail on the selected component. The layers menu is used to toggle the visibility of separate components of the model and the debug menu toggle is used to show additional information about the program such as frames per second (FPS) and the number of connected devices. The individualized view on each mobile device provides the trainee with a properly rendered 3D view of the anatomical model from the viewpoint of the individual trainee, allowing them to inspect the portions of the eye individually while being guided by the instructor.

In the inspection mode (available only on the mobile devices), the mobile device simulates the ophthalmoscope and provides the trainees with a "scope view" of the back of the cornea simulating the view that would be obtained with an actual ophthalmoscope (see Fig. 3(b)). In this mode, the trainee can zoom as desired and scroll the view of the back of the eye to highlight specific areas. Within this view, annotations can also be turned on in order to label different structural components of the cornea. The inspection mode allows the user to zoom the scope as well as pan the view of the cornea, whereby the anatomical structures of the cornea can be highlighted. The inspection mode interface consists of a main menu, static menu, inspect menu, captions toggle, and debug menu toggle. The main menu is used to switch to the anatomical mode and to reset the program, while the static menu is used to set the tabletop display into a "static" state where it will not affect the scoped view. The inspection mode menu allows the user to zoom the ophthalmoscope and pan the view of the cornea, while the captions toggle toggles the visibility of highlights showing the separate components of the cornea. Finally, the debug menu toggle is used to show additional information about the program including frames per second (FPS), and the number of connected devices.

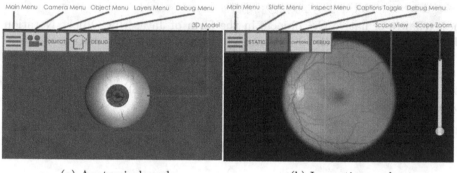

(a) Anatomical mode.   (b) Inspection mode.

Fig. 3. Two modes of operation to support ophthalmoscope training. (a) The anatomical mode allows the trainees to learn about the necessary anatomical aspects of the eye. (b) In the inspection mode, the trainees learn to use the ophthalmoscope.

The tabletop display and paired mobile devices interact on a tabletop-dependent basis. In other words, the position and rotation of the model in addition to the visible status of each individual component comprising the model are controlled at the tabletop display. Rotating the model on the tabletop display correspondingly rotates the world-space orientation of the eyeball on each mobile device's view. Similarly, hiding separate components of the model on the tabletop display also hides these components in the mobile device view.

3.5 Communication Architecture

An overview of the communication architecture is provided in Fig. 4. Each mobile device establishes a connection with the tabletop display and once this connection has been established, two-way communication between the mobile device and the tabletop display can take place. Communication is facilitated through

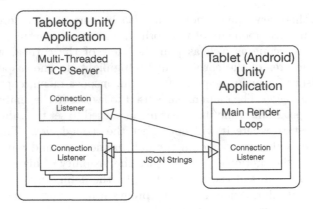

Fig. 4. Communication architecture overview.

the exchange of native C# objects in the form of Javascript Object Notation (JSON) strings [14]. Each JSON string contains sufficient information to reconstruct the object at the receiving end of the communication pipeline. This enables a common global state to be maintained across all of the rendering devices (tabletop display and mobile devices), and for interactions on the individual devices to be reflected in the display available on each.

4 Discussion and Future Work

Virtual simulation can provide a safe and cost-effective alternative to traditional medical education and training methods. However, virtual simulation rarely facilitate a learner-centric approach whereby the information presented to the trainees is customized/individualized to each trainee on a per-needed basis. Here we have described preliminary work towards the development of a novel display system that couples a tabletop display with mobile devices (e.g., one or more tablets or smartphones), that are allocated to each trainee, to promote learner-centered human anatomy education. Although coupling multiple devices is not necessarily novel, our contribution includes the novel infrastructure that allows the seamless interaction between the tabletop display and the individual mobile device to promote learner-centric simulation-based education.

An often identified advantage of a tabletop display is its ability to promote collaboration amongst its users (trainees) and therefore, it is a concern that providing each trainee with a mobile device that they interact with during the training session may interfere with the inherent collaborative nature of the tabletop computing platform. However, the benefits this interface provides, outweighs this potential drawback. The user interface is designed to provide flexibility to its users and to ultimately facilitate learner-centric simulation-based education. The mobile device is intended to augment the primary tabletop display and provide individualized information to the trainees as needed. Furthermore, it also allows the number of trainees to take part in a particular training session to be increased beyond the few that are located around the table and able to physically interact with it. Trainees can now participate in the training session remotely and can, through their mobile device, not only view the training session, but become active participants within it. Finally, the system can operate with the tabletop display alone with zero or more mobile devices and thus the instructor/educator ultimately has the freedom to choose how the training session is to proceed.

Although we have developed a functioning prototype, further work remains. More specifically, currently trainees are able to view their mobile devices as they wish. Future work will further investigate the interaction between the main tabletop display and the mobile devices and this will include examining various models of interaction between the tabletop display and the mobile devices. For example, rather than allowing each trainee to interact with their mobile device as they wish, perhaps the instructor should control when to activate a particular mobile device and determine what information to provide the mobile device with. Future work will also examine what, if any, effect the individual mobile devices (with their associated different view and augmented information), have on the collaborative nature of the tabletop display.

Informally, the Vuforia marker-based tracking platform that is used to synchronize the individual mobile devices with the tabletop display has demonstrated decent performance. However, relying on specific preregistered visual-based markers is prone to tracking errors depending on the ability of the mobile device to locate the target. Although we have surrounded the tabletop display with a large number of visual targets, there is a possibility that all visual targets will be occluded to one ore more mobile devices, particularly when considering a large number trainees positioned around the tabletop display. This is further complicated as the distance between the mobile device and the tabletop display is increased. In addition, localization and tracking of the target can be greatly influenced by various external factors including lighting conditions, and occlusion of the targets by objects and other users in the environment. Future work includes improving upon the Vuforia-based tracking method and conducting usability testing of the system to examine the functionality of the user interface, and user-based interactions. Finally, future work will also see more thorough pre- and post-testing of the eye simulation with medical students (including ophthalmology trainees), to quantify its effectiveness as a learning tool.

Acknowledgments. The financial support of the *Natural Sciences and Engineering Research Council of Canada* (NSERC), and the *Japan Society for the Promotion of Science*, is gratefully acknowledged. The financial support from a KAKENHI Grant (Number 25560109) and the Research Institute of Electronics, Shizuoka University, Japan in the form of a Cooperative Research Project grant is also acknowledged. We also appreciate the assistance of the Virtual Reality Center of the Mil. Nueva Granada University in Bogota, Colombia who provided us with their 3D eye model.

References

1. Allen, L.K., Bhattacharyya, S., Wilson, T.D.: Development of an interactive anatomical three-dimensional eye model. Anat. Sci. Educ. **8**(3), 275–282 (2014)
2. Anatomage: Eyesim: A virtual reality ophthalmic simulator for medical educators and students (2015). http://www.anatomage.com
3. Bay, B.H., Ling, E.A.: Teaching of anatomy in the new millennium. Singapore Med. J. **48**(3), 182 (2007)
4. Brown, J., Stonelake, S., Anderson, W., Abdulla, M., Toms, C., Farfus, A., Wilton, J.: Medical student perception of anatomage: a 3D interactive anatomy dissection table. Int. J. Surg. **23**, S17–S18 (2015)
5. Dubrowski, A., Kapralos, B., Kanev, K., Jenkin, M.: Interprofessional critical care training: interactive virtual learning environments and simulations. In: The Sixth IEEE International Conference on Information, Intelligence, Systems and Applications, Corfu, Greece (2015)
6. EON: Eyesim, a virtual reality ophthalmic simulator for medical educators and students (2015). http://www.eonreality.com
7. American Academy of Pediatrics: Pediatrics eye examination in infants, children, and young adults by pediatricians. Pediatrics **111**(4), 902–907 (2003)
8. Mustafa, M.S., Montgomery, J., Atta, H.R.: A novel educational tool for teaching ocular ultrasound. Clin. Ophthalmol. **2011**(5), 857–860 (2011)
9. Nacenta, M.A., Sakurai, S., Yamaguchi, T., Miki, Y., Itoh, Y., Kitamura, Y., Subramanian, S., Gutwin, C.: E-conic: a perspective-aware interface for multi-display environments. In: Proceedings of the 20th Annual ACM Symposium on User Interface Software and Technology, Newport, RI, USA, pp. 279–288 (2007)
10. Okita, A.: Learning C# Programming with Unity 3D. CRC Press (2014)
11. Papa, V., Vaccarezza, M.: Teaching anatomy in the XXI century: new aspects and pitfalls. Sci. World J. **2013**, 1–5 (2013). Article ID: 310348
12. Raftery, A.: Anatomy teaching in the UK. Surgery **5**(1), 1–2 (2006)
13. Smith, R.T., Piekarski, W.: Public and private workspaces on tabletop displays. In: 9th Conference on Australasian User Interface, Wollongong, Australia, pp. 51–54 (2008)
14. Sriparasa, S.S.: JavaScript and JSON Essentials. Packt Publishing, Birmingham (2013)
15. Vuforia: Augmented reality (vuforia) (2015). https://developer.qualcomm.com/mobile-development/add-advanced-features/augmented-reality-vuforia
16. Wagner, C., Schill, M.A., Hennen, M., Knorz, M.C., Hinckers, N., Mnner, R., Ruf, T.: A virtual reality simulator in development for training, teaching intraocular surgery. Ocular Surgery News (US Edition), 15 December 2000

Using a Short Video Animation to Assist with the Diagnosis of Sleep Disorders in Young Children

Blanca Guinea[1], Mario Alaguero[1], Fernando Melgosa[1],
and Andres Bustillo[2(✉)]

[1] Department of History and Geography, University of Burgos, Burgos, Spain
blanca.guinea@universidaddeburgos.es,
{malaguero, fmelgosa}@ubu.es
[2] Department of Civil Engineering, University of Burgos,
Avda Cantabria s/n, Burgos, Spain
abustillo@ubu.es

Abstract. A short video animation is designed to mitigate the fears of children admitted to hospital for the diagnosis of their sleep disorders. The video animation was produced following recommendations from medical staff involved in the diagnosis. Images taken from the animation decorated the hospital ward, to bring the video characters to life in the children's minds. Finally, standard diagnosis of sleep disorders was performed by means of polysomnography on two groups of children: a reference and an evaluation group. Both parents and children responded to questionnaires that measured their satisfaction and the perception of their experiences. Preliminary findings extracted from the polysomnography showed that the videos helped to relax nervous children, especially sensitive to the hospital environment, and shortened Sleep Onset Latency and Non-REM latency. Besides, the responses to the questionnaires suggested that the video also reassured the parents whose moods helped the children to accept their hospitalization.

Keywords: Short video animation · Sleep disorders · Children · Polysomnography · Blender

1 Introduction

Sleep-disorder diagnosis techniques for children can be helped by the use of non-intrusive methods such as questionnaires. Nevertheless, hospitalization is in all cases required to perform polysomnography during sleep time [1]. Polysomnography involves continuous, supervised monitoring of the patient's sleep and waking states, for over 6 night hours without pharmacologically induced sleep. But children suffer stressful situations in hospitalization that can affect the sleep process: late bedtimes, nighttime wakings, and shorter total sleep time; these difficulties have been identified in children of very different ages, from toddlers [2] to children [3]. Stress is intensified because the polysomnogram test is a very uncomfortable diagnosis technique that involves the connection of multiple electrodes to the child's head throughout the night.

© Springer International Publishing Switzerland 2016
L.T. De Paolis and A. Mongelli (Eds.): AVR 2016, Part II, LNCS 9769, pp. 13–29, 2016.
DOI: 10.1007/978-3-319-40651-0_2

Although the children could be monitored at home through the use of telediagnosis [4, 5], new ways of relaxing children during hospitalization would improve the diagnosis process. In the case of babies, the use of neuro-based music appears to be a suitable solution [6], but this technique is not so suitable for children, because their reasoning ability requires an understanding of the need for hospitalization. In the case of sleep disorder diagnosis, the children will hold some conception, within their limited capabilities, of what a sleep disorder is, and the need for polysomnography. This observation prompted staff at the Sleep Diagnosis Unit of the University Hospital of Burgos (Spain) and the University of Burgos to search for new ways of helping children to enter a relaxed state of sleep under polysomnography conditions in hospital environments.

This research proposes a solution from a perspective that is not usually associated with hospitals: the ad-hoc development of a short 3D video animation and its integration in the hospital environment where the children are treated. Children are eager to watch video animations that can stimulate the infantile imagination much more than non-fiction films, awakening greater empathy in the child with the characters in the video [7]. The use of short video animations to explain sleep disorders to children were first described in 2014 for jet-lag [8]. However, only 2D animations were created and no measurements were taken of its effect on the children's own understanding of jet lag in terms of a sleep disorder. The absence of any analysis of its effects is comprehensible as the video was designed for in-flight viewing; quite unlike the scientific context of a diagnosis based on a polysomnogram test while in hospital.

This research seeks to take a step further through the production of a short video animation; we propose the modification of the children's hospital environment to create an association between their immediate surroundings and the video animation. In this way, the positive feelings that relax the children while viewing the film may stay with them until they fall asleep in bed, allaying any fearfulness associated with the electrodes attached to their heads for the polysomnogram test. Besides, if the explanation convinces the children to accept the need for a polysomnogram test, it will reaffirm the parent's willingness to leave the children in hospital overnight, in such a way that the parents will in turn transmit confidence in the diagnostic process to the children. All in all, mutually reinforced confidence between parent and child will help to reduce stress and will improve sleep quality, the quality of the polysomnogram test and the eventual diagnosis of the sleep disorders.

The production of the short ad-hoc 3D video animation was limited to a very low budget. The idea was to produce the 3D video animation with only two modelers/animators over 3 months. If such an audiovisual product can be produced in the basis of a very low budget, it can open the production of very customized video animations for different purposes. Therefore the traditional workflow and the techniques in use had to be adapted to this requirement. In this study, some methodologies for the 3D modeling of cultural heritage items [9, 10] were used for 3D character modeling and shading, although their effect on final production costs were not as significant as planned. The main costs were due to the animation stage of the characters, as outlined in Sect. 2.

The paper is structured as follows: Sect. 2 describes the process of producing the short video animation with low-budget techniques; Sect. 3 shows its practical use to help in the diagnosis of sleep disorders in children; Sect. 4 summarizes the results of this experiment, using the surveys administered to both parents and children and the polysomnogram test results on both the reference and evaluation groups of children. Finally, Sect. 5 presents the conclusions and future lines of work.

2 Development of the 3D Video Animations

The production of a video animation includes many tasks that are usually grouped into 3 main stages: preproduction, production and postproduction. As it was a small-scale project, these 3 stages were simplified. Additionally, a making-of of the short film has been done and uploaded in Internet [11].

2.1 Pre-production

First, the identification of the main objectives of the video was done in collaboration with the Sleep Diagnosis Unit of the University Hospital of Burgos. The objectives of the video were as follows:

1. To induce feelings of happiness in children, within an age range of 3 and 6 years old, in such a way that the hospital ward is perceived as a harmless environment and the polysomnogram test as a beneficial technique.
2. To help the children understand the need for a polysomnogram test, so that they could vanquish their sleep disorders, associated with nightmares.
3. To prompt associations between the short video animation and the real hospital environment; between the avatars in the video animation and the medical staff caring for the children while in hospital; and, between the video scenarios and the real hospital wards.
4. To prompt a direct association between the main avatar in the video and the child, reproducing in a quiet and positive way the main steps that the children will follow while in hospital.

With regard to sleep disorders, the search to establish empathy and co-identity between the video viewer and the main avatar is a common objective in many other short video animations [8]. However, these videos are mainly designed for a more general use than in our case and marked associations with the hospital environment and secondary characters, such as doctors and nurses, is uncommon.

The short video animation of between 5–10 min was designed to respond to the above requirements. It included 3D animations, 2D animations and real recorded sequences. This mixture exploits the attraction that 3D animation exercises over children, the power to explain concepts and to lower production costs of 2D animation and the power that filmed sequences of real life have to provide quick identification of persons and places.

The second stage is to create the characters and storyboard. The short video animation included 5 characters: Alberto, a happy child as the main character, Morfea, the sweet and smiling Queen of Dreamsland, two warm and quiet fairies that help Morfea and, finally, Susto, the 'monster' in the short animation that lives in the child's nightmares. Morfea is meant to be identified with the doctor during the polysomnogram test and the fairies with the nurses. Susto is needed so that the children can make sense of their hospitalization. Figure 1 shows some preliminary drawings of some of the main characters.

Fig. 1. Some draft drawings of the fairies and the character of Morfea.

Four scenarios were likewise identified for inclusion in the storyboard: Dreamsland, the dreams-machine, Alberto's room, and the Forest. Dreamsland is a complex scenario that will be presented in 2D, 3D and real images, as it will include images of the Hospital (inside and outside). The dreams-machine is the place where the medical staff conducts the diagnosis and will be presented in the 3D video animation and in real images. Some concepts on sleep and the genesis of dreams are explained in Alberto's room at home that bridges the real life of children and the video narrative. Finally, the forest is the place where Susto is presented. It differs from the other scenarios as it separates the bad feelings that Susto represents from the hospital and home environments. Besides these three well-defined scenarios, some actions are presented in undefined scenarios: clear and well-lit for positive actions and dark scenarios for negative actions during the dream stages.

Finally, the storyboard was created including 2D, 3D, and real recorded sequences following the various previously presented strategies. The storyboard was divided into 3 stages: the characters and scenarios were presented first of all. Then the hows and whys of sleep-disorder diagnosis and, thirdly, the confrontation between the child and "Susto", the monster, during his sleep in the hospital drew the animation to a close giving it a happy ending after the child's nightmare.

2.2 Production

Although the short film also included real recorded sequences (8 %) and 2D sequences (48 %). only the production steps performed for the 3D animation sequences are presented in this research. Blender software (www.blender.org), 3D modeling and animation software developed as open-source software and distributed under GNU GPLicense was used for all of these production processes.

First, the 3D Modeling step was created. Different 3D models were built limiting both human and computational resources, by following previously developed methods for complex 3D Cultural Heritage reconstruction models [10], although some minor changes were introduced into the overall process. Most of the 3D meshes were created using standard 3D CAD tools that modify 3D standard meshes such as spheres and cubes, giving them a final smooth appearance through the application of smooth operators, see Fig. 2 as an example. The hair of each character, one of the most critical elements for final visual quality was created with meshes, without using real hair operators or Blender software plugins, as it would strongly increase the computational rendering time. Besides, this short video animation targets a public of children younger than 10 years old, a public that is not usually very critical of the visual appearance of characters. Instead, they tend to focus on the transmission of feelings, due to their empathy with the characters, which are evoked in the animation.

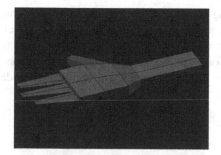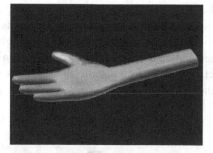

Fig. 2. The model of a character's hand: from easy geometrical meshes to final result.

Following 3D modeling, two different strategies were followed for the shading step, depending on the final appearance of the various 3D models. The first one shaded Susto's skin, the child's armor, the fairies wings and some objects in the rooms such as the bed and the walls in the hospital ward. Image textures were UV-mapped on the meshes of these objects [9], to improve their final visual quality, but without increasing the number of polygons that shape the meshes. In the case of Susto's skin, Fig. 3, a procedural noise texture for Normal Mapping was subsequently applied to give the avatar the appearance of a stuffed toy and, therefore, to attenuate the negative feelings that this character might arouse in the children. The second strategy was followed for the rest of the 3D meshes: only one-color materials without specular shaders were created. This technique simplified the shading step and was accepted because child spectators usually overlook this lack of realism. Only metal objects and the eyes

Fig. 3. UV mapping of Susto's character (Color figure online)

included specular shaders to reflect bright light when illuminated. Transparent objects were reduced as much as possible, due they increase the rendering computational time: only Alberto's glasses, the fairies' wings, and the windows of the hospital ward and Alberto's room included transparency levels.

Reductions in rendering time for lighting were achieved by using only one main soft spotlight and 2–3 secondary spotlights, to produce eye brightness and other elements. The main lighting was mainly a light warm (yellow or orange) color in all the scenes and cold colors (blue) were used in only two scenes, to increase the dramatic effect. Figure 4 shows some final renders of the main characters of the short video animation.

Fig. 4. Final renders of the main characters.

Finally, the animation of the 5 characters was done using standard armature techniques. Rigging and skinning were done first, followed by Weight Painting, to define the weight that each bone might have in the movement of each polygon of the mesh. Figure 5 shows two examples of Weight Painting of the hair of the Queen and the body of the child. It is worth mentioning that automatic skinning modifications, using the Weight Painting technique in joints, such as elbows and shoulders, created many problems. This stage requires substantial manual modification in the areas that use large deformations, to avoid undesired deformations when the character movements are exaggerated.

Fig. 5. Examples of Weight Painting of two characters.

Finally, some movement cycles were created (running of child and Susto) and shapekeys or morph keys were used for faces movements while speaking or expressing feelings. Figure 6 shows some examples of shapekeys for the 4 main characters. As happens with Weight Painting, this step was one of the most complex of the whole animation project. A very extended and exaggerated gestures gallery for each character was necessary, to obtain natural expressions on the faces of the characters with different refinements, which is necessary to overcome the artificiality of 3D-video animation characters.

Fig. 6. Examples of two shapekeys for each character.

Once the keyframing of the action was ready, the final renders were generated, before moving on to the postproduction stage.

2.3   Post-production

At this stage Premiere and After Effects software were used. The different frames were joined regardless of the technique: real recorded video, 2D animation and 3D animation. Then, the sound effects, the voices, and the music were included in the short film. Finally, some minor effects were included: the presence of Susto in real video scenes (using the chroma effect) or brightness on some objects in the 3D animation scenes when necessary to improve the visual quality of the final product. Some color management of certain scenes, to increase overall brightness increased the attractiveness of the video for children. Figure 7 shows some examples of postprocessed images of the short film. The short film has been also uploaded in Internet [12].

Fig. 7. Examples of two animated scenes after postproduction.

A study of workload distribution for the completion of this 3D animation short film appears in Fig. 8, showing the percentage allocation of working time for the different tasks. The whole virtual production described in Sect. 2 took 400 working hours. The distribution of working time between the different activities was as follows: preproduction stage (storyboard and character and scenario definition) 10 %, 3D modeling and shading 20 %, animation 40 %, rendering 20 % and post-production 10 %. Rendering time can not be considered a sequential task compared with the others. Ten computers with Intel Core 2 Quad processors (2.8 GHz, 4 GB RAM DDR2) from a 3D Editing Room [13] worked simultaneously on this task.

Finally, a comparison of workload distribution for 2D scenes and 3D scenes appears in Table 1. Although there were no significant differences between the time length of 2D and 3D animation in the video (around 3 min each), both human and computer time spent on 3D animation was at least 10 times higher than similar tasks for 2D animation scenes. This observation shows that as much 2D animation as possible in any short 3D animation will reduce the costs of the audiovisual product considerably.

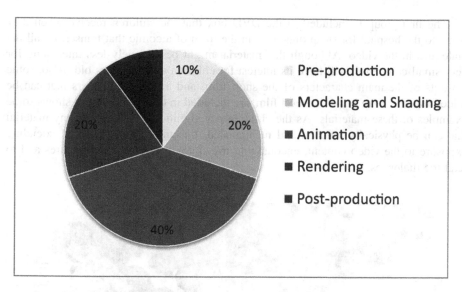

Fig. 8. Workload distribution for the 3D video animation

Table 1. Comparison of human and computer time in the 2D and 3D video animation process.

	Time in the video (s)	Working time per video's second (min)	Rendering time per video's second (min)	Total time per video's second (min)
2D Animation	186	12.6	4.16	16.76
3D Animation	170	141	35.4	176.4

3 Study Case: The Diagnosis of Sleep Disorders in Children

Once the short video animation was ready, the hospital rooms were decorated with characters and objects from the video so that the children would create associations with them in their minds. Then, the effect of the video view was evaluated with the two groups of children: first, 10 children slept in the hospital for sleep disorder diagnosis after viewing the video, the evaluation group, and then another 10 children who had not seen the video were evaluated, the reference group.

3.1 Creating a Full Environment Based on the Short Animation

Several complementary add-ins were designed to accompany the short video animation and to accentuate its effects on the children. On the one hand, material delivered to the child directly after having viewed the video and, on the other, material to decorate the hospital wards.

The first group is included in the DVD box that the children receive when they come to the hospital for sleep diagnosis in the form of a comic that transcribes all the dialogues in the video. Although this material might be relatively less interesting for very small children, it will have its interest for children up to 6 years old. Also, some cut-outs of the main characters of the short film, and a book of stickers that can be folded together to re-build the short film, are included in the box. Figure 9 shows some examples of these materials. As the children pay significant attention to any material that can be physically touched and manipulated, this material is aimed at extending exposure to the video content, encouraging the children to watch the pictures and to read the dialogues.

Fig. 9. Materials to boost the effect of viewing the video: stickers and cut-outs

The second group of materials was composed of posters and cut-outs of the different characters that were placed in the different hospital wards of the Sleep Diagnosis Unit -especially in the sleep rooms-. Some stickers are also included, to identify the medical equipment with the machines shown in the short video animation such as the dreams-machine. Figure 10 shows some examples of these materials. The idea is that, first of all, the children make the strongest associations between the real hospital environment where they are being diagnosed and the environment in the short film and, second, to create a positive and colored environment for children that is different from the children's neutral or hostile view of the standard hospital wards.

Fig. 10. Materials to boost the effect after having viewed the animation: decoration

3.2 Goals and Children's Profiles

The short film view and the full environment based on the characters in the video are intended to achieve the following objectives:

- Improve sleep disorder diagnosis by shortening SOL (Sleep onset latency), meaning a longer and more peaceful sleep
- Create a less hostile environment for the children during their hospitalization night
- Measure the effect of viewing the video on the sleep profiles of the children
- Evaluate the satisfaction with the experience among both parents and children, and their perception of the sleep

The children in the study were aged between 3 and 6 years. Twenty children diagnosed with sleep disorders at the University Hospital of Burgos were separated into two groups on the basis of age. The first group, the reference group, was formed of children from 3 to 5 years old (average age: 3.5 years), while the second group, the evaluation group, included children from 4.5 to 6.25 years old (average age: 6 years). Note that both groups had children between 4–5 years old. The reason for dividing the groups on the basis of age came from the medical staff, because they considered that the short animation was not suitable for very young children as Susto, the monster in the short video, might affect the children negatively. The small hospital wards reduced the number of children that could be evaluated, so the reference group in this case presented a significant difference with the evaluation group. With regard to gender, the reference group and the evaluation group had female populations of 60 % and 70 % respectively, therefore, the groups may be considered equally balanced, despite a slight imbalance. Table 2 shows the gender division, age and numbers of children in these groups.

Table 2. Profile of children in the reference and the evaluation groups

	Male	Female	Average age	Age range
Reference group	4	6	3.5	3–5
Evaluation group	3	7	6	4.50–6.25

3.3 Sleep Disorder Diagnosis Procedure

Before the children went to bed they were prepared for a standard overnight polysomnogram test. Standard overnight polysomnography identifies the time a person either spends in each sleep state or spends awake, by performing three simultaneous studies: electroencephalography (EEG), electrooculography (EOG), and surface electromyography (EMG). The standard procedure and the parameters these tests monitor are explained in detail in the bibliography [14]. The monitoring system records 12 channels, requiring the attachment of 12 wires to the patient's head. The electrodes provide a readout of the brain activity that is classified as REM (Rapid Eye Movement sleep), non-REM (NREM) and wakefulness. Usually NREM sleep is divided into three levels: N1, N2 and N3 (N1-REM, N2-REM and N3-REM, respectively).

Once the child is awake in the daytime, different parameters are extracted from the polysomnogram: total sleep time in REM, N1-REM, N2-REM and N3-REM stages, wakefulness time, sleep efficiency (night sleep duration expressed as percentage of total sleep time in bed), REM latency (period of time from sleep onset to the first appearance of REM stage), NREM latency (period of time between lights off and the first 30 s of N1 or sleep onset), number of sleep interruptions or wakefulness stages, Arousal Index (number of abrupt change from sleep to wakefulness, or from a "deeper" stage of NREM sleep to a "lighter" stage per hour of sleep), and RDI (Respiratory Disturbance Index). Sleep stages were scored according to the Rechtschaffen and Kales's criteria [15]. Arousals were defined as recommended by the American Sleep Disorders Association Task Force criteria [16].

Finally, the morning after the children's night in the hospital, the parents filled in a short survey while the children were asked 5 questions, the responses to which were recorded in another questionnaire. The questions related to the perceptions of both children and parents of the child's sleep experience in the hospital and the role of the video in relaxing and falling asleep. The questions included in both questionnaires are described below in Sect. 4. The use of questionnaires and polysomnograms are well-established techniques to evaluate sleep disorders in children [1].

4 Evaluation of the Influence of the Animation Film on Facilitating the Diagnosis

Both parents and children responded to 5 questions. All the questions had ten possible responses (on a scale from 1 to 10) to evaluate either agreement or disagreement with the proposed question. While the questions for the children referred to impressions on how they fell asleep (quietly, quickly, etc.) and their sleep (deep or light, dreams or nightmares or periods of wakefulness), the parents questions referred, also, to their impressions of the child's sleep and, besides, to their opinion of the effect of the short video animation and the clarity of the message transmitted to the child. The questions and the average scores of the answers for both groups are presented in Table 3.

The polysomnogram parameters are described in detail in Subsect. 3.3. The average values, mainly expressed in percentages, are also collected in Table 3 for both the evaluation and the reference groups.

Some conclusions can be directly extracted from Table 3. First, although average sleep efficiency and wakefulness time are the same for both groups, the dispersion of these parameters is somewhat smaller in the evaluation group: the cases with lower sleep efficiency and higher wakefulness time are presented in the reference group (e.g. the worst sleep efficiency was 74.5 % in the reference group and 80.2 % in the evaluation group and the longest wakefulness time dropped from 147 min in the reference group to 112 min in the evaluation group). These parameters therefore indicate that the short video animation had no effect on whether the children slept more during the night in average, but it did help the most nervous children who are especially sensitive to the hospital environment to relax.

Second, the time needed to fall asleep (NREM latency) was almost half in the case of the evaluation group (25 min to 46 min). It is interesting to note that this conclusion,

Table 3. Average values of polysomnography parameters and questionnaires.

Parameter/Question	Source	Group			
		Reference (average and range)		Evaluation (average and range)	
Sleep efficiency (%)	Polysomnography	84	(74.5 - 87)	84	(80.2 - 86.2)
NREM latency (min)	Polysomnography	46	(28.5 - 74)	25	(12.5 - 43.7)
REM latency (min)	Polysomnography	96	(61.7 - 120)	93	(71.5 - 133)
Wakefulness time (min)	Polysomnography	90	(58.7 - 147.5)	90.5	(80.5 - 112.2)
Number of sleep disruptions	Polysomnography	8	(5.5 - 17.7)	13	(7.7 - 16.2)
Arousal index	Polysomnography	11	(8.4 - 13.7)	93	(67.7 - 144)
Respiratory Disturbance Index (RDI)	Polysomnography	4	(1.4 - 8.7)	3.55	(1.2 - 12.05)
% Time in N1-REM	Polysomnography	7.3	(4.7 - 7.6)	10.3	(8.3 - 13.03)
% Time in N2-REM	Polysomnography	32	(29.2 - 41.9)	32.7	(27.6 - 44.5)
% Time in N3-REM	Polysomnography	35	(30.7 - 38.7)	34.55	(27.2 - 39.3)
% REM	Polysomnography	22	(20.4 - 25.1)	19.35	(17.03 - 24.9)
Q1. Child was quiet while sleeping (10 = I completely agree, 1 = not at all)	Parent questionnaire	7	(9 - 5)	7	(9 - 5)
Q2. Child slept like at home (10 = I completely agree, 1 = not at all)	Parent questionnaire	7	(8 - 6)	6	(8 - 5)
Q3. Sufficient information shared with the parents (10 = I completely agree, 1 = not at all)	Parent questionnaire	9	(10 - 8)	10	(10 - 10)
Q4. The test will help towards the improvement of the child's sleep (10 = I completely agree, 1 = not at all)	Parent questionnaire	8	(10 - 6)	10	(10 - 10)

(Continued)

Table 3. (*Continued*)

Parameter/Question	Source	Group			
		Reference (average and range)		Evaluation (average and range)	
Q5. Sufficient explanations were given to the child (10 = 100 % agree)	Parent questionnaire	10	(10 - 10)	9	(10 - 8)
Q6. How did you feel at night? (10 = very quiet, 1 = very nervous)	Child questionnaire	9	(10 - 8)	9	(10 - 8)
Q7. Was it easy to fall sleep? (10 = very easy, 0 = very difficult)	Child questionnaire	5	(8 - 4)	7	(9 - 6)
Q8. Did you sleep the whole night through? (10 = yes, 1 = not at all)	Child questionnaire	8	(10 - 6)	6	(10 - 5)
Q9. Did you dream? (10 = yes, 1 = no)	Child questionnaire	5	(10 - 6)	7	(10 - 6)
Q10. Did you have dreams (10) or nightmares (1)?	Child questionnaire	8.5	(10 - 6)	8.5	(10 - 6)

extracted from the polysomnography, agreed with the perceptions of the children (responses to question Q7), but it was not reflected in the answers from parents on their impression of their child's sleep (Q2).

Lastly, the other polysomnography parameters offered no clear conclusions; in some cases, they are very similar in both groups, %N2, %N3, %REM, RDI and REM latency, in others, they are very different, %N1, RDI, Arousal index and Number of sleep disruptions, but with no immediate explanation. In these cases, the age difference between the reference and the evaluation group can play an important role. For instance, if the presence of respiratory disorders was the main cause for sleep disorders among the children aged between 6–9 years but there would be other reasons among the younger children, these parameters would present a significant difference between both groups. Unfortunately, the small size of the groups under study provided no statistically significant conclusions to support this hypothesis.

The questionnaires provided further conclusions. The parents felt they had more information on the diagnosis procedure and more confidence in it when the short video animation was used rather than the oral explanations. Although there is no objective explanation for these perceptions, the influence of the parents' mood on their children towards acceptance of hospitalization was significant and more positive moods, in the case of the short video animation, can help to obtain a more reliable diagnosis, because the child will be more relaxed before falling asleep in bed. Moreover, the older children had more frequent and shorter interruptions in the night, which was also detected in the polysomnogram, that reflects the previously explained respiratory disorders, considered the main cause for sleep disorders in the evaluation group.

5 Conclusions and Future Works

This paper has presented the use of short video animations and adapted environments to mitigate the fear of hospitalization in the diagnosis of sleep disorders in children. The research followed 3 steps: in the first one, the video animation was designed following recommendations from the doctors; in the second, the hospital wards were decorated so that the children would associate the characters in the video animation with their immediate surroundings; finally, a standard polysomnogram test monitored the sleep disorders of a reference group and an evaluation group at the University Hospital of Burgos (Spain).

The short video animation included real recorded sequences (8 %), 2D animation sequences (48 %) and 3D animation sequences (46 %). Each technique is used with a different purpose: children are clearly attracted to 3D animation; 2D animation has a strong power to explain concepts and it has lower production costs than 3D animation sequences and real sequences help children to identify real scenarios of the short video animation while admitted to hospital.

When analyzing the human and computer efforts necessary to create the 3D and the 2D animation sequences, the results show that 3D animation requires around 10 times more efforts than 2D animation, meaning as many 2D scenes as possible in such projects to optimize final costs. Most work in the 3D animation process of this project is in the animation step. Two tasks are especially complex in the animation process: the Weight Painting of the skinning to avoid incorrect deformations in joints such as elbows or shoulders, when the character movement is very exaggerated and very extended exaggerated-gestures gallery for each character are needed, it is necessary to obtain natural expressions on the faces of the characters with different refinements, avoiding the common artificiality of 3D animation-created characters. Therefore an optimized definition of the characters in the pre-production stage, with fine and slender limbs (reducing the number of polygons in the joints) is fundamental to reduce the time consumed in the animation step.

Several complementary elements were created, so that the children can associate them with a short animation. These elements can be divided into two groups: on the one hand, material that will be delivered to the child directly after the viewing the short film and, on the other, material that will be used to customize the hospital wards where the study is conducted. The first group is included in the DVD box that the child receives on arrival at the hospital for sleep diagnosis and includes a comic, stickers and cut-outs of the main characters of the short animation with the idea of extending their exposure to the content of the animation. The second group of materials is composed of posters and cut-outs of the different characters of the short film that are attached to walls and furniture of the hospital wards of the Sleep Diagnosis Unit, to strengthen the children's association of the real environment and the environment shown in the short film, creating at the same time a positive and colored environment.

Sleep disorder diagnosis is monitored by overnight polysomnography. In addition, two short questionnaires are filled in by parents and children, to measure their satis-faction and the perception of their experience. Although a main difference in the age between the reference group and the evaluation group exists and the limited size of both groups (10 children each) makes it impossible to extract statistically significant conclusions, some preliminary findings can be extracted from the experience. The sleep efficiency and the wakefulness time, extracted from the polysomnogram, show that the video helps to relax the most nervous children who can be especially sensitive to the hospital environment. The time necessary to sleep (SOL latency) was half as long among the children who viewed the short film than among the children in the reference group. Finally, the questionnaires show that the parents thought that they were given more information on the diagnosis procedure and had more confidence in it, when the short video was used rather than the ordinary oral explanations. Although there is no objective explanation for these perceptions, the influence of the parents' mood in their children's acceptance of hospitalization is a strong influence on the children and these positive moods in the case of the short video animation can help to obtain a more reliable diagnosis, because the child will fall asleep in more relaxed way.

Further research will focus on extending this experience to larger numbers of children of specific ages, to gain reliable statistical significance of the conclusions. Moreover, the adaptation of the story to other plots that lead to interaction between the child and the story and its characters, such as games or augmented reality when smartphones and tablets are used, can increase the positive effect in the children's mood and a better sleep disorder diagnosis.

Acknowledgments. This work was partially supported by the Program "Impulso de la Industria de Contenidos Digitales desde las Universidades" of the Spanish Ministry of Industry, Tourism and Commerce. The authors would especially like to thank Dr. Joaquin Teran and his team at the Sleep Unit at the University Hospital of Burgos for performing the sleep disorders diagnosis included in this research.

References

1. Mouthon, A.L., Huber, R.: Methods in pediatric sleep research and sleep medicine. Neuropediatrics **46**(3), 159–170 (2015)
2. Bisogni, S., Chiarini, I., Giusti, F., Ciofi, D., Poggi, G.M., Festini, F.: Impact of hospitalization on the sleep patterns of newborns, infants and toddlers admitted to a pediatric ward: a cross-sectional study. Minerva Pediatr. **67**(3), 209–217 (2015)
3. Meltzer, L.J., Davis, K.F., Mindell, J.A.: Patient and parent sleep in a children's hospital. Pediatr. Nurs. **38**(2), 64–71 (2012)
4. Alonso-Álvarez, M.L., Teran-Santos, J., Ordax Carbajo, E., Cordero-Guevara, J.A., Navazo-Egüia, A.I., Kheirandish-Gozal, L., Gozal, D.: Reliability of home respiratory polygraphy for the diagnosis of sleep apnea in children. Chest **147**(4), 1020–1028 (2015)
5. Coma-Del-Corral, M.J., Alonso-Álvarez, M.L., Allende, M., Cordero, J., Ordax, E., Masa, F., Terán-Santos, J.: Reliability of telemedicine in the diagnosis and treatment of sleep apnea syndrome. Telemedicine e-Health **19**(1), 7–12 (2013)
6. Shoemark, H., Hanson-Abromeit, D., Stewart, L.: Constructing optimal experience for the hospitalized newborn through neuro-based music therapy. Front. Hum. Neurosci. **9**(9) (2015). Article no. 487, 5p

7. Ulusoy, K.: The effect of animation film application upon students' success and attitude in the process of history lesson. Energ. Educ. Sci. Technol. Part B: Soc. Educ. Stud. **3**(4), 701–712 (2011)
8. De Barros, M.P., de Pereira, E.C., de Carvalho, L.B.C., Ferreira, V.R., do Prado, L.B.F., Do Prado, G.F.: Educative animations for circadian rhythm sleep disorders. Revista Neurociencias. **22**(2), 278–285 (2014)
9. Bustillo, A., Martinez, L., Alaguero, M., Iglesias, L.S.: The church of the Charterhouse of Miraflores in Burgos: virtual reconstruction of artistic imagery. In: Fusion of Cultures, Proceedings of the 38th Annual Conference on Computer Applications and Quantitative Methods in Archaeology, CAA 2010, pp. 55–62. Archaeopress, Oxford (2013)
10. Alaguero, M., Bustillo, A., Guinea, B., Iglesias, L.S.: The virtual reconstruction of a small medieval town: the case of Briviesca (Spain). In: Proceedings of the 42nd Annual Conference on Computer Applications and Quantitative Methods in Archaeology, pp. 575–584. Archaeopress, Oxford (2015)
11. Making-of of the video animation. https://youtu.be/uYfuGhAmBT8
12. Video animation. https://youtu.be/IQjXl2qgqmo
13. Bustillo, A., Alaguero, M., Miguel, I., Saiz, J.M., Iglesias, L.S.: A flexible platform for the creation of 3D semi-immersive environments to teach cultural heritage. Digital Appl. Archaeol. Cult. Heritage **2**(4), 248–259 (2015)
14. Kushida, C.A., Littner, M.R., Morgenthaler, T., Alessi, C.A., Bailey, D., Coleman, J.: Practice parameters for the indications for polysomnography and related procedures: an update for 2005. Sleep **28**, 499–521 (2005)
15. Rechtschaffen A, Kales A.: Manual of Standardized Terminology, Techniques and Scoring System for the Sleep Stages of Human Subjects, vol. 204. Government Printing Office, Washington, D.C. (1968)
16. ASDA Standards of Practice: EEG arousals: scorning rules and examples. Sleep **15**(2), 173–184 (1992)

Configurable Software Framework
for 2D/3D Video See-Through Displays
in Medical Applications

Fabrizio Cutolo[1(✉)], Mentore Siesto[1], Stefano Mascioli[1],
Cinzia Freschi[1], Mauro Ferrari[1,2], and Vincenzo Ferrari[1,3]

[1] Department of Translational Research and New Technologies in Medicine and
Surgery, EndoCAS Center, University of Pisa, Pisa, Italy
`fabrizio.cutolo@endocas.org`
[2] Department of Vascular Surgery, Pisa University Medical School, Pisa, Italy
[3] Information Engineering Department, University of Pisa, Pisa, Italy

Abstract. Augmented Reality (AR) has already proven its worth in various
applications in the medical domain. However, most of the solutions proposed
were bound to specific hardware or software configurations, and/or their
application was limited to specific cases, thus lacking in flexibility. In this paper,
we present a software framework suitable for AR video see-through systems
conceived for medical applications: our solution allows merging of real world
images grabbed by one or more external cameras with computer-generated
sceneries coregistered to the acquired images. The software framework is highly
configurable and extensible thanks to the employment of two text configuration
files that make it suitable for many typologies of potential applications. The
proposed solution can be easily adapted to functioning with different tracking
and AR visualization modalities. The versatility of the software for video
see-through AR applications was already tested on various medical applications,
in conjunction with head-mounted displays or with external spatial displays.

Keywords: Augmented reality and visualization · Computer assisted
intervention · Interventional imaging

1 Introduction

Recent developments in the fields of medical imaging and computer vision related
technologies have encouraged the research for new visualization modalities of
patient-specific virtual reconstructions of the anatomy. Such visualization modalities
have been designed to act either as surgical guidance or as tools for surgical planning or
for diagnosis [1, 2]. In this framework, the idea of integrating in situ the surgeon's
perceptive efficiency with the aid of new AR-based visualization modalities has
become a dominant topic of academic and industrial research in the medical domain
since the 90's. The high expectations accrued among researchers, technicians, and
physicians regarding this fascinating new technology, were predominantly related to
the improvements potentially brought by AR-based devices to surgical navigation and
planning. In this context, AR visualization is indeed regarded as capable of providing

L.T. De Paolis and A. Mongelli (Eds.): AVR 2016, Part II, LNCS 9769, pp. 30–42, 2016.
DOI: 10.1007/978-3-319-40651-0_3

the surgeon with the ability to access the radiological images and surgical planning contextually to the real patient anatomy.

However, despite those ambitious targets, there are still few reasons why such systems are not yet routinely used in the medical workflow. Among them, there is the fact that most of these systems were and still are developed as proof-of-concept devices that were/are mostly conceived for research users more than for their immediate translation into immediate and reliable applications.

Many of those systems do not take into account the operational constraints imposed by the surgical context and often they do not satisfy the surgeons' practical needs and requirements. Generally, most of the AR systems have been regarded as disrupting the surgeon's act. This is because most of these systems have lacked of a systematic evaluation within a clinical context [3]. In fact, the basic condition for the acceptance of a new technology (as AR) in the operating room (OR) is related to its capacity of being smoothly integrated into the workflow of the intervention, without affecting and disturbing the user during the rest of the procedure [4, 5].

On this point, it is of utmost importance to move towards the implementation of devices and software platforms that are user-friendly and may not represent a too heavy burden for the surgeons to whom such new tools are addressed. Further, most of the proposed solutions are bound to specific hardware or software configurations and/or their application is limited to specific cases, thus rapidly falling into obsolescence as technological development goes on. This aspect limits the possibility of testing the efficacy of the same AR technology on medical applications that comprise different tracking approaches, visualization modalities, interaction paradigms, registration procedures, perception locations, display devices [3].

In this paper, we present a software framework suitable for AR (2D or 3D) video see-through systems conceived for medical applications. The software framework is highly configurable and extensible thanks to the employment of two text configuration files that make it suitable for many typologies of potential applications in terms of tracking methods, AR visualization modalities, display units and camera specifics.

2 Materials and Methods

2.1 Video See-Through Paradigm

In any AR-based application the key challenge is to ensure the highest degree of realism in merging computer-generated elements with live views of the real world. The unavoidable condition for achieving a perceptually coherent augmentation of the reality is to satisfy the geometric coherence in the augmented scene, namely to solve the registration problem [6]. For achieving a reliable geometric registration of the virtual content to the real scene, the process of image formation associated to the virtual viewpoint (i.e. the virtual camera) must perfectly mimic, both intrinsically and extrinsically, the one of the real viewpoint. In other words, the virtual content is to be observed by a virtual viewpoint whose view frustum and pose must be set equal to the real camera ones (Fig. 1).

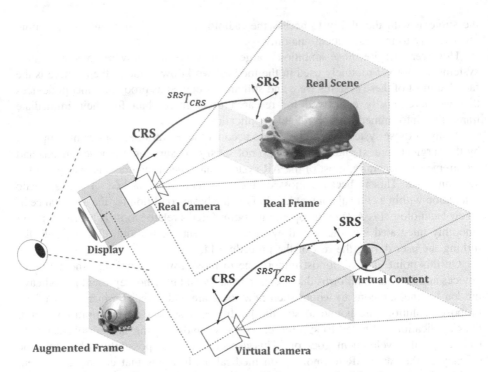

Fig. 1. The virtual content is mixed on real world frames acquired by the external camera. Geometric registration solely relies on the results of the camera calibration routine and on the real-time estimation of the camera pose, encapsulated by matrix $^{SRS}T_{CRS}$ (i.e. tracking).

The see-through displays fall into two categories depending on the AR mechanism they implement: video see-through displays and optical see-through displays. In optical see-through systems, the user's direct view of the real world is augmented with the projection of virtual information on a bean combiner and then into the user's line of sight [7]. In these systems, accurate geometric registration is difficult to achieve and frequent user-dependent calibrations are needed. The goal of such calibration routines are twofold: estimate the relative position between display and user's eye, which changes each time the position of the viewpoint is changed in relation to the display; estimate the projective model of the user's eye, which is however subject to change with the accommodation process in function of the focus distance [8–10].

Differently, in video see-through displays, be they head-mounted, hand-held or spatial, the real viewpoint corresponds to the one of the external camera, hence the spatial alignment of the virtual content with the real 3D world needs only for:

1. The definition of the intrinsic and extrinsic parameters of the virtual viewpoint so as to be consistent with those of the real camera. This condition is easily achievable as result of a one-off and robust camera calibration routine [11].
2. Real camera tracking in the scene reference system (SRS), encapsulated by matrix $^{SRS}T_{CRS}$ in Fig. 1, which is usually performed by means of an external tracker [12].

Here is a functional and logical description of the video see-through paradigm implemented: the external camera grabs video frames of the real scene; video frames, upon compensation of the radial distortion, are screened as backgrounds of the display; the virtual content, reconstructed offline from radiological images, is coherently merged to create the augmented scene. Due to the computational complexity of the whole video see-through paradigm, we implemented a multithreaded application to guarantee the synchronization of the views to be sent to display(s). A thread sets up the AR view, while the other one is dedicated to the tracking engine.

2.2   Hardware

Display Devices. Our software framework can be used with any 2D or 3D display device. For any stereoscopic device, the 3D mechanism can be set to anaglyph (i.e. alternating the left and the right view) or side-by-side. The application is independent of the chosen hardware and it can present the visually processed data on spatial, on hand-held, on head-mounted display (HMD), or on any other device able to acquire a computer video signal (e.g. a video streamer over a TCP/IP network). To date, we have primarily tested the software framework in combination with a set of stereoscopic HMDs (Fig. 2).

Fig. 2. Stereoscopic HMDs on which the software framework was tested. (A) Commercial video see-through AR visor by Vuzix (Vuzix WRAP 920AR). (B) First custom-made embodiment of stereoscopic HMD based on a commercial 3D visor by eMagin (eMagin Z800). (C) Second custom-made embodiment of stereoscopic HMD based on a commercial 3D visor by Sony (Sony HMZ-T2).

Video Input Devices. To capture the real-world scene, any DirectX/DirectShow™ camera can be used, provided that its intrinsic and extrinsic parameters have been estimated following the calibration procedure.

In our first applications we employed commercial (Fig. 2A) and custom-made stereoscopic HMDs (Fig. 2B–C) [13]. The custom-made embodiments were realized by mounting two external high-resolution USB 2.0 cameras on the top of commercial 3D visors at an anthropometric interaxial distance of ∼7 cm as done by [14, 15]. In such a way, the two cameras could be aligned with the user's eyes as to provide a quasi-orthoscopic view of the augmented scene mediated by the visor:

1. The first custom-made stereoscopic HMD (Fig. 2B) was based on a commercial 3D visor by eMagin (eMagin Z800) provided with dual OLED panels and featuring a diagonal field of view (FoV) of 40°. The two external cameras were two USB 2.0 cameras by IDS (uEye UI-1646LE) equipped with a 1.3 MP Aptina CMOS sensor (pixel pitch of 3.6 μm) that achieve a frame rate of 25 fps in freerun mode at full resolution (i.e. 1280 × 1024). A plastic frame (ABS) was built through rapid prototyping and fixed to the 3D visor as support for the two external USB cameras.
2. The second custom-made stereoscopic HMD (Fig. 2C) was based on a commercial 3D visor by Sony (Sony HMZ-T2) provided with dual 720p OLED panels and a horizontal FoV of 45°. The two external cameras were 2 USB 2.0 cameras by IDS (uEye XS) equipped with a 5 MP Aptina CMOS sensor (pixel size of 1.4 μm) that achieve a frame rate of 15 fps at 1280 × 720 resolution. In this embodiment, we also included a mechanism to modify the degree of convergence of the stereo camera setting [16]. The software was adapted to consider this feature.

2.3   Software

Our goal was to propose a configurable AR software framework suitable for medical applications that was capable of fulfilling the following requirements:

- **Versatility:** the software must be of use for as many operating scenarios as possible.
- **Ease-of-configuration:** one does not need to be a technician for using the software, neither for adapting it to different use cases.
- **Efficiency:** the system must be responsive, having to reach a compromise between frame rate and image quality (resolution);
- **Extensibility:** the system must be able to take advantage of new hardware solutions to achieve better performances and/or quality and to resist technological obsolescence.

The software framework was implemented in software libraries built in C++ through the open-source library for graphics editing OpenSG 1.8 (www.opensg.org).

The software framework consists of a GUI written in C++ (Fig. 3) exploiting the features of a class library specifically developed for AR applications (called OSGVisor3D). Most of the application-oriented aspects, on which the OSGVisor3D library acts, are configurable through two configuration files. As a whole, these aspects include:

- Cameras specifics, comprising the intrinsic and extrinsic camera parameters;
- Video equipment specifics (resolution, frame rate, synchronization if needed, mono/stereoscopic vision, stereovision method used);
- Loading of the specific components of the surgical case (see below);
- Composition of the virtual scenery. The whole virtual scene is called "scenegraph" (SG);
- Rendering in background or in foreground of the captured video scene (under development);

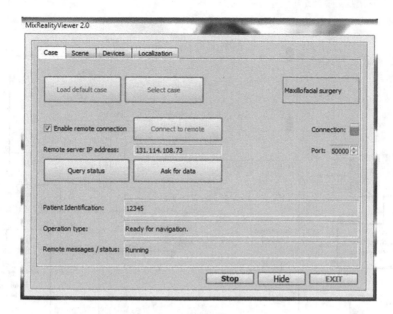

Fig. 3. Screenshot of the GUI component.

- Activation/deactivation of the tracking engine;
- Video-Based refinement of the registration to minimize errors of the registration procedure (only for video-based tracking methods);

The application uses two plain text configuration files: the first one (Augmented Reality Application or .ARA file) is a system-specific configuration file, while the second one (Augmented Reality Case or .ARC file) contains case-specific data. The . ARA file is loaded once by the application to configure its internals. The .ARA file contains the path to the folder containing the camera calibration files, the camera resolution, display specifics, the mechanism through which stereoscopy is delivered (only for HMDs). At runtime, different .ARC files can be loaded by the OSGVisor3D library to adapt the application to specific surgical case requirements (Fig. 4).

The application uses the class library to capture video data and register one or more virtual objects ("trackable objects" or TOs) to the real scene according to their associated tracking method (specified in the .ARC file).

The .ARC Configuration File. The content of the .ARC file is described in detail in the figure below (Fig. 5).

The .ARC file contains a series of directives specifying the details of the application and the components of the SG, together with their associated tracking and rendering requirements.

The "Rendering details" specify the rendering methodology for the camera images (background/foreground). The "Operation details" define the chosen case. The "Tracking engine global control" allows enabling or disabling the entire tracking component. The last part of the .ARC file contains a list of all the TOs, namely the

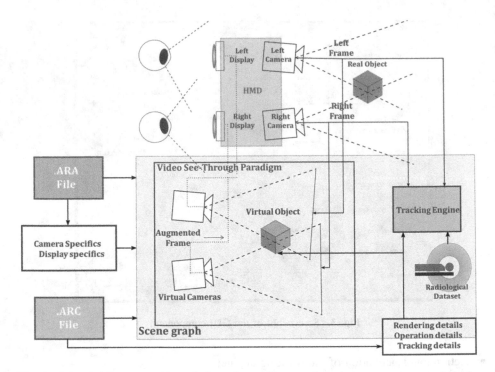

Fig. 4. Schematic representation of the software framework acting on a stereoscopic video see-through HMD. The scene graph library is configurable through two configuration files. The . ARA file is a system-specific configuration file that includes the camera specifics and the display ones. The .ARC file contains a series of directives specifying the details of the application and the components of the Scene Graph, together with their associated tracking and rendering requirements.

```
        -    Rendering details
        -    Operation details
        -    Tracking engine global control
        -    Trackable object 1 specific data:
             o    Name
             o    VRML file
             o    Tracking method
             o    Tracking method specific data
             o    Tracking enabled/disabled
             o    Maximum false results allowed
        -    Trackable object 2 specific data:
        -    ...
        -    Trackable object "n" specific data:
```

Fig. 5. Template of an ARC file.

single components of the SG. These directives define every TO in terms of their corresponding Virtual Reality Modeling Language (VRML) file and specific tracking characteristics (tracking method and its associated data).

Any TOs can be tracked independently one from another or excluded from the tracking process; this setting can be changed at runtime via the GUI for each object.

Each object has a set of tracking parameters associated with it. These parameters are related to the specific tracking engine used (e.g.: color segmentation thresholds for the video marker-based tracking method, grid geometries for the grid-based tracking method, etc.); this means that it is possible to tune the tracking engines singularly for every single TO via the GUI. It is also possible to turn off the entire tracking subsystem: this option, once excluded the cameras, allows direct interaction with the surgical map, which can be freely rotated, scaled, or moved. In such a way, the application can be used also for training or surgical planning purposes. A user can load the .ARC file in various ways (directly loading it via the "Select case" button or via network, if a remote client is connected). The application uses the OSGVisor3D library to parse the file and search for the data. It is important to note that it is possible to change the characteristics of any of the TOs used just by editing the .ARC file: this feature is replicated in the GUI, which holds all the necessary controls for the tracking engines and automatically shows them and keeps track of their state for every single TO in the scene. The .ARC file specifies also what tracking method associated to any particular TO.

Application Execution, Working Cycle, and Configurable Features at Runtime.
As soon as the application starts, each camera starts acquiring image frames at the resolution and frame rate dictated by the .ARA file. For any TO, the proper tracking engine is called, and the pose of the object is estimated accordingly (Fig. 4). The TOs excluded from the tracking are moved out of the scene. After tracking of the TOs, the scene is repainted and the application starts acquiring the next frame.

Important features that can be controlled at runtime are:

- Possibility to change the transparency of any component of the virtual scenario, making it simpler to adapt the AR visualization modality to the specific surgical task.
- Possibility to track more than one object on the captured area: it is also possible to decide in real-time which objects to localize, and fine-tune the localization engine for each object;
- Possibility to load different .ARC files to configure the software for different uses, without having to quit and restart (or, worse, recode and recompile) the application;
- A preliminary version of a "magic window" is under development. As in [16], the idea is improve user's depth perception by giving him/her the possibility of manipulating semi-transparent windows that show the virtual scenario under the patient skin as a function of the line-of-sight of the camera;
- Possibility to control the software via remote client, e.g. a web page communicating with it. This frees the user from any technical issue, allowing him to be focused only on his task.

3 Results: Use Cases

The application and the OSGVisor3D library have been adopted in a number of applicative cases. Here is a brief review of the most important ones.

3.1 Hybrid Simulator for Cholecystectomy

For educational purposes, we worked on a hybrid simulator for cholecystectomy, which could overcome the limitations of current simulators. The main goal of the work was to develop a new AR visualization method suitable for deformable structures. The hybrid simulator for cholecystectomy was developed through the combination of nitinol tubes with electromagnetic sensors so that the AR system were able to track the deformation of the unexposed tubular structures (Fig. 6) (e.g. arterial tree in a cholecystectomy intervention).

Fig. 6. AR frames of the replica of the arterial tree without (A) and with (B) a simulated connective tissue. The phantom comprises nitinol tubes and tin wires embedded with electromagnetic sensors.

The AR library OSGVisor3D was a key component in this application, providing useful AR support [17, 18]. In this application, the display unit was a standard 2D monitor, whereas the tracking was electromagnetic.

3.2 AR as Aid to Maxillofacial Surgery

In an in vitro study in maxillofacial surgery, the efficacy of the HMD as surgical navigator was validated in combination with an AR visualization modality allowing the definition of an ergonomic interaction paradigm within the augmented scene, named human-perspective-n-problem (hPnP) [19]. The system proved to be an effective surgical aid to bone repositioning [20]. Obtained results suggested that the proposed AR solution can effectively assist the surgeon, making easier and faster the performance of the surgical procedure. The ease-of-configuration of the software was particularly appreciated by the surgeons involved in the study, especially during the initial phase of the study, which was devoted to the definition of the most ergonomic AR visualization modality (Fig. 7).

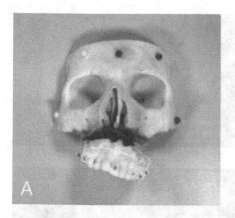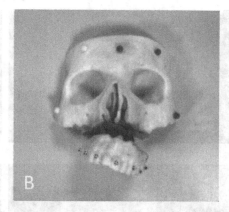

Fig. 7. Different AR visualization modalities tested for aiding maxillary repositioning. (A) Traditional AR interaction technique, featuring the superimposition of a semi-transparent virtual replica of the maxilla. (B) A more ergonomic form of visualization. The virtual information consists of a green asterisk for each coloured landmark on the maxilla.

3.3 AR as Aid to Kyphoplasty (Spine Surgery)

This study was aimed at testing in vitro the use of the HMDs as aid in reaching an intracorporeal target through percutaneous approach. Our goal was in particular to aid trocar insertion during a percutaneous transpedicular vertebroplasty procedure [21].

Several tests were conducted to evaluate the most ergonomic way with which the virtual content had to be displayed depending on one of the two specific subtasks involved in the procedure: the targeting of the entry point on the skin or the setting of the ideal trajectory of the trocar (Fig. 8). To this end, experienced and young surgeons were asked to perform the percutaneous task wearing the HMD with the AR guide running.

The software was particularly effective in speeding up the selection of the most ergonomic visualization modality.

3.4 The OPERA Advanced Operating Room Project

The remote control feature of our application has been exploited in the OPERA Advanced OPERAting Room project (www.progettoopera.it). The OPERA project is devoted to creating a highly automated operating room, with high security and efficiency levels. In this project, the single steps of a surgical workflow are all overseen by a software framework (OPERA Core) communicating with all the devices involved in it (patient monitor, cabinets, scialytic lamps, sliding doors, etc.). The AR support is an important part of the project goals.

During the assessment of the project results, a complete surgical workflow was simulated. Our AR system was tested in communication with the OPERA Core throughout the entire workflow, starting from patient preparation, going through the actual treatment and ending with the operating room cleaning and closing. The stages

40 F. Cutolo et al.

Fig. 8. Ergonomic AR visualization for aiding trocar insertion during a percutaneous transpedicular vertebroplasty procedure.

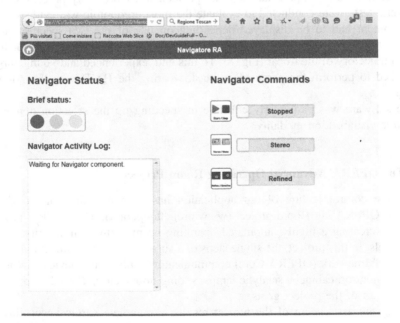

Fig. 9. Sample of the HTML page connected to the application.

of the process are shown in real-time on an HTML5 web page connected to the framework (Fig. 9) and the video output, sent to the HMD, is also replicated on an external display to allow for illustrative and educational purposes. The software was tested with our latest embodiment of HMD.

4 Conclusion

In this paper, we presented a software framework capable of managing flexible, efficient, and multi-purpose video see-through AR-based surgical navigation. The system is able to perform video see-through AR with commercial or custom-made equipment varying in a wide and constantly up-to-date list of devices. By means of video marker-based, template-based, infrared, or electromagnetic tracking methods the application can track several objects and register them to the acquired scene to enhance surgeon's perceptive efficiency.

The application is versatile: it can be coupled with a video see-through HMD (wearable solution) or a 2D/3D monitor. It is possible to use the system having either the monitor or the patient anatomy as perception locations. To improve depth perception and allow the designing of AR-based medical training applications it is possible to disable the tracking and turn off the video feed so as to show only the virtual scenario, which can then be freely rotated, moved and scaled. It is also possible to use more than one display device simultaneously by doubling the video output. The application is easily and highly configurable, thanks to the .ARC/.ARA files architecture. This allows the user to adapt the software framework for several different applicative scenarios and purposes. Any external camera provided with a Direct-Show™ interface and with known intrinsic parameters can be used. The same applies to the display part. The OSGVisor3D class library is highly scalable and takes advantage of multi-core CPUs and graphic card GPUs.

Acknowledgments. This work was funded by the Italian Ministry of Health grant SThARS (Surgical training in identification and isolation of deformable tubular structures with hybrid Augmented Reality Simulation, 6/11/2014–5/11/2017). Grant "Ricerca finalizzata e Giovani Ricercatori 2011-2012" Young Researchers – Italian Ministry of Health.

References

1. Peters, T.M.: Image-guided surgery: from X-rays to virtual reality. Comput. Meth. Biomechan. Biomed. Eng. **4**, 27–57 (2000)
2. Peters, T.M.: Image-guidance for surgical procedures. Phys. Med. Biol. **51**, R505–R540 (2006)
3. Kersten-Oertel, M., Jannin, P., Collins, D.L.: DVV: a taxonomy for mixed reality visualization in image guided surgery. IEEE Trans. Vis. Comput. Graph. **18**, 332–352 (2012)
4. Navab, N., Traub, J., Sielhorst, T., Feuerstein, M., Bichlmeier, C.: Action- and workflow-driven augmented reality for computer-aided medical procedures. IEEE Comput. Graph. **27**, 10–14 (2007)

5. Sielhorst, T., Feuerstein, M., Navab, N.: Advanced medical displays: a literature review of augmented reality. J. Disp. Technol. **4**, 451–467 (2008)
6. Holloway, R.L.: Registration error analysis for augmented reality. Presence: Teleoperators Virtual Environ. **6**, 413–432 (1997)
7. Rolland, J.P., Holloway, R.L., Fuchs, H.: A comparison of optical and video see-through head-mounted displays. Telemanipulator Telepresence Technol. **2351**, 293–307 (1994)
8. Kellner, F., Bolte, B., Bruder, G., Rautenberg, U., Steinicke, F., Lappe, M., Koch, R.: Geometric calibration of head-mounted displays and its effects on distance estimation. IEEE Trans. Visual Comput. Graph. **18**, 589–596 (2012)
9. Genc, Y., Sauer, F., Wenzel, F., Tuceryan, M., Navab, N.: Optical see-through HMD calibration: a stereo method validated with a video see-through system. In: Proceedings of the IEEE and ACM International Symposium on Augmented Reality, pp. 165–174 (2000)
10. Plopski, A., Itoh, Y., Nitschke, C., Kiyokawa, K., Klinker, G., Takemura, H.: Corneal-imaging calibration for optical see-through head-mounted displays. IEEE Trans. Vis. Comput. Graph. **21**, 481–490 (2015)
11. Zhang, Z.Y.: A flexible new technique for camera calibration. IEEE Trans. Pattern Anal. **22**, 1330–1334 (2000)
12. Navab, N., Heining, S.M., Traub, J.: Camera Augmented Mobile C-Arm (CAMC): calibration, accuracy study, and clinical applications. IEEE Trans. Med. Imaging **29**, 1412–1423 (2010)
13. Cutolo, F., Parchi, P.D., Ferrari, V.: Video see through AR head-mounted display for medical procedures. In: International Symposium on Mixed and Augmented Reality, pp. 393–396 (2014)
14. Hu, L., Wang, M.N., Song, Z.J.: A convenient method of video see-through augmented reality based on image-guided surgery system. In: 2013 Seventh International Conference on Internet Computing for Engineering and Science (ICICSE 2013), pp. 100–103 (2013)
15. Sauer, F., Vogt, S., Khamene, A., Heining, S., Euler, E., Schneberger, M., Zuerl, K., Mutschler, W.: Augmented reality visualization for thoracoscopic spine surgery. In: Proceedings of the Society of Photo-Optical Instrumentation, vol. 6141, p. 14106 (2006). Article no. 614106
16. Ferrari, V., Cutolo, F., Calabro, E.M., Ferrari, M.: HMD video see though AR with unfixed cameras vergence. In: International Symposium on Mixed and Augmented Reality, pp. 265–266 (2014)
17. Maria Viglialoro, R., Condino, S., Gesi, M., Ferrari, M., Ferrari, V.: Augmented reality simulator for laparoscopic cholecystectomy training. In: De Paolis, L.T., Mongelli, A. (eds.) AVR 2014. LNCS, vol. 8853, pp. 428–433. Springer, Heidelberg (2014)
18. Viglialoro, R., Condino, S., Freschi, C., Cutolo, F., Gesi, M., Ferrari, M., Ferrari, V.: Proceedings of the Twelfth IASTED International Conference on Biomedical Engineering. ACTA Press (2006)
19. Cutolo, F., Badiali, G., Ferrari, V.: Human-PnP: ergonomic AR interaction paradigm for manual placement of rigid bodies. In: Linte, C., Yaniv, Z., Fallavollita, P. (eds.) AE-CAI 2015. LNCS, vol. 9365, pp. 50–60. Springer, Heidelberg (2015)
20. Badiali, G., Ferrari, V., Cutolo, F., Freschi, C., Caramella, D., Bianchi, A., Marchetti, C.: Augmented reality as an aid in maxillofacial surgery: validation of a wearable system allowing maxillary repositioning. J. Cranio Maxillofac. Surg. **42**, 1970–1976 (2014)
21. Parchi, P.D., Piolanti, N., Andreani, L., Cutolo, F., Freschi, C., Mascioli, S., Ferrari, M., Lisanti, M.: Potentialities of wearable augmented reality in orthopaedics. In: 14th CAOS International (2014)

Application of a New Wearable Augmented Reality Video See-Through Display to Aid Percutaneous Procedures in Spine Surgery

Fabrizio Cutolo[1(✉)], Marina Carbone[1], Paolo D. Parchi[1,2],
Vincenzo Ferrari[1,3], Michele Lisanti[1,2], and Mauro Ferrari[1,4]

[1] Department of Translational Research and New Technologies in Medicine
and Surgery, EndoCAS Center, University of Pisa, Pisa, Italy
fabrizio.cutolo@endocas.org
[2] 1st Orthopaedic Clinic, University of Pisa, Pisa, Italy
[3] Information Engineering Department, University of Pisa, Pisa, Italy
[4] Department of Vascular Surgery, Pisa University Medical School, Pisa, Italy

Abstract. In mini-invasive surgery, the surgeon operates without a direct visualization of the patient's anatomy. In image-guided surgery, solutions based on augmented reality (AR) represent the most promising ones. The aim of this study was to evaluate the efficacy of a new wearable AR system as aid in the performance of percutaneous procedures in spine surgery. Our solution is based on a video see-through head mounted display (HMD) and it allows the augmentation of video frames acquired by two external cameras with the rendering of patient-specific 3D models obtained elaborating radiological images. We tested the system on an in vitro setup intended to simulate the reaching of a lumbar pedicle. An experienced surgeon performed the percutaneous task wearing the HMD. System accuracy was evaluated through post-operative CT scan, measuring the maximum distance between the planned and obtained trajectories inside the pedicle canal. The mean insertion error was of 1.18 ± 0.16 mm .

Keywords: Minimally invasive surgery · Augmented reality and visualization · Computer assisted intervention · Interventional imaging · Spine surgery

1 Introduction

Minimally invasive surgery techniques allow the performance of complex procedures with minimized incisions, increased accuracy, and reduced trauma to the patient, and have become the gold standard for the treatment of specific pathological conditions in different surgical disciplines, as in general surgery [1, 2] and spine surgery [3]. In mini-invasive surgery the surgeon performs the procedure under medical imaging guidance (endoscope, X-Ray, US, etc.) and he/she is often forced to work with an unnatural and restricted view of the surgical field and of the patient's anatomy, with the additional information visualized on an external monitor.

© Springer International Publishing Switzerland 2016
L.T. De Paolis and A. Mongelli (Eds.): AVR 2016, Part II, LNCS 9769, pp. 43–54, 2016.
DOI: 10.1007/978-3-319-40651-0_4

In orthopaedic surgery, Vertebroplasty (VP) and Kyphoplasty (KP) are percutaneous procedures widely used for the treatment of osteoporotic or pathologic fractures. Compared to open procedures they bring several advantages as less bleeding, less pain, less risk of infection, small skin incision, early recovery and shorter hospital stays [4–6].

Vertebral augmentation procedures (VAPs) include three main steps: localization of the correct vertebral level; instrumentation of the vertebral body, either transpedicularly or extrapedicularly (cannula insertion); injection of the cement [7]. Fluoroscopic Guidance (FG) is essential in each step, and a substantial exposure to ionizing radiation for surgeon, patient, and medical staff is unavoidable [8, 9].

Furthermore, FG provides only bi-dimensional projective images, thus forcing the surgeon to carry out complex processes of mental elaboration and hand-eye coordination. Technological advances in medical imaging technologies (CT, MRI, 3D Ultrasound) have helped to overcome some of the shortcomings and limits hindering the mini-invasive procedures by providing physicians with increasingly detailed information on the anatomy and physiology of the patient. Several research activities have been proposed to move towards the development of surgical navigation systems that could aid the physician throughout all the phases of the procedure.

Surgical navigation systems have been proposed also for VAP, based either on direct intraoperative 3D imaging and a navigation software [10, 11] or on Augmented Reality (AR) strategies [12–14]. In a recent work by Sembrano J., et al. [15], the authors compared navigated (through Stealth computer navigation system by Medtronic) and non-navigated needle placement in 30 balloon kyphoplasty procedures. Their results proved the efficacy of navigated VAP in reducing needle malposition rate, but they were not conclusive in terms of cement leakage rates and clinical benefit for both patient and clinical staff (e.g. radiation exposure to the surgeon and patient). The authors claimed that further studies are still needed to conclusively prove the efficacy of the well-established methods for surgical navigation also in VAPs. On this point, the AR-based approaches may represent a promising breakthrough solution for allowing the smooth integration of surgical navigation into the VAP workflow.

AR-based image guided surgery allows the contextual enrichment of the real view of the surgical scene with a virtual content consisting in specific 3D models of the patient's anatomy extracted from medical dataset [16–18].

This paper aims to propose the use of a new wearable AR video see-through navigation system as an aid in the placement of a working cannula through transpedicular approach into the vertebral body, without the aid of X-ray imaging. The aim of the study is to preliminarily test the accuracy of the system in aiding the reaching of lumbar pedicles, as in a VAP, on a newly designed patient-specific spine phantom. Special focus has been devoted to the evaluation of the ergonomics and the effectiveness of the augmented information to be proposed to the operating surgeon throughout the procedure.

2 Materials and Methods

In this section, we shall provide a detailed description of the experimental set-up comprising the HMD system and the patient-specific spine phantom that was designed as testing platform for our AR-based surgical navigation system. Further, we also briefly outline the video see-through paradigm implemented for solving the image-to-patient registration problem.

2.1   AR Navigation System

Our custom-made stereoscopic video see-through HMDs comprises the following two major components (Fig. 1) [19–21]: a commercial 3D visor and a pair of external USB cameras. The commercial 3D visor is a Sony HMZ-T2, provided with dual 720p OLED panels and a horizontal field of view of 45°. The 2 external USB cameras (uEye XS by IDS) are equipped with a 5 Megapixel CMOS sensor (pixel size of 1.4 μm) achieving a frame rate of 15 fps at 1280 × 720 resolution. The two external cameras are mounted on the visor aligned with the user's eyes as to provide a quasi-orthoscopic view of the surgical scene mediated by the visor (in a video see-through fashion). The AR application was implemented in custom-made software library built in C++ on the top of the multipurpose EndoCAS Navigator Platform modules [22].

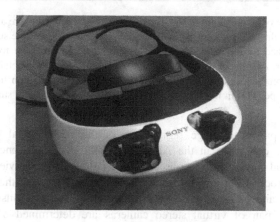

Fig. 1. Our custom-made stereoscopic video see-through HMD based on a commercial 3D visor by Sony (Sony HMZ-T2).

The management of the virtual 3D scene was carried out through the open-source software framework OpenSG 1.8 (www.opensg.org), while regarding the machine vision routines, needed for implementing the video-based tracking method, we adopted Halcon 7.1 software library developed by MVTec®.

The whole system ran on a gaming laptop Alienware® M14 provided with an Intel Core i7-4700 @ 2.4 GHz quad core processor and 8 GB RAM. The graphics card is a 1 GB nVidia® GeForce GTX 765 M.

Here is a functional and logical overview of the video see-through paradigm underpinning our AR mechanism: the two external cameras grab video frames of the real scene; the video frames are screened as backgrounds onto the corresponding display of the visor; the software application elaborates the grabbed video frames to perform the real-time registration of the virtual content, defined during the surgical planning, to the underlying real scene (Fig. 2).

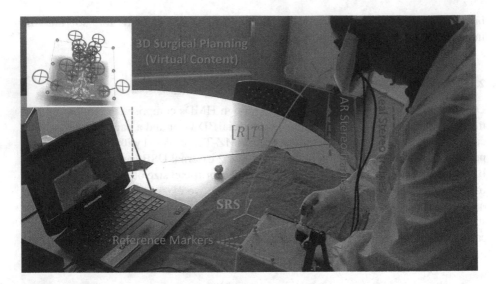

Fig. 2. Video see-through paradigm of the stereoscopic HMD. The software application merges the 3D surgical planning (virtual content) with the stereoscopic views of the surgical scene (real stereo frames) grabbed by the stereo rig. The AR stereo frames are sent to the two internal monitors of the visor. Alignment between real and virtual information is obtained by a tracking modality that relies on the localization of three reference markers rigidly constrained to the spine phantom and whose position in the virtual scene (SRS) is recorded during surgical planning.

The accurate patient-to-image registration is the fundamental prerequisite for yielding geometric coherence in the AR view of the surgical scene. To fulfill this condition the virtual content is to be observed by a couple of virtual viewpoints (virtual cameras) whose processes of image formation must mimic those of the real cameras in terms of intrinsic and extrinsic parameters. To this end, the intrinsic and extrinsic parameters of the pair of virtual stereo cameras are determined offline through a standard calibration routine [23].

Further, to perform a real time registration of the virtual content to the real scene, our system exploits a video-based tracking modality that relies on the localization of at least three physical markers rigidly constrained to the patient and whose position in the virtual scene (i.e. scene reference system or SRS) is recorded during planning. The video-based tracking algorithm computes in real time the rigid transformation encapsulated by matrix $[R|T]$, between the camera reference system (CRS) and the SRS [19].

The key characteristic of the implemented strategy for registering the preoperative planning to the live views of the surgical scene is that it does not rely on the adoption of a bulky external tracker. Standard surgical navigation systems, featuring the use of external infrared trackers, may in fact introduce unwanted line-of-sight constraints into the operating room as well as add error-prone technical complexity to the surgical workflow [24]. Our video-based algorithm provides sub-pixel fiducial registration accuracy on the image plane.

2.2 Spine Phantom

The accuracy and ergonomics of our AR-based surgical navigation system has been tested on an experimental setup that simulates the reaching of lumbar pedicles as in a standard VAP.

An acrylonitrile butadiene styrene (ABS) replica of a patient-specific phantom comprising the lumbar spine (L1-L5) was created. At first, the 3D model of the lumbar spine was obtained from the segmentation of a preoperative computed tomography (CT) dataset: the DICOM files were segmented using a semi-automatic segmentation tool integrated into the open-source platform Insight Segmentation and Registration Toolkit [25].

The resulting 3D virtual anatomic details of the spine were then imported in a CAD environment (PTC® CREO 3.0) to layout the complete phantom. For each of the five vertebrae, the pair of pedicle canals (left and right one) were identified and artificially created in the form of two cylindrical holes with 6 mm diameter. The 3D model of the spine was incorporated in a square box that was designed to contain the anatomy and for acting as a support for 8 spheres taken as reference markers for the tracker-less registration (Fig. 3). The obtained CAD model, in the form of a STL file, was then printed with a 3D rapid prototyping machine (Stratasys® Elite Dimension).

A silicone rubber was injected inside each pedicle in order to replicate the different consistence of the pedicle in respect to the simulated cortical bone. The whole model was then filled with polyurethane foam and covered with a skin-like layer of silicone

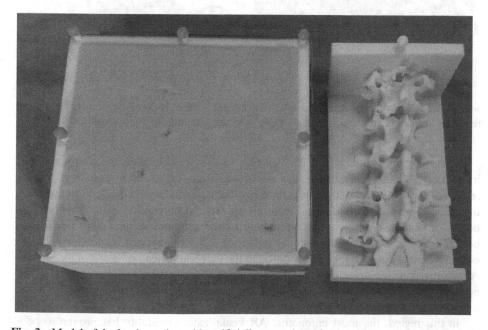

Fig. 3. Model of the lumbar spine with artificially created canals along the pedicles. On the left the ABS replica of the patient-specific phantom was filled with polyurethane foam and covered with a skin-like layer of silicone rubber. On the right the "naked" replica of the spine is shown.

rubber in order to hide the anatomical target, thus for allowing the simulation of a percutaneous intervention [26].

2.3 Surgical Planning and AR Visualization Modality

The visually processed data of the AR visualization modality [27] were all conceived to aid the surgeon in planning the optimal trajectory for accessing the surgical target. The 3D virtual reconstruction of the lumbar spine, together with the purely geometrical elements useful for elaborating the visualization modality, were individually exported to a 3D graphics-modelling tool (Right Hemisphere® Deep Exploration) to elaborate the surgical planning.

Several tests were conducted to evaluate the most ergonomic AR visualization modality in function of the task to be accomplished. In this phase, experienced and young surgeons were asked to perform the percutaneous task wearing the HMD with the AR guide running (Fig. 4).

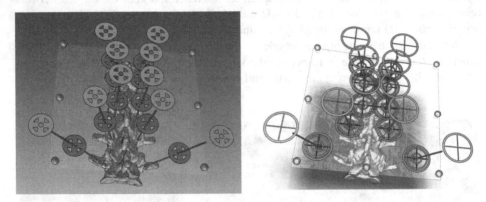

Fig. 4. Complete virtual surgical planning. The figure on the right comprises a more elaborated rendering of the viewfinders, allowing a more accurate definition of the planned trajectory.

As in previous studies [19, 28–30], also in this specific task, the traditional AR interaction technique, featuring the superimposition of a semi-transparent virtual replica of the spine, did not prove to be very effective in aiding the surgeon in targeting the pedicle canal. This is due to the surgeon's limited perception of the relative distances of objects within the AR scene and to the presence of unnatural occlusions between real and virtual structures. Further, the presentation of a too detailed and complex virtual content, proved to confound the surgeon instead of being of assistance. A major issue in the designing of AR-based surgical navigation system is related to the need of providing consistent visual cues for correct perception of depth and spatial relations in the augmented scene [31].

In this regard, the most ergonomic AR visualization modality has proven to be a view indicating the ideal trajectory for targeting each pedicle through a pair of virtual viewfinders: the first at the level of the skin, the second at the level of the bottom of the trocar. The first viewfinder indicates the ideal insertion point for the surgical tool, whereas the second viewfinder defines, once coaxially aligned with the first one, the optimal trajectory of trocar insertion. With such AR guide, the surgeon must simply align the tip of the needle to the center of the first viewfinder on the patient's skin (hence managing 2 positional degrees of freedom).

The second viewfinder is then used by the surgeon to pivoting the trocar around the entry point so that it can be aligned to the planned insertion direction into the pedicle (managing 2 rotational degrees of freedom) (Fig. 5).

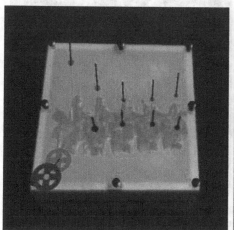

Fig. 5. AR Visualization with the rendering of the spine, the skin, the ideal trajectories, and a pair of viewfinders defining an optimal trajectory of insertion.

2.4 Evaluation Study

In the preliminary evaluation tests, an experienced surgeon performed 4 trial sessions. Each test session consisted in the insertion of 10 Kirshner-Wires (K-Wires) in the pair of pedicles of the 5 lumbar vertebrae included in the phantom. The tests were performed with the aid of the stereoscopic HMD and using the above described AR Visualization modality. The surgeon repeated the test 4 times for a total of 40 percutaneous insertions.

These preliminary tests were aimed at assessing the efficacy of the AR-based guide in terms of accuracy in needle insertion. In this in vitro study, we have not evaluated the registration accuracy, since the in vitro setup did not give rise to any issue related to a preoperative registration procedure: the fiducial markers were rigidly constrained to the ABS box used as support for the replica of the spine.

The surgeon, once planned the ideal trajectory, started the trial whilst wearing the HMD device. The first viewfinder on the external surface of the phantom (i.e. the skin) helped the surgeon finding the insertion point; the second viewfinder, at the bottom of the trocar, was intended to aid the surgeon in defining the optimal trajectory of insertion. Once the surgeon considered the trajectory as satisfying, the K-wire could be inserted.

For each session, system accuracy was evaluated by using post-operative CT scans of the model of the lumbar spine with the 10 needles inserted (Fig. 6). After registering the preoperative and the postoperative reconstructions of the lumbar spine, three different engineers evaluated insertion errors for each K-wire at the upper and lower surface of each pedicle canal by comparing the planned trajectories (green lines in Fig. 6) with the real ones (red lines in Fig. 6). Likewise, the angular insertion error in the axial and sagittal plane was measured. Insertion errors were computed by means of the values collected by the three technicians.

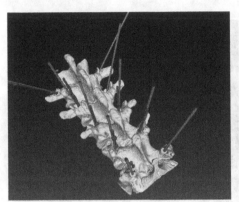 

Fig. 6. Evaluation of the insertion error between planned trajectories (green lines) and reached trajectories (red lines). The light green cylinders indicate the pedicle canals. (Color figure online)

It is important to highlight that, from session 2, a different approach for needle insertion was adopted: a clamping arm was introduced to hold the trocar steady in the defined trajectory during the insertion phase. This strategy was adopted following on surgeon's feedback on the difficulty encountered in maintaining the trajectory steady during the needle insertion. By means of the clamping arm, the trocar can in fact be fastened once the planned trajectory is reached, thus allowing a straight trocar insertion. Therefore, the surgical tasks can be summarized in (1) align the tip of the trocar to the center of the first viewfinder and (2) align the trocar bottom to the second viewfinder (Fig. 7).

3   Results

Results of the tests are reported in Table 1. The results obtained in all the 4 test sessions (10 K-wires implanted for each session) show an overall mean error of 1.18 mm (range of misplacement: 0.01–2.45 mm) with 2 K-wires misplaced (L1Sx and L3sx) in the first session, the one in which the clamping arm was not used.

After the introduction of the clamping arm (i.e. in the last 3 test sessions) we recorded a reduction of the overall mean error from 1.42 to 1.1 mm. As for the angular errors, we obtained an average error of 1.48° (range of angular error: 1.20°–1.97°) in the axial plane and 1.08° (range: 0.75–1.26°) in the sagittal plane.

Fig. 7. The AR-aided surgical tasks. Upper row: The surgeon first aligns the tip of the trocar to the center of the red viewfinder he/she sees in the AR scene; in the zoomed image the red viewfinder and the centered tip are shown. Lower row: the surgeon coaxially aligns the handle of the trocar to the two viewfinders (blue and red). The two viewfinders define the ideal trajectory of insertion; in the zoomed image the two viewfinders and the handle of the trocar are shown optimally aligned. (Color figure online)

The errors reported are encouraging and comparable with those reported in literature. A similar AR-guided approach was described by Abe et al. in 2013. They presented the results of a study conducted on phantoms and on 5 patients in which they adopted a modified commercial HMD (Epson® Moverio) as an AR-based aid in the definition of the optimal trajectory path towards the pedicle canal. Their system uses a single webcam and a template-based tracking method. Throughout the study, they inserted 40 K-wires in a phantom with two vertebrae with and without the navigation system. Axial and sagittal angular errors of insertion for each K-wire were measured by means of a control CT. The overall average angular error reported was of about $0.75 \pm 0.61°$ on the axial-plane and $0.61 \pm 0.70°$ in the sagittal-plane. The results highlighted a statistically significant improvement of the accuracy with the guidance system.

Fritz et al. in 2014 reported their experience with a MRI guided approach. In their study, they performed 25 PVP on a cadaver study reporting a final target error of

Table 1. Insertion errors of the needle inside the pedicles. err US: error at the upper surface. err LS: error at the lower surface. AxA err: Axial Angular error. SagA err: sagittal angular error. mean errors and standard deviation are reported for each session test and globally.

	err US [mm]	err LS [mm]	Overall Mean	AxA err [°]	SagA err [°]
Test 1 (hands free)	1.27±0.71	1.58±0.60	**1.42±0.66**	1.97±1.53	1.26±0.95
Test 2	1.13±0.50	1.04±0.36	**1.08±0.43**	1.20±0.61	0.75±0.45
Test 3	1.03±0.70	1.29±0.43	**1.16±0.58**	1.32±0.89	1.24±0.54
Test 4	1.03±0.40	1.11±0.44	**1.07±0.41**	1.44±0.78	1.09±0.68
Overall MEAN	**1.11±0.12**	**1.25±0.24**	**1,18±0.16**	**1.48±0.34**	**1.08±0.23**

6.1 ± 1.9 mm [14]. Braak et al. in 2013 [10] proposed a Cone Bean CT-based AR guided approach. In that work, the planned trajectory, with a 5-mm safety margin for the needle path, is defined directly in the operating room. The planned path is then projected onto the fluoroscopy image producing a highly accurate real-time image of needle positioning and progression toward the target. The authors tested the system on a spine phantom for a total of 44 needles inserted reporting an overall accuracy of 2.61 ± 1.72 mm.

4   Conclusion

There is a growing interest on the use of AR systems as new surgical navigation systems. The introduction of AR in orthopedic surgery, both for training purposes and as surgical navigators, can lead to positive and encouraging results in terms of increased accuracy and reduced trauma to the patient.

Wearable AR systems based on HMDs allows the surgeon to have an ergonomic viewpoint of the surgical field and of the patient's anatomy and reduce the problems related to eye-hand coordination [19].

In this study, we have presented a wearable AR navigation system as aid to percutaneous VAPs. Results of the in vitro tests were encouraging in terms of insertion accuracy, system usability and ergonomics. Quantitative results confirmed the feasibility of this approach: although our testing platform did not comprise any registration phase, our results, in terms of insertion accuracy, were comparable to similar studies from the published literature. The next appropriate steps will be to proceeding to testing on humans to assess, under real clinical conditions, surgical accuracy and real benefits for the patient. To this end, we think that an improvement of the graphical interface and the designing of a robust intraoperative registration procedure will be key steps to be addressed to improve system accuracy and ergonomics.

Acknowledgments. This work was funded by the Italian Ministry of Health grant SThARS (Surgical training in identification and isolation of deformable tubular structures with hybrid Augmented Reality Simulation, 6/11/2014-5/11/2017). Grant "Ricerca finalizzata e Giovani Ricercatori 2011-2012" Young Researchers – Italian Ministry of Health.

References

1. Soper, N.J., Stockmann, P.T., Dunnegan, D.L., Ashley, S.W.: Laparoscopic cholecystectomy: the new 'gold standard'? Arch. Surg. **127**, 917–921 (1992). Discussion, 921–913
2. Legorreta, A.P., Silber, J.H., Costantino, G.N., Kobylinski, R.W., Zatz, S.L.: Increased cholecystectomy rate after the introduction of laparoscopic cholecystectomy. JAMA **270**, 1429–1432 (1993)
3. Oppenheimer, J.H., DeCastro, I., McDonnell, D.E.: Minimally invasive spine technology and minimally invasive spine surgery: a historical review. Neurosurg. Focus **27**, E9 (2009)
4. Deramond, H., Sebert, J.L., Rosat, P., Fardellone, P., Romero, C.A., Berlemont, F.: Destructive spondyloarthropathy in chronic haemodialysis patients: current data and radiological aspects. J. Neuroradiol. **14**, 27–38 (1987)
5. Peh, W.C., Gilula, L.A.: Percutaneous vertebroplasty: indications, contraindications, and technique. Br. J. Radiol. **76**, 69–75 (2003)
6. Garfin, S.R., Yuan, H.A., Reiley, M.A.: New technologies in spine: kyphoplasty and vertebroplasty for the treatment of painful osteoporotic compression fractures. Spine **26**, 1511–1515 (2001)
7. Peh, W.C.G., Gilula, L.A.: Percutaneous vertebroplasty: indications, contraindications, and technique. Br. J. Radiol. **76**, 69–75 (2003)
8. Ortiz, A.O., Natarajan, V., Gregorius, D.R., Pollack, S.: Significantly reduced radiation exposure to operators during kyphoplasty and vertebroplasty procedures: methods and techniques. AJNR Am. J. Neuroradiol. **27**, 989–994 (2006)
9. Choi, H.C.: Fluoroscopic radiation exposure during percutaneous kyphoplasty. J. Korean Neurosurg. Soc. **49**, 37–42 (2011)
10. Braak, S.J., Zuurmond, K., Aerts, H.C., van Leersum, M., Overtoom, T.T., van Heesewijk, J.P., van Strijen, M.J.: Feasibility study of needle placement in percutaneous vertebroplasty: cone-beam computed tomography guidance versus conventional fluoroscopy. Cardiovasc. Intervent. Radiol. **36**, 1120–1126 (2013)
11. Hoheisel, M., Skalej, M., Beuing, O., Bill, U., Klingenbeck-Regn, K., Petzold, R., Nagel, M. H.: Kyphoplasty interventions using a navigation system and C-arm CT data: first clinical results, pp. 72580E–72588. (2009)
12. Bichlmeier, C., Ockert, B., Heining, S.M., Ahmadi, A., Navab, N.: Stepping into the operating theater: ARAV - augmented reality aided vertebroplasty. In: 7th IEEE International Symposium on Mixed and Augmented Reality 2008, Proceedings, pp. 165–166 (2008)
13. Abe, Y., Sato, S., Kato, K., Hyakumachi, T., Yanagibashi, Y., Ito, M., Abumi, K.: A novel 3D guidance system using augmented reality for percutaneous vertebroplasty. J. Neurosurg. Spine **19**, 492–501 (2013)
14. Fritz, J., Paweena, U., Ungi, T., Flammang, A.J., Kathuria, S., Fichtinger, G., Iordachita, I.I., Carrino, J.A.: MR-guided vertebroplasty with augmented reality image overlay navigation. Cardiovasc. Intervent. Radiol. **37**, 1589–1596 (2014)
15. Sembrano, J.N., Yson, S.C., Polly Jr., D.W., Ledonio, C.G., Nuckley, D.J., Santos, E.R.: Comparison of nonnavigated and 3-dimensional image-based computer navigated balloon kyphoplasty. Orthopedics **38**, 17–23 (2015)

16. Kersten-Oertel, M., Jannin, P., Collins, D.L.: The state of the art of visualization in mixed reality image guided surgery. Comput. Med. Imag. Graph. **37**, 98–112 (2013)
17. Cutolo, F., Badiali, G., Ferrari, V.: Human-PnP: ergonomic AR interaction paradigm for manual placement of rigid bodies. In: Linte, C., Yaniv, Z., Fallavollita, P. (eds.) Augmented Environments for Computer-Assisted Interventions, vol. 9365, pp. 50–60. Springer, Heidelberg (2015)
18. Sielhorst, T., Feuerstein, M., Navab, N.: Advanced medical displays: a literature review of augmented reality. J. Disp. Technol. **4**, 451–467 (2008)
19. Cutolo, F., Parchi, P.D., Ferrari, V.: Video see through AR head-mounted display for medical procedures. In: International Symposium on Mixed and Augmented Reality, pp. 393–396 (2014)
20. Ferrari, V., Cutolo, F., Calabro, E.M., Ferrari, M.: HMD video see though AR with unfixed cameras vergence. In: International Symposium on Mixed and Augmented Reality, pp. 265–266 (2014)
21. Ferrari, V., Megali, G., Troia, E., Pietrabissa, A., Mosca, F.: A 3-D mixed-reality system for stereoscopic visualization of medical dataset. IEEE Trans. Bio-Med. Eng. **56**, 2627–2633 (2009)
22. Megali, G., Ferrari, V., Freschi, C., Morabito, B., Turini, G., Troia, E., Cappelli, C., Pietrabissa, A., Tonet, O., Cuschieri, A., Dario, P., Mosca, F.: EndoCAS navigator platform: a common platform for computer and robotic assistance in minimally invasive surgery. Int. J. Med. Robot. Comp. **4**, 242–251 (2008)
23. Zhang, Z.Y.: A flexible new technique for camera calibration. IEEE Trans. Pattern Anal. **22**, 1330–1334 (2000)
24. Navab, N., Heining, S.M., Traub, J.: Camera Augmented Mobile C-Arm (CAMC): calibration, accuracy study, and clinical applications. IEEE Trans. Med. Imaging **29**, 1412–1423 (2010)
25. Ferrari, V., Carbone, M., Cappelli, C., Boni, L., Melfi, F., Ferrari, M., Mosca, F., Pietrabissa, A.: Value of multidetector computed tomography image segmentation for preoperative planning in general surgery. Surg. Endosc. **26**, 616–626 (2012)
26. Condino, S., Carbone, M., Ferrari, V., Faggioni, L., Peri, A., Ferrari, M., Mosca, F.: How to build patient-specific synthetic abdominal anatomies. An innovative approach from physical toward hybrid surgical simulators. Int. J. Med. Robot. **7**, 202–213 (2011)
27. Kersten-Oertel, M., Jannin, P., Collins, D.L.: DVV: a taxonomy for mixed reality visualization in image guided surgery. IEEE Trans. Vis. Comput. Graph. **18**, 332–352 (2012)
28. Badiali, G., Ferrari, V., Cutolo, F., Freschi, C., Caramella, D., Bianchi, A., Marchetti, C.: Augmented reality as an aid in maxillofacial surgery: Validation of a wearable system allowing maxillary repositioning. J. Cranio Maxill Surg. **42**, 1970–1976 (2014)
29. Parrini, S., Cutolo, F., Freschi, C., Ferrari, M., Ferrari, V.: Augmented reality system for freehand guide of magnetic endovascular devices. Conf. Proc. IEEE Eng. Med. Biol. Soc. **2014**, 490–493 (2014)
30. Ferrari, V., Viglialoro, R.M., Nicoli, P., Cutolo, F., Condino, S., Carbone, M., Siesto, M., Ferrari, M.: Augmented reality visualization of deformable tubular structures for surgical simulation. Int. J. Med. Robot. Comput. Assist. Surg. (IMRCAS) (2015)
31. Bichlmeier, C., Wimme, F., Heining, S.M., Navab, N.: Contextual anatomic mimesis hybrid in-situ visualization method for improving multi-sensory depth perception in medical augmented reality. In: 6th IEEE and ACM International Symposium on Mixed and Augmented Reality, ISMAR 2007, pp. 129–138 (2007)

Challenges in the Effectiveness of Image Tagging Using Consumer-Grade Brain-Computer Interfaces

Christopher Bellman[✉], Ruba AlOmari, Albert Fung,
Miguel Vargas Martin, and Ramiro Liscano

University of Ontario Institute of Technology, Oshawa, Canada
{christopher.bellman,ruba.alomari,miguel.vargasmartin,
ramiro.liscano}@uoit.ca, albert.fung@uoit.net

Abstract. Image tagging in the Internet poses a challenge for search engines. We performed two image tagging experiments using brain-computer interface devices. Both experiments were aimed at testing the feasibility of detecting significant changes in the subjects' electroencephalogram signals upon seeing two classes of visual stimuli. In the first experiment, participants focused on reading web articles while we disguised the images as web advertisements. The second experiment explicitly asked the subjects to think of a word that best described each of the images shown to them. We found that the accuracy of classifying either a rugby or soccer image using a purely Event-Related Potential-based (ERP) classification method produced statistically similar results whether the classification was done with the participant being aware of the classification, or unaware. This may suggest that ERP-based individual image classification using consumer-grade brain-computer interface devices may not be feasible regardless of the method of stimulation.

Keywords: Brain-computer interfaces · Image tagging · Aware image tagging · Unaware image tagging

1 Introduction

With the proliferation of smart-phones and social media, millions of new images are uploaded to the Internet everyday. Classifying these images for content-based image retrieval is challenging even if they are tagged by the user or the uploading application (see e.g. [24]). We hypothesized that both the unaware and aware mind is capable of tagging images and that it is possible to capture such tagging with some level of accuracy using off-the-shelf hardware.

We performed an image tagging experiment whereby electroencephalography (EEG) signals were captured by a consumer-grade Brain-Computer Interface (BCI) while human subjects engaged in reading movie synopses and the images flashed on both sides of the screen disguised as web ads. The participants were

© Springer International Publishing Switzerland 2016
L.T. De Paolis and A. Mongelli (Eds.): AVR 2016, Part II, LNCS 9769, pp. 55–64, 2016.
DOI: 10.1007/978-3-319-40651-0_5

unaware that image tagging was taking place so we called this part of the experiment *unaware*. To make sure subjects were unaware of tagging, this part of the experiment used deception to conceal from the real purpose of the experiment, and subjects were asked to read the synopses carefully as they would be quizzed at the end. We also ran an experiment with the same human subjects and the same set of images where we explicitly asked the subjects to think of a word that best described each image (i.e. "rugby" or "soccer"). Since they were aware that image tagging was taking place, we call this part of the experiment *aware*. These two experiments allowed us to view the results of image tagging using two different methods of stimulation.

Contributions. We provide evidence that consumer-grade BCIs are potentially incapable of interpreting EEG signals as to enable tagging of images that are not necessarily related to the core ERP-based visual stimuli in both unaware and aware scenarios. We found that there is no statistical difference in tagging accuracy between image classes (rugby vs. soccer) when performing unaware and aware tagging.

2   Related Work

In recent years, a staggering number of images are being shared every day online. As of June 2015, Instagram reported 30+ billion photos uploaded since its launch in 2006 with an average of 70+ million photos a day [17]. Flickr reported in May 2015 its photo library contained 10 billion photos [14]. In 2013, a white paper published by Facebook revealed users uploaded a quarter of a trillion photos to Facebook, and an average of 350 million uploads per day [11]. In this section we summarize our efforts to tag images while a participant is unaware of the tagging, i.e., without a human being actually providing a tag explicitly. We classify these efforts into task-based and EEG-based.

2.1   Task-Based Image Tagging

It has been suggested that humans outperform computers in some semantic problems such as image tagging, and a number of crowd-sourcing approaches have been proposed, including embedding the task of tagging or labeling in games known as Games With A Purpose (GWAP) and micro tasks (e.g., Amazon Mechanical Turk, a human intelligence coordination system where people get paid for performing specific tasks on the computer).

Von Ahn et al. [35] proposed and deployed the "ESP" game, a GWAP that aims at tagging images based on a two-player game. The goal of the game is to guess what the other player types about an image that is shown to both players. Players first choose the images they will use. Then for each of the chosen images each player tries to guess what the other player typed, getting points for each correct guess. The game ends when they have gone through all the chosen images, and the player with most points wins the game. Other GWAPs have been proposed. For example, von Ahn et al. [1] proposed Peekaboom, a two-player web-based game that helps identify the location of objects within images. A similar GWAP called "Guess That Face" was proposed by Marques et al. [25] whereby severely blurred photographs of famous people are gradually de-blurred and players have to determine who the face belongs to.

2.2 Using EEG in Image Tagging

Consumer-grade BCIs emerged as a cheap and innovative way to capture and analyze the brain's electrical activity without having to resort to more invasive and expensive technologies such as electrocorticogram, magneto- encephalography, single photon emission computerized tomography, functional magnetic resonance imaging, or lab-grade BCI systems [23]. BCI devices used in EEG recordings can vary from 1-channel headsets (e.g., [27]) to 72-channel headsets [7].

Shenoy et al. [32] ran an experiment in which they used EEG recordings to categorize faces versus non-faces, faces versus images of animals, and faces versus images of inanimate objects. The choice of image categories was based on work showing that different types of objects evoke spatially and temporally different responses [15]. They used Regularized Linear Discriminant Analysis (RLDA) to classify the collected data, and show that the EEG data can be used to categorize images with reasonable accuracy. Kapoor et al. [20] combined EEG data with another method based on Pyramid Match Kernel using a convex kernel alignment algorithm. This combined method outperformed each method individually.

Koelstra et al. [21] assigned affective tags according to the valence-arousal model (see [16]) to videos based on EEG signals elicited by subjects during an experiment. They call their tagging "implicit" because tags are generated implicitly from EEG data as opposed to explicitly expressed by the subjects. A similar system, focused on images instead of videos, was proposed by Apostolakis et al. [2].

Yazdani et al. [37] presented a system that tagged images based on elicited emotions measured with a BCI. A related system using facial point tracker to tag images based on facial geometric information (as opposed to EEG signals) was proposed by Jiao et al. [18].

2.3 Computer Classification

While our focus is on the use of consumer-grade BCI headsets for image classification, it is important to examine efforts on the other side of the spectrum using computers for classification.

Work done by Songhao et al. [33] discuss a method for classifying and tagging images within an individual's photo album on a social media account. The authors propose a three-step method for the automatic tagging of images: First, images are manually selected that are good examples of images that represent a general image within the database. Next, applicable tags are added to the images selected. Finally, using the tag relevance within and between the image tags, tags are automatically added to the unknown images remaining in the set [33]. They found that using their system, average Precision and Recall values exceeded existing algorithms in the literature by as much as 20–50% [33].

Yang et al. [36] propose a novel approach to image tagging and image sub-classification where they were able to sub-classify individual features of specific images from a variety of pre-assembled image databases. They highlight and compare a number of different algorithms and show that they can achieve classification accuracies ranging from 40 % up to over 80 %, depending on the algorithm [36]. These accuracies are taken from images where multiple classifications have been applied to objects within them while in our experiment we only attempt to classify the image as a whole.

In our study we utilize both aware and unaware image tagging to gather results about the tagging quality from the "players" as we can gather data both from their unaware minds when they are actively doing a different task, as well as from when they are aware of directly classifying the images in front of them.

3   Experiment

To determine the feasibility of tagging images using BCIs, we conducted two experiments with human subjects. In the first experiment (we will refer to this experiment as "unaware") we showed the participants images disguised as web advertisements while they focused on reading movie synopses (we refer to these synopses as "articles"). In this experiment subjects had not been informed of the purpose of the experiment and were instructed to pay attention to the article as they would be quizzed about its contents. In the second experiment (we will refer to this experiment as "aware") we specifically asked the same subjects to think of a word that best described each of a series of images showed to them (the same set of images presented during the unaware experiment). These two experiments were conducted in the same session. The experiments were approved by the University of Ontario Institute of Technology's Research Ethics Board (REB # 14–136).

3.1   Stimuli and Apparatus

Both experiments used the Emotiv EPOC headset [10] and captured data at 128 Hz. The EPOC headset has 14 electrodes located according to the 10–20 system of electrode positioning [31]. The 14 electrodes are: AF3, F7, F3, FC5, T7, P7, O1, O2, P8, T8, FC6, F4, F8, and AF4.

Unaware Experiment. In this experiment 24 subjects used a web interface which was designed to look similar to a standard web page a user may come across in their average browsing and consisted of a brief article and two images, one on each side of the article. The articles were synopses of movies taken from Wikipedia (modified to fit on the screen). The images shown on the sides of the articles belonged to one of two classes: soccer or rugby. The images were taken from the results of a Google search of the words soccer and rugby. The images in both sides were shown in a pre-selected, but random order and making sure that at any given time both images corresponded to the same class. Each pair of images was shown for 3 s and then immediately replaced by a new pair of images. A button at the bottom of the screen indicated that the subject was done reading the article and was ready to move forward and be quizzed. The quizzes were evaluated during the analysis to see to what level participants were paying attention to the articles. Each subject went through 6 articles (7 articles total; the first article was not recorded). The number of pairs of images shown varied per article and per subject depending how long it took them to read the article. On average, each of the 6 articles showed 31.28 images (standard deviation of 11.74), yielding a total of 187.71 images per subject.

Aware Experiment. In this experiment the same 24 subjects used a web interface again, but the interface only showed the same set of images used in the unaware experiment for each particular subject, one at a time in random order for 1 s each. This time the subject was specifically asked to think of a word that best described the image shown.

During both of these experiments, the BCI headset was recording EEG data. In the unaware experiment, EEG data was recorded from the time that a participant began reading an article to the time that they clicked the button to indicate they finished reading the article. For the aware experiment, EEG data was recorded for the length of the experiment as there was no stopping in between each image.

3.2   Subjects

A total of 24 participants were recruited from the University of Ontario Institute of Technology's community to participate in the experiment. Test subject candidates were provided with an initial questionnaire to determine eligibility in the experiment. Our inclusion/exclusion criteria included a number of questions relating to any issues reading an article or wearing a BCI headset. The subjects in our experiment were 17 males and 7 females between the ages of 18 and 34 (averaging 22.84 years of age with a standard deviation of 5.12).

3.3   Procedure

We made use of deception to hide the real purpose of the unaware experiment to help reduce active consideration of the images on screen. In the unaware experiment, subjects were told that the purpose was "to conduct research on BCI devices and how the brain interacts with concentration-based tasks." The real purpose of the experiment was explained in the aware experiment. In the aware experiment, subjects were simply asked to think of a word that describes the image they were seeing (i.e. soccer or rugby).

3.4 Data Pre-processing

In total, we removed the data of five subjects due to poor quality data. In addition to these removals, individual data of images were removed if the data exhibited amplitudes of $\pm 50\,\mu V$ (generally caused by blinking or excessive movements). As a result of the pre-processing, we ended up with a total of 19 participants' data (12 males and 7 females). In the unaware experiment there was an average of 30.56 images shown per article per person (with an average standard deviation of 5.37). Roughly 50 % of these images were soccer, 50 % rugby. For the aware experiment, each participant was presented with a total of 209 images. Due to the static nature of this part of the experiment, a constant number of images were shown to each participant. The number of images remaining after pre-processing this set of images (average 45.56) depended on the quality of the data received just as with the unaware experiment image data.

To process the data, we used EEGLAB, a MATLAB toolbox, which allows for efficient analysis of raw EEG data. EEGLAB was chosen due to its mature open source nature, large development community, and extensive library of available plug-ins developed by the EEG research community. We used a band-pass filter of 0.1–15 Hz, as recommended by Bougrain et al. [5], which includes δ (1–3 Hz), θ (4–7 Hz), and α waves (8–12 Hz) [34].

4 Analysis and Results

Our analysis focused on finding tempo-topographic patterns in EEG data that allow for accurate tagging of images belonging to two classes, soccer and rugby. The analysis was conducted separately for the unaware and aware experiments.

4.1 Method for Processing EEG Data

The BCI2000 P300 classifier [29] uses Stepwise Linear Discriminant Analysis [22] (SWLDA), an extension of Fisher's linear discriminant analysis [13], first used to classify P300 waves by Farwell et al. [12]. Nevertheless, since we were classifying a number of ERPs besides P300, we used a linear support vector machine [19] (SVM) with the sequential minimal optimization method to optimize a separating hyperplane as it has been shown to have a competitive performance compared to SWLDA [22]. The features used for SVM classification were the voltage values from the 14 channels.

We trained and tested the SVM for the following epochs: 50–90 ms (VEPs, see Seeck et al. [30]), 130–200 ms (N170, see Eimer [9], Bentin et al. [3], and Caharel et al. [6]), 190–600 ms (visual evoked potentials VEP, see Boehm et al. [4]), 200–300 (P2, see Caharel et al. [6]), 200–350 ms (N200, see Rosburg et al. [28]), 250–500 ms (P300, N400, see Martinovic et al. [26] and Bentin et al. [3]), 300–500 ms (N400f, see Eimer [9] and Currana et al. [8]), 500–750 ms (P600f, see [9]), and 0–999 ms (other ERPs, see [8]). We are not claiming the discovery of a particular ERP for unaware or aware image tagging, as that is a controversial area

Table 1. Unaware experiment F1 scores.

ERP	Average	Max	Min
VEPS1	0.46461	0.57143	0.28571
N170	0.45596	0.58824	0.33333
VEPS2	0.46544	0.61538	0.36364
P2	0.47027	0.57143	0.36364
N200	0.46101	0.57143	0.36364
P3N400	0.46412	0.58824	0.36364
N400F	0.44908	0.61538	0.33333
P600F	0.45187	0.61538	0.25
OERPS	0.43231	0.54545	0.2

Table 2. Aware experiment F1 scores.

ERP	Average	Max	Min
VEPS1	0.44244	0.60714	0.23529
N170	0.47239	0.5614	0.33058
VEPS2	0.49361	0.57534	0.39604
P2	0.46928	0.54902	0.29474
N200	0.45316	0.58278	0.33613
P3N400	0.49876	0.59494	0.384
N400F	0.48574	0.58407	0.34545
P600F	0.44997	0.57325	0.2716
OERPS	0.46241	0.56115	0.32353

we are not targeting in this work. Nevertheless, our results revealed the similar performance of classifying images of a similar nature using machine learning techniques. So, by choosing certain epochs, we are not attempting to detect any specific ERP, as determining ERP tempo-topology is still an ongoing effort of the research community.

4.2 Support Vector Machines

An SVM classifier built-in to MATLAB was used for each of the ERP ranges for both the unaware and aware data. For SVM features, we used the individual voltage values throughout each of the ERPs considered individually. SVMs were trained with the same 1/3 of the total number of images from their corresponding data. To evaluate the performance of image tagging, we use binary classification metrics.

Tables 1 and 2 show the average, maximum, and minimum F1 scores from the SVM classifications. This study suggests that the tagging of images of similar contents using consumer-grade BCIs may be impossible.

5 Discussion and Future Work

The unaware experiment was designed in such a way that subjects were not supposed to notice that the web advertisements were fake. At the end of the experiment, we asked them if they noticed that the imaged disguised as ads were fake. All of the participants responded that they noticed they were fake. This may have skewed our results if participants paid attention to the images and not the articles. However, it turned out that they performed well in the post-article quizzes (average mark was 72 %), which may confirm that they did pay attention to the articles. To make sense of this phenomenon, we would need to conduct further experiments where images would be better concealed.

To deploy a BCI tagging system, we envision an environment where volunteers would wear headsets while using computers as they normally would. These volunteers could be motivated to use the system if they were offered something in return such as free or discounted access to certain services like Internet connection or computer applications.

In the future, a look into wave-based classification (as opposed to ERP-based) may prove useful in finding more accurate and efficient methods of classifying images.

6   Conclusions

We studied the accuracy of image tagging using BCIs. To this end we conducted two experiments with 24 subjects who were shown images of rugby and soccer. In the first experiment, participants focused on reading an article while we flashed images concealed as web advertisements. To make sure they paid attention to the articles and not the images, we used deception by not disclosing the real purpose of the experiment, and furthermore, we quizzed them on the articles they read. In the second experiment, we disclosed the real purpose of the experiment and then showed them the same set of images (no articles to read this time) one by one and asked them to think of a word that best described each image. The results show that using the mind to classify images shows no statistical differences whether or not the participant is aware of whether or not the participant is tasked with thinking of a word that best tags the image, suggesting that image tagging using ERPs as a method of classification is not feasible on such similar images (e.g. rugby images vs soccer images). To address this, further research may be done comparing the performance of ERP-based images (e.g. faces, familiar scenes, etc.) with images that may not be as effective at eliciting ERPs such as just the soccer or rugby balls as well as comparing the differences in produced EEG signals rather than analyzing only the time frames associated with ERPs.

Acknowledgments. This work was partially supported by the Natural Sciences and Engineering Research Council of Canada and the R. Howard Webster Foundation.

References

1. von Ahn, L., Liu, R., Blum, M.: Peekaboom: a game for locating objects in images. In: Proceedings of the SIGCHI Conference on Human Factors in Computing Systems, CHI 2006, pp. 55–64, Montreal, Canada (2006)
2. Apostolakis, K., Daras, P.: A framework for implicit human-centered image tagging inspired by attributed affect. Vis. Comput. **30**(10), 1093–1106 (2014)
3. Bentin, S., Deouell, L.: Structural encoding and identification in face processing: ERP evidence for separate mechanisms. Cogn. Neuropsychol. **17**(1), 35–55 (2000)
4. Boehm, S., Sommer, W.: Neural correlates of intentional and incidental recognition of famous faces. Cogn. Brain. Res. **23**(2–3), 153–163 (2005)

5. Bougrain, L., Saavedra, C., Ranta, R.: Finally, what is the best filter for P300 detection? In: TOBI Workshop lll- Tools for Brain-Computer Interaction, Würzburg, Germany (2012)

6. Caharel, S., Poiroux, S., Bernard, C., Thibaut, F., Lalonde, R., Rebai, M.: ERPs associated with familiarity and degree of familiarity during face recognition. Int. J. Neurosci. **112**(12), 1499–1512 (2002)

7. COGNIONICS: EEG hardware platforms (2015). http://www.cognionics.com/index.php/products/hd-eeg-systems/mobile-eeg-cap. Accessed 7 Apr 2016

8. Currana, T., Cleary, A.: Using ERPs to dissociate recollection from familiarity in picture recognition. Cogn. Brain. Res. **15**, 191–205 (2003)

9. Eimer, M.: Event-related brain potentials distinguish processing stages involved in face perception and recognition. Clin. Neurophysiol. **111**(4), 694–705 (2000)

10. Emotiv: EPOC (2015). https://emotiv.com/cpoc.php. Accessed 7 Apr 2016

11. Facebook: Focus on efficiency white paper (2013). http://newsroom.fb.com/news/2013/09/focusing-on-efficiency/. Accessed 7 Apr 2016

12. Farwell, L., Donchin, E.: Talking off the top of your head: toward a mental prosthesis utilizing event-related brain potentials. Electroencephalogr. Clin. Neurophysiol. **70**(6), 510–523 (1988)

13. Fisher, R.: The use of multiple measurements in taxonomic problems. Ann. Eugenics **7**(2), 179–188 (1936)

14. Flicker: Flicker stats (2015). http://blog.flickr.net/en/2015/05/07/flickr-unified-search/. Accessed 7 Apr 2016

15. Grill-Spector, K.: The neural basis of object perception. Curr. Opin. Neurobiol. **13**(2), 159–166 (2003)

16. Hanjalic, A., Xu, L.: Affective video content representation and modeling. IEEE Trans. Multimedia **7**(1), 143–154 (2005)

17. Instagram: Instagram press (2015). https://instagram.com/press/. Accessed 7 Apr 2016

18. Jiao, J., Pantic, M.: Implicit image tagging via facial information. In: Proceedings of the 2nd International Workshop on Social Signal Processing, SSPW 2010, pp. 59–64, Florence, Italy (2010)

19. Kaper, M., Meinicke, P., Grossekathoefer, U., Lingner, T., Ritter, H.: BCI competition 2003-data set IIb: support vector machines for the P300 speller paradigm. IEEE Trans. Biomed. Eng. **51**, 1073–1076 (2004)

20. Kapoor, A., Shenoy, P., Tan, D.: Combining brain computer interfaces with vision for object categorization. In: IEEE Conference on Computer Vision and Pattern Recognition, CVPR 2008, pp. 1–8. IEEE (2008)

21. Koelstra, S., Patras, I.: Fusion of facial expressions and EEG for implicit affective tagging. Image Vis. Comput. **31**(2), 164–174 (2013)

22. Krusienski, D., Sellers, E., Cabestaing, F., Bayoudh, S., Mcfarland, D.: A comparison of classification techniques for the P300 speller. J. Neural Eng. **3**(4), 299–305 (2006)

23. Lee, J., Tan, D.: Using a low-cost electroencephalograph for task classification in HCI research. In: Proceedings of the 19th Annual ACM Symposium on User Interface Software and Technology, UIST 2006, pp. 81–90 (2006)

24. Liu, D., Hua, X.S., Zhang, H.J.: Content-based tag processing for Internet social images. Multimedia Tools Appl. **51**(2), 723–738 (2011)

25. Marques, O., Snyder, J., Lux, M.: How well do you know Tom Hanks? Using a game to learn about face recognition. In: CHI 2013 Extended Abstracts on Human Factors in Computing Systems, pp. 337–342 (2013)

26. Martinovic, I., Davies, D., Frank, M., Perito, D., Ros, T., Song, D.: On the feasibility of side-channel attacks with brain-computer interfaces. In: 21st USENIX Security Symposium, pp. 143–158, Bellevue, USA (2012)
27. NeuroSky: EEG hardware platforms (2015). http://store.neurosky.com/pages/mindwave. Accessed 7 Apr 2016
28. Rosburg, T., Trautner, P., Dietl, T., Kral, T., Erich, C., Kurthen, M.: The influence of repetition and famousness on the intracranially recorded temporobasal N200. Behav. Neurosci. **119**(4), 876–883 (2005)
29. Schalk Lab: BCI2000 Wiki (2015). http://www.bci2000.org/wiki/index.php. Accessed 7 Apr 2016
30. Seeck, M., Michel, C., Mainwaring, N., Cosgrove, R., Blume, H., Ives, J., Landis, T., Schomer, D.: Evidence for rapid face recognition from human scalp and intracranial electrodes. Cogn. Neurosci. Neuropsychol. **8**(12), 2749–2754 (1997)
31. Sharbrough, F., Chatrian, C., Lesser, R., Luders, H., Nuwer, M., Picton, T.: American electroencephalographic society guidelines for standard electrode position nomenclature. Neurophysiology **18**, 200–202 (1991)
32. Shenoy, P., Tan, D.S.: Human-aided computing: utilizing implicit human processing to classify images. In: Proceedings of the SIGCHI Conference on Human Factors in Computing Systems, pp. 845–854. ACM (2008)
33. Songhao, Z., Zhiwei, L., Xiaoyuan, J.: Tags tagging. In: Control Conference (CCC), pp. 3066–3069. IEEE (2011)
34. Szafir, D., Mutlu, B.: Pay attention! designing adaptive agents that monitor and improve user engagement. In: Proceedings of the SIGCHI Conference on Human Factors in Computing Systems, CHI 2012, pp. 11–20 (2012)
35. von Ahn, L., Dabbish, L.: Labeling images with a computer game. In: Proceedings of the SIGCHI Conference on Human Factors in Computing Systems, CHI 2004, pp. 319–326, Vienna, Austria (2004)
36. Yang, Y., Huang, Z., Yang, Y., Liu, J., Shen, H.T., Luo, J.: Local image tagging via graph regularized joint group sparsity. Pattern Recogn. **46**(5), 1358–1368 (2013)
37. Yazdani, A., Lee, J.S., Ebrahimi, T.: Implicit emotional tagging of multimedia using EEG signals and brain computer interface. In: Proceedings of the First SIGMM Workshop on Social Media, WSM 2009, pp. 81–88, Beijing, China (2009)

Development of a Virtual Simulator for Microanastomosis: New Opportunities and Challenges

Valerio De Luca, Antonio Meo, Antonio Mongelli[✉],
Pietro Vecchio, and Lucio T. De Paolis

Department of Engineering for Innovation, University of Salento, Lecce, Italy
{valerio.deluca,antonio.mongelli,
lucio.depaolis}@unisalento.it

Abstract. The paper deals with the development of virtual surgical simulator for microanastomosis developed within the INTERREG (Italy-Greece) MICRO project. Microanastomosis is a surgical technique that involves, under optical magnification, the conjunction of blood vessels of a few millimeters diameter and is used also to support the surgical treatment of tumours. This manuscript describes the two principal solutions analysed during the progress of the MICRO project. The first step concerns the development of the simulator using the Unity3D engine; the second step describes an evolution of the surgical simulator to support remote control by a haptic interface via web using the WebGL platform based on JavaScript code. For both, a force feedback module has been implemented that reads data coming from the simulator and converts them to generate a servo control action on the haptic interface. For both solutions, some results of the implemented simulator are described .

Keywords: Surgical simulator · Microanastomosis · Virtual reality

1 Introduction

According to the AIRTUM 2013 (Italian Association of Cancer Registers) report, head and neck malignant tumours are in fifth place in order of frequency in Italy. Every year they record about 7,200 new cases among men and 2,100 among women (in addition, the percentages related to skin cancers has to be considered).

About 90 % of these neoplasms are represented by squamous-cell carcinoma departure from the epithelium lining the mucous membranes of the various districts. Less frequently, tumours may originate from different types of tissues such as the salivary glands, thyroid, skin, lymph tissue and bone tissue. More various can be the onset locations: the mouth, throat, nose, sinuses, larynx, pharynx, salivary glands, thyroid gland, eye sockets, or bones of the facial region.

At present, surgery is still the method of choice in most cases. The surgical removal of the tumour, when possible, gives the best chance of healing, especially if associated with radio-chemotherapy combined treatments. Moreover, thanks to the improvements in recent years in the anaesthetic techniques and postoperative care of patients the number of patients who are candidates for surgical treatment is increasing.

© Springer International Publishing Switzerland 2016
L.T. De Paolis and A. Mongelli (Eds.): AVR 2016, Part II, LNCS 9769, pp. 65–81, 2016.
DOI: 10.1007/978-3-319-40651-0_6

Due to the aesthetic-functional importance of the involved structures, however, it is of fundamental importance not only tumour resection, but also performing an adequate reconstruction. Otherwise, sometimes, the results of this type of intervention can be extremely deleterious. At present, the best reconstructive methods to optimize surgical resections are based on the use of free flaps. This method, born in the 70 s, has revolutionized the oncologic and reconstructive surgery. Today, the use of this method allows, in fact, to adequately reconstruct different areas of the face and different types of tissues, thus allowing the recovery of adequate function and an often optimal aesthetic appearance.

However, this technique requires specialized surgical centres, and it is a procedure that involves the use of a microscope with a specific ability to operate in diameter vessels very few millimetres in size. For this reason, it is important to act in the setting up of a specific training, which today, in Italy, can be done on synthetic or animal models. Both these methods have major limitations and they are not often used. The synthetic models, based on the simulation of micro-sutures of silicone models, do not constitute a faithful representation of reality. The use of animal models is rather limited by ethical issues, since it needs special structures with high costs, and at present in Italy there are few centres that could benefit from them.

These factors constitute a big obstacle to the training of the surgeons who would perform microsurgery and to refresher courses for them.

The simulator developed in this project, by virtually recreating the conditions of the operating field and of the microscope, can allow the surgeon to perform a training session to learn and perfect microsurgical techniques, thus facilitating clinical practice. The use of a virtual system allows one to avoid the problems related to synthetic and animal models, thus increasing the number of specialists that could perform reconstructive surgeries based on microsurgical techniques.

The paper treats the development of a virtual surgical simulator for microanastomosis developed within the INTERREG MICRO project. Microanastomosis is a surgical technique that involves, under optical magnification, the conjunction of blood vessels of a few millimeters in diameter (Fig. 1). This technique is used to support the surgical treatment of tumours, consisting in bone reconstruction after demolition, and is one of the surgical procedures used in maxillofacial surgery.

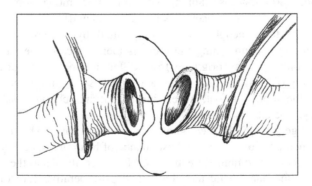

Fig. 1. Surgical technique for microanastomosis

Also in the medical field, virtual simulators are excellent training tools that allow improvement in surgical performances. In recent years, advances in engineering and information technology have allowed for the development of more and more detailed and realistic simulation models. These innovations therefore provide new tools for diagnosis, preoperative surgical planning and training, allowing surgeons to perform procedures on virtual patients that are realistic replicas of real ones.

The serious game represents a new trend in the development of virtual surgical simulators. Serious games are games whose main purpose is not entertainment, but teaching and learning. Although virtual simulations and serious games are conceptually similar and can use the same technology (hardware and software), serious games introduce an element of entertainment and include some of the main aspects of video games including challenge, risk, reward and defeat.

Within the MICRO Project, we carried out the development of a simulator for surgical training in the microanastomosis procedure. Section 2 presents the architectures of the MICRO simulator based on the Unity3D [1, 2] and WebGL [3, 4] platforms. It describes also the algorithms and the structures implemented to obtain a standard surgical simulator.

Section 3 describes the virtual simulator in terms of both the architectures and the Mass-Spring based algorithm used to simulate the penetration of the needle in the tissue.

Finally, Sect. 4 contains the conclusions with future improvements of the surgical simulator in order to be realized as a serious game.

2 Related Works

Several works about surgery simulators can be found among the literature. Some review papers [5, 7] analysed the potential benefits of virtual reality simulators for microsurgery, neurosurgery and robot-assisted surgery. They highlighted that virtual reality provides a safe, cost-effective and portable environment for surgical training.

Reference [8] evaluated the advantages and disadvantages of virtual simulators for open surgical procedures compared to more traditional techniques such as those based on bench models, live animals and cadavers. The main concern about virtual reality simulators is related to the sense of realism that they could provide.

A strong improvement in users' performance and appreciation is provided by stereo viewing and it leads to an accurate navigation and faster decision-making [9, 10].

An example of an anastomosis simulator [11] is the one developed by Boston Dynamics Inc. By means of a needle holder and forceps attached to force feedback devices, it allows the user to grasp, poke, pluck and suture flexible tube organs. It uses a mirror system to show the 3D surgical scene at the hand level of the trainee.

Mimic Technologies released MSim 2.1 [12], a software upgrade that adds anastomosis exercises to dv-Trainer [13], a training tool for the da Vinci surgical system. It provides also an evaluation of training performance based on data collected from more than 100 experienced surgeons.

MicroSim [14] provides a virtual environment for microanastomosis training. It uses real instruments as input interface and detects their position through an optical tracking system. It uses also a stereo display to simulate the surgical scene viewed through a microscope.

The microsurgery training system presented in [15] allows a physics-based suture between two blood vessels running at 500 Hz. The hardware involved in the virtual interaction includes also a pair of haptic forceps.

Other significant virtual simulators deal with the anastomotic technique of Coronary Artery Bypass Grafting (CABG) [16] and ventriculostomy [17, 18].

Some other virtual environments [19, 20] simulate guidewire insertions along the centre line of blood vessels.

Some important algorithms [21] were designed to improve visual realism in virtual environments for surgical training: they concern object deformations due to external forces and collisions among deformable and rigid objects.

Some libraries and frameworks have been designed to support the development of applications based on haptic interactions. The QuickHaptics microAPI [22] provides a wide range of features that can be used to develop graphics applications involving also force feedbacks. The Penn Haptic Texture Toolkit [23] is a public repository containing 100 haptic textures and friction models: each of them is based on a ten-second recording of the force, speed, and high-frequency acceleration perceived through a handheld tool. Another component-based haptic framework [24] was designed as an extension for Unity3D.

None of the mentioned works focused on the suitable developing frameworks and technologies. Our work tries to make a comparison between a desktop (based on Unity3D) and a WebGL (based on Javascript) implementation of a microanastomosis simulator. We focused on the technical challenges faced in these two development environments. In particular, we analysed the feasibility of the implementation of a surgical simulator as a web service.

3 Architectures and Technologies

3.1 Unity3D Architecture

The research into the development of the simulator has seen two distinct phases. At first, the development of the simulator was experienced using Unity3D [1, 2]. Unity3D is an integrated platform for creating 3D videogames or other interactive contents such as virtual reconstructions or 3D animations in real time. The SDK [25] of Unity3D can run on both Microsoft Windows and OS X, and the games produced can be run on Windows, Mac, Linux, Xbox 360, PlayStation 3, PlayStation Vita, Wii, iPad, iPhone, Android. Unity3D allows using an editor for both development and content design. Figure 2 shows the simulator architecture based on Unity.

Analysing the stack from the bottom to the top, you can see the first module is the interface that communicates directly with the haptic Open Haptics Library [26, 27] for full hardware management. This library implements a process with a loop for rendering in about 1000 Hz that are necessary for a correct simulation of the forces. Following, a Middleware communication was adopted for the communication between the Haptic Server and the Unity3D platform. The haptic Server communicates via ZeroMQ [28] that allows a rapid deployment of complex communication systems using C++ codes.

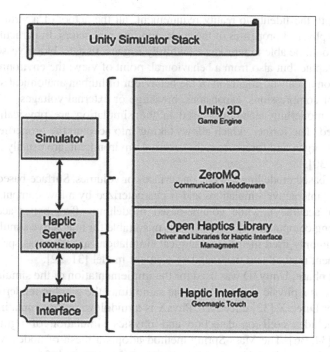

Fig. 2. Proposed architecture based on Unity3D

The ZeroMQ communication layer allows uncoupling the management of the interface haptic simulator. In this way, you can use the device with any rendering graphic engine. The Haptic Sever implements an internal loop and contains a buffer to allow the correct simulation of the forces. Information about handle positions and forces is delivered to the communication layer on the physics engine. Figure 3 shows the scheme of the Haptic Server.

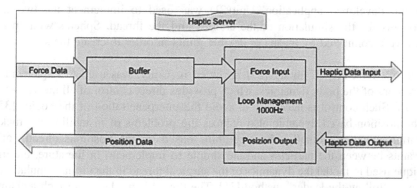

Fig. 3. Haptic server scheme

According to the fidelity-to-reality requirement, all the actors of a virtual simulator have the same physical properties of the corresponding real actors. In particular, surgical simulations should be able to reproduce faithfully organs, tissues, blood vessels, etc. not only from a graphic, but also from a behavioural, point of view: the environment should give the surgeon a realistic cognition of the behaviour of human anatomical structures in the presence of compressions, expansions, breakage or external voltages.

The main modelling techniques used in the simulation are physically-based or geometry-based. The former, which allows taking into account the properties of matter constituting an organ and forces from the external environment, are usually preferred to the latter [29, 30].

Physically-based modelling can rely on surfaces or volumes. Surface-based modelling is indicated for interactive simulations and is characterized by a low computational load (with a lower accuracy), while volume-based modelling offers better accuracy, but involves a strong computational load, which is unsuitable for interactive simulations [30]. The most commonly used methods in surgical simulations are the mass-spring method, the finite element method and the boundary element model [31, 32].

In the first phase, Unity3D was used for the implementation of the simulator. It uses NVidia PhysX as a physic engine and, at the same time, the graphic rendering contains the OpenGL or DirectX [33] directives. PhysX is a middleware for simulating real-time physics. It includes collision detection and physics simulation of rigid bodies as explained in [34, 36]. The Mass-Spring method adopts a mesh of nodes with specific mass connected through springs with specific damping factors [32].

The model can be deformed when an external force is applied. The offset of each node can be calculated as:

$$m_i \ddot{r}_i = -d_i \dot{r}_i + \sum_j^i f_{ij} + F_i^e + f_i^u \tag{1}$$

where m_i and r_i are the mass and the offset of the node i, while d_i is the damping factor, while f_{ij} is the external force between the node i and node j, F_i^e is the external force on the node i and f_i^u is the initial force applied on the node i.

In the developed application, Unity3D was used to implement the two main components for the simulation of the arteries and the thread. Spheres with specific masses were connected by means of flexible joints in order to create the shape of the body.

The NVIDIA PhysX library [37], included in Unity, was used to implement the management of the body dynamics, which provides direct control of all the vertices of the mesh. Such control is necessary to avoid the interpenetration of the bodies [35].

The position-based dynamic also reduces the problems of instability that make a simulation unnatural. Finally, the algorithms based on the positions directly affect constraints between the particles and are simple to implement. In literature, the main technique used to model the dynamics of the surgical thread in the virtual simulations is known as "follow-the-leader" method [31]. The thread is modelled through a chain of N cylinders of length L and radius R = L/2. The connection of the cylinders is obtained by means of joints, which allow the bending of the thread.

3.2   WebGL/JavaScript Architecture

The MICRO project went through several phases: it started with the development of a standard simulator with the characteristics of a serious game as in [38, 39], but then it focused on the design of a cloud-based simulator. In order to enable remote control through a haptic interface on a web service platform, we implemented a WebGL version of the surgical simulator using the JavaScript language [3, 4].

The implemented modules are shown from the bottom to the top of the left column (Fig. 4).

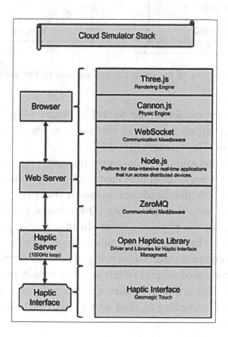

Fig. 4. Cloud-based 3D architecture

The Haptic Server communicates through the ZeroMQ library [28] with the JavaScript Web Server based on Node.js middleware [40]. The Node.js framework allows the development of server-side web application using the same syntax of JavaScript.

The framework offers several advantages: the most important of which is the possibility to develop server-side applications without the need to learn any "traditional" language. Since a strong point of Node.js is software scalability, the framework could be used for both small projects and enterprise applications. The simulator was developed as a Single Page Web Application with two specific libraries: Cannon.js [41] as a physics engine and Three.js [42] as a graphic engine.

The diagram in Fig. 5 shows the application deployment.

The client application includes a haptic Server communicating through ZeroMQ with the web server based on Node.js. The client browser queries the web server

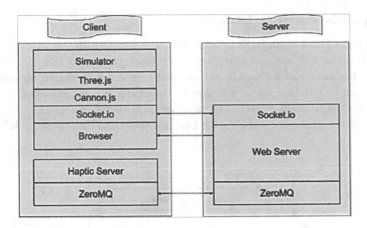

Fig. 5. Block diagram of the implemented system in the WebGL platform

through the Web Socket protocol with the Socket.io library [43]. The algorithms for the modelling of tissue and suture thread are the same as those implemented in Unity (Mass-Spring and Follow-The-Leader) [31, 32].

In the proposed architecture, physics and rendering engines are handled as two different processes. In this way, an improvement of the system's general performance can be obtained due to the independence between the two modules. Each worker implements a proprietary loop that provides a 30 Hz frame rate for the graphic engine and a 60 Hz frame rate for the physics engine. In this way, a proper rendering and a realistic simulation of the virtual environment can be achieved.

The worker code implements the mass-spring algorithm generating the vessels and the thread structure by means of several spheres with a well-defined mass connected by elastic constraints [30]. The primary worker updates information about position and orientation of the meshes according to data sent by the secondary worker.

3.3   Haptic Server and Force Feedback System

In the MICRO project, the setup and configuration of a GeoMagic haptic interface with the related SDK was implemented [26, 27]. The APIs described in the haptic interface manual allows a direct control of the hardware system regarding position, rotation matrix and friction components, mass and density characterizing the force feedback.

In order to provide support to the surgical instrumentation with modules for the interaction with the haptic interface we used the ZeroMQ (ØMQ) [28] communication protocol. In this sense, we studied procedures for the real-time data transmission as a support to surgical environments and we implemented an application based on the ZeroMQ libraries, which are compliant with the Web-Socket protocol. The application uses the ZeroMQ libraries and the haptic interface API to elaborate position and interaction data and to implement real-time transmissions. The ØMQ API provides general-purpose sockets, each of which can represent many connections between endpoints with force feedback system.

Within this activity, we detected the system calls needed for a force feedback implementation in the server module of the haptic interface simulation and then we have successfully implemented the force feedback system. The force feedback system reads the data coming from the Unity Platform and converts them to generate a servo-haptic control action on the haptic interface.

Even though in a rough form, the force feedback allows remote management during the wire penetrations through the blood vessel. We implemented a Publish/Subscribe [44] channel based on the ZeroMQ libraries between the haptic interface control system and the Unity-based client. In this way, data provided by the Unity client with the API calls of the haptic interface can be used to reproduce a force feedback in real-time even for remote sessions.

Figure 6 shows the prototype of the implemented simulator.

Fig. 6. The prototype of the implemented simulator

The code for this force feedback was implemented on a C++ platform and it was entirely integrated with the API calls of the GeoMagic haptic interface SDK. Data transfer is realized by sending and receiving data strings into particular communication sockets. The output represents a continuous data string containing spatial localization, rotational and control data.

The Unity3D framework allows the addition of a force impulse for each rigid body of the medical rope using their mass. It can detect the collisions of the medical rope with the blood vessel in real time; therefore, we can intercept the feedback force impulse instantly with a single system call.

These feedback force impulses have various behaviours in accordance with the mass value of rigid body that has generated it, for this reason the force applied on objects to push or to twist rigid bodies should be equalized on the different values of mass in order to avoid too much amplifications or attenuations of force impulses in the virtual model.

These effects are useful for applying forces that instantly happen, such as forces from explosions or collisions and are applied to the rigid body as its mass*distance/time. Such data, which represent a measure of the force feedback, are sent from the Unity3D platform to the Haptic Server to generate a servo-haptic control action on the interface. Below you can find an extract of the implemented code for transmitting the force impulses from the Unity3D platform toward the haptic server:

```
Vector3 impulse2 = CollisionManager.impulse;
float xx = impulse2.x;
float yy = impulse2.y;
float zz = impulse2.z;
string data2 = xx + "*" + yy + "*" + zz + "*";
NetMQMessage message2 = new NetMQMessage();
message2.Append(data2);
byte[] data3 = System.Text.Encoding.UTF8.GetBytes(data2);
socket2.SendMore("CHANNEL2", true).Send(data3);
```

We declare a variable of type Vector3 to which we assign the values of the force impulse retrieved by the Unity3D platform. Then we declare three variables of type float to exact the measures of collisions on the 3D space. Then, these data are sent from the Unity3D to the haptic server by a socket web connection using the NetMQ library [45]. In this way, the haptic server module will send and receive data on two different sockets contemporaneously in real time.

Some libraries were already available for the Unity3D engine to link the haptic interface control system and the Unity-based client.

On the contrary, for the WebGL/JavaScript platform, we had to implement on our own some new software routines to emulate the force feedback of the haptic interface by estimating strength and permanence of the rope with needle inside the blood vessel. In particular, we identified some measures to bind the movements of the haptic interface with the deformations of the blood vessel during the penetration of the medical needle through the blood vessel. The measures of the deformation and then of the force feedback are obtained by calculating the offsets of each elementary structure that the blood vessel model realized with respect to predetermined positions; and adding to them other coefficients calculated basing on the crossing of the medical rope inside the blood vessel.

Below it is reported the essential code to calculate the feedback force components for the WebGL platform. In particular, in the extract of the implemented code there are three principal variables: Ind1, Ind2 and the Vector3d feedbackForce.

```
if(((Ind1+Ind2) < threadLength) ) {
  if (Ind1<Ind2) {
      for(var i=0;i<=(Ind1-1);i++){
          bodies["thread-"+i].velocity.set(-1*normalP2.x,-1*normalP2.y,0);
          feedbackForce = bodies["vesselAxes-" + indexASSE[i]].position.vsub
          (bodies["thread-"+i].position));
      }
      for(var i=Ind1;i<=(mInd-1);i++){
          bodies["thread-"+i].velocity.set(-1*normalP2.x,-1*normalP2.y,0);
          bodies["thread-"+i].position.set(PointOrigine2.x+0.1*normalP2.x,Point
          Origine2.y+0.1*normalP2.y,PointOrigine2.z+0.1*normalP2.z);
          feedbackForce = bodies["vesselAxes-" + indexASSE[i]].position.vsub
          (bodies["thread-"+i].position));
      }
      if (Iscarto>=4) {
          for(var i=Ind1; i<=((Ind1+Math.floor(Iscarto/2))-1); i++){
              bodies["thread-"+i].velocity.set(1*normalP2.x,1*normalP2.y,0);
              bodies["thread-"+i].position.set(bodies["vesselAxes-" +
              indexASSE[0]].position.x+0.1*normalP2.x,bodies["vesselAxes-" +
              indexASSE[0]].position.y+0.1*normalP2.y,bodies["vesselAxes-" +
              indexASSE[0]].position.z+0.1*normalP2.z);
              feedbackForce = bodies["vesselAxes-" +
              indexASSE[i]].position.vsub(bodies["thread-"+i].position));
          }
          for(var i=(Ind1+Iscarto); i<=(Ind1+Math.floor(Iscarto/2));i--){
              bodies["thread-"+i].velocity.set(1*normalP1.x,1*normalP1.y,0);
              bodies["thread-"+i].position.set(bodies["vesselAxes-" +
              indexASSE[0]].position.x+0.1*normalP1.x,bodies["vesselAxes-" +
              indexASSE[0]].position.y+0.1*normalP1.y,bodies["vesselAxes-" +
              indexASSE[0]].position.z+0.1*normalP1.z);
              feedbackForce = bodies["vesselAxes-" + indexASSE[i]].position.vsub
              (bodies["thread-"+i].position));
          }
} } } }
```

The Ind1 and Ind2 variables record and manage the penetration of the medical rope inside the blood vessel by teaching each body of the structure to follow some specific directions; while tVector3d feedbackForce is used to calculate the force feedback by estimating the deformation of the blood vessel with respect to the fixed position of the its axes points.

The Vector3d feedbackForce variable will be used to implement the servo-haptic control action on the haptic interface using a different socket to transmit in real time the control data between the haptic server and the graphic client WebGl/JavaScript.

3.4 Unity3D Architecture

A screenshot of the obtained simulation results is given in Fig. 7, which shows an example of a latero-lateral anastomosis during a session of the surgical simulator based on the Unity3D platform.

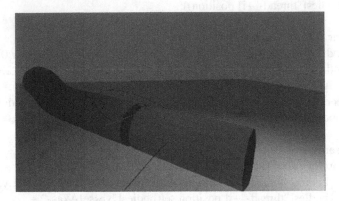

Fig. 7. A possible latero-lateral anastomosis

Fig. 8. A possible latero-lateral anastomosis

3.5 WebGL/JavaScript Architecture

Figure 8 shows an example of a latero-lateral anastomosis during a session of the surgical simulator based on WebGL/JavaScript.

4 Conclusions and Future Work

The manuscript has dealt with the development of virtual surgical simulator for micro anastomosis developed within the INTERREG (Italy-Greece) MICRO project. The development of the simulator has seen two distinct phases. At first, the development of the simulator was experienced using the Unity3D platform [2, 25].

In the second phase, to overcome some of the limitations of the Unity3D platform and support remote control by a haptic interface via the web, an evolution of the surgical simulator was implemented using the WebGL platform with JavaScript code [41].

In particular, the advantages of using the Unity3D environment lie in the multi-platform features: it allows implementations for various operation systems and hardware support. The SDK of the Unity3D [25] can run on both Microsoft Windows and OS X, and the games produced can be run on Windows, Mac, Linux, Xbox 360, PlayStation 3, PlayStation Vita, Wii, iPad, iPhone, Android.

The disadvantages in the use of Unity3D lie in the NVidia PhysX engine [33, 37]. The implementation of the suture thread in Unity3D based on the NVidia PhysX engine did not produce a satisfying result because the simulation diverges under some stress conditions. In particular, it could be noticed that the lack of high fidelity articulated physics support often manifests itself in the following problems:

- Two rigidly joined rigid bodies can be pulled apart under huge force;
- The mass ratio between two joined rigid bodies is limited to less than 1:10 in order to maintain joint stability;
- A heavy weight at the end of a long rope makes the rope springy, jumpy and unstable;
- Motors are soft and cannot deliver enough power to drive multi-level articulated robotics;
- Doors, hands, wheels wobble around their joint axis under a heavy load;
- Simulation step size (time interval) should be made too small to provide the needed accuracy, which destroys performance.

For these reasons, we decided to develop the simulator also with a new software architecture based on a new physical engine, in particular with WebGL platform [3, 4, 41].

On the other hand, the advantages in using the WebGL/JavaScript architecture are the access, via the web, to the surgical simulator, also by a haptic interface in remote position and an optimal multi-platform for different and various pieces of hardware.

In a WebGL/JavaScript environment, the whole surgical simulator is loaded into a normal browser for navigation on the Internet and in this sense, only a local or remote Internet connection with specific cloud access via web would be needed.

Moreover, the WebGL graphic engine is very stable and can control all the kinetics of the rigid bodies, of the joined rigid bodies and of the surgical rope with an acceptable simulation step size.

The disadvantages in using of the WebGL/JavaScript architecture lie in ensuring an adequate internet connection needed to run the communications between the ZeroMQ [28] server with the simulator client with an optimal frame-rate and in setting up an opportune SubScribe/Publisher mechanism to manage the interaction between the haptic interface and the rendering engine WebGL during remote control.

Nevertheless, other disadvantages may lie in the requirement for hardware platforms that are more advanced in the sense of computational complexity and a JavaScript code unsuited for the debugging of the surgical simulator or to update it.

With the help of the maxillo-facial surgery medical staff of the "Casa Sollievo della Sofferenza" Hospital in San Giovanni Rotondo, other improvements were identified to make the virtual simulator as close as possible to the real operating environment. In particular, the main issues deal with the enhancement of the surgical suture realism, the possible insertion of a vascular clamp to interrupt the blood flow and the modelling of bleeding in the case of the non-tightness of microanastomosis as in [38, 39, 46].

In the MICRO project, the "Touch" haptic interfaces provided by Geomagic were used as input devices, even though they were not integrated with the typical surgical instruments used by surgeons during the microanastomosis procedure.

Therefore, a further improvement to this project would be to provide the use of haptic devices that simulate in a more correct way the movements of the surgeon and the internal forces during the microanastomosis operation [15].

Currently, the trend in simulation is to implement virtual training system as a serious game [47, 48]. A serious game is a simulator able to rate skills through a final score. This total score is obtained from the analysis of different parameters appropriately defined and integrated in the simulator in order to produce an assessment of the training session.

In the light of the above, an improvement could be the addition of a score that will index the performance of the procedure. The score will be obtained by considering a number of parameters that must be provided by doctors (for example the elapsed time, the suture precision, the distance variability of needle insertion points, etc.).

Acknowledgements. The presented simulator has been developed in the Italy-Greece INTERREG Project titled "A cross-border microsurgery centre of excellence for the promotion of research, training and education - MICRO".

The partners of the MICRO Project are:

- Microsurgery Lab of the Foundation for Research and Technology (FORTH), Greece;
- University of Ioannina, Greece;
- Augmented and Virtual Reality Laboratory (AVR Lab) of the Department of Engineering for Innovation, University of Salento, Lecce, Italy;
- "Casa Sollievo della Sofferenza" Hospital in San Giovanni Rotondo, Italy.

References

1. Xie, J.: Research on key technologies base Unity3D game engine. In: ICCSE 2012 - Proceedings of 2012 7th International Conference on Computer Science and Education, pp. 695–699 (2012)
2. Unity3D_Guide, http://docs.unity3d.com/Manual/UnityManual.html
3. webgl_Guide, http://ptgmedia.pearsoncmg.com/images/9780321902924/samplepages/0321902920.pdf
4. webgl_homepage, http://www.khronos.org/webgl/
5. Erel, E., Aiyenibe, B., Butler, P.E.M.: Microsurgery simulators in virtual reality: review. Microsurgery **23**, 147–152 (2003)

6. Alaraj, A., Lemole, M.G., Finkle, J.H., Yudkowsky, R., Wallace, A., Luciano, C., Banerjee, P.P., Rizzi, S.H., Charbel, F.T.: Virtual reality training in neurosurgery: review of current status and future applications. Surg. Neurol. Int. **2**, 52 (2011)
7. Malone, H.R., Syed, O.N., Downes, M.S., D'ambrosio, A.L., Quest, D.O., Kaiser, M.G.: Simulation in neurosurgery: a review of computer-based simulation environments and their surgical applications. Neurosurgery **67**, 1105–1116 (2010)
8. Davies, J., Khatib, M., Bello, F.: Open Surgical Simulation - a Review. J. Surg. Educ. **70**, 618–627 (2013)
9. Ricciardi, F., Pastorelli, E., Paolis, L.T.D., Herrmann, H.: Scalable medical viewer for virtual reality environments. In: Augmented and Virtual Reality - Second International Conference, AVR 2015, Lecce, Italy, 31 August – 3 September 2015, Proceedings, pp. 233–243 (2015)
10. Livatino, S., De Paolis, L.T., D'Agostino, M., Zocco, A., Agrimi, A., De Santis, A., Bruno, L.V., Lapresa, M.: Stereoscopic visualization and 3-D technologies in medical endoscopic teleoperation. IEEE Trans. Industr. Electron. **62**, 525–535 (2015)
11. O'Toole, R.V., Playter, R.R., Krummel, T.M., Blank, W.C., Cornelius, N.H., Roberts, W.R., Bell, W.J., Raibert, M.: Measuring and developing suturing technique with a virtual reality surgical simulator. J. Am. Coll. Surg. **189**, 114–127 (1999)
12. Mimic Technologies MSim 2.1 software upgrade enables dV-Trainer customers to perform tube anastomosis and tube closure exercises. http://www.prweb.com/releases/2013/8/prweb10999321.htm. Accessed 25 Feb 2016
13. dV-Trainer - Proven, cost-effective training for the da Vinci Surgical System. http://www.mimicsimulation.com/products/dv-trainer/. Accessed 25 Feb 2016
14. Hüsken, N., Schuppe, O., Sismanidis, E., Beier, F.: MicroSim-a microsurgical training simulator. In: Studies in Health Technology and Informatics, pp. 205–209 (2013)
15. Wang, F., Su, E., Burdet, E., Bleuler, H.: Development of a microsurgery training system. In: 30th Annual International Conference of the IEEE Engineering in Medicine and Biology Society, EMBS 2008, pp. 1935–1938 (2008)
16. Park, Y., Shinke, M., Kanemitsu, N., Yagi, T., Azuma, T., Shiraishi, Y., Kormos, R., Umezu, M.: A surgical training simulator for quantitative assessment of the anastomotic technique of coronary artery bypass Grafting. In: IFMBE Proceedings, pp. 1179–1182 (2009)
17. Brown, N., Natsupakpong, S., Johannsen, S., Manjila, S., Cai, Q., Liberatore, V., Cohen, A. R., Cavusoglu, M.C.: Virtual environment-based training simulator for endoscopic third ventriculostomy. Stud. Health Technol. Inform. **119**, 73–75 (2006)
18. Lemole, G.M., Banerjee, P.P., Luciano, C., Neckrysh, S., Charbel, F.T.: Virtual reality in neurosurgical education: part-task ventriculostomy simulation with dynamic visual and haptic feedback. Neurosurgery **61**, 142–148 (2007)
19. Huang, D., Tang, W., Ding, Y., Wan, T., Chen, Y.: An interactive 3D preoperative planning and training system for minimally invasive vascular surgery. In: 2011 12th International Conference on Computer-Aided Design and Computer Graphics (CAD/Graphics), pp. 443–449 (2011)
20. Huang, D., Tang, W., Wan, T.R., John, N.W., Gould, D., Ding, Y., Chen, Y.: A new approach to haptic rendering of guidewires for use in minimally invasive surgical simulation. Comput. Anim. Virtual Worlds **22**, 261–268 (2011)
21. Brown, J., Sorkin, S., Bruyns, C., Latombe, J.-C., Montgomery, K., Stephanides, M.: Real-time simulation of deformable objects: tools and application. In: Conference Proceedings on Computer Animation, pp. 228–236 (2001)

22. Chen, D., Gourishankar, V., Rawley, C., Grinstein, G.: The QuickHaptics microAPI: enabling haptic mashups. In: 2010 IEEE Haptics Symposium, HAPTICS 2010, pp. 269–272 (2010)

23. Culbertson, H., Lopez Delgado, J.J., Kuchenbecker, K.J.: One hundred data-driven haptic texture models and open-source methods for rendering on 3D objects. In: 2014 IEEE Haptics Symposium (HAPTICS), pp. 319–325 (2014)

24. Yamaguchi, T., Oshima, K., Hirano, Y., Makishima, A., Harada, T., Richard, P.: Component-based authoring tool for haptic navigation. In: Proceedings of the 10th International Conference on Computer Graphics Theory and Applications (VISIGRAPP 2015), pp. 486–491 (2015)

25. Unity3D_SDK_Guide, http://docs.unity3d.com/Manual/android-sdksetup.html

26. Geomagic-Touch_Device_Guide, http://dl.geomagic.com/binaries/support/downloads/Sensable/3DS/Geomagic-Touch_Device_Guide.pdf

27. OpenHaptics Toolkit - Programmer's guide, http://www.geomagic.com/files/4013/4851/4367/OpenHaptics_ProgGuide.pdf

28. The ZeroMQ Guide - for C Developers, http://zguide.wdfiles.com/local–files/main%3A_start/zguide-c.pdf

29. Müller, M., Chentanez, N.: Solid simulation with oriented particles. In: ACM SIGGRAPH 2011 Papers, British Columbia, Canada, pp. 92:1–92:10. ACM, Vancouver (2011)

30. Chen, X.: Real-time Physics Based Simulation for 3D Computer Graphics, http://scholarworks.gsu.edu/cs_diss/79, (2013)

31. Maggiorini, D., Ripamonti, L.A., Panzeri, S.: Follow the leader: a scalable approach for realistic group behavior of roaming NPCs in MMO games. In: Proceedings of the Twelfth European Conference on the Synthesis and Simulation of Living Systems: Advances in Artificial Life, ECAL 2013, Sicily, Italy, 2–6 September 2013, pp. 706–712 (2013)

32. Liu, T., Bargteil, A.W., O'Brien, J.F., Kavan, L.: Fast simulation of mass-spring systems. ACM Trans. Graph. 32, 214:1–214:7 (2013)

33. nvidia_SDK_Guide, http://download.nvidia.com/developer/cuda/seminar/TDCI_PhysX.pdf

34. Hernandez-Belmonte, U.H., Ayala-Ramirez, V., Sanchez-Yanez, R.E.: A mobile robot simulator using a game development engine. In: Proceedings of the 1st Robotics Summer Meeting, 27–28 June 2011, pp. 5–11 (2011)

35. Craighead, J., Burke, J., Murphy, R.: Using the unity game engine to develop SARGE: a case study. Computer 4552, 366 (2008)

36. Cadavid, A.N., Ibarra, D.G., Salcedo, S.L.: Using 3-D video game technology in channel modeling. IEEE Access. 2, 1652–1659 (2014)

37. nvidia_library_Guide, https://developer.nvidia.com/physx-sdk

38. Qin, J., Chui, Y.P., Pang, W.M., Choi, K.S., Heng, P.A.: Learning blood management in orthopedic surgery through gameplay. IEEE Comput. Graph. Appl. 30, 45–57 (2010)

39. Lin, Y., Wang, X., Wu, F., Chen, X., Wang, C., Shen, G.: Development and validation of a surgical training simulator with haptic feedback for learning bone-sawing skill. J. Biomed. Inform. 48, 122–129 (2014)

40. nodejs_Guide, http://www.tutorialspoint.com/nodejs/pdf/nodejs_express_framework.pdf

41. Nazarov, J.G.R.: Native browser support for 3D rendering and physics using WebGL, HTML5 and Javascript. In: BCI 2013, 19–21 September 2013, Thessaloniki, Greece, pp. 21–24 (2013)

42. tree_homepage, http://mrdoob.github.com/three.js/

43. websocket, https://www.ietf.org/proceedings/80/slides/hybi-2.pdf

44. Mitchell, J.D., Siegel, M.L., Schiefelbein, M.C.F., Babikyan, A.P.: Applying publish-subscribe to communications-on-the-move node control. Lincoln Lab. J. 16(2), 413–430 (2007)

45. Netmq_homepage, http://netmq.readthedocs.org/en/latest/
46. Birr, S., Mönch, J., Sommerfeld, D., Preim, U., Preim, B.: The LiverAnatomyExplorer: a WebGL-based surgical teaching tool. IEEE Comput. Graph. Appl. **33**, 48–58 (2013)
47. Tommaso De Paolis, L., Ricciardi, F., Giuliani, F.: Development of a serious game for laparoscopic suture training. In: Paolis, L.T., Mongelli, A. (eds.) AVR 2014. LNCS, vol. 8853, pp. 90–102. Springer, Heidelberg (2014)
48. Ricciardi, F., De Paolis, L.T.: A comprehensive review of serious games in health professions. Int. J. Comput. Games Technol. **2014**, e787968 (2014)

Improving Endovascular Intraoperative Navigation with Real-Time Skeleton-Based Deformation of Virtual Vascular Structures

Giuseppe Turini[1,2](✉), Sara Condino[2], Matteo Postorino[2],
Vincenzo Ferrari[2,3], and Mauro Ferrari[2]

[1] Computer Science Department, Kettering University, Flint, MI, USA
gturini@kettering.edu
[2] Department of Translational Research on New Technologies in Medicine
and Surgery, EndoCAS Center, University of Pisa, Pisa, Italy
{sara.condino,matteo.postorino,vincenzo.ferrari,
mauro.ferrari}@endocas.unipi.it
[3] Information Engineering Department, University of Pisa, Pisa, Italy
vincenzo.ferrari@unipi.it

Abstract. Endovascular surgery requires acquisition of intraoperative X-ray images, exposing patient and surgical staff to a considerable dose of radiations. This disadvantage, and the difficulty in using bidimensional projective images, motivates the integration of endovascular navigators in the clinical practice. This paper presents a real-time vascular deformation system to enhance the standard static virtual environment usually used in endovascular navigation. Our approach is based on a skeleton representation of the virtual vessel, linked to the 3D vascular structure via vertex color masks applied on the target vascular branches. This method allows the usage of multiple partial skeletons, each with its own deformation function and linking strategy; so, we can model different kind of deformations due to several factors (e.g., heartbeat, breathing etc.). The system has been tested modeling the deformation of renal arteries due to patient breathing: showing a good visual realism, and ensuring the necessary updating frequency for real-time simulation.

Keywords: Computer-assisted surgery · Endovascular navigation · Virtual reality · Skeleton-based deformation · Real-time simulation

1 Introduction

Endovascular interventions are usually performed exploiting real-time images of the vascular structure of the patient, through the use of a fluoroscope. This approach allows the intraoperative guidance of the surgical instruments, fusing the projection of the target vessel and the surgical instruments in a single picture. Although this technique reduces the invasiveness of endovascular procedures allowing a shorter recovery time for the patient, it also presents some issues.

© Springer International Publishing Switzerland 2016
L.T. De Paolis and A. Mongelli (Eds.): AVR 2016, Part II, LNCS 9769, pp. 82–91, 2016.
DOI: 10.1007/978-3-319-40651-0_7

One of the main disadvantages is the exposure of the patient and the surgical staff to a significant amount of X-rays (i.e., ionizing radiations). Furthermore, endovascular procedures require the surgeon to navigate inside the vascular tree relying only on a bidimensional image: the projection of the patient anatomy. Finally, other difficulties may arise from the injection of the nephrotoxic contrast medium: required to visualize the vascular structure using a fluoroscope.

In order to overcome these issues, innovative methods to track and visualize endovascular tools in MRI environments have been proposed. In spite of promising results (acquisition of 3D/4D anatomical models using radiation-free imaging), the transfer of MR-guided techniques into the clinical practice has been limited by the lack of MR-compatible instrumentation (e.g., guidewires) with mechanical charactcristics similar to standard surgical tools [3,4].

A possible solution consists in combining MRI with live fluoroscopy: hybrid X-ray and MR imaging systems (i.e., XMR) can benefit from 3D information on vascular structures offered by MRI along with a large armamentarium of X-ray compatible catheters/guidewires [2,16].

Finally, intraoperative navigation platforms have been proposed to ease endovascular surgical procedures, and to reduce the usage of fluoroscopy; limiting in this way, the procedural radiation dose by using electromagnetic localization strategies, or rather: tracking in real-time the insertion of endovascular instruments inside the patient vasculature [1,14,15,17,18].

Furthermore, these software tools are usually based on a *static* virtual 3D vascular anatomy of the patient, registered with the real patient position just before the catheter insertion.

The method we propose is an extension for this kind of endovascular navigators (Fig. 1a). The real-time fusion of the 3D vascular structure of the patient with the surgical instruments provided with sensors (Fig. 1b), is improved using a vascular deformation system for the virtual vessels. The continuous tracking of the position, orientation, and configuration of the surgical instruments, is coupled with the real-time updating of the vascular tree (e.g., coherently with the heartbeat and the breathing of the patient).

Our approach is based on a *compact* representation of the vessels: a skeleton describing the structure of the vascular anatomy, properly linked to the virtual vessel wall. Therefore during each simulation cycle, a deformation is firstly applied to the vessel skeleton, and then transmitted to the virtual vessel wall via skeleton-vessel links: modifying the shape of the 3D vascular structure.

2   The Vascular Deformation System

The proposed deformation module has been developed to be integrated in our endovascular navigator with an architecture, including: hardware devices, software modules, and the "Real-Time Deformation" system (Fig. 2) [5,6].

The preliminary test has included the modeling of the deformations of the renal arteries due to the patient breathing. Afterwards, we have performed a visual validation of the real-time updating of the vascular structure, monitoring

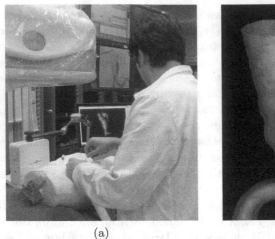 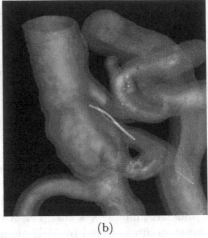

(a)   (b)

Fig. 1. Overview of the endovascular navigation system: (a) shows a photo during the preliminary test using a synthetic phantom, whereas (b) illustrates a screenshot of the virtual 3D environment during the catheter insertion.

at the same time: the breathing of the patient using a position sensor, and the patient anatomy through an ultrasound scanner.

2.1 Endovascular Navigation System Overview

The endovascular navigation platform is a system providing intraoperative guidance (Fig. 1a), allowing the reduction of the radiation dose and the injection of nephrotoxic contrast medium [6].

Intraoperative 3D rotational angiography is acquired in the initial phase of the endovascular intervention, and the volumetric dataset is used to generate the 3D vascular structure of the patient (Fig. 3a and b). Endovascular catheters and guidewires, provided with 5 DOF electromagnetic sensors, are tracked using an NDI Aurora Electromagnetic Tracking System (Figs. 1a and 5a). Initially, the virtual anatomy is registered to match the real patient position. Then, the endovascular navigation system is able to visualize the 3D virtual environment: fusing together the 3D vascular tree of the patient with the endovascular instruments, coherently with the real surgical scenario (Fig. 2) [6].

The endovascular navigation system has shown an overall *spatial accuracy* of $1.2\,\text{mm} \pm 0.3\,\text{mm}$, and has demonstrated a good usability during the preliminary evaluation by a group of expert surgeons [5,6].

2.2 Real-Time Skeleton-Based Vascular Deformation

In order to deform the shape of the vessels in real-time, we have designed and implemented a compact representation of the vascular structure: the *vessel skeleton*. This mainly consists in an approximation of the vessel *centerline*: or rather

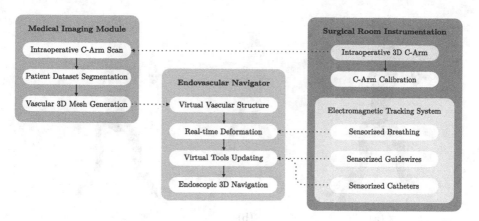

Fig. 2. The endovascular navigation platform architecture, including: hardware devices, software modules, and the "Real-Time Deformation" system.

a tree structure (i.e., *undirected graph*) described using *nodes* (3D points) and *links* (3D line segments). Moreover, the skeleton includes also special connections (i.e., *skeleton-vessel links*) between its elements (nodes and/or links) and the vertices of the virtual vessel wall. These allow to reshape the vessel wall considering the skeleton deformation.

The automatic generation of the vessel skeleton is performed through the computation of the centerline of the patient vascular structure. Although in this paper we use a different algorithm, in other publications we demonstrated how to automatically generate the vessel centerline processing ultrasound 3D datasets [13, 21].

Automatic Generation of the Vessel Centerline. The strategy to determine the vessel centerline, is based on the algorithm proposed by Cornea et al. [7]. Initially, the volumetric dataset (e.g., a C-arm scan) is analyzed and the relative 3D force field, represented using a 3D array storing a force vector for each volume cell (*voxel*), is generated. Then, once the topological features of the field are computed, the connected centerline of the vascular structure is created.

Vessel Skeleton Generation and Linking. Once obtained the vascular structure centerline, we can generate the vessel skeleton. In our approach, we approximate the centerline using only its core structure (e.g., avoiding curve links).

Afterwards, the vessel skeleton can be manually optimized: reducing the number of nodes, or adjusting their position.

Finally the skeleton has to be linked to the virtual vessel wall. In particular, the user can define a specific function to connect the vessel skeleton to the vertices of the 3D vascular structure. We have paid particular attention to the development of a versatile solution for the vessel skeleton, in order to enable the connection of both skeleton nodes and links using a wide range of strategies. For

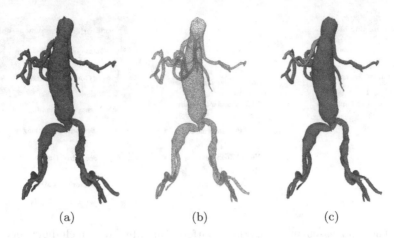

(a)   (b)   (c)

Fig. 3. An example of virtual vascular structure: (a) shows the raw high resolution 3D model generated segmenting the medical dataset, (b) illustrates the same model after the optimization process (artifact removal, simplification, and smoothing), and (c) represents the two color masks applied to the vertices of the virtual renal arteries in order to use two different partial vessel-skeletons. (Color figure online)

example: in order to test the deformation of the renal arteries, we have connected each vertex of the virtual vessel with the two nearest skeleton nodes.

Enabling Multiple Partial Vessel Skeletons. Sometimes, only part of the vascular structure requires a real-time updating: for example when adhesions between the vessels and the surrounding anatomy constrain the position of the main part of the vascularization. In these cases, it would be useless to compute the deformation of the whole vascular structure; instead we can restrict the updating to the vessels undergoing a significant deformation.

Our solution consists in the usage of *multiple partial vessel skeletons*, each attached to a specific branch of the vascular structure. The identification of the proper region of the 3D virtual vessel, linked with a partial vessel skeleton, is done using *color vertex masks* (see Fig. 3c). This means that each skeleton is tagged with a color, and linked only to mesh vertices matching that color.

This strategy allows not only to use multiple partial vessel skeletons, but also to apply different deformation functions to each part of the vascular structure.

Deforming the Virtual Vessel Wall. During each iteration of the interactive simulation, we update the vessel skeleton configuration applying the deformation function to all its nodes. Subsequently, we modify the position of the virtual vessel vertices linked to at least one skeleton element (a node or a link).

In our preliminary tests, each vertex is linked to a pair of skeleton nodes. So, we have defined an update function f_{upd} based on a *weighted distance mean* of the displacement vectors of the two linked vessel skeleton nodes.

In particular, if i is the index of a virtual vessel vertex, $\mathbf{V}_i$ is its original (*rest state*) 3D position vector, j and k are the indices of the vessel skeleton nodes linked to the vertex i, $\mathbf{N}_j$ and $\mathbf{N}_k$ are their original 3D position vectors; we can define the two *distance weights* α and β as:

$$\alpha = \frac{\|\mathbf{V}_i - \mathbf{N}_j\|^n}{\|\mathbf{V}_i - \mathbf{N}_j\|^n + \|\mathbf{V}_i - \mathbf{N}_k\|^n} = 1 - \beta. \tag{1}$$

$$\beta = \frac{\|\mathbf{V}_i - \mathbf{N}_k\|^n}{\|\mathbf{V}_i - \mathbf{N}_j\|^n + \|\mathbf{V}_i - \mathbf{N}_k\|^n} = 1 - \alpha. \tag{2}$$

where: α and β are the *distance weights* associated respectively to skeleton-vertex links (i, j) and (i, k) of the vertex i, and n is the exponential factor used to enhance the effect of the vertex-node distances.

So we can compute the updated position $\mathbf{V}'_i$ of vertex i applying the update function f_{upd} defined as:

$$f_{upd}(i) = \mathbf{V}_i + (\alpha\,(\mathbf{N}'_j - \mathbf{N}_j) + \beta\,(\mathbf{N}'_k - \mathbf{N}_k) = \mathbf{V}'_i. \tag{3}$$

where $\mathbf{N}'_j$ and $\mathbf{N}'_k$ are the updated position vectors of the linked skeleton nodes j and k.

Even if we have chosen an update function based on a weighted distance mean of the displacement vectors of the two linked skeleton nodes, the deformation system has been designed to integrate any user-defined function: exploiting the linking strategy selected by the user to attach the vessel skeleton elements to the vertices of the virtual vascular structure.

3 Experimental Validation

We have decided to validate the vascular deformation system considering the distortion inducted by the breathing of the patient on the renal arteries. This choice allows the testing of two different partial skeletons (one for each renal artery), avoiding the deformation of the aorta: constrained by the adherencies with the backbone, and therefore considered stable (with no significant deformation).

3.1 Modeling Renal Arteries Deformation Due to Breathing

Several studies have been proposed to model the respiratory motion of the patient in order to enable the correction of endovascular imaging roadmaps, through the deformation of a preoperative representation of the patient anatomy.

King et al. proposed a motion correction for X-ray guided cardiac catheterisations: a subject-specific affine motion model generated analyzing few high resolution MRI slices and a general model of the cardiac respiratory motion [11].

Takemura et al. studied digital angiographies taken during patient breathing. The visceral branches of the abdominal aorta were divided in groups: hepatic arteries, splenic arteries, and celiac arteries; associating each group to an artery bifurcation point. Then, the motion of these points was tracked, and ranges of vertical and horizontal movements for each group were obtained [19].

In this work we have used the results reported by Draney et al. [8] and by Lujang et al. [12] to model respectively: the maximum displacement of the skeleton nodes of the renal arteries, and the temporal evolution of the skeleton nodes position during the respiratory cycle. According to Draney et al. [8], the maximum displacement of the points belonging to the renal arteries centerlines can be modeled using a hyperbolic function (Fig. 4), as described by the formula:

$$T_{max}(\mathbf{N}_j) = \frac{a\,\|\mathbf{N}_j - \mathbf{N}_0\|}{b + \|\mathbf{N}_j - \mathbf{N}_0\|}. \tag{4}$$

where T_{max} is the maximum translation of a generic point j belonging to the renal artery centerline, $\mathbf{N}_j$ is the 3D position of the point j, $\mathbf{N}_0$ is the position of the *renal artery ostia*, whereas a and b are constant parameters controlling the shape (i.e., slope of the function, asymptotic value) of T_{max}.

According to Lujang et al. [12] the position of a generic abdominal organ (e.g., the kidney in our case) can be modeled using a function of the time t:

$$T_z(t) = T_{z\,0} - c\cos^{2n}\left(\frac{\pi}{\tau}t - \phi\right). \tag{5}$$

where: $T_{z\,0}$ represents the position of the organ at exhale, c is the amplitude of the motion wave function, $(T_{z\,0} - c)$ defines the position at inhale, τ is the period of the respiratory cycle, n is a constant value controlling the shape of the motion function, and finally ϕ is the initial phase of the respiratory cycle.

Assuming that the same parametric function is applicable to points belonging to the renal artery centerline, and that the translations along the X and Y axes (*latero-lateral* and *anterior-posterior* direction respectively) are negligible; we

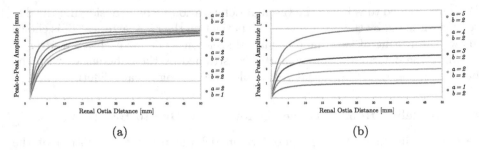

(a)   (b)

Fig. 4. The T_{max} function, modeling the renal artery maximum displacement: (a) shows the change in shape of the function varying the parameter b (from 1 to 5) while maintaining a constant ($a = 2$ mm), whereas (b) illustrates the different T_{max} functions changing the value of a (from 1 to 5 mm) while maintaining b constant ($b = 2$). (Color figure online)

can describe the motion of vessel skeleton nodes during the respiratory cycle as:

$$T_z(t, \mathbf{N}_j) = T_{z\,0} - T_{z\,max}(\mathbf{N}_j) \cos^{2n}\left(\frac{\pi}{\tau}t - \phi\right). \qquad (6)$$

where: $T_z(t, \mathbf{N}_j)$ is the position of the input skeleton node, $T_{z\,0}$ represents a constant offset (mm) along the Z (*superior-inferior*) axis, n is a constant value, and $T_{z\,max}(\mathbf{N}_j)$ is the maximum displacement of the node along the Z axis derived by (4), or rather: the approximation of $T_{max}(\mathbf{N}_j)$ neglecting the X and Y displacement components.

3.2 Preliminary Tests of the Vascular Deformation System

Preliminary tests have been performed in order to visually evaluate the "Real-Time Deformation" module developed.

A MRI dataset has been segmented using the EndoCAS Segmentation Pipeline [9, 10] based on ITK-SNAP [20], and the 3D model of a segment of the abdominal aorta has been generated and optimized. Afterwards, a vertex color mask has been applied to each renal artery, and the relative vessels skeletons have been defined and linked.

A 5 DOF electromagnetic sensor (NDI Aurora Tracking System) has been placed on the chest of the patient, in correspondence to the diaphragm. This enable the tracking of the patient breathing frequency, used as input parameter (i.e., $1/\tau$ in (6)) for the "Real-Time Deformation" system.

An ultrasound scanner (Esaote MyLab One) has been used to verify the maximum displacement (along the Z axis) of the patient kidneys during the respiratory cycle. This experimental value has resulted compatible with the maximum displacement of the renal arteries as reported by Draney et al. [8], so it has been used to estimate the constants a and b of (4).

All the tests have been performed running the endovascular navigator [6] on a consumer notebook: Intel Core i7 1.73 GHz CPU with 8 Gb RAM running a

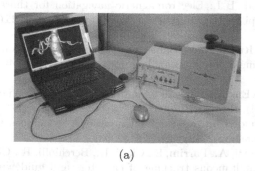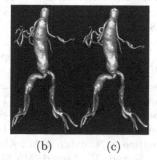

(a)   (b)   (c)

Fig. 5. The endovascular navigation system during the preliminary tests: (a) shows an overview of the system, whereas (b) and (c) illustrate the virtual vascular 3D model (back view) during the real-time deformation of both renal arteries.

64 bit Microsoft Windows 7; using a NDI Aurora system for the electromagnetic tracking. Figure 5 illustrates the endovascular navigation system during the preliminary testing of the real-time vascular deformation module.

4   Conclusions and Discussion

This article presents a real-time vascular deformation module integrated in our endovascular navigation system. The approach described is based on the concept of vessel skeleton: a compact representation of a virtual vessel derived directly from the centerline of the vascular structure of the patient. Furthermore, the deformation system supports the usage of multiple partial vessel skeletons, exploiting vertex color masks applied to the virtual vascular structure during the generation of the 3D model.

The method proposed has proven to be a good tradeoff between an accurate vascular deformation and the performance required for an interactive simulation system. Moreover, the deformation module is versatile, since the software has been designed to enable the user to customize both the skeleton deformation function and the skeleton-mesh linking strategy. In this way, it is possible to model different kind of vascular deformations, for example those due: to the heartbeat, to the abdominal insufflation, or to the patient decubitus.

Acknowledgments. The research leading to these results has been partially supported by the scientific project LASER (electromagnetic guided *in-situ* laser fenestration of endovascular endoprosthesis, November 2014–November 2017) funded by the Italian Ministry of Health and Regione Toscana through the call "Ricerca Finalizzata 2011–2012".

References

1. Abi-Jaoudeh, N., Glossop, N., Dake, M., Pritchard, W.F., Chiesa, A., Dreher, M.R., Tang, T., Karanian, J.W., Wood, B.J.: Electromagnetic navigation for thoracic aortic stent-graft deployment: a pilot study in swine. J. Vasc. Interv. Radiol. **21**(6), 888–895 (2010)
2. Andersson, T., Söderman, M., Ruijters, D., Babic, D., Homan, R., Mielekamp, P.: 3D-multimodality roadmapping in interventional neuroradiology. MedicaMundi **53**(2), 58–62 (2009)
3. Bartels, L.W., Bakker, C.J.G.: Endovascular interventional magnetic resonance imaging. Phys. Med. Biol. **48**(14), R37–R64 (2003)
4. Bock, M., Wacker, F.K.: MR-guided intravascular interventions: techniques and applications. J. Magn. Reson. Imaging **27**(2), 326–338 (2008)
5. Condino, S., Calabrò, E.M., Alberti, A., Parrini, S., Cioni, R., Berchiolli, R., Gesi, M., Ferrari, V., Ferrari, M.: Simultaneous tracking of catheters and guidewires: comparison to standard fluoroscopic guidance for arterial cannulation. Eur. J. Vasc. Endovasc. Surg. **47**(1), 53–60 (2014)

6. Condino, S., Ferrari, V., Freschi, C., Alberti, A., Berchiolli, R., Mosca, F., Ferrari, M.: Electromagnetic navigation platform for endovascular surgery: how to develop sensorized catheters and guidewires. Int. J. Med. Robot. Comput. Assist. Surg. **8**(3), 300–310 (2012)
7. Cornea, N.D., Silver, D., Yuan, X., Balasubramanian, R.: Computing hierarchical curve-skeletons of 3D objects. Vis. Comput. **21**, 945–955 (2005)
8. Draney, M.T., Zarins, C.K., Taylor, C.A.: Three-dimensional analysis of renal artery bending motion during respiration. J. Endovas. Ther. **12**(3), 380–386 (2005)
9. Ferrari, V., Cappelli, C., Megali, G., Pietrabissa, A.: An anatomy driven approach for generation of 3D models from multi-phase CT images. Int. J. Comput. Assist. Radiol. Surg. **3**(1), S271–S273 (2008)
10. Ferrari, V., Carbone, M., Cappelli, C., Boni, L., Melfi, F., Ferrari, M., Mosca, F., Pietrabissa, A.: Value of multidetector computed tomography image segmentation for preoperative planning in general surgery. Surg. Endosc. **26**(3), 616–626 (2012)
11. King, A.P., Boubertakh, R., Rhode, K.S., Ma, Y.L., Chinchapatnam, P., Gao, G., Tangcharoen, T., Ginks, M.R., Cooklin, M., Gill, J.S., Hawkes, D.J., Razavi, R.S., Schaeffter, T.: A subject-specific technique for respiratory motion correction in image-guided cardiac catheterisation procedures. Med. Image Anal. **13**(3), 419–431 (2009)
12. Lujan, A.E., Larsen, E.W., Balter, J.M., Ten Haken, R.K.: A method for incorporating organ motion due to breathing into 3D dose calculations. Med. Phys. **26**(5), 715–720 (1999)
13. Parrini, S., Zhang, L., Condino, S., Ferrari, V., Caramella, D., Ferrari, M.: Automatic carotid centerline extraction from three-dimensional ultrasound doppler images. In: 36th Annual International Conference of the IEEE on Engineering in Medicine and Biology Society (EMBC 2014), pp. 5089–5092 (2014)
14. Pujol, S., Frerichs, K., Norbash, A., Kikinis, R., Westin, C.F.: Preliminary results of nonfluoroscopy-based 3D navigation for neurointerventional procedures. J. Vasc. Interv. Radiol. **18**(2), 289–298 (2007)
15. Pujol, S., Pecher, M., Magne, J.L., Cinquin, P.: A virtual reality based navigation system for endovascular surgery. Stud. Health Technol. Inform. **98**, 310–312 (2004)
16. Saikus, C.E., Lederman, R.J.: Interventional cardiovascular magnetic resonance imaging: a new opportunity for image-guided interventions. JACC: Cardiovas. Imaging **2**(11), 1321–1331 (2009)
17. Sidhu, R., Weir-McCall, J., Cochennec, F., Riga, C., DiMarco, A.N., Bicknell, C.D.: Evaluation of an electromagnetic 3D navigation system to facilitate endovascular tasks: a feasibility study. Eur. J. Vasc. Endovasc. Surg. **43**(1), 22–29 (2012)
18. Solomon, S.B., Dickfeld, T., Calkins, H.: Real-time cardiac catheter navigation on three-dimensional CT images. J. Interv. Cardiac Electrophysiol. **8**, 27–36 (2003)
19. Takemura, A., Suzuki, M., Sakamoto, K., Kitada, T., Iida, H., Okumura, Y., Harauchi, H.: Analysis of respiration-related movement of upper abdominal arteries: preliminary measurement for the development of a respiratory motion compensation technique of roadmap navigation. Radiolog. Phys. Technol. **1**, 178–182 (2008)
20. Yushkevich, P.A., Piven, J., Hazlett, H.C., Smith, R.G., Ho, S., Gee, J.C., Gerig, G.: User-guided 3D active contour segmentation of anatomical structures: significantly improved efficiency and reliability. NeuroImage **31**(3), 1116–1128 (2006)
21. Zhang, L., Parrini, S., Freschi, C., Ferrari, V., Condino, S., Ferrari, M., Caramella, D.: 3D ultrasound centerline tracking of abdominal vessels for endovascular navigation. Int. J. Comput. Assist. Radiol. Surg. **9**(1), 127–135 (2014)

A Wearable Augmented Reality Platform for Telemedicine

M. Carbone[1(✉)], C. Freschi[1], S. Mascioli[1], V. Ferrari[1,2],
and M. Ferrari[1]

[1] Department of Translational Research and New Technologies in Medicine
and Surgery, EndoCAS Center, University of Pisa, Pisa, Italy
marina.carbone@endocas.org
[2] Department of Information Engineer, University of Pisa, Pisa, Italy

Abstract. This paper describes the development of the prototype of an Augmented Reality based tele-consultation platform settled with a wearable video see through Head Mounted Display (HMD) with the aim to provide specialist consult to low specialist remote area without the need to move the patient. The platform prototype has the donning advantage that gives the user an immersive experience, moreover the video see through HMD allows for intrinsic coherence of the scenes shared between the users (the mentor and the proctored clinician). The platform has been preliminarily evaluated from a technical point of view and two different scenarios were identified for future clinical testing: ambulatorial (gynecologic) and surgical (orthopaedic).

Keywords: E-health · Telemedicine · Information systems, collaboration

1 Introduction

The terms tele-presence and tele-assistance have been evolving rapidly in the last decades thanks to technology evolution. "Telepresence" used to refers to audio and, occasionally, video interaction between a remote expert supervising a local technician in doing a specific task, while today the concept evolved implying the concept of immersive tele-presence thanks to the Augmented Reality (AR) systems.

AR tele-presence (or tele-consultation/tele-mentoring) platforms are widely and commercially diffuse in industry for maintenance purposes [1, 2], indeed AR has the capacity to deliver hands-on training where users receive visual instructions in the context of the real-world objects [3].

In the context of healthcare, from the concept of tele-consultation towards tele-mentoring and tele-surgery, AR based systems are starting to spread in literature even if commercial applications are sparse [4, 5].

Rizou et al. [6] defines a general telemedicine system as "Telemedicine is the use of electronic information and communication technologies to provide and support health care when distance separates the participants (physicians, providers, specialists and patients)". In such a definition AR based systems seems to be the best way to provide the needed information in a telemedicine context.

© Springer International Publishing Switzerland 2016
L.T. De Paolis and A. Mongelli (Eds.): AVR 2016, Part II, LNCS 9769, pp. 92–100, 2016.
DOI: 10.1007/978-3-319-40651-0_8

A lot of existing tele-consultation platforms rely on systems that allow the mentor to overlay with AR technique graphic or textual annotations onto imagery of the environment where the proctored clinician is. These images are displayed to the trainee typically on a nearby computer monitor. It is an important issue to enhance the ability of the mentor to demonstrate proper actions of the trainee in a manageable way.

Vera et al. [7] implemented and validated an augmented reality tele-consultation platform for laparoscopic surgery, which overlaid a live view of the surgical instruments manipulated by a remotely located mentor onto the laparoscopic monitor viewed by a trainee to conduct the intervention. This approach showed the effectiveness of overlaying mentor guidance directly onto the trainee's view of the operating field; because the trainee normally views the operating field through the laparoscopic monitor, there was no active focus shifting [7]. In fact in a very recent work Andersen et al. [4] underlined how it is important to provide to the mentor and the trainee the same point of view in order to improve the efficacy of the communication. They propose a display based platform that interpose a transparent display between the surgeon's eyes and the patient so to offer directly in the right point of view the mentor indications.

Another interesting approach to augmented reality tele-consultation or tele-mentoring has been presented by Shenai et al., it is called Virtual Interactive Presence and Augmented Reality and uses a set of videoscopes through which both trainee and mentor could view the operating field augmented with mentor-provided overlays. This system allowed a mentor to "see what the local surgeon sees," and was used successfully while performing a cadaveric carotid endarterectomy and a craniotomy; a major disadvantage, however, was the bulky eyewear of the apparatus that forced the trainee to operate from a fixed, rigid location [5].

Considering what abovementioned the requisite for a comprehensive and practical tele-consultation system are:

- High-definition visualization and depth perception by both the remote and local clinician;
- Ability of the remote clinician to "see what the local sees";
- Ability to provide AR facilities to both clinicians;
- An interface that deploy standard and available internet protocol guaranteeing real time, high quality interaction.

In this respect this article presents a wearable AR-based platform that tries to address the need for immersive tele-presence and a real-time platform for tele-mentoring with the aim of provide specialist consult to low specialist remote area without the need to move the patient.

2 Methods

In this section we provide the description of the developed platform and its initial testing.

2.1 Augmented Reality Platform

The platform proposed consists of two dedicated workstations: the Local Calling Clinician (LCC) workstation and the Remote Expert Clinician (REC) workstation.

Both workstations are provided with a video see through Head Mounted Display (HMD) shown in Fig. 1. The device entails a commercial stereoscopic HMD (Sony HMZ-T2) modified with two external cameras (IDS uEye XS), one for each eye. The cameras capture real world and stream images on the internal HMD monitors so that the user feels to observe the reality with its own eyes, the internal monitors are used to display virtual information to augment the reality perceived by the user [8–10].

Fig. 1. Modified HMD display. The two external cameras can be moved to adjust eye convergence and field of view.

The HMD has been developed in the mainframe of a multipurpose platform for image guided surgery, and its custom AR software libraries are used to develop the tele-mentoring platform [8].

The LCC workstation is provided by a laptop and the HMD. The clinicians, whenever he/she needs a second opinion or a mentoring, just wear the HMD, start the application and call the REC.

The REC workstation is organized as a green room (Fig. 2) for field background subtraction. In this case the visor is mounted in a fixed position and the mentor can sit and comfortably lean his/her head on the visor.

A key element of the system is represented by the fact that the two platforms are configured with exactly the same hardware in particular regarding the HMD and the external cameras configuration.

The two external cameras are mounted with a strategy that allows to vary camera convergence depending on the needed working distance. From a perceptive point of view camera convergence regulates the stereoscopic perception of the scene, as it allow to adjust the screen disparity of the displayed images for viewer comfort, to optimize depth perception or to otherwise enhance the stereoscopic experience [11]. In our application is important to set the camera convergence depending on the needed working distance, that can vary if the clinical scenario changes but it's otherwise defined for each clinical scenario.

We decided to mount the cameras with a strategy to vary camera convergence in function of the application needed in a range of three different predefined positions. All the parameters are registered in a configuration file that allows to coherently adapt the convergence of the virtual cameras to consistently compose the virtual scene [12].

Fig. 2. REC Workstation. The workstation is arranged to ensure ergonomics and comfort for the operator and to maximize efficiency for background subtraction. In the red circle the HMD highlighted. Professional lighting (red arrow) to minimize shadows or chromatic aberrations for a maximum efficiency of Chroma-key, green screens highly absorbent and low reflectivity for a good result of the Chroma-key. (Color figure online)

The fact that the two workstations share the same hardware with exactly the same camera convergence configuration automatically solves the issue related to the consistence of the two different scenes and allows to avoid the registration problem. In fact both the REC and the LCC moves their hands and instruments in the same field of view and at the same focal distance: the augmented scene is naturally aligned and intrinsically consistent in terms of focus and object dimensions.

2.2 Network and Communication Protocol

As said high quality, real-time, video streams are a fundamental technological prerequisite for the implementation of tele-medicine applications, and relies on the availability of a broadband solid network.

The aim of the project is to bring specialist support in remote areas that does not have specialist medical facilities. It is important to underline that it could be logistically unfeasible to implement a dedicated network infrastructure, so the system has to work properly with available internet facilities. Starting from the open source available libraries for developing Voice Over IP (VOIP) platforms [13–15] we decided to move towards what already used in literature to develop platforms for telemedicine [16–18].

We selected and tested four VOIP software: Skype™ (Microsoft Corporation), ooVoo™ (ooVoo LLC), VSee (Vsee Lab Inc.), Hangouts (Google inc.). The platforms were tested in terms of video resolution, bandwidth occupation and robustness of the communication. In Table 1 you can see the comparison between the identified software solutions and highlighted the selected software: VSee. VSee software revealed a secure, high-resolution video-conferencing software. The VSee video-collaboration software met all the requirements by providing extremely low bandwidth video-calling, control of bandwidth utilization with robust high resolution and strong data security features. Moreover, the Vsee company provides (commercially) the API of the software so to develop tailored platforms.

Table 1. Selected VOIP software comparison

Resolution \ Bandwitdh (Upload/Download)	skype www.skype.com	ooVoo www.oovoo.com	VSee www.vsee.com	Google Hangouts www.hangouts.com
Default (240p)	150/300 Kbps	190/216 Kbps	50/150 Kbps	150/300 Kbps
High Resolution (480p)	225/600 Kbps	504/592 Kbps	70/250 Kbps	256/600 Kbps
High Definition (720p)	600/2000 Kbps	960/2000 Kbps	300/1000 Kbps	512/2000
FIXED Video Resolution (no bandwidth dependant)	No	Yes	Yes	Yes

As for now we decided to develop the platform maintaining the Vsee software external, but in the future we intend to integrate the VOIP facilities in a unique platform.

In Fig. 3 a schematic diagram of the system is shown. The core of the platform is the QRSAR software developed on the top of the custom developed AR libraries [8]. Its role is too performs the stereo image composition both from the REC and the LCC side and build the AR scene.

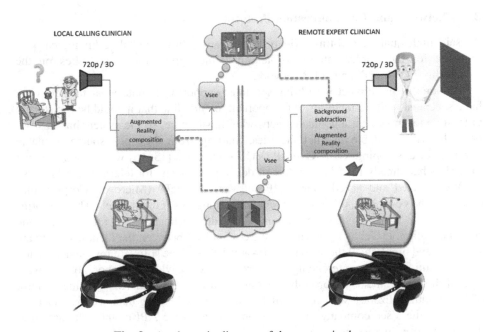

Fig. 3. A schematic diagram of the system is shown

More in details the QRSAR software automatically calibrate for background sub-traction at the REC side and the stereoscopic frames of the segmented hands or surgical instruments moved by the mentor are composed with the LCC stream in order to provide on both side the same view: the remote mentor hands or instruments over-lapped to the real local scene so to provide an immersive visual feedback that allows for an effective proctoring. In Fig. 4 an image taken during a phantom [19] test is shown that explain the afore-described process. On the right it is possible to observe the side-by-side 3D left and right eye stream once the AR scene has been composed.

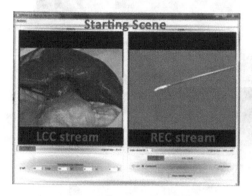
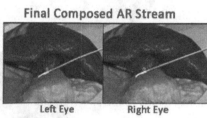

Fig. 4. Example application of the platform in a simulated laparoscopic scenario. Left: the LCC and REC stream are showed before Chroma-key subtraction and AR composition. The remote clinicians moves in the green room a surgical instrument to guide the movements of the local clinician; Right: once calibrated both clinicians share the same view: the Augmented Reality composition of the scene.

2.3 Preliminary Testing

Initial tests of the platform consisted in a preliminary technical evaluation of the system to qualitatively assess technical aspects such as connectivity, assessment of the video frame rate, and usability.

In particular 10 non clinicians and 2 clinicians tested the platform in three different network condition (ADSL, 4G, 3G) for a 30 min call.

The overall video frame rate ranged from 23 to 58 fps with a medium fps value of 32 fps, that means that the real-time target is reached. The video quality was fixed at 720p (HD) and maintained for the whole time of the call and the audiostream was constant.

The clinicians users report that the user interface could be improved in term of intuitivity and that the HMD could result a bit cumbersome for long calls.

Two test in two different clinical environments were conducted too.

As said our target application areas are the clinical environments, including rural medical centers. In particular it was selected a mountainous area of Tuscany, the Garfagnana, where only a generalist hospital is available; in this context a lot of patients are often required to move to more specialistic hospitals for a second opinion or for more specilistic exams.

We selected two different scenarios: an ambulatorial one, where routines control are executed that could sometimes require a second more specialistic opinion; and the orthopaedic trauma unit, where sometimes for serious trauma or fractures external fixation has to be placed before to move the patient.

In the first scenario, the ambulatorial one, we tested the system during a gynechologic control (Fig. 5), the LCC called the REC (that in this trial was simply in another room) for help during an external observation of a pregnant woman.

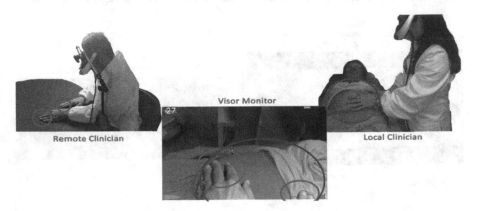

Fig. 5. Early system testing: gynecologic setup. On the right: the clinician during an exam asked for advice to an expert: On the left the expert hands guide the local clinician for effective palpation. In the center the image proposed on both the HMD is shown: the hands of the remote doctor (red circles) are superimposed perfectly and consistently to the actual scene (blue circle) and the local doctor can easily follow the instruction. (Color figure online)

For the second scenario we tested the system with an expert clinicians guiding remotely a resident to mount an external femoral fixator: in that case we do not involve a real patient but proved the feasibility on a phantom. Such a scenario revealed very interesting in terms of possible outcome and usefulness. External fixation is a viable alternative to attain temporary rigid stabilization in patients with multiple injuries. It is rapid, causes negligible blood loss, and can be followed by subsequent nailing when the patient is stabilized. Although demonstrated benefits the mounting of an external fixator is a challenging task, especially when performed by non-expert clinicians [20]. The possibility to proctor this task through a tele-mentoring platform has been explored in literature [21, 22], and our application can reveal very useful as it allows the proctored clinicians to be effectively guided by the hands of the expert clinician in an immersive way.

Such application scenario will be further investigated and a structured clinical trial will be conducted to assess effectiveness of the platform for this task.

3   Conclusion

Our project is a step in the direction of providing specialist healthcare facilities to remote rural areas through tele-consultation. An Augmented Reality (AR) based platform for tele-health over a standard internet connection has been proposed that proved to offer a real opportunity to enhance clinical outcome.

From a technical point of view the platform revealed effective for the purposes, allowing a real-time high quality video communication and the AR application added significative effectiveness and immersive guidance.

Further testing are needed for a clinical assessment and to elaborate clinical protocols and logistic strategies for actual implementation. We also intend to explore the local impact of the telehealth service, considering the improvement of the health care delivered.

Acknowledgments. This work was funded by the Fondazione Cassa di Risparmio di Lucca.

References

1. Webel, S., Bockholt, U., Engelke, T., Gavish, N., Olbrich, M., Preusche, C.: An augmented reality training platform for assembly and maintenance skills. Robot. Auton. Syst. **61**, 398–403 (2013)
2. Olwal, A., Gustafsson, J., Lindfors, C.: Spatial augmented reality on industrial CNC-machines. Eng. Reality Virtual Reality **2008**, 6804 (2008)
3. Gavish, N., Gutiérrez, T., Webel, S., Rodríguez, J., Peveri, M., Bockholt, U., Tecchia, F.: Evaluating virtual reality and augmented reality training for industrial maintenance and assembly tasks. Interact. Learn. Environ. **23**, 778–798 (2015)
4. Andersen, D., Popescu, V., Cabrera, M.E., Shanghavi, A., Gomez, G., Marley, S., Mullis, B., Wachs, J.P.: Medical telementoring using an augmented reality transparent display. Surgery **79**(5), 741 (2015)
5. Shenai, M.B., Dillavou, M., Shum, C., Ross, D., Tubbs, R.S., Shih, A., Guthrie, B.L.: Virtual interactive presence and augmented reality (VIPAR) for remote surgical assistance. Neurosurgery **68**, 200–207 (2011)
6. Rizou, D., Sesma, L., Salvatore, L.: Doctors mobility covered by TraumaStation. In: 2010 10th IEEE International Conference on Information Technology and Applications in Biomedicine (ITAB), pp. 1–4 (2010)
7. Vera, A.M., Russo, M., Mohsin, A., Tsuda, S.: Augmented reality telementoring (ART) platform: a randomized controlled trial to assess the efficacy of a new surgical education technology. Surg. Endosc. **28**, 3467–3472 (2014)
8. Cutolo, F., Parchi, P.D., Ferrari, V.: Video see through AR head-mounted display for medical procedures. In: International Symposium Mix Augment, pp. 393–396 (2014)
9. Ferrari, V., Viglialoro, R.M., Nicoli, P., Cutolo, F., Condino, S., Carbone, M., Siesto, M., Ferrari, M.: Augmented reality visualization of deformable tubular structures for surgical simulation. Int. J. Med. Robot. (2015)
10. Parchi, P., Piolanti, N., Andreani, L., Cutolo, F., Ferrari, V., Ferrari, M., Lisanti, M.: Potentialities of wearable augmented reality in orthopaedics. In: Computer Aided Orthopaedics Surgery International (2015)

11. Allison, R.S.: The camera convergence problem revisited. Stereoscopic Displays Virtual Reality Syst. Xi **5291**, 167–178 (2004)
12. Ferrari, V., Cutolo, F., Calabro, E.M., Ferrari, M.: HMD video see though AR with unfixed cameras vergence. In: International Symposium Mix Augment, pp. 265–266 (2014)
13. Herlein, G.: The OpenPhone project–internet telephony for everyone! Linux J. **2000**, 2 (2000)
14. De Luca, M.: Integrazione di un protocollo per la moderazione in un client open source per una piattaforma di videoconferenza basata su IP (2006)
15. Bansal, A., Kulkarni, P., Pais, A.R.: Effectiveness of SIP messages on SIP server. In: 2013 IEEE Conference on Information and Communication Technologies (ICT), pp. 616–621 (2013)
16. Zhang, K., Liu, W.-L., Locatis, C., Ackerman, M.: Mobile videoconferencing apps for telemedicine. Telemed. e-Health **22**, 56–62 (2015)
17. Miller, D.J., Miljkovic, N., Chiesa, C., Callahan Jr., J.B., Webb, B., Boedeker, B.H.: Telemedicine using free voice over internet protocol (VoIP) technology. Stud. Health Technol. Inform. **163**, 369–371 (2011)
18. Lu, Y., Zhao, Y., Kuipers, F., Van Mieghem, P.: Measurement study of multi-party video conferencing. In: Proceedings Networking, vol. 6091, pp. 96–108 (2010)
19. Condino, S., Carbone, M., Ferrari, V., Faggioni, L., Peri, A., Ferrari, M., Mosca, F.: How to build patient-specific synthetic abdominal anatomies. an innovative approach from physical toward hybrid surgical simulators. Int. J. Med. Robot. **7**, 202–213 (2011)
20. Scalea, T.M., Boswell, S.A., Scott, J.D., Mitchell, K.A., Kramer, M.E., Pollak, A.N.: External fixation as a bridge to intramedullary nailing for patients with multiple injuries and with femur fractures: damage control orthopedics. J. Orthop. Trauma **18**, S2–S10 (2004)
21. Ricci, W.M., Borrelli, J.: Teleradiology in orthopaedic surgery: impact on clinical decision making for acute fracture management. J. Orthop. Trauma **16**, 1–6 (2002)
22. Vladzymyrskyy, A.V.: Four years' experience of teleconsultations in daily clinical practice. J. Telemed. Telecare **11**, 294–297 (2005)

eBSim: Development of a Low-Cost Obstetric Simulator

Andrea Paci[1], Simone Marcutti[1(✉)], Serena Ricci[1], Maura Casadio[1],
Gianni Viardo Vercelli[1], Pierangelo Marchiolé[2],
and Massimo Cordone[3]

[1] Department of Informatics, Bioengineering, Robotics and Systems
Engineering, University of Genova, Genoa, Italy
andrea.paci90@gmail.com, simone.marcutti@simarlab.it,
ricci_serena@ymail.com,
{maura.casadio,gianni.vercelli}@unige.it
[2] ASL3 Genova - Gynecology and Obstetric Villa Scassi Hospital, Genoa, Italy
pmarchiole@yahoo.com
[3] Centre of Advanced Simulation, University of Genova, Genoa, Italy
massimocordone@gaslini.org

Abstract. This work presents the design a low cost obstetric simulator allowing
precise identification of the fetal position in a simulated birth canal. The system
consists on a female pelvis, a custom-made fetal mannequin, a virtual 3d representation, a visual display and an user interface to show in real time what
happens inside the birth canal. Students are often unable not only to identify
correctly the fetal head position, but also to discriminate between the two
fontanels, for this reason the simulator eBSim can help them to train this ability
and could be an important instrument for the instructors to objectively assess the
clinical skill of each student.

Keywords: Simulation · Obstetric · Medical training · Arduino · RaspberryPi

1 Introduction

The knowledge of the correct position and orientation of the fetal head is important for
obstetricians and midwives during spontaneous and operative vaginal deliveries.
Nevertheless, these parameters are estimated in a subjective way. This fact leads to
discordant evaluations, errors and failures in ventouse extraction and forceps application, worse outcomes for mother and newborn, increased use of urgent and emergent
cesarean section.

Nowadays, students can practice deliveries only in cases where there is no danger
for both the mother and the fetus. However, when they start their career, they could
come across emergency situations in which they have to act quickly [1].

Simulation is widely used in medicine because it allows students and doctors to
train their skills without any risk; moreover a simulator is an important tool to
objectively assess students' abilities.

© Springer International Publishing Switzerland 2016
L.T. De Paolis and A. Mongelli (Eds.): AVR 2016, Part II, LNCS 9769, pp. 101–110, 2016.
DOI: 10.1007/978-3-319-40651-0_9

The most important studies concerning obstetrical simulation started about thirty years ago, in fact in 1988–1989 R. H. Allen, J. Sorab and G. Gonik from the Huston University used sensors applied on a clinician's hand in order to investigate the relation between applied forces and risk of birth injury [2, 3].

In 2002 C. M. Pugh and P. Youngblood, from the Stanford University, implemented the simulator "E-Pelvis" to simulate pelvic examinations; it consists of a partial mannequin instrumented internally with electronic sensors that are interfaced with a data acquisition card and a graphic software to visualize the examinations [4].

In 2003 the "Laboratoire Ampère" of Lyon (France) developed the Birth simulator: it includes a fetal mannequin; the maternal anatomically correct pelvic model; an interface pressure system mimicking the pelvic muscles; a software to visualize in real time the head location [5, 6].

One of the main problems of the commercially available simulators is their high price. Moreover, most of them do not allow detecting the fetal position and its orientation with respect to the female ischial spines [5]. The birth simulator presented in this article is a low cost model that overcomes this problem allowing an identification of the fetal position.

2 Clinical Problem

Delivery is defined as the ejection or the extraction of the fetus from the maternal birth canal, which is composed by the pelvis and the soft tissue.

The pelvis consists of four bones: sacrum, coccyx and two innominate bones, formed by the fusion of the ilium, ischium and pubis. The pelvic cavity can be divided into the false and the true pelvis. The false pelvis is bounded posteriorly by the lumbar vertebra and laterally by the iliac fossa, whereas the true pelvis is bounded above by the sacrum, the linea terminalis, and the upper margins of the pubic bones, and below by the pelvic outlet.

Extending from the middle of the posterior margin of each ischium are the ischial spines. These are of great obstetrical importance because the distance between them usually represents the shortest diameter of the pelvic cavity. They also serve as valuable landmarks in assessing the level to which the presenting part of the fetus has descended into the true pelvis.

Fetus could be seen as the union between two parts: the body and the head joined by the neck. The fetal head is composed of two frontal, two parietal, and two temporal bones, connected by a thin layer of fibrous tissue and separated by membranous spaces termed sutures. Where several sutures meet, an irregular space, called fontanel, forms. The greater, or anterior, fontanel is a lozenge-shaped space that is situated at the junction of the sagittal and the coronal sutures. The lesser, or posterior, fontanel is represented by a small triangular area at the intersection of the sagittal and lambdoid sutures [7].

If the fetal head is located in correspondence with the ischial spines, or under them, the birth canal is defined "engaged". The engagement level is determined according to the eleven stations postulated by the American College of Obstetrician and Gynecologists (ACOG), i.e. eleven positions inside the birth canal (Fig. 1). The position '0'

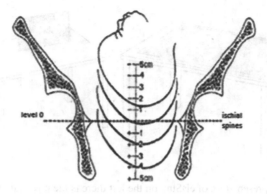

Fig. 1. Head levels with respect to maternal ischial spines according to ACOG classification [10]

corresponds to the vertex at the ischial spines and then there are five stations over and five under it. Each fifth station is located a centimeter above or below the spines. Thus, as the presenting fetal part descends from the inlet toward the ischial spines, the designation is −5, −4, −3, −2, −1, then 0 station. Below the spines, as the presenting fetal part descends, it passes +1, +2, +3, +4 and +5 stations to delivery [7–9].

3 Background

Our goal is to develop a prototype to train the ability in internal examination during labor, discriminating between the two fetal fontanels and estimating correctly the fetal head position and descent with respect to the female ischial spines.

An analysis of commercially available birth simulators revealed that most of them are not able to detect and display the position of the fetus in the birth canal; moreover they are very expensive. For these reasons we decided to implement a birth simulator able to detect physically and visually the position of the fetus with respect to maternal ischial spines and the forces applied on the fetal fontanels. Our aim is to create a didactical system usable both by students, to improve their skills, and by teachers which can objectively evaluate juniors' performances [11]. The prototype we developed has four parts (Fig. 2):

- Physical model of the fetus and the pelvis
- Graphic model corresponding to the physical one
- Desktop application which allows users' authentication and students' performances
- Server-side subsystem to manage communications among the physical model, the graphic model and the desktop application

Importantly, the first prototype uses only low-cost electronic component and it is a wireless simulator, it means that there are no cables coming out from the physical model. Thus it is a space-saving and plug and play system.

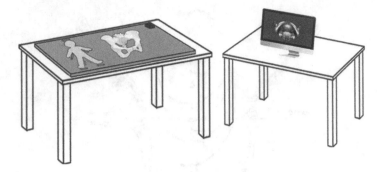

Fig. 2. Schematic representation of eBSim: on the left there is the physical model, the black box in the middle represents the communication system and the screen on the right corresponds to the user interface, i.e. graphical model and desktop application

3.1 Maternal Pelvis Model

The maternal pelvis model includes a pelvis skeleton and an overlay (Fig. 3). The first one is a female pelvis skeleton model distributed by 3b Scientific, having the same dimensions as a real pelvis. It is placed on a wood surface and it is covered by a wood overlay which has two openings both to locate the fetus and to perform a simulated internal examination.

The pelvis model is equipped with eleven magnetic hall effect sensors (US 1881), located inside the birth canal to measure the engagement level of fetal head. The fetus neck has a magnetic strip detected by sensors when the fetus passes through the birth canal. The sensors position simulates the ACOG classification, i.e. eleven levels in which the birth canal is divided, as described before. For this reason the distance between two adjacent sensors is 1 cm.

Fig. 3. The complete physical model

ACOG classification postulates that the engagement level is determined starting from the head position of the fetus; however we detected the neck position because the head can't have any artifact detectable by users. Thus we shifted the system 11,5 cm upwards, as shown in Fig. 4, according to the distance between the neck and the farthest head point.

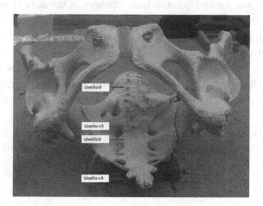

Fig. 4. Correspondence between ACOG classification and sensors' position. Red lines show the ACOG levels 0 and +5, whereas the green lines highlight the sensors corresponding to the same levels. (Color figure online)

3.2 Fetus Model

The fetal mannequin is composed by a custom-made body and a 3d printed head (Fig. 5). Starting from a free fetus model, available online, we realized a simulated fetal head.

Fig. 5. The fetal head: on the left there are the groves created to contain the electronic components, on the right a suture is visible

In particular we edited the model changing the head's dimensions so that they were compatible with our pelvis; then we cut the head at the beginning of the neck, so that it can join an existing body and we divided it in two parts, both to make the printing process easier and to locate sensors correctly. Moreover we edited the model adding the main anatomical landmarks, i.e. sutures and fontanels, which are required to a correct training.

After the editing we looked for the best sensors. Our aim is to build a wireless prototype able to determine the fetal position and orientation inside the birth canal and to detect the force applied on the fontanels. Thus, we chose small sensors so as they could be placed easily in the head.

The orientation is determined by an Inertial Measurement Units (IMU MPU6050), whereas the contact force of the user's hand on the mannequin's fontanels is detected by two pressure sensors (FSR) located in correspondence with the anterior and posterior fontanel.

All sensors previously mentioned, together with a Bluetooth module (nRF8001) used to send data to the communication subsystem, are connected to an Arduino Mega inside the head.

3.3   Communication System

The communication sub-system is based on a Raspberry Pi 2 model B, which acts as a bridge connecting physical and virtual simulator. Raspberry Pi 2 model B is a low cost single-board computer that plugs into a computer monitor. It has various functionalities including the ability to interact with the outside world thanks to 40 pins GPIO (General Purpose Input/Output).

Data coming from the fetal head are received and transmitted to Raspberry via Bluetooth, whereas the magnetic sensors located in the pelvis are physically connected to Raspberry which sends information to the client via Wi-Fi (Fig. 6).

The software is implemented with Node.js, that is a platform used to build applications based on JavaScript V8 runtime. It uses sockets (software abstraction) such as Socket.IO or UDP to communicate in real time: in release mode and development mode, respectively. Socket.IO enables real-time bidirectional event-based communication; UDP is used to connect Node.js and the graphic editor Unity that is a graphical shell for a desktop environment. It is a cross-platform game engine known for its ability to target projects to multiple platforms.

3.4   User Interface

User interface includes a graphical model, i.e. a virtual representation of the fetus and the birth canal, and a desktop application which makes it possible to use eBSim as a didactic instrument (Fig. 7).

The graphic representation consists of a female pelvic 3D model and a fetus 3D model. The first one is a free model available online, edited so that its dimension are the same as the physical pelvic model; the second one is the model used to build the fetal

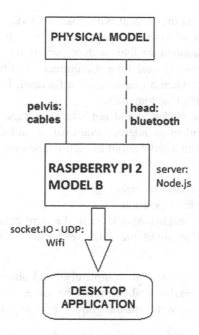

Fig. 6. The communication architecture

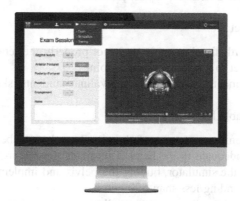

Fig. 7. User interface includes a graphic representation of the birth canal, shown on the right and a desktop application for students and teachers

head which is mentioned before. It translates and rotates as the real mannequin because it receives data from the IMU and the magnetic sensors. Thus, the graphic representations shows in real time what happens inside the simulated birth canal allowing users to train and test their abilities.

eBSim will also include a desktop application which, at the present time, is just designed. After authentication teachers and students will access to their personal page: the student's page will give information about previous sessions and it will allow students to start a training or simulation session. Teacher's page will have information about the whole class allowing each teacher to start an exam session.

During a training session the student will make a pelvic examination and he will check his skills by a feedback provided on a screen. In particular, he will detect the correct position and orientation of the fetus with respect to the ischial spines. Moreover, the graphic model will show in real time the correct identification of the fontanels thanks to pressure sensors: when a user touches a fontanel, i.e. a pressure sensor, the graphic model will highlight that fontanels.

In simulation mode the student could not take advantage of the virtual representation; in fact he will simulate an internal examination and then he will complete a checklist which will give him a score about his skills. The evaluation checklist consists of multiple choice questions aimed to evaluate:

- The correct detection of the fontanels
- The recognition of the fetus position
- The identification of the engagement level in the birth canal
- The student's knowledge about the safest extraction maneuver for the current clinical situation

During an exam mode the student, completely blind about the fetus, will start an internal examination. The teacher will complete the same checklist mentioned above, according to the student's answers and the graphic representation.

4 Conclusion and Future Development

The aims of the project are:

- To implement a birth-simulator able to detect properly the fetal head position and descent with respect to the female ischial spines
- To create an instrument that can train and evaluate students' skills to improve their obstetrical abilities
- To develop a portable low-cost device

Thus, each electronic component of the simulator had to be low-cost and with dimension that were adequate to the head. This made the research hard, but we succeeded in sensorizing the simulator, buying the pelvis and implementing the software using free tools by spending less than 500 euros.

The development of the first prototype allows us to analyze the main problems linked to the simulator's feasibility and to determine the future development of the project.

As we mentioned above, we used eleven magnetic sensors located on the pelvis to determine the position of the fetus inside the birth canal. Although these sensors work well, i.e. they are small and able to determine properly the head location, their electronic connection are very complex: each sensor has five physical connection, this means that there are fifty-five cables coming out from the pelvis. For this reason it could be useful to find a new technology that could replace the magnetic system.

At present eBSim has a simple physical model made of wood (Fig. 3) which has to be replaced by a more realistic overlay, i.e. a woman's mannequin. In addition the physical and graphical pelvis could be equipped with soft tissue, since it is normally present in the birth canal.

The fetus mannequin has a custom-made body made of cloth, connected to a head which is 3d printed starting from a 3d model. However, the head's material (ABS) is too much stiff and it could be replaced with a softer one, i.e. rubber like material, in order to be similar to the human skin. Finally, it will be useful to mechanize the fetus's positioning inside the birth canal and to measure the force applied on whole head during the delivery.

As we explained before, the desktop application has not developed yet, so it will be important to create it, giving a comparison with a web application, so that it can be possible to study advantages and disadvantages of both solutions.

Finally, another important step will be to test and validate the prototype of the simulator, in that occasion a selected group of doctors and students will be asked to use and became familiar with the prototype in order to give us some feedback and suggestions to improve the simulator, including an evaluation process with scores and penalties so that the assessment will be as objective as possible.

Acknowledgment. Andrea Paci, Simone Marcutti and Serena Ricci contributed equally to this work.

The authors thanks Andrea Canessa, Agostino Gibaldi, Filippo Sante, Edoardo Bellanti and Giorgio Carlini for their help in the inizial stage of the work.

References

1. Macedonia, C., Gherman, R., Satin, A.: Simulation laboratories for training in obstetric and gynecology. Obstet. Gynecol. **102**, 388–392 (2003)
2. Allen, R., Sorab, J., Gonik, B.: Measuring clinician-applied forces during birth using tactile sensing technology. IEEE Eng. Med. Biol. Soc. **3**, 1285–1286 (1988)
3. Sorab, J., Allen, R.H., Gonik, B.: Tactile sensory evaluation of clinician-applied forces during delivery of newborns. IEEE Trans. Biomed. Eng. **35**, 1090–1093 (1988)
4. Pugh, C., Youngblood, P.: Development and validation of assessment measures for a newly developed physical examination simulator. J. Am. Med. Inf. Assoc. **9**, 448–460 (2002)
5. Dupuis, O., Silveira, R., Zentner, A., Dittmar, A., Gaucherand, P., Cucherat, M., Redarche, T., Rudigoz, R.: Birth simulator: reliability of transvaginal assessment of fetal head station as defined by the American College of Obstetrician and Gynecologists classification. Am. J. Obstet. Gynecol. **192**, 868–874 (2005)
6. Moreau, R., Ochoa, V., Pham, M.T., Boulanger, P., Redarche, T., Dupuis, O.: A method to evaluate skill transfer and acquisition of obstetric gestures based on the curvatures analysis of the position and the orientation. J. Biomed. Inf. **41**, 991–1000 (2008)
7. Cunningham, G., Leveno, K., Bloom, S., Hauth, J., Rouse, D., Spong, C.: William Obstetrics, 23rd edn. McGraw-Hill Medical, New York (2010)
8. Hagadorn-Freathy, A., Yeomans, E., Hankins, G.: Validation of the 1988 ACOG forceps classification system. Obstet. Gynecol. **77**, 356–360 (1991)
9. Robertson, P., Laros, R., Zhao, R.: Neonatal and maternal outcome in low-pelvic and midpelvic operative deliveries. Am. J. Obstet. Gynecol. **162**, 1436–1444 (1990)

10. Moreau R.: Le simulateur d'accouchement BirtSIM: un outil complet pour la formation sans risque en obstétrique. Ph.D. thesis. National Institute of Applied Sciences of Lyon (2007)
11. Ricci, S., Paci, A., Marcutti, S., Marchiolè, P., Torre, G., Casadio, M., Vercelli, G., Cordone, M.: The development of a low-cost obstetric simulator to train midwifery students and test objective examinations' skills. In: The 4th International Workshop on Innovative Simulation for Healthcare, pp. 66–72 (2015)

Applications of VR/AR in Cultural Heritage

Interactive Painting and Lighting
in Dynamic Multi-Projection Mapping

Vanessa Lange, Christian Siegl$^{(\boxtimes)}$, Matteo Colaianni, Philipp Kurth,
Marc Stamminger, and Frank Bauer

Computer Graphics Group, University of Erlangen-Nuremberg, Erlangen, Germany
`vanessa.lange@fau.de,christian.siegl@cs.fau.de`

Abstract. Digital Art and Design is a major part of our culture. Creating assets in a completely digital environment is well established and understood. Currently we see a rise in mixed-reality applications that aim to combine the traditional real-world based way of working with their digital counterparts. In this paper we present a non-destructive, immersive, fully dynamic mixed-reality painting system for real-world objects that combines the workflow of a traditional airbrush artist with the power of digital media. With this system we can completely alter the appearance of any Lambertian object.

1 Introduction

Digital painting is currently the method of choice when coloring 2D and 3D digital assets. Recently, 3D printing technology is pushing into the main stream market. Being able to produce real-world copies of any asset allows us to bring 3D painting back from the digital into the physical world. Painting 3D assets on a 2D screen is often a cumbersome task requiring a high level of abstraction and a trained artist. Using the same skills on a real-world object liberates from this indirection.

In this paper we present a system that allows us to paint real-world 3D surfaces with digital tools. We achieve this by employing a state of the art projection mapping system that can power multiple projectors and allows us to relight complex, moveable objects in a fully dynamic setup. Our system compensates shading artifacts produced by the projectors, giving artists a neutral canvas to work with. We use an airbrush style metaphor to interact with a given surface. Digital painting in our context is not limited to applying colors to a surface. To create rich assets, painting complex materials and setting a light stage is a crucial part of our system, as can be seen in Fig. 1.

Interacting with arbitrary, real-world objects in this way makes texturing 3D assets accessible to untrained users. In experiments with our students, we found that the interaction is not only simple to learn but also fun to use (see our video at https://vimeo.com/161289655). It allows to play with a blank object without having a permanent impact on its actual design. A system like this is useful in various fields. In archeology for example, it is often desirable to simulate the

© Springer International Publishing Switzerland 2016
L.T. De Paolis and A. Mongelli (Eds.): AVR 2016, Part II, LNCS 9769, pp. 113–125, 2016.
DOI: 10.1007/978-3-319-40651-0_10

Fig. 1. Designing complex lighting scenarios with our real-time multi-projector painting system on real-world objects.

materials of replicated statues both for research and in a teaching environment. Texturing real-world objects is also important when designing new products. Instead of manufacturing a series of prototypes from digital 3D assets, where the actual texture is often painted on a 2D parametric surface, a simplified stand-in can be printed. With our system the color and material design can be applied using natural interaction in the real world. This helps to improve turnaround times in the designing process and also enables customers to easily create their own designs.

After giving a brief overview of the previous work in Sect. 2, we introduce the basic workflow and hardware of our system, as well as some technical details on the underlying projection mapping system in Sect. 3. In Sect. 4 we detail our painting framework and subsequently present additional modes of interaction and some results in Sects. 5 and 6. Finally we give an overview of all our results and a brief discussion in Sect. 7.

2   Previous Work

Using projection mapping for digital painting is a well described idea. Raskar et al. described painting using their shader lamps application back in 2001 [2]. While they showed convincing results, modern hardware allows us to employ more realistic effects while painting. Tracking and user input were improved as well over the years allowing us to build a complete system with customer grade hardware.

In 2012 Aliaga et al. demonstrated a system that enabled high resolution projection mapping [1]. However, while still impressive, the system was not able to generate the images at interactive rates at the time.

We created our system around a very flexible projection system described in [13]. This system ensures (per projected pixel), that the light contributed by multiple projectors on a complex surface is mixed such that viewers will not perceive any visual seams. This technique provides a great level of immersion altering the complete appearance of white diffuse real-world objects.

A simplified version of projection mapping with a single projector was used in [5]. The authors describe a system that helps traditional painters by augmenting the canvas with visual guides. Supporting artists in achieving their goals by means of projection mapping and therewith extending the digital world into the real world is also demonstrated in [3,4,14,15]. Their work shows, that bringing back the advantages of digital media into the real world can increase creativity.

While the system we use is markerless, other mixed-reality implementations like [11] rely on color or IR-markers. The presence of markers in general improves the reliability of a tracking system. However, the need for markers contradicts our purpose of having a simple workflow allowing users to paint on 3D printed objects.

Allowing users to interact digitally with real-world objects is an emerging field in state of the art research. For example in [12] an ultra wide angle projector as well as a `Microsoft Kinect` depth sensor are used to augment the physical appearance of clothing allowing users to design their own garments.

3   System Overview

The base for our painting system is a state of the art multi-projection framework that consists of two parts as depicted in Fig. 2. Before the system is usable, all hardware components (depth sensor and projectors) need to be calibrated. This is a crucial step, since relighting relies on the exact location for every pixel of our projection on the target object. After calibration, the pipeline shown on the right

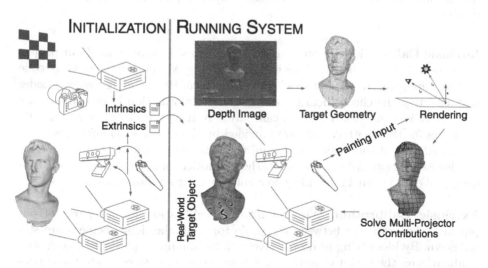

Fig. 2. The two parts of our system. First, all components need to be calibrated. The actual projection mapping system is markerless and can generate complex and immersive alterations of the target object.

side of Fig. 2 takes over. The depth image is used for rigid tracking to determine the position and orientation of the real-world target object. This transformation is transferred to the target geometry. Based on this, we can project every arbitrary appearance for the object that also contains the user's painting input and lighting. The images passed to the projectors have to be altered subsequently by our multi-projector solver, such that no artifacts are visible (see Fig. 4).

Hardware Setup. Our hardware setup consists of a standard desktop workstation with an `Intel Core i7 4771 (3.5GHz)`, 32 GB of RAM and an `NVidia GeForce 980` graphics card. As projectors we use two `NEC NP-P451WG`, with a resolution of 1280 by 800 pixels. For object tracking, an `ASUS Xtion PRO Live` depth sensor is utilized. The projectors' intrinsic calibration is performed with a `Canon 5D Mark III` camera. An exemplary setup is depicted in Fig. 3a.

(a)   (b)

Fig. 3. (a) An exemplary setup of our system with two projectors, a depth camera for tracking and our Augustus bust as the target object. (b) The `Razer Hydra` we use for painting.

Intrinsic Calibration. In order to find the intrinsic parameters of our projectors we employ the calibration method presented by Moreno et al. [8]. Gray-code patterns are projected onto a checkerboard pattern. By decoding the gray-codes and detecting the checkerboard corners, enough information is gathered to use the widely known `OpenCV` camera calibration routine presented by Zhang [16]. Intrinsics for the depth camera are provided by the sensor's manufacturer.

An additional calibration step required for a setup with multiple projectors is color calibration. All our projectors showed noticeable differences in color rendering. We utilize an `i1 Display Pro` colorimeter to obtain color profiles.

Extrinsic Calibration. With an intrinsic calibration for all parts of our pipeline, the extrinsics between the projectors and the depth camera are still unknown. By identifying projector pixels which illuminate predefined geometric landmarks on the target object, we get correspondences to estimate the extrinsic calibration. This has to be performed only once per setup. The subsequent tracking does not rely on markers.

Object Tracking. We track the projectors' positions and orientations relative to the target object based on the depth image and a known 3D scan of the target geometry. To achieve this, we use a projective iterated closest point algorithm based on a point-to-plane metric. In a similar fashion to previous works on 3D reconstruction [6, 9, 10], the problem is iteratively linearized around the last solution estimate. The corresponding linear system is built on the GPU resulting in a small 6 × 6 system that is solved on the CPU, using singular value decomposition (SVD) [7].

Painting Device. For painting on the object, we use the `Razer Hydra` device depicted in Fig. 3b. The two controllers are tracked magnetically and offer a range of about 1.5 m to the base station. Using the provided API, position, orientation and button events of the controllers are available. For registration, we point one controller at predefined geometric landmarks on the target object and employ the previously described extrinsic calibration.

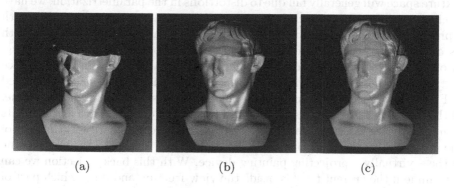

(a)   (b)   (c)

Fig. 4. Our multi-projector system: (a) The result of only a single projector. Note the limited coverage and self shadowing. (b) Simply adding a second projector leads to artifacts in the overlapping regions. (c) With the implemented multi-projector solver, the projection is correct at every surface point.

Multi-projector. With a single projector, only a very limited amount of the target object's surface can be covered (see Fig. 4a). Even remotely complex geometry will introduce self shadowing, which breaks the user's immersion. By adding a second projector, those shadows can be filled. Additionally, a larger area on the target object is covered (see Fig. 4c). These two factors greatly impact the level of immersion for the user. One might argue that a larger coverage is also achieved by placing the projector at a larger distance and therefore increasing the projection area. However, this contradicts the level of quality we want to achieve. By placing the projector farther away, the pixel footprint on the target surface increases, leading to a more blurred projection.

While all those advantages convinced us to use a multi-projector framework, the drawback of such a system is its complexity. In a fully dynamic setup, where the object can be moved around, the correct blending between projectors has to be computed per frame. Otherwise artifacts in the overlapping areas would occur as can be seen in Fig. 4b. We used a multi-projector solver based on the work presented by Siegl et al. [13]. In this system, the contribution of every projector regarding every surface patch is solved on a per-pixel level, which leads to a very high projection quality. Also surface effects like object-to-projector distance and Lambert's cosine law are considered, providing a clean canvas for painting. However, the resulting non-linear system is very complex and has to be solved on the GPU to meet the real-time constraint needed for the fully dynamic setup in this paper.

4   Painting

Intuitive and correct painting on a 3D object is a challenging task. First, we need a parameterization of the surface. Since a simple projection of a brush into texture space will generally fail due to distortions in the parametrization, we have to choose a different approach for painting. When drawing onto the surface with a predefined brush, we think of the painting device as a virtual projector, with its own view-frustum. A good real-world analogy to this is airbrush painting. In order to avoid sampling artifacts when projecting the brush into the surface texture, we render the model into its own parameterized UV space, as depicted in Fig. 5. This means, we issue exactly one fragment shader evaluation per texel of the target texture. By this sampling in the target domain, we avoid artifacts from differences in resolution. For every texel we need to identify if it is part of the projected brush. Therefore, we backproject every texel onto the image plane of the – virtually – projecting painting device. With this backprojection we can determine if the current texel is inside the view-frustum and if so, which part of the brush hits the texel.

Considering the generally small brush size, issuing one fragment shader per texel will generate massive overdraw. Therefore, we implemented an additional

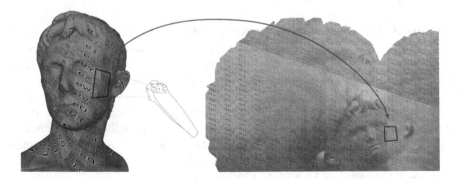

Fig. 5. Painting on a model by rendering it into its UV space. Every texel in the UV space issues a fragment shader that decides on how to paint into the texture.

triangle clipping inside the geometry shader stage of the rendering pipeline.

Brushes. Our system is capable of using arbitrary brushes. On the one hand, simple images with alpha channel can be used. They are mapped onto the image plane of the virtual painting projector. On the other hand, we can also handle parametric brushes, like Gaussian brushes, noise brushes, etc.

The virtual view-frustum of the painting device has another advantage. By altering the field of view, the brush size can be changed. Additionally – like in real airbrush painting – moving away from the target object increases the size of the painted region on the object.

For asymmetric brushes, rotating the input device will directly translate into the brushes' rotation on the surface.

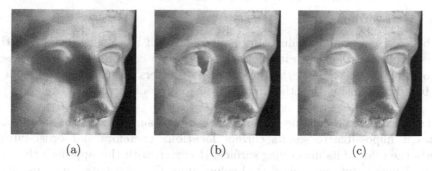

(a)　　　　　　　　(b)　　　　　　　　(c)

Fig. 6. Pointing the painting device at the nose from the right side. (a) No clipping is applied. (b) Texels with too much normal deviation and (c) texels with too much normal and depth deviation are clipped.

Clipping. Without additional clipping in the fragment shader, our brush will exhibit unexpected behaviour. When mimicing the behavior of a real-world brush, most notably one would not expect to draw onto backfacing geometry (see Fig. 6a). To remedy this, we need to know where the central ray of the painting view-frustum hits the target surface (center-point). Given this center-point's normal, we can clip every texel with a surface normal that differs more than a predefined epsilon (see Fig. 6b). In most cases, this still leads to unwanted artifacts. In our example such an artifact is visible on the eye. Using an additional depth test, relative to the center-point, these regions can be clipped (see Fig. 6c).

Razer Hydra. For our painting system we use the previously introduced `Razer Hydra`. Its resemblence of an airbrush pistol suits our needs perfectly. While we use this input device for showing results in this work, any other device, for example a `PlayStation Move` controller would be possible.

For interaction, we use the button configuration shown in Fig. 7. The right trigger buttons are used for painting and erasing. Using the four buttons on top,

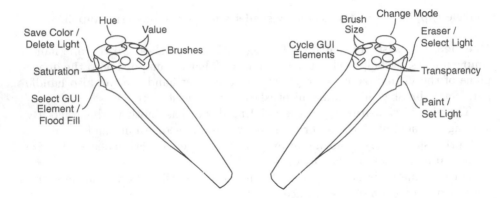

Fig. 7. Button assignment on the Razer Hydra.

the brush size and alpha value can be altered. With the analog joystick of the left controller, a color value inside the circular HSV color model can be chosen by rotating the stick. The other two color parameters – saturation and value – can be adjusted using the other four buttons on top of the left controller.

Virtual Palette. Rendering a colored brush on a surface with the same color makes it impossible to see its current location. Therefore, our brush-cursor inverts the color of its underlying surface. However, with this approach the user can no longer determine the selected color. Since digital artists are accustomed to visual cues, we include a user interface in form of a virtual palette.

We decided to use a simple box as the canvas for this palette. By placing the target object on this box, it is always close to the painted region. Also having four distinct sides, gives us a natural way of introducing four toolboxes. In general, every trackable or stationary surface with a known position is suitable for this task.

The first palette is color, with the currently selected color in the upper left (see Fig. 8). For ease of use, the two slots to the right show the color triad for the active color. The bottom three slots can be used to store custom colors. On the second palette, the user can choose different materials. The third palette offers

(a)   (b)   (c)   (d)

Fig. 8. Renderings of our virtual palettes. (a) A simple color palette. (b) Available brushes. (c) Material selection palette. (d) Mode switching toolbox (Color figure online).

(a)   (b)

Fig. 9. Material editing results of our system (Color figure online).

the selection of different interaction modes: painting and light design. Using the forth side, the user can choose various brush options.

For ease of use, the toolbars can be digitally rotated such that the needed palette is directly accessible, without rotating the target object.

5   Material Editing in Projection Mapping

Up to this point we described a system for simple color painting using different brushes. Since we use a digital system we are not limited to color editing. By introducing custom shaders we can simulate complex surface materials (see Fig. 9). From a user's perspective this is as simple as selecting a different color. Especially for one of our main focuses, painting in cultural heritage, this is very beneficial. When trying to figure out the original appearance of artifacts, archeologists want to experiment with materials, for example gold platings. In design applications, designers can get a quick feel for the appearance of different material combinations on a product. While presenting to a client, changes to a prototype can quickly be visualized. Our system supports a multitude of materials (for example gold, granite, limestone, linen, leather, cotton, etc.), best seen in the accompanying video.

The previously described brushes are also used to apply materials. This allows us to emulate different crafting techniques (for example gold plating). As customary in digital painting, brushes also enable the artist to seamlessly blend between materials.

To enable large scale alterations, which is of special importance in material editing, a floodfill operation is implemented.

6   Light Design in Projection Mapping

An important aspect of the physical appearance of objects is lighting. By giving the user the possibility to add and edit virtual lights in the scene, complex lighting situations can be created (see Fig. 10). Generally the placement of lights

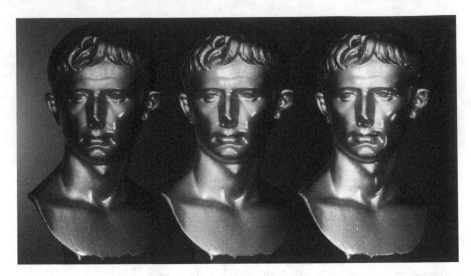

Fig. 10. Different lighting scenarios created with our system (Color figure online).

is not a very intuitive task. Our system provides real-time feedback and tangible control which makes the problem much more approachable, even for less experienced users.

After switching to the light editing mode, the user can press the right trigger button to add a virtual light to the scene. While holding the button and moving the controller, the light position updates in real-time. Upon releasing the button, the light is permanently placed in the scene. The color of the light can be changed with the same interaction as previously described for the brush's color. Since the actual position of the lights is not visible in the physical world, a new mode to pick lights is required. When the user enters the light picking mode, our system locates the light closest to the controller. By letting this light flash, the user gets an immediate response and a good idea which light is about to be picked. In addition, the influence of the light for the complete scene is clearly visible. After picking a light, it can be placed at a different location and the color/brightness can be changed. Furthermore, picked lights can be deleted.

With this very intuitive interaction mode for light design, complex and compelling lighting situations can be created. These more advanced lighting scenarios greatly add to the immersion of the user in our mixed-reality system.

7   Results and Discussion

With the system for painting, material editing and light design presented in this paper, we can produce compelling results.

Figure 11 shows the intermediate result of a short painting session. The result combines light editing, material and color painting. On the bottom, different sides of the palette box can be seen in action.

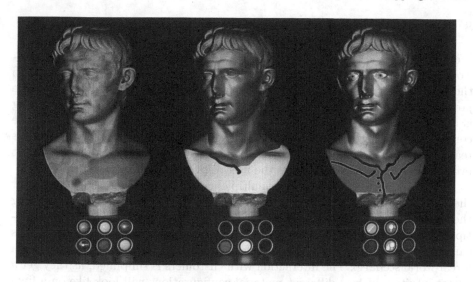

Fig. 11. Intermediate results of a quick painting session.

Figure 9 shows further material editing results. The Augustus bust is painted with blue car paint and weathered limestone. On the right, an exemplary design application is depicted using a soccer shoe as the target object.

The results of the light design capabilities can be seen in Figs. 1 and 10. In Fig. 10, the leftmost bust shows our startup lighting setup, in the middle a green light from the top left was added. On the rightmost side an additional blue light fills in from the bottom right.

While developing and testing the presented framework in real-world scenarios, we found that our painting application is very engaging. In contrast to virtual reality, the shared mixed-reality experience naturally added a social component which immediately sparked discussions revolving around the design.

Limitations and Future Work

Of course, our system shows some limitations. When the hand interacting with the scene is within the view frustum of the projector, a shadow is cast on the target object. This not only interferes with the user's immersion, but can render the desired task of painting impossible as the painted region may be within the shadow. Since we have multiple projectors, one feasible approach to remedy this in the future is to detect this case and fill in the shadow from another projector.

Another drawback is the accuracy of the chosen painting device. The magnetic tracking of the `Razer Hydra` proved to be vulnerable to adjacent electronic devices. Especially the large and powerful projectors tended to disturb the tracking. Switching to an optically tracked device like the `PlayStation Move` controller would help with this problem. However these systems suffer from occlusion by the user.

8 Conclusion

We have presented a multi-projector system for altering the appearance of real-world objects in a mixed-reality setup. With our system, the user can paint onto the object in a completely non-destructive way. Editing material gives artists the power to create complex surface effects with the stroke of a brush. Since lighting is added to the scene in a physically correct manner, artists can freely explore compelling lighting scenarios. With our multi-projector setup and markerless real-time tracking, the object can be moved around while maintaining a correct projection at all times. This gives the user a great level of immersion.

With this system, we can cover multiple use cases: Archeologists can recover the native appearance (including realistic lighting) of artifacts without altering the actual object. In teaching environments, our mixed reality system gives multiple users the possibility to jointly explore and alter an object. Product designers can quickly iterate through different ideas and easily collaborate with others in a real-world scenario. The interaction with customers is simplified, as they get a better intuition of how different material configurations will look like on a final product. This makes our system a great tool for agile design development.

References

1. Aliaga, D.G., Yeung, Y.H., Law, A., Sajadi, B., Majumder, A.: Fast high-resolution appearance editing using superimposed projections. ACM Trans. Graph. **31**(2), 13:1–13:13 (2012). http://doi.acm.org/10.1145/2159516.2159518
2. Bandyopadhyay, D., Raskar, R., Fuchs, H.: Dynamic shader lamps : painting on movable objects. In: IEEE and ACM International Symposium on Augmented Reality, 2001, Proceedings, pp. 207–216 (2001)
3. Binder, T., De Michelis, G., Gervautz, M., Jacucci, G., Matkovic, K., Psik, T., Wagner, I.: Supporting configurability in a mixed-media environment for design students. Pers. Ubiquitous Comput. **8**(5), 310–325 (2004)
4. Fiorentino, M., de Amicis, R., Monno, G., Stork, A.: Spacedesign: a mixed reality workspace for aesthetic industrial design. In: Proceedings of the 1st International Symposium on Mixed and Augmented Reality, p. 86. ISMAR 2002, IEEE Computer Society, Washington, DC (2002)
5. Flagg, M., Rehg, J.M.: Projector-guided painting. In: Proceedings of the 19th Annual ACM Symposium on User Interface Software and Technology. UIST 2006, NY, USA, pp. 235–244. ACM, New York (2006)
6. Izadi, S., Kim, D., Hilliges, O., Molyneaux, D., Newcombe, R., Kohli, P., Shotton, J., Hodges, S., Freeman, D., Davison, A., et al.: Kinectfusion: real-time 3D reconstruction and interaction using a moving depth camera. In: Proceedings of UIST, pp. 559–568. ACM (2011)
7. Low, K.L.: Linear least-squares optimization for point-to-plane icp surface registration. University of North Carolina, Chapel Hill (2004)
8. Moreno, D., Taubin, G.: Simple, accurate, and robust projector-camera calibration. In: Second International Conference on 3D Imaging, Modeling, Processing, Visualization and Transmission (3DIMPVT), 2012, pp. 464–471, October 2012

9. Newcombe, R.A., Davison, A.J., Izadi, S., Kohli, P., Hilliges, O., Shotton, J., Molyneaux, D., Hodges, S., Kim, D., Fitzgibbon, A.: Kinectfusion: Real-time dense surface mapping and tracking. In: Proceedings of ISMAR. IEEE (2011)
10. Nießner, M., Zollhöfer, M., Izadi, S., Stamminger, M.: Real-time 3D reconstruction at scale using voxel hashing. ACM TOG **32**(6), 169 (2013)
11. Punpongsanon, P., Iwai, D., Sato, K.: Projection-based visualization of tangential deformation of nonrigid surface by deformation estimation using infrared texture. Virtual Reality **19**(1), 45–56 (2014). http://dx.doi.org/10.1007/s10055-014-0256-y
12. Saakes, D., Yeo, H.S., Noh, S.T., Han, G., Woo, W.: Mirror mirror: an on-body clothing design system. In: SIGGRAPH 2015: Studio. SIGGRAPH 2015, NY, USA, pp. 39:1–39:1. ACM, New York (2015)
13. Siegl, C., Colaianni, M., Thies, L., Thies, J., Zollhöfer, M., Izadi, S., Stamminger, M., Frank, B.: Real-time pixel luminance optimization for dynamic multi-projection mapping. ACM Trans. Graph. (TOG) **34**(6), 237:1–237:11 (2015)
14. Simões, B., Prandi, F., De Amicis, R.: Creativity support in projection-based augmented environments. In: De Paolis, L.T., Mongelli, A. (eds.) AVR 2015. LNCS, vol. 9254, pp. 168–187. Springer, Heidelberg (2015)
15. Wilson, A.D., Benko, H.: Combining multiple depth cameras and projectors for interactions on, above and between surfaces. In: Proceedings of the 23nd Annual ACM Symposium on User Interface Software and Technology. UIST 2010, NY, USA, pp. 273–282. ACM, New York (2010)
16. Zhang, Z.: A flexible new technique for camera calibration. IEEE Trans. Pattern Anal. Mach. Intell. **22**(11), 1330–1334 (2000)

Briviesca in the 15th c.: A Virtual Reality Environment for Teaching Purposes

David Checa[1], Mario Alaguero[1], Miguel A. Arnaiz[1],
and Andres Bustillo[2(✉)]

[1] Department of History and Geography, University of Burgos, Burgos, Spain
{dcheca@ubu.es,malaguero,arque}@ubu.es
[2] Department of Civil Engineering, University of Burgos,
Avda Cantabria s/n, Burgos, Spain
abustillo@ubu.es

Abstract. The virtual visualization of historical sites opens the door to a variety of new classroom teaching methods for students. Two of these methods are semi-guided tours around 3D immersive environments and the screening of videos rendered from 3D models. Both are compared in this research that integrates a 3D model, designed for off-line rendering, in a 3D immersive environment, operating on Oculus Rift. First, the hardware and the software associated with the immersive environment are described. Then, the suitability of the 3D teaching environment is assessed in relation to historical knowledge, urban layout, and the portrayal of everyday medieval life. The evaluation of undergraduate student experiences, by means of post-session surveys, points to the effectiveness of both methods: higher scores were awarded to video screenings with background narrative in relation to the acquisition of historical concepts, while the virtual tour was the best means of transferring visually acquired knowledge such as urban concepts.

Keywords: Virtual reality · Teaching · Cultural Heritage · Immersive environments · Oculus Rift

1 Introduction

Over recent years, the use of virtual environments for teaching purposes has become a reality, through the development of hardware, such as Oculus Rift™, and its marketing to the general public. Virtual environments increase receptivity and learning rates among students [1, 2], especially among young students [3, 4]. Knowledge acquisition processes are, however, highly complex human activities. It is therefore necessary to identify the best way of using virtual environments for teaching purposes, taking into account the topics that should be acquired and the capabilities and interests of the students. The majority of studies published on teaching experiences in relation to Cultural Heritage refer to virtual museums [5], Virtual Reality 3D rooms [6] and serious games [7]. The first step in such a teaching experience is the development of the virtual environment, which comprises three elements: the hardware, the 3D models, and their integration in a game engine.

© Springer International Publishing Switzerland 2016
L.T. De Paolis and A. Mongelli (Eds.): AVR 2016, Part II, LNCS 9769, pp. 126–138, 2016.
DOI: 10.1007/978-3-319-40651-0_11

Various computer hardware systems have been proposed for the generation of the virtual environments over the past twenty years: 3D animations with interactive dialogues [8], real construction of the 3D meshes by means of 3D printers [9], 3D caves and 3D immersive environments [4, 10–12], and easy virtual environments rendered on-line with a web engine for visualization on the Internet [2, 6, 8]. The case of 3D immersive environments is especially interesting, because it is an option that exercises greater attraction over young students [3, 4]. Up until 2015, most published research referred to very expensive solutions such as 3D caves [4, 10–12]. Over the past few years, the launch of low-cost, high-fidelity, head-mounted displays (HMDs), such as Oculus Rift™, have opened up new horizons for the application of 3D-immersive environments in many different sectors. Although some simulator-sickness problems had to be overcome before their acceptance in long-term experimental programs ready for audiences of all ages [18, 19], these immersive systems have been proposed for gaming. They improve the feeling of immersion in the 3D world, in comparison with 2D displays, as well as the feelings of amazement, astonishment, and excitement in users [19]. If these systems were used for teaching purposes, their characteristics would make it reasonable to expect higher learning rates. However, 3D immersion blurs both the picture frame and the distance of the teaching content for the student, which raises various questions: will 3D immersion leave students at a loss in the visual experience? Will they either lower their learning rates or will these environments open up new opportunities for the narration of historical events? [20].

Different approaches have been proposed to create 3D digital reconstructions of Cultural Heritage, depending on the accessibility of the historical object [11]. In the case of huge items with complex geometries, such as a late-medieval church or small medieval town, only three techniques may reasonably be considered: topographic techniques using a Geodesic Station, laser scanning, and photogrammetry [6]. The most common technique is laser scanning for the generation of the 3D model and the acquisition of high-resolution images for texturing the 3D model [6]. However, if the object is mainly destroyed or lost, these techniques are of little or no use. In such cases, the most common approach is the use of CAD tools [4, 11–15].

Mainly designed for off-line rendering, most 3D CAD Models used in 3D environments are unsuitable for real-time rendering, due to their large size and high surface-detail. The use of light 3D models in 3D environments is a key factor for successful teaching experiences, because the size of the 3D models clearly limits interactivity between the end user and the virtual reconstruction [11].

This paper reports and experimentally validates a teaching experience with undergraduate students created through the integration of a 3D model, designed for off-line rendering and video creation, in a 3D immersive environment running on Oculus Rift™, with Unreal Engine virtual-reality development tools. The integration of such a 3D model implies many manual and semi-automated tasks, to improve experiential performance, optimization of which depends strongly on the workflow design, including shading, lighting, polygonal load, creation of tiled textures, and secondary UV channels for the light cache, among others. First, we briefly describe the hardware and software associated with the 3D immersive environment to outline the difficulties that might arise when a 3D model designed for off-line rendering and video creation has to be adapted to real-time VR HMD. The study then moves on to investigate the suitability of the environment for teaching in different areas: from historical knowledge to Medieval urban layout and the customs and traditions of the Middle Ages. It identifies the strengths and the weaknesses of this immersive environment for teaching Cultural Heritage through a comparison with videos in a real case: narrating the foundation and the initial development in the 14th and 15th c. of the new town of Briviesca (Spain). Therefore, this study takes a step forwards in relation to previous research, most of which has focused on the software tools and the hardware needed to generate a 3D immersive environment [5, 10–12]. Very few works [1–3] have evaluated their effect or suitability for final use and even fewer have done so in the context of teaching Cultural Heritage topics [4, 8], as their disciplines are mainly in such areas as second languages [2], architecture [16], history [12], and archaeology [11].

Briviesca is located in Northern Spain in an area that was formerly the old Kingdom of Castile. According to the extant documentation, the main town of Briviesca was, up until the 13th c., located on a hillside, on the same site of the Roman town of Virovesca; although several small hamlets little more than a few hundred meters from the main town had sprung up since then. From around the 13th c., the dominance of the Christian fiefdoms in the Kingdom of Castile assured a period of stability and prosperity for the region, during which time the nascent bourgeoisie and the nobility began to exercise greater influence. In the early 14th c., Doña Blanca de Portugal purchased an inheritance of a cluster of hamlets around Virovesca from Juana Gómez de Manzanedo. Doña Blanca is recognized as the founder of Briviesca and was actively involved in planning the construction of a new villa on the plain, regrouping farmers from the small hamlets nearby. In 1313, she granted the Fuero de Briviesca (Charter of Briviesca) to the town, to encourage new town dwellers to settle within its walls. She also decided on its organized layout, in imitation of the classic Roman urban grid, highly unusual in the medieval urban centers of the Iberian Peninsula. The grid structure was only slightly modified by the presence of a small settlement in the south-west of the new town. Finally, she promoted the construction of defensive buildings and other infrastructure to attract new inhabitants. Figure 1 shows the spatial distribution of Briviesca nowadays and its urban layout in the 15th c. [14]. This unusual urban model lends special interest to the explanations given to students on historical developments and daily life in Briviesca in the late Middle Ages.

In this study, we used a 3D model of the town of Briviesca at the beginning of the 15th c., almost a century after its foundation, to create a teaching activity for undergraduate students that shows the growth of the town, from its foundation until its consolidation as the main town in the area, a century later. The 3D model, composed of 1,771,882 triangles, includes around 300 ordinary buildings, such as houses and stables, and over 20 singular buildings, such as churches and gateways in walls.

The paper is structured as follows: Sect. 2 describes the hardware and software that comprise the virtual environment and the process followed to import the 3D models; Sect. 3 discusses the practical teaching experience with undergraduate students following two methodologies: a guided visit to the virtual environment and the screening of the animation video, Sect. 4 summarizes the teaching objectives achieved by each methodology comparing their strengths and weaknesses. Finally, Sect. 5 presents the conclusions and future lines of work.

Fig. 1. Briviesca nowadays and its urban layout in the 15th c.

2   3D Virtual Environment and Adaptation of 3D Models

The 3D models that recreate the village of Briviesca in the 15th C. have previously been presented in a former work [14]. Historical-archaeological research cites records of around 300 ordinary buildings in Briviesca at the turn of the 15th c. (including houses, stables, sheep pens and sheds) and over 20 singular buildings. Besides, some urban accessories, like signposts, fences, plants and wells, were also modeled. The 3D model consists of 1,771,882 triangles, among which the normal houses each have an average of 3,000 triangles, with many more in such singular buildings as the Colegiata of Saint Mary (89,000 triangles) and the church of Saint Martin (31,000 triangles).

The 3D models strike a balance between visual quality and size that permits suitable real-time visualization in a game engine. However, the original 3D models were conceived for off-line rendering and are therefore not optimized for real-time rendering. So, the design of the following 3-stage methodology was necessary to import the existing 3D models into the game engine. First a visualization project analysis was performed. In this step, the complexity of the 3D models was analyzed, so as to decide which 3D models should maintain high complexity, due to their historical importance or their proximity to the guided walk that the user will follow. This approach preserved a level of detail that the user can view during the walk, which would not be preserved in the mesh quality of other 3D models further away from the walk. The second step was the integration of the 3D models in the selected game engine, Unreal Engine. Based on the particularities of this game engine, the 3D models underwent different manual or semi-automated tasks, to obtain their best display. These tasks included: adjusting the orientation of normals, checking whether the 3D models were completely closed, and creating collision meshes to cover those models closer to the guided walk. In this step, the adjustments of the textures on the 3D models by UV mapping and the creation of tiling and additional texture maps were performed. Finally, in the third step, the virtual environment was created, through the integration of the 3D models into the virtual environment. First of all, in view of the large number of objects, a proper management procedure was necessary to import the project into folders and to structure it. Then, the 3D models were placed in the virtual world, after checking that they had been properly scaled, to create an optimal virtual reality experience. Before the first tests could be performed, the lighting was positioned and the interactions and the animations were introduced.

The main problems encountered in this process were with the technology, which is still at a very early stage of its development; both the software and the hardware have no commercial versions and each new release is not always compatible with its former versions. A further problem that appeared was simulator sickness, as previously reported in other studies [18, 19]. We reduced this effect in our virtual reality experience in various ways by setting a continuous rate of 75 fps, by game-engine optimization and by controlling the exposure time of the students.

Blender is a 3D modeling and animation software developed as open-source software and distributed under the GNU GPLicense (www.blender.org). It was used for the original 3D meshes and was our chosen tool for 3D modeling. The choice of Unreal Engine as the game engine was motivated by the easy-to-achieve photorealistic appearance of the virtual environments that it can create and its ability to create large virtual maps; an indispensable requisite for this project in view of the size of the villa of Briviesca. Although other game engines, like Unity, have a larger user community and variety of web-based learning resources, their implementation is tied to Oculus SDK. Complete projects may be created for students with Unreal Engine and Unity, which in both cases operate under an open-source license.

In terms of hardware, Oculus Rift Development Kit 2 was used as the HMD. The choice was fairly easy, because it is the only development hardware of its type available to final users. Since the expansion of this technology over recent years, almost anybody can now acquire a copy, although we should remember that is a development-oriented unit, for experimental work with this new technology, which is as yet not on the market for the final consumer. The computer used for running the 3D environment had the following specifications: Intel(R) Core(TM) i7-4790 CPU 3.60 GHz, 32 GB RAM with a NVIDIA GeForce GTX 780 graphic card.

Table 1. Summary of time spent on the development of the virtual environment

Steps	Tasks	Software tools	Time (%)
Visualization project analysis	Analysis of modeling complexity and possible tiling geometry	Blender	10
Game engine adaptation	Orientation of normals, closing objects, collision mesh, textures (additional UV channels and maps) and materials	Blender, Unreal Engine	35
Creation of the virtual environment	importation and classification, model refinement, virtual reality optimization, placing objects, lighting, interaction and animation, final revision	Unreal Engine	55

Table 1 summarizes the different characteristics of the 3-step methodology for the development of the virtual environment: the time spent (as a percentage of total time) on each task, the main tasks included in each step, and the software tools required for its running.

3 Study Case: Teaching Session on the History of Briviesca in the 14th c.

Once the 3D Model of the town had been integrated in the virtual environment, a teaching session was designed for its validation with undergraduate students following two different strategies. Its objective was to detect the strengths and weaknesses of both teaching methodologies: a video [17] explaining the town in the 15th c. with off-line renders of the 3D model and a guided visit to the town through the virtual environment that includes the screening of short video clips.

3.1 Teaching Session Goals and Student Profiles

The teaching experience was designed so that the students could progress towards the following goals:

- Assimilation of the main historical aspects relating to the re-establishment of the town of Briviesca, its urban layout and its influence in medieval life
- Evaluation of the visually-acquired knowledge: information not explicitly included in the teaching narrative, which can be extracted from the images visualized by the student such as building materials and the structures of houses, etc.
- Stimulation of the interest of students in History, Urbanism and Virtual Reality, through the use of Information Technologies

It involved 50 undergraduate students on the Communications Media Bachelor Degree at the University of Burgos. The students were randomly divided into two groups. The first group watched the video, while the second group followed an individual guided tour around the town through the virtual environment that included viewing short video clips. Both groups were gender balanced: 60 % of the first group and 44 % of the second group were female. The students were aged 21−28 in the first group and 21−29 in the second group, sizes that were similar to those reported in research with the same HMD [19].

3.2 Description of the Teaching Session

First of all, both groups of students received a short introduction to the goals of the teaching experience. Then, the first group (25 students) watched the video [17], while the second group followed a virtual tour with the HMD through the virtual environment, Fig. 2. Finally, all the students were afterwards asked to fill in an anonymous survey.

Fig. 2. Students from both groups during the teaching experience

For this second group, a tour was designed through the virtual town of Briviesca. As the same teaching goals were valid for both groups, the students might be able to acquire the same historical content, so the 15-minute-video was edited into 7 clips of approximately 2 min each. These seven clips were located at various milestones around the virtual tour, in such a way that, at the end of the teaching experience, all the students would have received similar amounts of information. The virtual tour also takes the student on a walk close by all of the unique buildings in the town. On arrival at each milestone, a 2D map of the actual position on the map is shown to the student. The definition of a fixed virtual tour was selected for two reasons: it ensures that all the students spend comparable lengths of time exposed to the virtual environment and they also receive the same information (by watching all the video clips on the compulsory itinerary). In this way, the learning rates achieved by the students might be comparable. The quality of the 3D model of the town is greatly reduced in all those areas without close-up views, to which the student is not taken on the tour; this makes it possible to reduce the computing requirements of the virtual environment, as previously outlined. Figure 3 shows the itinerary of the students through the virtual environment and the locations of each milestone.

There are two options to create a fixed virtual tour: the user avatar can either travel on a means of transport (a horse and cart, for example) with no control over its movement or the avatar can follow a signposted route on foot, which the avatar is unable to vary. We chose the second option, because it permits the user to control speed of movement and to take time to enjoy the virtual tour, which can result in a better acquisition time. Only when the user arrives at a milestone is any further movement blocked, so that the video clips may be viewed. A path of grass and flowers is shown in the design of the virtual tour to indicate the right pathway. Two complementary strategies were applied to limit user navigation around the virtual environment: first, some shields at the beginning of the virtual tour inform the user about the path of grass and flowers that should be followed, and, second, transparent walls were located at the entrance of the forbidden secondary streets so that the users would not lose their way. Figure 2 shows a student during the virtual tour with the HMD. On arrival at the end of the virtual tour, the student is asked to fill in a survey to provide feedback and

Fig. 3. Itinerary of the students through the virtual environment and video-clip locations

conclusions on the learning experience. The average duration of the virtual tour was between 30-to-40 min.

3.3   Evaluation of the Teaching Session

The survey consisted of 15 questions. The first question inquired into overall satisfaction with the teaching experience. The remaining survey questions were split into three groups, to evaluate whether all the goals of the session had been fulfilled. In all the questions, the student had to select one answer from three options. A first group of five questions evaluated the knowledge acquired by the students (on historical aspects, use of the main buildings and population distribution within the town); these snippets of information were only transmitted in the video narrative. The second group was composed of five questions on visual knowledge: information not explicitly included in the video narrative, although it can be extracted from the rendered images (e.g. the average height of village buildings, the main materials used in the construction of the poorest houses, etc.). Finally, the third group was composed of four questions that evaluated student capability to recall the main buildings/services of the town (e.g. the main building next to the town gateway to the Burgos road, the location of the inns of the town, etc.).

4   Analysis of the Teaching Activity

All of the 50 students who attended the session filled in the survey, although in some cases the option of "Don't know/No answer" was selected to answer some questions. The responses were normalized to the number of valid surveys for analysis and representation. The main results of the surveys are shown below.

The first question evaluated overall student satisfaction with the teaching experience on a scale from 1 (not at all satisfied) to 5 (highly satisfied). Figure 4 shows the average score for both teaching experiences. The virtual reality experience scored an average of 4.84 and the video view an average of 4.76 (over 5 in both cases). The difference is not so large, but is sufficient to ensure that the overall satisfaction is higher for the virtual tour, perhaps due to its novelty for the students.

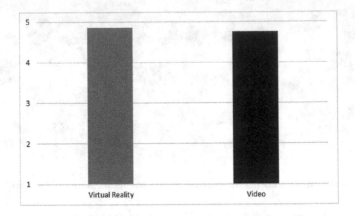

Fig. 4. Student's overall satisfaction with the teaching experience.

The students who viewed the video obtained better marks (an average of 81.4/100) in the 5 questions on the topics relating to the knowledge transmitted by the video narrative (on historical aspects, use of the main buildings and population distribution within the town) than the students who followed the virtual tour (59.9/100). Figure 5 shows the average marks for each question and the overall average score for the responses from both groups of students. Although the students on the virtual tour gave more incorrect answers in general to all the questions, their low result is mainly due to

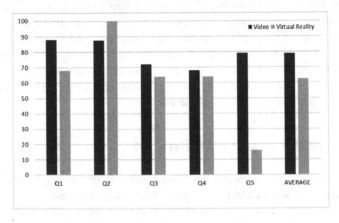

Fig. 5. Knowledge acquired from the video narrative.

their answers to the last question of this group. If the responses to question 5 are left out, the marks are not so very different: 79.7 and 70.9, respectively. The reason for this poor result was because of a mistake in the design of the virtual tour: the students were able to complete the virtual tour without viewing one of the video clips, losing the chance of listening to the information required for a correct answer to this last question.

Quite unlike the results of the previous group of questions, the marks for the responses to questions on visually-acquired knowledge were as follows: the group of students who followed the virtual tour obtained better marks to the 5 questions (an average mark of 69.3/100) than the students who watched the video (51.7/100). Figure 6 shows the average mark for each of the responses from the two groups of students to this set of questions and their average scores. It is important to note that the difference in the average mark (17.6 points) in this second set of questions was higher than in the first when only 4 questions (9.2 points) were considered.

Finally, the third group of questions tested the students' recall of the main buildings and services of the town. Once again, the student group that followed the virtual tour obtained better marks in the 4 questions (an average mark of 52.5/100) than the student group that watched the video (32.0/100). Figure 7 shows the average mark for each response from the two groups of students and the average score. It is important to note that the difference in the average mark, although both groups present relatively low marks, was significantly better for the virtual tour (21.0 points, almost 40 % better). Although it might be thought that this result was due to the limited spatial allocation of the viewer in the video projection, the video was designed to show different bird's eye views of the city, so as to facilitate student awareness of the main buildings of the village and their locations; the effect of viewer limitations in the video projection case might therefore be negligible in this teaching experience.

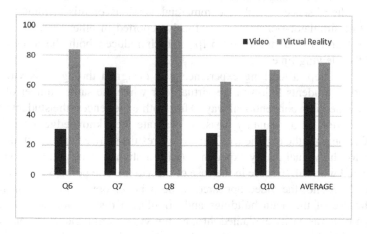

Fig. 6. Visually-acquired knowledge.

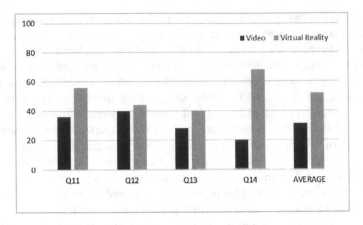

Fig. 7. Students' abilities to position the main buildings

5 Conclusions and Future Works

Undergraduate students studying for the Communications Media Bachelor Degree have followed a teaching experience, to evaluate knowledge-acquisition rates from two separate IT techniques: watching a video generated with renders from a 3D Animation software and a virtual tour through a 3D model showing the same video in short clips.

This research covered 2 steps: in the first, an existing 3D model of the town of Briviesca (Spain) in the 15th C. created for off-line rendering was adapted to a 3D game engine and implemented in a 3D HMD. Although it is not the main objective of this research, it is interesting to note that the main problems encountered in this process were due to the absence of stable, commercial versions of this technology and the appearance of simulator-sickness as previously reported in other research. The game engine was therefore optimized to 75 fps, which reduced both the aforementioned effect and the viewing time.

In a second step, a teaching experience was designed through this virtual environment and 25 students followed the virtual tour while the same number of students watched the video in a conventional way. After both experiences, the students had time to fill in a survey, on a voluntary basis, to evaluate their knowledge acquisition and their satisfaction with the experience. The survey results showed that the students had a preference for the virtual reality experience (with a slightly better satisfaction score of 4.84 compared with a 4.76 score in the case of the video), due perhaps to its novelty for the students. Second, the video appeared to be a better option to transmit historical aspects, the use of the main buildings and population distribution within the town; information that was easily explained through the video script and visual appreciation. Third, the virtual tour was a more effective medium for the transmission of visually-acquired knowledge and information on the main buildings in the town. The virtual tour was clearly appreciated as a better medium for knowledge acquisition by undergraduate students. So, we may clearly conclude that a virtual tour with video clips is a balanced solution for knowledge acquisition on Cultural Heritage by undergraduate students. Finally, the design of a virtual tour is a critical task where any mistakes, such as the one mentioned in this article, may result in a drastic reduction of potential acquired knowledge.

Further research will focus on extending this teaching experience to a wider group of students and people of different ages and personal interests to reinforce the significance of our conclusions and to extend their scope of application. Moreover, presentation of the off-line renders to a group of students in a lecture and an analysis of their acquired knowledge might help to generalize both the advantages and the limitations of this methodology and the virtual environment for Cultural Heritage teaching.

Acknowledgments. This work was partially supported through the Program "Impulso de la Industria de Contenidos Digitales desde las Universidades" of the Spanish Ministry of Industry, Tourism and Commerce. The authors would especially like to thank Mr. Mario Alaguero for the development of the 3D models.

References

1. Chen, S., Pan, Z., Zhang, M., Shen, H.: A case study of user immersion-based systematic design for serious heritage games. Multimedia Tools Appl. **62**, 633–658 (2013)
2. Katsionis, G., Virvou, M.: Personalised e-learning through an educational virtual reality game using Web services. Multimedia Tools Appl. **39**, 47–71 (2008)
3. Korakakis, G., Pavlatou, E.A., Palyvos, J.A., Spyrellis, N.: 3D visualization types in multimedia applications for science learning: a case study for 8th grade students in Greece. Comput. Educ. **52**, 390–401 (2009)
4. Bustillo, A., Alaguero, M., Miguel, I., Saiz, J.M., Iglesias, L.S.: A flexible platform for the creation of 3D semi-immersive environments to teach Cultural Heritage. Digit. Appl. Archaeol. Cult. Heritage **2**, 248–259 (2015)
5. Bonis, B., Stamos, J., Vosinakis, S., Andreou, I., Panayiotopoulos, T.: A platform for virtual museums with personalized content. Multimedia Tools Appl. **42**, 139–159 (2009)
6. Chow, S.K., Chan, K.L.: Reconstruction of photorealistic 3D model of ceramic artefacts for interactive virtual exhibition. J. Cult. Heritage **10**, 161–173 (2009)
7. Anderson, E.F., McLoughlin, L., Liarokapis, F., Peters, C., Petridis, P., de Freitas, S.: Developing serious games for Cultural Heritage: a state-of-the-art review. Virtual Reality **14**, 255–275 (2010)
8. Champion, E.M.: Otherness of place: game-based interaction and learning in virtual heritage projects. Int. J. Heritage Stud. **14**, 210–228 (2008)
9. Wachowiak, M.J., Karas, B.V.: 3D scanning and replication for museum and Cultural Heritage applications. Techniques de balayage et de reproduction en trois dimensions pour applications muséales et culturelles **48**, 141–158 (2009)
10. Bruno, F., Bruno, S., De Sensi, G., Luchi, M.L., Mancuso, S., Muzzupappa, M.: From 3D reconstruction to virtual reality: a complete methodology for digital archaeological exhibition. J. Cult. Heritage. **11**, 42–49 (2010)
11. Lucet, G.: Virtual reality: a knowledge tool for Cultural Heritage. In: Ranchordas, A., Araújo, H.J., Pereira, J.M., Braz, J. (eds.) VISIGRAPP 2008. CCIS, vol. 24, pp. 1–10. Springer, Heidelberg (2009)

12. De Paolis, L.T.: Walking in a virtual town to understand and learning about the life in the middle ages. In: Murgante, B., Misra, S., Carlini, M., Torre, C.M., Nguyen, H.-Q., Taniar, D., Apduhan, B.O., Gervasi, O. (eds.) ICCSA 2013, Part I. LNCS, vol. 7971, pp. 632–645. Springer, Heidelberg (2013)

13. Styliadis, A.D., Sechidis, L.A.: Photography-based façade recovery & 3-d modeling: a CAD application in Cultural Heritage. J. Cult. Heritage **12**, 243–252 (2011)

14. Alaguero, M., Bustillo, A., Guinea, B., Iglesias, L.S.: The virtual reconstruction of a small Medieval town: the case of Briviesca (Spain). In: Archaeopress (ed.) CAA2014 21st Century Archaeology, Concepts, Methods and Tools. Proceedings of the 42nd Annual Conference on Computer Applications and Quantitative Methods in Archaeology, pp. 575–584. Archaeopress (2015)

15. Alaguero, M., Bustillo, A., Iglesias, L.S., Martinez, L.: The Church of the Charterhouse of Miraflores in Burgos: virtual reconstruction of artistic imagery. fusion of cultures. In: Proceedings of the 38th Annual Conference on Computer Applications and Quantitative Methods in Archaeology, Granada, Spain, April 2010 (BAR International Series 2494) (2013)

16. Styliadis, A.D., Konstantinidou, D.G., Tyxola, K.A.: eCAD system design - applications in architecture. Int. J. Comput. Commun. Control **3**, 204–214 (2008)

17. Link to the final video. https://www.youtube.com/watch?v=dwa7-94Y_Qw

18. Treleaven, J., Battershill, J., Cole, D., Fadelli, C., Freestone, S., Lang, K., Sarig-Bahat, H.: Simulator sickness incidence and susceptibility during neck motion-controlled virtual reality tasks. Virtual Reality **19**, 267–275 (2015)

19. Hupont, I., Gracia, J., Sanagustín, L., Gracia, M.A.: How do new visual immersive systems influence gaming QoE? A use case of serious gaming with Oculus Rift. In: 2015 Seventh International Workshop onQuality of Multimedia Experience (QoMEX), pp. 1–6 (2015)

20. Fitter, B.: VR and the death of the screen plane. In: 2015 International Conference on 3D Imaging (IC3D), pp. 1–5 (2015)

VR for Cultural Heritage

A VR-WEB-BIM for the Future Maintenance of Milan's Cathedral

Francesco Fassi[1(✉)], Alessandro Mandelli[1], Simone Teruggi[1],
Fabrizio Rechichi[1], Fausta Fiorillo[2], and Cristiana Achille[1]

[1] ABC, Politecnico di Milano, Via Ponzio, 31, 20133 Milan, Italy
{francesco.fassi,alessandro.mandelli,
fabrizio.rechichi,cristiana.achille}@polimi.it,
simone.teruggi@mail.polimi.it
[2] DICIV, Università degli studi di Salerno, Via Giovanni Paolo II, 132,
84084 Fisciano, SA, Italy
ffiorillo@unisa.it

Abstract. The work presented here is the final step of a multidisciplinary research project conducted on the Milan Cathedral for eight years (2008–2015). Three main topics, consequentially related, will be here addressed: (i) the survey of the structure, meant to update the old drawings; (ii) the construction of an accurate and detailed 3D model to be used to produce measurements at a 1:20–1:50 representation scale; (iii) the development of a Building Information System (BIM) to collect all the data relating to the restoration projects, as well as all information relating to past, current and future maintenance activities of the cathedral.

The result of this research project is a complex and accurate digital 3D model of the main spire of the cathedral and of other parts of the building. This model can be visualized, navigated and used by the Veneranda Fabbrica technicians as an info-data catalogue, thanks to a common web browser connected with the remote BIM System Server and the modelling software where *ad hoc* I/O plugins are implemented.

The last step of this long project was to take advantage of the nascent potential of immersive visualization techniques and to transpose the BIM system in a VR environment, thus obtaining two main results. The first was a high-appeal visualization system that allows a virtual visit of the Main Spire of the cathedral, the building's highest part that has been closed to visitors since the beginning of the XX century. The second was the possibility to use this technology to virtually explore the cathedral from a technical point of view: by using an immersive visualization technology, operators can improve their understanding of the structure and obtain real-time information about the state of conservation, including current and past maintenance activities, in a sort of "augmented reality system in a virtual environment".

Keywords: Survey · 3D reality-based modelling · Immersive visualization · Virtual reality · BIM · Architecture

© Springer International Publishing Switzerland 2016
L.T. De Paolis and A. Mongelli (Eds.): AVR 2016, Part II, LNCS 9769, pp. 139–157, 2016.
DOI: 10.1007/978-3-319-40651-0_12

1 Introduction

"Virtual Reality is a computer technology that gives the illusion, to those who use it, of being immersed in a virtual environment that does not really exist. It is a computer simulation of a real situation where the human subject may interact with the virtual environment, sometimes by means of non-conventional interfaces like glasses and helmets on which the scene is represented and the sounds reproduced. A data glove is equipped with sensors to simulate tactile stimuli and to translate the movements into instructions for the software. The purpose of virtual reality is to simulate a real environment in order to give the impression of being truly immersed in that environment" [1].

Initially, in the wide world of Cultural Heritage, the aim of Virtual Reality was to implement (i) high-impact applications and (ii) functional purposes. The first corresponded to beautifully performed virtual reconstruction without 'metric' accuracy; the second to reconstructions of sites with the relocation of environment and objects, used, for example, when they are closed to the public and/or no longer exist. Today the trend is to 'mix' all aspects by creating scientific virtual reconstructions (metric) that are, at the same time, able to convey an impressive effect.

A virtual model of Cultural Heritage can have different values (scientific, educational, historical, ...) depending on the information that it provides, and it can also be used to assess the evolution of the environment by comparing 3D reconstructions made at different times in the object's life. It thus becomes easy to compare present and past, and to assess and quantify the changes caused by time.

The reality-based model of the Main Spire of Milan Cathedral was commissioned by the Veneranda Fabbrica del Duomo[1] (from here onwards abbreviated as VDF); made with great care and designed to support the ordinary and extraordinary maintenance operations, it is used not only to allow 'the virtual tour' (typical case of cultural heritage not accessible to the wide public) but also as a support for the display of information (technical, historical, ...) georeferenced on the single piece (single block of marble). In this sense, it is not just a virtual visit, but also a real exploration of the 3D model. In other words a virtual visit to a restoration yard.

In the virtual scenario of the geometric model of the Main Spire the work in progress on its pieces, it is linked in a sort of Augmented Reality inside the Virtual Reality. The substantial difference between Virtual Reality (VR) and Augmented Reality (AR) is that, in the first case, the reconstruction of an entirely fictional world and consisting of virtual objects is observed on a screen; the second case is not tied to a video display, but to any surface/object that can become a support to visualize the additional information of the scene; what we observe is an integration between real images and virtual objects. In the case of the Duomo, VR and AR models are blended. The user is immersed in the virtual model and can access computer-generated information contained in the Database. The virtual world is 'increased', and further enriched

---

[1] "Veneranda Fabbrica del Duomo di Milano" (VFD) is the historic organisation responsible for preservation and restoration of the Cathedral. Gian Galeazzo Visconti established VFD in 1387, for design and construction of the Cathedral, and it has been operating for over six hundred years to ensure the preservation and architectural and artistic restoration of the Duomo, safeguarding and providing services for the Cathedral's religious activity [2].

by additional information (graphic and textual) georeferenced and synchronized on the model. It is possible to virtually visit the Spire and simultaneously know how the operations are carried out by the VFD staff (consolidation, cleaning, replacement, tessellation, etc.). The careful organization of the data will allow the public to visit the monument and understand its complex organization; in this sense, therefore, the virtual tour will help visitors to understand the complexity of the preservation of Cultural Heritage.

In a futuristic scenario, the combination of VR and AR will allow the technical staff to simulate the start and the arrangement of the restoration yards. These virtual operations made on reality-based models managed in a BIM process will help to improve the prediction of costs and the duration of operations, as well as to simulate future scenarios, etc. The complex system of information (structured DB) visible on the model will allow technicians to optimize all operations, helping to identify the needs of the yard.

The use of the model by VFD will contribute to the dissemination of innovative systems for the use of data and will simultaneously allow VFD to self-evaluate needs-time-cost-answers.

VR and AR will become a management tool of complex Cultural Heritage yards both for researchers and users in general. It is necessary to overcome the initial effect of 'wonder' that this system inspires, and learn to use it effectively as a new work tool, and thus create the necessary professionals and specializations. VR and AR models will never replace the *in situ* visit, but they will certainly increase the understanding of the Cultural Heritage by the visitor as well as support studies and scientific analyses.

This paper starts with a brief description of the previous research activities regarding the survey and modelling phase of the project that led to the creation of the accurate 3D model of the Main Spire of the Milan Cathedral. Then it moves on to briefly describe the WEBBIM system, created *ad hoc* and already in use by the Veneranda Fabbrica del Duomo to support its continuous maintenance activities. Finally, it will describe the process necessary to modify and adapt this 3D model to a VR immersive environment.

The paper does not aim at presenting new technical developments in the VR technologies. Rather, as the final chapter of a long and multidisciplinary research work, it aims at illustrating the investigation that the team carried out over the years whilst exploring the possible uses of high detailed BIM 3D model inside VR and AR, as support for professional activities in the field of Cultural Heritage conservation.

1.1   Virtual Reality for the Cultural Heritage (State of the Art)

The integration of the research in the area of computer graphics, computer vision and 3D survey systems found as a common action field the virtual reconstructions of Cultural Heritage. A 2004 paper by Jiri Zara [3] presented an overview of techniques for the creation and visualization of cultural heritage objects and site on the web. The discussion included dealing with acquiring techniques, modelling, optimization, and final presentation of digital reconstructions using Virtual Reality paradigms that are still relevant today. The study was illustrated by practical experience from the implementation of the EU project Virtual Heart of Central Europe [4]. The aim of the project were: (i) the digital reconstruction of selected historical buildings of four cities from different countries – Bratislava (SK), Graz (AT), Maribor (SI), and Prague (CZ); (ii) the creation of a digital storytelling; (iii) and the publication of the results on the web. The pioneering experiment was the Virtual Old Prague project [5], a web application based on progressive downloading city parts in correspondence to current user's position and consists of several components: 3D scene; HTML document, and 2D navigation map synchronized with the user's movement in simulated scene. Although today the technology is evolved and the interface used for the navigation in the virtual space is old-fashion and not very user-friendly, topics discussed and conclusions are still current: "The web definitely has a potential to bring cultural heritage on the screen of any interested Internet users".

The article "Visualization and Virtual Reality for Cultural Heritage Diagnostic" [6] promoted the use of Virtual Reality in Cultural Heritage applications for diagnostic purpose, introducing the term of Virtual Cultural Heritage. The work developed within into the SIDART (Integrated System for Cultural Heritage Diagnostic) project and its objective was the development of hardware and software package to acquire, process, integrate and visualize information produced by different survey instruments (laser scanner, multi-spectral camera, calibrated metric photogrammetric camera, thermography). Using a VR device (Table Projector Baron with a workstation equipped with nVidia Quadro 4500 graphic card), the system allowed passive and active stereoscopic visualization. In order to correctly visualize the model, the user had to wear a special eyewear (HMD). The most innovative idea of the study was the possibility to not only visualize but also work interacting with the survey data in an immersive 3D environment: "This lets the operator perceive the third dimension and the virtual investigation of the object becomes more realistic. This lets us take into consideration in a more simple, natural and correct way and also reduce the possibility to make wrong evaluation due to the false prospective of the classic visualization."

The current virtual technologies (VR and AR), devices and sensors are able to immerse the user in a virtual environment, offering the possibility of interacting with additional contextual heritage data (reality-based 3D model, pictures, technical documents, historical information, tourist guides, etc.) [7]. The VR applied to Cultural Heritage has already become a potential tool for 'tourist' users to navigate and interact in a virtual scene in total symbiosis with the environment. The system has an attractive impact for dissemination purposes because it adds extra information and allows a direct and intuitive access of digital objects [8].

VR offers more than a replica of the real context; it allows virtual hypothetical reconstructions of the past aspect that can be developed for different epochs and can be related or overlaid with the archaeological surviving evidences [9]. VR creates a direct connection between tangible data (museum collection, archaeological remains etc.) and ancient invisible space, reproducing the scene, the environment and the atmosphere (i.e. ancient illumination condition and sound) of past context in an immersive ad attractive mode [10].

The potentiality of VR applications to promote knowledge Cultural Heritage is proven by the development of a significant number of projects in this research area [11]. An increasingly large number of museums possess a virtual gallery where the users can explored online digital reproductions enriched with technical and/or historical documentations [12] and organized in a virtual rooms of the collections [13].

The "museum of the future" [14] developed by European and ArchiVision contains the 3D models of the masterpieces from the Dutch Rijksmuseum. Using a development kit for the Oculus Rift virtual reality glasses, the user can visualize and walk around the paintings at much closer range than would be possible in reality.

Furthermore, in order to make digital contents available to the Europeana collection portal, the 3D-ICONS project was founded [15]. The aim is the definition of a standard workflow for the creation of a 3D replica from the selection of methods and tools, data acquisition, post-processing, online publication of content, and metadata capture.

Virtual Museum Transnational Network (V-MusT) [16], instead, was created to provide the heritage sector with tools and support to develop virtual museums with communicative and educational purposes using VR technologies and devices.

"Apa Game" [17] is a case-study selected by V-MUST project to address the issues of re-use of digital assets in online and mobile applications. The first case study was the project "Apa discovering Bologna" made by CINECA for the museum of Bologna Genus Bononiae, which in ITABC CNR participated for the reconstruction of the Etruscan and Roman age landscape of the city. The result is a 3D cartoon on the history of Bologna that combines high-performance graphics and rigorous virtual reconstruction (based on laser scanner and photogrammetry integrated system) [18]. Since its release in 2011, Apa was considered an innovation in the panorama of educational museum movies, it is the first 3D stereoscopic movie with historical references applied to an entire city with four different geo-referenced scenarios and seven historical periods: Etruscan, Roman, Medieval, Renaissance, XVII and XVIII century and the present day.

"Ati discovering Veio" [19] is the successive short 3D animation of the CINECA; the 3D reconstructions are the result of joint work of archaeologists and experts in modelling and computer vision [20]. The protagonist Ati (Apa's cusin), guides the tourists in the rooms of Villa Giulia museum (Rome) dedicated to the masterpieces of Etruscan sculpture, with the famous Apollo of Veii, and in the sanctuary of the "Portonaccio", leading them to the roof of the temple.

The preview of the animation film was made during the inauguration of the exhibition "Apa, Etruscan lands in Rome" [21] at the National Etruscan Museum of Villa Giulia. The initiative was the result of a partnership between the Roman museum and Genus Bononiae, and a scientific and technological project coordinated by CINECA. At the same time, the exhibition "The journey beyond life. The Etruscans and the afterlife among masterpieces and virtual reality" was opened in Palazzo Pepoli-Museum of the History of Bologn [22]. The starting point of these initiatives is always a complete historical and scientific study combined with the application of the most advanced reality-based reconstructions, thus combining science, art and spectacular effects.

One of the attractions of the exhibition "Apa Etruscan lands in Rome" was the holographic life-size installation of "Situla della Certosa" [23] (precious bronze vase symbol of Northern Etruria). Virtual animations include the actual geometry of the vase rich in decorative details, and an artificially restored version, that brings it back to the time of its production. In the same way, the "Sarcofago degli Sposi" [24], symbolic monument of the Etruscan civilization (permanently exhibited at Villa Giulia) was the subject of a virtual reconstruction in the museum of Bologna. The digital survey of the sarcophagus was built starting from the fourth team of researchers acquisition campaigns (3DOM-Fondazione Bruno Kessler [25], CNR-ISTI, CNR-ITABC, Leica, and University of Bologna), coordinated by CINECA. The installation was a performance combining holography, projections 3D video mapping, sound and advanced visualization techniques in an immersive audiovisual environment.

In conclusion, it is possible to summarize the principal purpose of a VR application in function of the final consumer: (i) the 'technical user' can use metric data and functional information for preservation and maintenance purpose; (ii) the 'common user' can take advantages for knowledge and dissemination purpose. In any case, the 3D reconstructions of the present and of the past require a reality-based acquisition and modelling, connected with spatial and geographical data.

2   The Case-Study: The Milan Cathedral

The case study presented here is the Milan Cathedral: to be precise, the research activities that accompanied the restoration works of the monument over the last 8 years. The original purpose of the work, commissioned by VFD, was to update the old drawings and produce new plans, sections and elevations of the Main Spire of Milan Cathedral [26]. The occasion was represented by the extraordinary maintenance activities that were about to be implemented on that part of the monument. Over the years, however, the research project evolved into something more stimulating and challenging. The classical approach was immediately abandoned in favour of testing new solutions: in particular, survey methods able to directly reproduce the 3D geometry of the structure, as well as different modelling strategies. The final, ambitious aim became building a complete high resolution and high accuracy three-dimensional virtual model of the entire structure. The idea was to adopt a method that would generate plans, sections, elevations and, in general, all measurements at every point of the building. The resulting virtual model would respect, in fact, the requirements of metrical accuracy, as well as the richness of details, and would easily allow various representation scales, including 1:50 for structural parts and 1:5 for the statues and decorations.

It was clear that a mere extraction of 2D drawings from a very complex 3D model was important and mandatory (and immediately useful for to Veneranda Fabbrica del Duomo), but reductive in relation to the inherent high potential of the high-resolution 3D model [27].

An important point was how to take advantage of a detailed three-dimensional model and make it usable for all the operators and workers involved in the Cathedral's maintenance. A careful study was conducted in order to better understand the modus operandi of VFD. Its main activities are the supervision of the monument, in order to cyclically identify the damaged parts, and the consequent maintenance operations, which consists of the restoration of the cracked or chipped marble blocks or the complete substitution in the most extreme cases. The restoration of the monument is an endless, continuous work of repairing, cleaning and replacement that has to be documented to help future activities. The modern answer to this necessity is the management of all the works inside a BIM system, as it combines the digital three-dimensional or multidimensional representation of an object with an information database (spatial position, technical features, properties of the materials, realization phases, maintenance operation, etc.) [28]. Thanks to this working method, it is possible to create a proper geographic and informative system of the heritage, including the management of its life cycle, from the phase of the project, to the phases of the use and maintenance.

Therefore, the main effort was spent in the last years to build a dedicated BIM system with this specific goal: supporting to the operations of the restoration yard.

Since 2009, the research work involved different areas of the Milan Cathedral following or, to be more precise, anticipating the restoration yards. As of today (2016) the system includes the Main Spire, the Dome Cladding, the two Altars of the Transept, the 18th Spire, the Lantern and the Big Dome.

2.1   The Survey: Measuring and Modelling Gothic Architecture

The Milan Cathedral is one of most important example of Gothic architecture in Italy. It is an architectural style born and developed in the early and late medieval period; it evolved from Romanesque architecture and ended with the advent of Renaissance architecture. This style had great influence in ecclesiastical architecture. Churches, abbeys and monasteries were built using a unique combination of existing technologies such as ogival or pointed arches, ribbed vaults, buttresses, window traceries, clustered columns, towers, pinnacles and spires. When applied to religious buildings this style emphasizes the verticality and the light. Pointed arches gave greater flexibility to architectural form allowing a vertical visual result; they are used in every location (doorways, windows, arcades and galleries), both for structural and decorative purposes. Externally, towers and spires, both large and small, are characteristics of Gothic churches. Gothic architecture and especially its characteristic decorations exhibit quite elaborated geometric shape configurations. This is achieved by combining only a few basic geometric patterns, namely circles and straight lines. The results are obtained combining them with one another thanks to a limited set of operations, such as intersection, offsetting and extrusions.

It was not possible to preventively decide which were the correct and more efficient methods and tools in order to study such a complex architecture. Therefore, the survey phase involved different approaches and instrumentations and evolved over the time. Although a first topographic survey was not sufficient to completely describe the building, these measurements were essential to georeference all data together. The use of a laser scanner (2009) seemed to be the obvious choice to complete an exhaustive survey of the Cathedral [27]. Over the years (2010–2015) the laser approach was substituted by the photogrammetric method. This technique permitted to overcome problems linked to the penetration of the laser beam in the structure that prevents accurate and reliable measurement of structures. Moreover, photogrammetry is more flexible, as it allows to better negotiate with the presence of narrow spaces, and can be easily used on moving scaffoldings. As a result, a high number of photos were acquired and were useful not only to build the 3D model but also to complete the description of the Cathedral with the addition of information about the state of health, degraded parts and colour of the marble surfaces. These data also allowed to elaborate high definition orthophoto, useful to subdivide the models according the disposition of the constructive elements. This represented the starting point to build up a multi-scale model aimed at the precise description of every single marble block of the yards involved in the maintenance activities.

2.2 The Modelling

The goal of the modelling part was to develop a method to generate 3D models of complex objects starting from dense point clouds generated from range or image based techniques. The modelling phase nowadays still represents the bottleneck of the entire workflow, especially when it comes to reality-based modelling objects rich of details and freeform shapes [29].

The model was created using Rhinoceros, a widespread 3D software working with NURBS curves and surfaces. It is capable to manage the complexity of the information obtained from the survey phase and it shows flexibility both in the modelling phase as well as in importing/exporting file formats. It can be integrated with external plug-ins able to manage dense point clouds (Pointools[2]) or to apply aided parametric design (Grasshopper). Moreover it is possible create some *ad hoc* personalized processes using SDK tools free for developers.

The protagonist of all the maintenance activities is the marble block: for this reason, every single marble block is singularly modelled. The whole model results in a big LEGO structure composed by simple (structural) and complex (artistic) blocks that are close and topologically connected elements. If all objects are closed and valid (there are no auto-intersecting surfaces), it is possible to calculate the volume, the external surface and the mass of each element. These values, properly organized, provide useful information that can be employed in the daily activities of the yard: for economic, logistics and structural analysis purposes.

An interesting aspect of this system is that it provides not only information on each object, but also on their position and their proximity, thus resembling a geographic information system, and therefore allowing the user to operate spatial queries.

During the modelling phase, three types of objects were identified as requiring different modelling strategies. Line-based items compose the first family: this is the case of structural elements, that are normally quite simple and with a geometry easily mouldable with sweeping, revolution and extrusion operations. The second family is that of freeform objects, which include all round statues, ornaments and decorations with no straight lines at all [29]. Every component of this category is different from one another, so they were acquired one by one moving from point clouds obtained by image-based techniques to meshes, to mesh and finally to NURBS, editable in Rhinoceros. The transformation is realized through re-topology operations and reverse engineering software. It is a mandatory step in order to lighten the model inside the modelling software and to merge different family models. This allows to virtualize the last type of objects born from the combination of the two previous ones: they are "mixed" elements in which appear at the same time geometric and free form shapes. Usually, these correspond to high-decorated structural elements.

---

[2] Today no longer available.

Concerning the modelling strategies, two different approaches were tested: direct and parametric. Today, the most used modelling technique to create reality-based complex 3D objects is the direct approach. This working method is based on the extraction of features from surveyed data and on the extrusion of these profiles along tracks. The parametric approach is used to model similar object avoiding the time consuming work to model separately one by one blocks that are different to the extent but identical in shape. This approach can reduce the time requested for modelling because it allows to adapt a first parametric model to all similar objects, thus allowing the creation of an abacus of *ad hoc* parametric models that include elements belonging to a specific architectonical family.

2.3   The WebBIMDuomo

A dedicated system called WebBIMDuomo was developed in order to manage all the restoration activities of the yards through a BIM system.

WebBIMDuomo is an *ad hoc* system created for Cultural Heritage applications, as the BIM commercial software are not yet capable to handle completely the uniqueness and the complexity of the objects belonging to this field to be described by three-dimensional models. It promotes a shared knowledge of an architectural or artistic object among different participants. It allows to collect and share information and data useful for the study of the past and to design the interventions for the future.

The system is divided into three parts: the I/O plug-in inside Rhinoceros, the database and a web-based visualization system. The first part belongs to the realm of the technical officers, who have the possibility to load parts or the whole model, through specific queries, as well as to modify the 3D model itself, update or add information to the imported objects in any file formats. The second module is the database, which collects all the 3D models, all the information and files related to the objects, both in the NURBS original format and the JSON one, which is used for the web visualization. The database, remotely installed on the cloud, allows the users to share and to synchronize of all reviews in real time [30]. The web module has been developed for non-technical users and to be used during the works in the yard. In fact, through any mobile device endowed with an internet connection it is possible to add information, photos and notes taken during inspections directly on the model, to plan replacement of parts of the cathedral and to "create all type of maintenance operations". For each planned activity, the system is able to create the corresponding records in the database, to register the input data and share it in real time, allowing the updating of the virtual model in function of the real physical modification of the structure. Web-BIMDuomo was developed taking into account the specific needs expressed by the workers of VFD: the system was designed to be able to manage all the ordinary and extraordinary activities or interventions that daily occurs in the yards of the Cathedral [31]. Usually, the main interventions regard the substitution, in whole or in part, of the degraded marble blocks, anchorages and reinforcement structures.

When an intervention is created inside the system, automatically, a "father-son" relationship is established between original and modified object; in this way, it is possible to derive in real-time the history of modifications for each single element.

All the relations are included in the system: one-to-one, one-to-many, many-to-many, many to one. This feature allows to cover all possible interventions, from cleaning and tessellation to partial or entire substitutions. The BIM system automatically prepares all the necessary records in the DB to insert images and information about the maintenance operation and about the new objects (3D model, data and info) that will up uploaded in the system only. The changes are modelled by the technical office on the basis of the data and instructions stored in the system during the yard activity. The process ends when the new block is housed in its position in the yard and the 3D model is uploaded into the system with the related information. In this way, the visualized model is always up-do-date, as it also includes the latest modifications.

A precise color-coding was adopted in order to simplify the understanding of the blocks involved in the restoration activities and to have an immediate perception of the progress on a specific date: the opening procedure of an intervention is highlighted in blue, the survived part and the tessellation in red and green (Fig. 1).

Fig. 1. (a) Main Spire 4.825 blocks; (b) North Altar 3.358 blocks; (c) South Altar 2.883 blocks; (d) (e) Dome Cladding + Big Dome 4.194 blocks; (f) 18th Spire 379 blocks (Color figure online)

3 The VR System

As anticipated, the main aim of this branch of the research was to investigate the possibility to develop a specific VR application in order to use the BIM system in an immersive environment. Using this type of technology not only for general public dissemination but also for technical purposes would represent an important

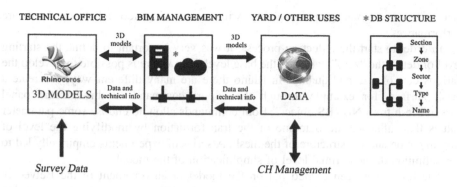

TECHNICAL OFFICE   BIM MANAGEMENT   YARD / OTHER USES   *DB STRUCTURE

Fig. 2. Synthetic scheme of WebBIMDuomo system performance

achievement. The most obvious and immediate application, in fact, is using the model for museum, virtual navigation, game, virtual reconstruction, documentation or teaching purposes. The following step, however, that is creating a VR immersive system for a professional use in the cultural heritage field still represents a significant challenge. The direct fruition of the virtual model through a fully immersive VR tour could open the path for an innovative development in the field of architectonic maintenance, improving our understanding of the spaces and allowing to immediately georeference the information.

The idea was to focus on the highest part of the Milan Cathedral because it has been closed since the beginning of XX century. It is also hardly accessible, the only access now being represented by yard elevators. For this reason, a system that would allow a virtual visit of this area could be attractive both for a general public and for technician that are not allowed to enter in the yard.

The chosen development tools are Unity 3D, well-known software designed for videogame development, and Oculus DK2, the Head Mounted Display (HMD), cheap and fast, and endowed with an open development kit.

The main idea was to use the data that already exist (3D model and info) and adapt them in order to build an immersive system. The main issue was the huge amount of data due to the high details of the 3D reality-based model. In order to solve this issue, it was necessary to implement a multi-step simplification process:

1. A fix mesh decimation that allows a fix carefully considered reduction of the number of polygons forming the initial NURBS model.
2. A logical segmentation of the model following the natural distribution of the structure of the cathedral and following the subdivision in Area-Zone–Sector-Type used in the technical BIM system.

3.1 The Mesh Simplification

The first process of simplification has been carried out directly inside Rhinoceros 3D. The expected result was a system of simplified objects topologically well connected that retained a good graphic quality without stressing too much on hardware performances.

In order to start the reduction process, it was very important to define the starting level of detail, the "zero", which is the base level from where is possible to develop the various cuts of size and quality. In Rhino there are many different ways to create a mesh surface, for example through the export command or through the panel "Mesh/Mesh from NURBS object". Both commands allow to choose some parameter values that influence the outcome of the transformation by modifying the level of simplification and the structure of the mesh. A series of experiments empirically led to the definition of the optimal level of simplification of the model.

The tests have been carried out on the model of an ornament of the Belvedere balcony. The aim was to evaluate the behaviour of the different parameters in connection with the typology of the object, taking care in particular of the degree of complexity (linear simple object or artistic freeform surface) and of the dimensions. The ornament is a good test object because shows both linear simple surfaces and complex free-form shapes. The two main objectives were: on the one hand, to decimate the mesh as much as possible without losing accuracy and detail, and in particular paying attention to preserve the continuity between all the parts that compose the models; on the other hand, to find common parameters for every type of object in order to simplify the two processes of automatization of the decimation, and exportation of the models.

The conducted tests suggest that not only the number of the polygons affects the handling of a model's heaviness, but that also the orderliness of the mesh is very important. In fact, a structured mesh is more manageable by the software compared to a disordered one, and ordering the structure is essential during the decimation process when the simplification algorithm is being applied to a large amount of data.

It became clear that some parameters had more influence in decimating the polygons than others. The "maximum angle parameter" sets the maximum allowable angle between the input surface normal and the neighbouring mesh vertices. It defines a substantial change in the computed mesh by establishing the curvature degree of simplification. Within the range between 0 and 90°, after checking which portion of the test sample is further simplified and which is not, the value 45° resulted optimal. The second relevant field is the "aspect ratio of the surface", which varies between 1 and 100. Smaller values result in slower meshing and a higher polygon count with more equilateral and nicely shaped polygons. This value directly influences the degree of regularity that the structure of the mesh will retain during the computation of the new simplified model. Since it affects the proportions of the polygons, it is important that this number remains close to 1 as much as possible: this means that the mesh triangles approach the shape of an equilateral triangle after decimation process. The parameter was set to 5, the best compromise between quality, regularity of mesh structure.

Directly tied to the aspect ratio there are the maximum and minimum edge lengths that directly control the dimensions of the polygons forming the surface. The choice was to keep the same values for the two parameters, so that the resulting polygon would remain as regular as possible. The selection of the best value for these fields was carried out by taking into account the scale of representation of the processed model; however, the optimal theoretical value (0,008–0,01 m) resulted in a mesh surface still difficult to navigate. The chosen minimum appreciable distance was reduced drastically at 0.08 m, resulting in a lower definition of the initial surface (in particular for decorated objects) but that nevertheless preserved enough quality and resolution for more simple and linear objects. The test comparisons on this elaborated 3D model with the original detailed model demonstrate that this value guarantees a representation scale of about 1:50 typical of large-scale architecture. To keep the reduction of details within an acceptable interval, the "minimum initial grid quad" was set on value 10. This parameter represents the initial resolution of mesh grid that is a quad mesh that Rhino creates on each NURBS surface in the first stage of meshing. In practice, Rhino will use at least this number of polygons to describe each surface. This parameter controls the minimum number of polygons of a surface and consequently its final definition.

In order to conduct the simplification tests, a zero level mesh was used. This was the mesh automatically created by Rhino using default parameters. It is a not regular mesh and present 110949 polygons. The surface, after the application of the simplification algorithm resulted as composed of 34741 polygons. The reduction has been substantial (66 %) and the processed mesh surface keeps the desired acceptable level of detail.

On the ornament of the Belvedere section the algorithm for simplification proved to be quite successful so the work proceeded by testing its effectiveness on a larger part of the 3D model, precisely on the central cylindrical staircase section of the Main Spire.

3.2   Other Simplification Methods

Other simplification methods were tested starting from how videogames techniques manage environments and objects: that is, their Level of Approach to Details (LOD) and their logical sequential segmentation of the scene. These two methods have been applied to the Milan Cathedral as a case study (Fig. 3).

Fig. 3. Central cylindrical staircase decimated using first experiment parameters (on the left) and the same parts using new parameters (on the right)

LOD Levels. The LOD approach, applied to the VR tour development, simulates the effect of human vision for which the eye catches more details on near objects than on distant ones. For this reason, objects can be loaded in the scene with a different level of detail: farther objects are shown at a lower definition while near objects are formed by more dense and accurate surfaces. The different quality between near and far objects goes unnoticed, because of the effect of distance and the fact that the scene moves fast. Unity can simulate automatically the effect thanks to the "LOD Group" component.

It must be properly tuned depending on the scale of the different pieces that form the model. A different number of meshes with different levels of details can be assigned. This depends on the desired range of zoom in which they become active, that is a percentage corresponding to the ratio between bounding box and screen heights.

In our case, to produce a substantial improvement in performance, the component needs at least three versions of the same mesh. The first (high definition - LOD 0) is the decimated mesh automatically exported from Rhinoceros following the previously described consideration. The second and the third retain a lower amount of detail (LOD 1 and LOD2) that reciprocally correspond to a reduction of 70 %. The result was two very light meshes with a great amount of defects and deformations due to their strong simplification. They have been taken into account only for objects really far from the observer where only the silhouette and approximate shape of the block are important.

A LOD approach works very well in this kind of situation due to the outdoor environment, the dimensions and the high degree of verticality of these structures. The application of human sight rules surely further lightened the impact of the model on the system, but the complexity of the Main Spire proved still too heavy to be computed as a whole. This approach needed to build an *ad hoc* scene subdivision and to design a correct setup.

Scene Set Up. The logical solution was to subdivide the environment into levels as for videogames, so that only the blocks related to a specific section would be loaded at the same time at higher definitions.

The whole complex of Milan Cathedral can be seen as formed by different constituting areas, and the same concept can apply to the Main Spire. The Spire has been divided into its four constituting areas as in the technical BIM environment. Each one corresponds to a specific scene: upper cladding of the dome, first balcony, central cylindrical staircase and Belvedere. Each has been assigned to a specific scene inside Unity creating four virtual container for objects and each scene is initially separated and independent from the others. There are many advantages in choosing this segmentation. First, in each section there are few pieces with a lot of details, significantly reducing the time computation and generally making the system faster; secondly in this way it is possible to load just the interesting area allows for easier and faster consultation.

To create the whole version of the tour, all the scenes have to be connected so that the user can automatically tour through the whole Main Spire. "Triggers" handle the connection between different areas. The position of the triggers follows the sequential order of the areas of the main spire. From the upper cladding of the dome the user passes to the first balcony, than to the central cylindrical staircase and only after going through all the sections reaches the Belvedere and vice versa from the top of the Spire, it is possible to descend until the cladding level (Fig. 4).

Layer Structure. Since the application is thought also for the facility management and the restoration works of the Milan Cathedral by the Veneranda Fabbrica, it is important to maintain the name and the layer structure of the blocks coming from the NURBS model inside Rhinoceros and used for the technical application of the BIM system [30]. It is required to connect the application to the central database, that is the core of the BIM system where are stored data, info, photos and the original high-resolution models of the marble blocks. Maintaining the correct naming of the blocks is important for yet

Fig. 4. Background seen from the upper cladding of the dome

another reason: in the original model, the marble blocks are named according to the elapsed intervention works. There are three different name types, an integer number (i.e. 1), a number followed by an underscore (i.e. 1_1) and the letter "n" followed by a three digits number (i.e. n532); changes in this convention would result in the wrong identification of the marble blocks and of the corresponding maintenance activity. Keeping this information during the export operation is not an automatic and easy task, due to different behaviour of Unity and Rhino in managing objects and their names. The problem lies in the fact that whereas Rhinoceros automatically accepts objects with the same name but on different layers, Unity 3d does not. Therefore exporting the model (from Rhino to Unity) using a spatial "area based" query, as logically, resulted in an automatic random variation of the names assigned to the blocks. The solution to avoid this unacceptable situation was found by taking advantage of the LEGO structure of the model and by importing the pieces from the subclass "typology". In this way the software does not meet blocks with the same name inside the same asset and keeps the correct structure of the blocks. This implies that the export has to be done piece by piece and in the future needs to be automated in order to easier and faster export a huge number of 3D blocks.

Collisions. A general common task in this type of applications is the definition of the "physics rules" inside the virtual environment. The tour, to be effective, must be realistic, which means that the interactions between objects must follow real world physics rules. The main scope is to create useful interactions between the user and the model in order to (i) navigate the complex space of the spire, (ii) display information about the marble blocks, statues and decorations. Inside the software, the correct use of "Colliders" represents the basis for both interactions. Different types of colliders (static and convex) are available. The choice obviously fell on the static type of collider. This is a key point because on this assumption the Unity engine regulates the physics of the object and makes useful optimizations. It is possible to assign automatically a single static collider to each object, so that they are selectable in order to get the specific data related to the marble piece and its conservation process. For static object that sometimes need to be moved or scaled inside the application it is possible to add to the desired block a "RigidBody" component with the "IsKinematic" property set to active, this would be necessary for example for the implementation of interaction through a "Leap Motion" device (Fig. 5).

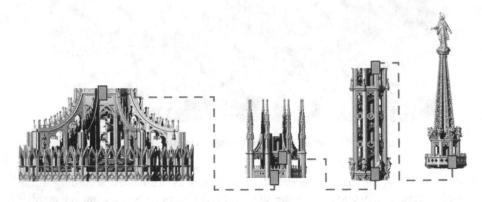

Fig. 5. Trigger sequence

Model User Interactions. Interactions between the user and the model are thought for the facility management of the cathedral. Before the models are displayed through the Oculus device, a special function takes care of colouring objects involved in maintenance activities: green blocks are the remaining parts of large blocks that survived the interventions, while red ones are the new additions, following the same encoding used in the BIM system (Fig. 6).

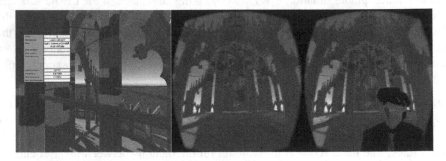

Fig. 6. Result of the process and general view through Oculus device (on screen display) (Color figure online)

The user interaction with the model is very simple: it is enough to look at the desired object and click on it for its selection. To retrieve the right object, it is necessary to shot the RayCast directly from an object inside the model space, starting from the crosshair cursor. The crosshair cursor is a custom version adapted to be used inside the stereoscopic rendering used by the oculus device, managing the problems of double vision, offset from the centre of the screen, facing the camera changing its position and orientation in space according to head movements.

When an object is selected, the marble block is highlighted in yellow. It is necessary to take into account of all multipart meshes as well as different models of the same block imported for LOD level purposes, changing the colour for all of them.

After the selection, the system displays the connected BIM data on screen. Tabs have been designed *ad hoc*, covering all corresponding fields of the WebBIMDuomo. Some tabs are also designed to display the image gallery: one for the images of the object, one dedicated to the performed restoration works and one for the post-intervention, in the same way as is the WebBIMDuomo technical release.

All information is gathered in real time from the database of WebBIMDuomo, through an internet or local connection to the database. The connection to the database was not always smooth because Unity is still locked to a very old version of Mono 2.0 and it has an incomplete support of system.data.dll. This leads to the inability to use the .NET ODBC class, which is not fully implemented, thus preventing the connection to the PostgreSQL database, used for WebBIMDuomo. To solve this problem, it was necessary to use an old version of Npgsql, compiled for the old .NET corresponding to Mono 2.0, and to mix the Npgsql class with system.data general class. Npgsql must be used only to the connection, while for the commands and readers it is required to use IDbCommand and IDataReader. Otherwise, the queries are executed, but the connection closes unexpectedly when the system tries to access the data. At first, the object is identified using its layer structure and its name; then a set of queries are executed onto the database and all data table are filled with the results.

4   Conclusion

The research presented here aimed at applying new VR immersive techniques to the field of architecture and facility management. The main goal was to evaluate how VR could be used in the sector of Cultural Heritage as a support for conservation and maintenance activities. The work represented the follow-up of the previous research activities of survey and modelling of the Main Spire of the Milan Cathedral. The research work led to the creation of a complete high-resolution 3D model, currently used as a support of the maintenance activities of the Milan Cathedral. Furthermore, in order to promote a wider use of the 3D virtual model to a larger group of users also including non-experts of 3D, an *ad hoc* BIM system has been developed. This system is able to connect the modelling software with an external navigation system that encourages a simple and shared use of the 3D model by different stakeholders of the conservation process. It works like a catalyst that collects and connects data and information. The presented work succeeded in adding a further step in terms of virtualization by creating a VR immersive system that not only allows the classical virtual visit of the object, but also provides the technical information stored in the BIM system.

The research was split into different steps ranging from the optimization and simplification of the original real-based models for VR environment, to the creation of the VR system inside Unity software, and finally to the connection of the VR application to the technical BIM database. The mix of high accuracy 3D survey, reality-based modelling, information system and virtual navigation allows a multidisciplinary professional use of the final virtual model. Differently from the industrial realm, the immersive virtualization of a BIM system in the Cultural Heritage field is nowadays not as widespread as the current technology could, in theory, allow. As of today, for the Milan's Cathedral it is perhaps still a futuristic vision. The research demonstrated how high resolution models with a given maximal representation scale, that have been created for technical purposes, can nevertheless be easily adapted to the use in virtual environments without an excessive loss of detail; it also shows how the connection with external BIM data can create an augmented system inside a virtual environment. Moreover, this type of systems is surely optimal to better understand the geometry of a very complex and extensive architecture, and to immediately georeference the information. In perspective, the tested system may represent a fundamental tool to address the main difficulties faced by the VFD: the enormous dimension of the cathedral, and the consequent huge amount of "objects" and information that must be managed during the endless works of maintenance.

The next phase of this line of investigation will have to focus on improving the graphic quality and performances, and to add more interactive functions. The future developments of our work will head in the following directions: (i) the development of the automatic exporting of the optimized model and its LOD levels for VR visualization, (ii) the possibility, as in the BIM system, to dynamically load the object from the cloud without restrictions or pre-constituted sub-divisions, and give the possibility to the user to choose from time to time what to display, (iii) the integration of external devices as "Leap motion" to improve the immersive experience and interaction with the model, (iv) the possibility to actively interact with the VR BIM system not only in reading- but also in writing-mode.

References

1. Encyclopaedia Treccani. http://www.treccani.it
2. Veneranda Fabbrica del Duomo di Milano. http://www.duomomilano.it/en/
3. Zara, J.: Virtual reality and cultural heritage on the web. In: 7th International Conference on Computer Graphics and Artificial Intelligence, pp. 101–112 (2004)
4. Virtual Heart of Central Europe project site. http://www.sccg.sk/~projects/virtual-heart
5. Virtual Old Prague project site. http://www.cgg.cvut.cz/vsp
6. Fassi, F., Colizzi, L., De Pascalis, F.: 3D visualization and virtual reality for cultural heritage diagnostic. Conserv. Sci. Cult. Herit. **7**, 31–42 (2007)
7. Calori, L., Camporesi, C., Pescarin, S., Guidazzoli, A.: Open heritage: an integrated approach to web 3D publication of virtual landscapes. 3D-ARCH 2005: Virtual Reconstruction and Visualization of Complex Architectures, pp. 1–5 (2005)
8. Forte, M., Pescarin, S., Pujol Tost, L.: VR applications, new devices and museums: visitor's feedback and learning: a preliminary report. In: 7th International Symposium on Virtual Reality, Archaeology and Cultural Heritage VAST (2006)
9. Forte, M., Danelon, N.: Regium@Lepidi 2200 Project. Archeomatica **6**(1), 42–48 (2015)
10. Navvab, M., Bisegna, F., Gugliermetti, F.: Experiencing the tangible past through virtual reconstruction: cultural heritage of buildings and their environmental boundaries. Archeomatica **4**(3), 36–41 (2013)

11. Pescarin, S., Pagano, A., Wallergard, M., Hupperetz, W., Ray, C.: Evaluating virtual museums: archeovirtual case study. In: 40th Conference on Computer Applications and Quantitative Methods in Archaeology (2012)
12. Smithsonia X3D. http://3d.si.edu/
13. The virtual museum of Iraq. http://www.virtualmuseumiraq.cnr.it/prehome.htm
14. Europeana. http://blog.europeana.eu/2013/12/virtual-reality-and-the-museum-of-the-future
15. DICONS home page. http://3dicons-project.eu/
16. Virtual Museum Transnational Network. http://www.v-must.net/
17. Apa Game. https://hpc-forge.cineca.it/files/visit_Dissemination/public/ApaGame/ApaGame 2013/
18. Guidazzoli, A., Baglivo, A., De Luca, D., Imboden, S., Liguori, M.C., Rivalta, A.: Crossmedia integration of 3D contents for cultural communication. In: 3DTV-Conference: The True Vision - Capture, Transmission and Display of 3D Video (2014)
19. ATI alla scoperta di Veio. http://www.glietruschielaldila.it/ati-alla-scoperta-di-veio
20. Russo, A., De Lucia, M.A., Cosentino, R., Guidazzoli, A., Imboden, S., De Luca, D., Liguori, M.C., Verri, L., Bellavia, G.: Apa l'Etrusco sbarca a Roma e passa il testimone ad Ati. Un cortometraggio tridimensionale per raccontare il santuario di Portonaccio a Veio. Archeomatica 6(2), 42–47 (2015)
21. CINECA. http://www.cineca.it/it/comunicatistampa/apa-letrusco-sbarca-roma
22. Mostra. http://www.glietruschielaldila.it/la-mostra
23. La situla della certosa. http://www.glietruschielaldila.it/la-situla-della-certosa
24. Il sarcofago degli sposi. http://www.glietruschielaldila.it/il-sarcofago-degli-sposi
25. FBK news. http://www.fbk.eu/news/sarcophagus-spouses-reconstructed-3d-fbk-researchers
26. Fassi, F., Achille, C., Fregonese, L., Monti, C.: Multiple data source for survey and modelling of very complex architecture. In: The International Archives of the Photogrammetry, Remote Sensing and Spatial Information Sciences, vol. XXXVIII, Part 5, pp. 234–239 (2010)
27. Fassi, F., Achille, C., Fregonese, L.: Surveying and modelling the main spire of milan cathedral using multiple data sources. Photogram. Rec. 26, 462–487 (2011)
28. Achille, C., Fassi, F., Fregonese, L.: 4 year history: from 2D to BIM for CH. In: 18th International Conference on Virtual Systems and Multimedia, pp. 377–382 (2012)
29. Mandelli, A.: Surveying, modelling and management of cultural heritage. Definition of good practices through applications on monuments and artworks. Ph.D. thesis (2016)
30. Fassi, F., Achille, C., Mandelli, A., Rechichi, F., Parri, S.: A new idea of BIM system for visualization, web sharing and using huge complex 3D models for facility management. In: The International Archives of the Photogrammetry, Remote Sensing and Spatial Information Sciences, vol. XL-5/W4, pp. 359–366 (2015)
31. Fassi, F., Parri, S.: Complex architectures in 3D: from survey to web. Int. J. Herit. Digit. Era 1(3), 379–398 (2012)

A Virtual Experience Across the Buried History

Antonina Canzoneri[1], Gaia Pavoni[1], Marco Callieri[1(✉)],
Matteo Dellepiane[1(✉)], Paolo Pingi[1], Manuela De Giorgi[2],
and Roberto Scopigno[1]

[1] Visual Computing Laboratory, ISTI-CNR, Pisa, Italy
{marco.callieri,matteo.dellepiane}@isti.cnr.it
[2] Universitá del Salento, Lecce, Italy
http://vcg.isti.cnr.it

Abstract. The Sant'Angelo cave church is an underground medieval Benedictine complex in the south of Italy, affected by serious structural and chemical degradation. In the context of a documentation campaign promoted by the local Superintendence and supported by the IPERI-ONCH.it project, we carried out an accurate 3D and photographic survey, and reconstructed a detailed 3D model of the site (encoding shape and colour). While the primary purpose of this large amount of collected data was to provide a metric documentation of the site, the completeness and the high detail of the survey suggested also a possible use for dissemination and virtual presentation. Thus, we exploited the 3D digital models to design and build a virtual visit of the church, oriented to scholars, museums and tourists. This paper describes the design and implementation of this educational experience, closely related to the bibliographic sources of the artistic heritage, fully enriched with hyper-textual information, intuitive and easy to use for all users regardless of their level of familiarity with the 3D medium.

Keywords: Virtual tour · 3D reconstruction · Interactive experience · 3D web

1 Introduction

Located in Casalrotto, Taranto (IT), the Sant'Angelo cave church is a peculiar structure, since it is a completely hypogean complex. The Benedictine church has been carved in the tuffaceous rock between the IX and XV century a.C.; its structure and decoration constitute an exceptional evidence of the Greek and Byzantine influences in the art of southern Italy [5, 7].

The complex is composed by two underground floors, divided by pillars into three absidate naves, following the traditional structure of the Cappadocian, Caucasian and Byzantinium funerary crypts. Some of these naves have Greek altars, others are decorated by various frescoes with multiple style contaminations. The upper floor was mainly intended to liturgical private functions, the lower (accessible by a flight of stairs from the back of the right nave at the first

© Springer International Publishing Switzerland 2016
L.T. De Paolis and A. Mongelli (Eds.): AVR 2016, Part II, LNCS 9769, pp. 158–171, 2016.
DOI: 10.1007/978-3-319-40651-0_13

Fig. 1. Sant'Angelo church. Top row: entrance and upper floor. Bottom row: details of the structure.

floor), slightly smaller, served for funeral rites, as shown by the presence of seven tombs carved into the floor. Over the centuries the architectural structure suffered several changes: most probably, it was initially composed by one floor of two aisles and the third one was excavated later; the lower level was a later addition as well. The detachments of some painted portions from the walls revealed chronological stratification of paints.

Cave churches are an amazingly interesting heritage: the arrangement of spaces and the decorations were related to very strong symbolic meanings, and they can tell a lot about the local culture and the influences from the Greek and Byzantine worlds. Unfortunately, they are only partially known by the wide public. One of the reasons for this is that most of the churches are difficult to reach (see Fig. 1), and due to their structure, they often lack the proper safety requirements to allow visitors. Additionally, a massive amount of tourists may impact on the already critical humidity and stability conditions.

The Sant'Angelo church is affected by serious physical and chemical degradation phenomena mainly due to the high level of humidity of the underground that permeates the friable rock of water. In recent years, a number of targeted restoration actions and physical-chemical surveys have been carried out aiming at preserving both the paintings and the rock structure. The latest of these surveys was supported by the IPERIONCh project.

In this framework, the Visual Computing Lab of ISTI-CNR performed a 3D laser scanning campaign of the Sant'Angelo cave church, coupled with a photographic survey. Then, since the frescoes are the most affected by the degrading effects of moisture, a detailed photographic survey covered a set of six frescoes, among the most historically and artistically relevant. This detailed coverage has been used to generate 3D-from-photos model, then integrated with the laser scanner data to produce models with higher detail.

The main purpose of this survey was the creation of technical metric documentation of the current state of the church structure as a whole, but also of the frescoes. The aim was the mapping on the 3D digital models of the different analysis and observation done by the restorers and curators. The 3D models will then be used as a support for the planning and the mapping of future analysis and restoration actions.

After fulfilling this primary goal, the availability of the 3D digital models suggested a different work direction. Given their completeness and level of detail, it seemed natural to exploit them as a way to create a virtual visit of the church.

2   3D Data Acquisition and Processing

The upper floor of the church covers approximately 14 m by 12 m, while the lower 10 m by 10 m, the height of walls is approximately 2.3 m on average. In addition to the two main areas, the architectural complex includes a sloped depression at the ground level, leading to the entrance, and another small external room. Given this considerable size, the device used to acquire its global shape was the phase-shift laser scanner Faro Photon 120, that is a device used for architectural end engineering survey.

To overcome self occlusion problems related to the presence of pillars, niches, altars and loose materials, 29 scan positions have been used. In order to obtain a sufficiently detailed coverage of the church without having an excessively large amount of data, the resolution of the range scans was set to 1–2 cm. The resulting pointcloud, after cleaning and alignment, had around 175 million points with a global resolution of less then 1 cm (due to the overlapping among scans). A triangulated surface 3D model of the entire church was obtained using Poisson reconstruction [8]. The final 3D model id made of 56 million triangles (see Fig. 2). All the processing stages were performed using the open source tool MeshLab [4].

As previously mentioned, Sant'Angelo church walls are adorned by frescoes, full of symbolic meanings. The precise color reconstruction is not an aesthetic need, but it helps the historical interpretation. Two sets of images were captured using a Nikon5200 using external diffusive flash or spotlights: 152 pictures for the global coverage and 221 for an higher resolution color mapping for the six most significant frescoes. After the pre-processing stages, the pictures for the global covering were registered and projected onto the 3D geometry using MeshLab (see results in Fig. 4). The other set was processed using Photoscan [1]: the image-based reconstruction was used to achieve an higher color resolution (see Fig. 3) in the painted regions, and an easier alignment and color mapping on the 3D scanned geometry.

Fig. 2. The processed 3D data, after scans alignment and 3D reconstruction

Fig. 3. First nave's Deésis and San Pietro fresco: 3D models renderings

3   Designing an Interactive Education Experience

The increased availability of high quality 3D models is a major breakthrough also for Cultural Heritage, both for the technical use and the dissemination. While their use as a technical tool is slowly becoming a consolidated workflow, the way the 3D model are used when presented to the public still needs specific care, because non-technical users are involved. It is always necessary to explicitly design the interactive experience, the type of information that has to be conveyed, the target audience, the interaction modality.

Before choosing how to display the collected data, we had to better understand which were the storytelling needs related to this particular subject, exploring the bibliographic material, and what type of visualization fit better to its

Fig. 4. A rendering of the 3D model of Sant'Angelo's cave church.

shape. Historical and cultural overview derived from literature sources provided explanations about the church architecture and the meaning of the internal placement of the artworks. These historical interpretation had to be contextualized within the model.

3.1 How the Visualization of the 3D Metric Data Might Influence Perception

When working with an object, may it be a vase or a statue, simply displaying it on the screen, and letting the user spin it around may be enough to effectively convey its shape in a way that mimics the real viewing experience. Buildings, and especially complex decorated environments, are not so simple to manage. Ideally, in those cases, one would like to show both the building as a whole *and* its detail in a more focused way. This is not an easy task, as each level of navigation would require a different interaction paradigm. At the same time, there is the problem of accessibility: an interface that offers a completely free navigation makes possible a complete exploration of the artwork, but may prove to be too complex to use for the generic user; conversely, a constrained navigation is easier to use, but may be too limited and boring. Leveraging all these aspects (generality versus specificity, freedom versus guidance) in a single navigation scheme is difficult.

Instead of trying to create a multi-purpose visualization with a complex interface that tries to show all the available data (an approach that, in our experience, is never really working), we decided to implement different viewers, each one tailored to a specific aspect of the church that we wanted to convey. In this way, it was possible to choose, for each kind of data, the best possible interface.

Offering multiple way to explore the environment also makes the experience more approachable for the user, that may choose its own path to explore the church.

We then applied the Hypertext principle, interconnecting the different visualizations, letting the user go jump between the different layer of information and presentation paradigms. In this way, the user can experience each facet of the building using the most suitable interaction method, but at the same time he is able to create its own exploration path across the data.

3.2 From Global to Details

The Sant'Angelo church has interesting aspects at several "levels": from the global structure to the single painted surfaces. For this reason, the interactive experience was structured to covey these multiple perspectives of the church, by using a *multiscale* integrated presentation.

This idea was developed in the context of a website, where interactive three-dimensional components were obtained using *3D Heritage Online Presenter* (3DHop [11]), an open-source software package for the creation of interactive Web content, oriented to the Cultural Heritage field. 3DHOP is fully customizable, and is basically a toolkit to create interactive 3D presentation; this feature was really important, as we wanted each visualization to use a specific interface and interaction. Another important feature of 3DHop is the use of multi-resolution algorithms [10], that makes possible the visualization of very high resolution 3D models on the web, by streaming the model during the navigation, adapting the experience to the device and available band.

The general structure, visible also in the main page of the website, is shown in Fig. 7. The *global* navigation layer provides two modalities: one to visualize the structure "from the outside", and one to navigate the interior of the church. The *relationship* layer, where analogous portions of the church can be compared, and the *detail* layer, where each one of the frescoes may be examined individually.

A Global Perspective. In the global perspective, the overall structure is displayable both from the outside and from the inside. Again, trying to show the environment from these two perspectives using a single interface would result in a limited experience not able to effectively convey the idea of a "walkable" space, nor the idea of a complex building structure. Thus, we designed two visualization pages, following two different paradigms, each tailored to the specific perspective (inner space/outer space).

A Navigation Designed for the Audience. Sant'Angelo church is normally closed to the public for safety and conservation reasons; only a limited number of visitors is allowed in the church, and only by appointment. For this reason, we decided to create, as our first exploration method, a virtual visit that mimics the way the church is explored by foot. At the same time, we exploited the possibilities of the interactive media: linkong the 3D geometry to the church's artistic contents, and fully enriching it using hypertextual information. This feature uses the 3DHOP hotspots: Fig. 9(a) shows red areas indicated on the 3D model; by clicking on the red area, the user can obtain additional information about the details in the church. Other hotspots are used to connect this visualization to each separate frescoes (see Sect. 3.4).

The cave is pervaded by an intimate and liturgical atmosphere, concordant with the functions of gathering the believers and taking care of the deads. This feeling could be well experienced much more easily by a virtual environment visit than the by mere two-dimensional image observations. A number of recesses and the entire lower floor are almost totally immersed in darkness, so that the real physical experience is limited by the poor visibility (and frescoes are hardly discernible). Virtual visitors have the possibility to adjust the light direction both to have a better visibility and to obtain a suffused lighting.

One issue was related to the navigation of the three-dimensional space. Given the wide range of potential users, the exploration should have been intuitive and easy to use for all, regardless of the level of familiarity with the 3D medium. When dealing with complex architectural environment, free navigation in a videogame-like style can be devised, but this usually needs a massive amount of work to prepare the model, possibly leading to lower geometric detail. Alternative solutions [2] try to provide free navigation where the user can easily control movements. A different strand of research removes the plain 3D rendering, using alternative solution like panoramas [6].

In this case, we opted for a constrained path navigation, where the user can move inside the environment following an invisible pre-defined track. As in a guided tour, starting from the outside square the user enters through the gate to the left along the first nave, comes in front of three apses to get down to the subterranean burial and finally return to the starting point. The user may move along the path on its own, using the mouse wheel, or follow it with an "autopilot". At any time, (both in manual or automatic mode) the user may change the facing direction, to look around. In the automatic mode, when the user reaches an interesting point (marked by a hotspot), the path stops, and the view direction is rotated automatically to face the point of interest.

Methods for automatic determination or improvement of constrained navigation have been investigated [3,9]. In this case, we decided to set the track in a manual way, given the type of information we wanted to convey, and the structure of the church (see next sections).

Advantages of a Three Dimensional Representation. The virtual visit outlined in the previous section mimics something that can be done in reality; however, 3D models may be used to show aspects that cannot be fully appreciated on-site. In this case, something related to the underground nature of the site. The overall structure, hidden underground, is hardly intelligible from standing on the ground level, but also from the inside in a simple visit; conversely, by looking at the 3D model from the "outside", we perceive much more better the spaces and the relationships between them. We can for example notice that the two levels (Fig. 6) are slightly misaligned, and have an idea of the thickness of

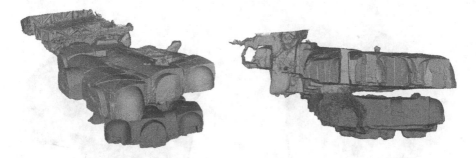

Fig. 5. Left: the misalignment between the two floors. Right: an image showing the floor thickness

the floor (see Fig. 5). So, we decided to create a viewer using the digital model of the church as a "maquette", with the 3D geometry viewed from the outside.

However, looking a the 3D model in this way is not enough to convey the relationship between its structure and the inside space: for this reason, still following the "maquette" paradigm, we subdivided the church in slices, and the **external navigation** (Fig. 8) allows to "switch on and off" the visualization of each slice of the church (using the interface on the right side). Clicking on a layer makes that slice transparent, while all the ones above it are made invisible, and all the ones below it are made visible and solid. In this way, the user may *peel away* the structure slice by slice, exploring it from top to bottom. Several important aspects of the church can be seen with this visualization: among them, the carving of the higher ceiling the first floor plant, the mutual positioning of the columns, the arched entrances, the altars and the opening to the floor below.

This solution represents an added value compared to the direct experience or to other forms of documentation. It allows the user to overcome the problem of non-visible offering in the same time the perception of the shapes and occupied spaces, difficult to reach by a simple site visit.

3.3   A Comparative Perspective

A different level of exploration of the church is focused towards the comparison of recurring elements of the church. The underground environment is full of recurring elements: altars, frescoes, apses. In many cases, there are several variations of the same elements, and exploring them side-by side could help understanding the analogies and the differences between them.

Among the different recurring elements in the church, we chose to work on the two Deésis frescoes on the upper floor. A third one, on the lower floor, is severely damaged. The Deésis (from the greek δέησις, "supplication") is an iconographic Byzantine theme, closely linked to the funerary functions, representing the intercession of the Virgin and the Baptist, in the presence of Christ, for the humankind during the Final Judgment. The two reviewed Deésis (one located in the right apse and the other in the central one) show a number of

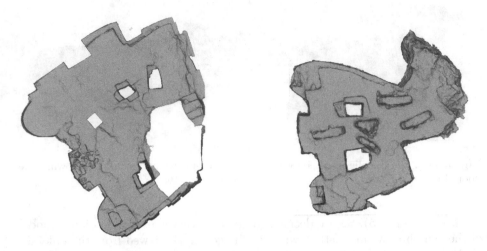

Fig. 6. Plants of the first and the second floor, extracted from the 3D model.

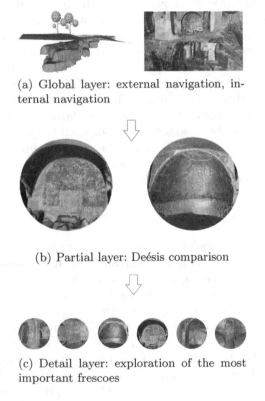

(a) Global layer: external navigation, internal navigation

(b) Partial layer: Deésis comparison

(c) Detail layer: exploration of the most important frescoes

Fig. 7. The *three perspectives* visualization criterion: from the global to the detail.

Fig. 8. The external navigation. Top: the whole 3D model. Bottom: the ceiling of the first floor is made transparent to show the structure of the church.

differences and similarities, that are source of debate for the scholars. For example in the right aisle the figure of St. John the Baptist was replaced by St. James probably for the devotion of the client to the saint and the benedictory Christ, central in both cases, assumes a whole different attitude. Colours for themselves are drastically different.

The *partial* layer gives the possibility to visualize them at the same time (Fig. 10), from corresponding viewpoints. Each difference and similarity is highlighted and discussed in the partial display mode through a simultaneous comparison on two juxtaposed panels.

This visualization is peculiar because it gives the possibility to compare two portions that cannot be seen at the same time in the church. Again, the 3D model offers a visualization that overcomes the limits of the physical space.

At the moment, this type of comparison only involves two of the Deésis, but ideally should also be extended to some other architectural and decorative elements that are present in multiple variants in the church. For example, it would be useful to create a similar side-by-side comparison for the different altars (which are of two types: Greek and Latin), but also for the different kind of ceilings geometries.

(a) Visible hotspots

(b) Clicked hotspot

Fig. 9. The internal navigation (Color figure online)

Fig. 10. Deésis comparison: the analysis of the same portion of the two Deésis to show similarities and differences.

3.4 A Particular Perspective

Finally, it is possible to use the 3D models of the single frescoes to explore the church following its details. In this last navigation mode, it is possible to separately examine the multi-resolution models of the most important frescoes. As they are not just flat images, we used the detail 3D model to also show the relationship between the icon and the shape of the wall. Each of the artworks is presented on its own, in a simple visualization page, that enables the user to pan across the 3D, change light direction, look at the surface from any angle, get close to the picture. The view panel is accompanied by a general description and a number of hotspots with additional information.

Figure 11 shows the visualization of the Pope Silvester fresco. In this case, the navigation mimics the on-site experience (moving in front of the fresco, looking at the wall from different directions, getting close to the surface), with the additional possibilities to visualize the smallest details and to be guided by the hotspots.

Fig. 11. Visualization Pope Silvester's fresco, with two hotspots.

3.5   A *Spatial* Navigation Through Visualizations

One of the interesting mechanisms implemented in the viewers is the interconnection of the various visualizations using a "spatial" navigation. Since all the layers are referenced to a common three-dimensional space (the church), the user can pass from one layer to the other following different paths.

For example, the user can select the visualization of a detail, and from the detail 3D fresco page there's the possibility to switch back to the website structure, as one would expect, but also to jump in the global internal navigation, in the place where the detail is located, just in front of the fresco. The user can move inside the 3D model, find another detail, and jump to the dedicated detail page. The global external viewer is similarly connected to the details, and the details of the Deésis are connected to the comparison visualization.

In this way, the analysis of the information can follow different paths, and the website and the 3d space are perfectly integrated. We believe that this has a big potential as a way to really integrate three-dimensional data in the context of websites, museum kiosks, mobile applications.

4   Conclusions and Future Perspectives

This paper presented the results of the uses of 3D data acquired in the context of a 3D scanning campaign for the monitoring and preservation of an ancient cave church. The main effort was focused on the discussion about a possible reuse of the data, in order to construct a virtual experience through an ancient and buried world only conceived for didactic purposes.

The available metric data collected by Visual Computing Lab were easily integrated with other types of data from all the investigations conducted on the site. The navigation of the site was structured in a multi-level fashion, trying to provide information at different *granularity* (a global, comparative and detail layer). While the application was mainly intended for the wide public, it might be interesting to combine this application with one addressed to an audience of researchers and restorers, useful for the purpose of monitoring the church and to constitute a comprehensive documentation of all the previous surveys.

The website (http://vcg.isti.cnr.it/activities/mottola) could be a very good starting point for further integration of other types of information: for example, the evolution of the structure of the church, or the separation of the different layers on the frescoes. In order to obtain this additional information, further study of the historical data, and processing of data would be needed.

Acknowledgements. The research leading to these results has received funding from Iperion CH-It Italian initiative. The authors would like to thank Marco Potenziani for the collaboration in data acquisition.

References

1. Agisoft. Photoscan (2009). http://www.agisoft.com
2. Callieri, M., Dellepiane, M., Scopigno, R.: Remote visualization and navigation of 3d models of archeological sites. In: ISPRS Archives, Proceedings of 3D-ARCH Conference, vol. XL-5/W4, pp. 147–154, March 2015
3. Eisemann, E., Thormählen, T., Seidel, H.-P., Kurz, C., Ritschel, T.: Camera motion style transfer. In: 7th European Conference on Visual Media Production (CVMP), London, UK, 17–18 November 2010 (2010)
4. Cignoni, P., Callieri, M., Corsini, M., Dellepiane, M., Ganovelli, F., Ranzuglia, G.: Meshlab: an open-source mesh processing tool. In: Sixth Eurographics Italian Chapter Conference, pp. 129–136 (2008)
5. Dell'Aquila, F., Messina, A.: Le chiese rupestri di Puglia e Basilicata. Mario Adda (1998)
6. Di Benedetto, M., Ganovelli, F., Rodriguez, M.B., Villanueva, A.J., Gobbetti, E.: Scopigno. R.: Exploremaps: efficient construction and ubiquitous exploration of panoramic view graphcs of complex 3d environments. Comput. Graph. Forum **33**(2), 459–468 (2014)
7. Fonseca. C.D.: Civiltà rupestre in terra Ionica. Milano-Roma (1970)
8. Kazhdan, M., Hoppe, H.: Screened poisson surface reconstruction. ACM Trans. Graph. **32**(3), 29:1–29:13 (2013)

9. Nieuwenhuisen, D., Overmars, M.H.: Motion planning for camera movements. In: Proceedings of the International Conference on Robotics and Automation (ICRA), vol. 4, pp. 3870–3876, July 2004

10. Ponchio, F., Dellepiane, M.: Fast decompression for web-based view-dependent 3d rendering. In: Proceedings of the 20th International Conference on 3D Web Technology, Web3D 2015, pp. 199–207. ACM (2015)

11. Potenziani, M., Callieri, M., Dellepiane, M., Corsini, M., Ponchio, F., Scopigno, R.: 3dhop: 3d heritage online presenter. Comput. Graph. **52**, 129–141 (2015)

Cyberarchaeology: Improved Way Findings for Archaeological Parks Through Mobile Augmented Reality

Roberto Pierdicca[1]([⊠]), Emanuele Frontoni[1], Primo Zingaretti[1],
Eva Savina Malinverni[2], Andrea Galli[3], Ernesto Marcheggiani[3,4],
and Carlos Smaniotto Costa[5]

[1] Department of Information Engineering, Universitá Politecnica delle Marche,
Via Brecce Bianche 12, 60131 Ancona, Italy
{r.pierdicca,e.frontoni,p.zingaretti}@univpm.it
[2] Department of Civil Engineering, Building and Architecture,
Universitá Politecnica delle Marche, Via Brecce Bianche 12, 60131 Ancona, Italy
e.s.malinverni@univpm.it
[3] Department of Agricultural, Food and Environmental Sciences,
Universitá Politecnica delle Marche, Via Brecce Bianche 12, 60131 Ancona, Italy
{a.galli,e.marcheggiani}@univpm.it
[4] Department of Earth and Environmental Research, KU Leuven, Leuven, Belgium
[5] CeiED Interdisciplinary Research Centre for Education and Development,
Universidade Lusona, Campo Grande, 376, 1749-024 Lisboa, Portugal
p900911@ulusofona.pt

Abstract. Latest improvement on mobile devices capabilities definitively changed the way people experience their surroundings. Thanks to the improvement of built in sensors, devices are able to sense the environment at users' location. The ability to provide contextual services to the visitors is a key aspect to make public parks more accessible, comprehensible end enjoyable. The paper outlines the application of Augmented Reality technologies in a real case scenario. The aim is to equip visitors with an ICT tool able to enhance their perception visiting open spaces and parks. The reporting area chosen for the study case is an Archaeological park, the Cardeto, located within an urban green open space in the outskirts of Ancona, a city in central Italy. Ensuring the success of the experiment has required an hybrid approach, with the main objective of providing visitors with an endless flow of information, anytime and anywhere. To reach this result, a mobile application has been developed, exploiting two different tracking systems: location-based and edge-based. The first one helps users to move along with a network of given Points of Interest disseminated within the park. At the same time, the second system displays a rich set of information each time a user came in close the proximity with artefacts or valuable heritages. This work is part of a wider ongoing project aiming at a better understanding of the potentials inherent the design space for smartphones in context-aware AR applications for tourists. Our experiment demonstrates the validity of purposed methodology as a promising solution for Cultural Heritage purposes.

© Springer International Publishing Switzerland 2016
L.T. De Paolis and A. Mongelli (Eds.): AVR 2016, Part II, LNCS 9769, pp. 172–185, 2016.
DOI: 10.1007/978-3-319-40651-0_14

Keywords: Augmented reality · Cyber archaeology · Smart tourism · Way-finding · Mobile · Edge-based tracking · GPS

1 Introduction

Location-based Augmented Reality (AR) has successfully grabbed the tourism industry. This is because, among other peculiarities, AR has the capability of changing users' sight of the environment. The growing potentials of mobile devices are definitively changing the way in which tourists gather and access information, especially in outdoor environment [10]. The traditional orientation, guides and way-finding maps, have been overridden by the relentless diffusion of mobile orientation devices and on-line maps, more suitable and accessible to users needs. Built-in cameras, global positioning system (GPS) sensors and Internet connection open the way towards a new manner of experiencing public spaces, thanks to contextual information. Context-awareness is a powerful way to create an interactive on-line environment in which tourists, even if with little knowledge of a certain area, can naturally experience unfamiliar places. A trivial and common thought, preventing AR from being a world-wide reference in this domain, is that mobile maps are a good solution to find places and interesting areas in outdoor spaces. However, even if well-established solutions, are not optimally designed for urban exploration and provide limited capabilities to access data; moreover, and more important, they oblige the user to look away from the reality. Another issue of currently available 3D maps is that the camera view of the object is often occluded by nearby structures, which is especially problematic in densely built-up areas [19]. AR represents instead a natural choice for exploring location-based information of real world, mainly because information can be superimposed onto the display, with the same sight of the user. Simply by framing his/her surroundings, the user can easily access additional information about a building, in urban environment, by pointing an AR-enabled mobile device into its direction, regardless of the visual barriers. In [22], the authors have listed a set of challenges that developers have to take into account designing AR browsers for outdoor environments; many objects can be augmented with information; each object can be a source of a substantial amount of information; contents might be visually heterogeneous and dynamic; users are into unfamiliar environment; tourists have information needs which differ from those of dwellers. These considerations represent a useful reference also dealing with archaeological heritage [2].

Cyberarchaeology aims to build a spatial-temporary environment able to reconnect the current archaeological landscape with the ancient one, following a validated and transparent methodological path [8]. Despite Cyberarchaeology concept was originally conceived for virtual tours in an indoor museum space [3], is nowadays possible to develop the "simulation process" on site, by AR applications. AR, which enriches the real world by adding virtual entities, offers great potential and opens towards new opportunities for mobile applications. In recent years, many AR systems have emerged. However, the vast majority of these systems are intended for small indoor environments, easier to control because of the limits derived by known issues (e.g. brightness variation, occlusion, 3D registration, etc.) [24]. The development of AR applications for outdoor scenario implies the use of built in sensors, handy and spread for the majority of devices, but error prone in terms of accuracy.

To this end, the main objective of this work is the development of an AR experience for cultural communication, designed for mobile devices in outdoor environments. The project aims to the enhancement of the Cardeto park, focusing on personal experience to provide tourists and visitors with an interactive tool to discover the hidden secrets of the park. This research underpins two main aspects. The first one, theoretical, is that AR and mobile technologies would represent the milestone for the promotion, the use and the conservation of archaeological parks. We propose a shift, through new technological tools and new contents, with the twofold objective of making visit experience easier and complete, with a greater involvement of visitors, bridging the gap between existing and accessible, between visible and invisible. The second aim, more technical, is to challenge the development of an application by merging a well established state of art location-based services with an edge-based tracking system. The idea is to use an hybrid approach, integrating into the same application the two aforementioned tracking techniques. Our test demonstrates that the latter is a performing tracking system also in outdoor scenarios, where lighting condition and the variety of landscape hamper an affordable use of marker-less solutions based on image matching. We also outlined best practices suitable to be adopted for further exploitations of open-air cultural heritages.

The paper is outlined as follow: Sect. 2 provides a description of the operational background, highlighting related works and guidelines adopted for the development of our system. Section 3 focuses on the description of the experimental application, while Sect. 4 gives details about the architecture of application, with special focus on the tracking systems. Results of experiments and discussion on future developments are provided in Sects. 5 and 6 respectively.

2   Background and Related Works

In addition to offering a revolutionary new concept of cultural enjoyment, AR can attract a growing number of visitors; it is also an affordable and simple solution for insiders (e.g. tourist guides, administrators etc.) who can enable new solutions, offering new information and management methodologies to simplify access to historical areas, expanding the range of promotion and dissemination services. In some cases [15] existing GIS platforms have been extended into mobile services. Starting from the territory, AR can take the user into other domains, evaluating the entirety of the cultural heritage (CH), encouraging a deeper exploration of diffused heritage goods [9]. From the e-learning standing point, Mobile Augmented Reality (MAR) has proved of being a winning solution [7]. However, some technological and anthropological issues still exist, preventing MAR from becoming a broadly used tools for open spaces. External variables that influence user acceptance include enjoyment, personal innovativeness, perceived benefits, costs and information quality [20]. In the following, a brief state of art review is reported, useful as a comparison with our work.

The problem of using AR for tourism purposes, highlighting the benefits offered to the tourists, is widely discussed in [11]. Authors state that the core idea behind the use of AR for tourism is the enhancement of user's perception of reality and of the surrounding environment. As tourists in fact, we are often exposed to unfamiliar environments where the fast retrieval of information is fundamental for our decision-making. Access to relevant contents through location-based services not only facilitates this process, but also changes the way we perceive destinations, creating more memorable and unique experiences. Recently, a lot of attention was directed towards AR interfaces as a suitable visualization paradigm, especially within the domain of travel and tourism. AR browsers deliver (geo)spatial and attribute information about physical objects through spatially registered virtual annotations. Such interfaces reduce the need to translate abstract information (for example, encoded in maps), or oblige switching gaze between information and physical space. This happens with guidebooks or list-based mobile interfaces. This scenario is particularly beneficial for time-pressured visitors to unfamiliar locations. In [23], interesting consideration have been done, with respect to the criteria that should be used when developing an AR service for tourism. Four features should be followed:

- Readability: labels should be readable at all times and should not overlap;
- Unambiguous association: labels should clearly refer to their target objects;
- Aesthetics: labels should be placed in a way that prevents visual clutter;
- Frame-coherency: the system should provide a seamless transition of content among frames.

The aforementioned criteria are effective also when dealing with archaeological sites [5]. In fact, these areas are generally wide, and findings are scattered among the landscape. Some commercial existing solutions prove the validity of the method. CorfuAR[1] is a tourist city guide using the strengths of the AR technology, by placing information about surroundings on reality. The experience of visiting Corfu is enhanced with virtual information about sights, museums, monuments, religious sites, nature and many more. AR have been adopted also for the visualization of ancient buildings to be viewed and explored in real-time [4]. Some interesting example of visualization of 3D models during a visit can be found in [1] for city environment, and in [13] for remote archaeological sites. In spite of this, location-based services are error prone, and are more suitable for way finding purposes, rather than for precise registration of virtual objects. Object-centered design with edge-based tracking [16], [24] is the state of art technique that better fits with the problems of outdoor environments, and could represent (together with cloud computing services [21]) the only effective alternative to deepen the knowledge of cultural goods, scattered and diffused in our parks.

---

[1] http://www.corfuar.com, last accessed: April 12, 2016.

3 The Project

This project is concerned with the proposal of a change in the use of the park: new technological tools and new contents communicate with the dual objective of making the visit easier and straightforward, improving the involvement of visitors. Even if the development has been carried out at a local level and is ongoing, the discussion is backed by the first knowledge and experiences exchanges carried out within the European COST Action Project Cyberparks[2], which provides a forum for cross-sector working among researchers, urban designers and developers, ICT experts, urban anthropologists and sociologists, creative industries experts, from 29 countries. Actually, the park presents some weaknesses such as the complete lack of orientation and the inaccessibility for the majority of the buildings. With the introduction of digital service, the expectation is that there will be a change in the use of the park, bridging this way the gap between existing and accessible, between the visible and invisible. The current condition of the trails is of semi-abandonment, with few sporadic way findings along the way (Fig. 1).

Fig. 1. One of the main entrance of the park. The lack of care and signs makes the park inaccessible and difficult to visit.

---

[2] http://www.cost.eu/domains_actions/tud/Actions/TU1306.

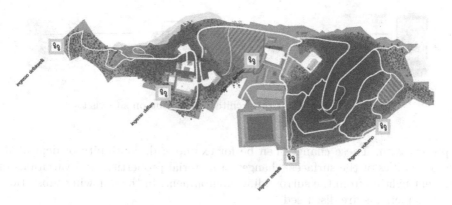

Fig. 2. Map of the park with all the starting point highlighted in yellow. (Color figure online)

The App, accessible by smartphone or tablet, allows visitor to choose from different visit trails. Accordingly with his position, the tourist can chose among different pathways. By different tracking techniques, further information are made available every time a user gets close to a point of interest. The site's map, with highlighted the main entrance points, is shown in Fig. 2.

4   Methodology and Technology

For the development of the proposed application, we have chosen to adopt two tracking systems. Location-based tracking and edge-based tracking. The first one is based on the user location and enables the smartphone retrieving context information accordingly. The second one is an *Object-centric* approach categorized as marker-less tracking, based on geometrical edge features [12]. The reason why we have chosen to merge two tracking system into the same application, lies in the possibility to exploit the potentials of both systems. Location-based helps way finding, triggering services only at a specified distance from the Point of Interest (POI). Furthermore, in absence of signage, as for this study case, it helps a visitor to follow his preferred path according to the POIs typology. On the contrary, once the tourist is close to the cultural good, the location-based service cannot provide in-depth analysis of cultural objects. The development of Augmented Reality experiences, in fact, is strictly dependent on the type of registration (i.e. overlaying of virtual contents) that one choose. Delivering in-depth analysis of specific objects, requires robust tracking techniques able to anchor the real object with the one displayed in the camera of the device. With edge-tracking, enabled only at a certain distance from the POI, the user is provided with a more precise registration of digital contents. It is a state of art method used to mark the points of digital image in which the light intensity changes abruptly. Abrupt changes of the properties of an image are usually the symptom of important events or changes in the physical world in which images are the

Fig. 3. The steps of the architecture during on site visit.

representation. These changes can be for example: discontinuity of depth, the discontinuities of the surfaces, changes in material properties, and variations in ambient lighting from the surrounding environment. In the following subsection, the two methods are discussed.

4.1 Location-Based AR

This functionality has been developed to permit the user activating the augmented reality browser and to search for all the POIs close to him/her.

All the POIs have been stored into a Relational Database Management System (RDBMS), with a classical web-server which hosts php pages. For this experiment we have chosen an open source MySQL server. POIs have been stored within the database by assigning them a table with specific parameters like latitude and longitude (to correctly register geo-location), title, description, link to external resources, metadata and other information of interest for the user. A web-service is needed to collect the POI information (in JSON format) and get it back to the AR platform. These parameters are computed by the application, permitting to overlay the labels into the real scene. To retrieve these points according to user's location it also necessary that the application generate a php script that returns the POIs. Performing a series of asynchronous calls to activate the php script it is possible to transfer the user's location coordinates as parameters. A brief explanation of the architecture can be found in Fig. 3.

All the features of the app have been implemented by using libraries provided by API LayarSDK[3], a static library that implements augmented reality and geo-localization functions. A compass, displayed on the screen, helps the user in orienting among the different POIs. In this way, the user is guided to reach the area where the wanted item (a building or a specific finding) is located. To implement this feature we took advantage from the set of embedded sensors of mobile devices (e.g. compass, gyroscope, accelerometer and GPS receiver). For adjusting the search area, the user can set a search radius from the device. Within this radius, the application looks for relevant POIs. This is particularly helpful during the visit to retrieve information of a limited set of POIs nearby the user. Moreover, the application allows displaying, in a popup window, more information (the title, description, footnote and image) associated with the selected, as well as the cultural good typology.

---

[3] https://www.layar.com, last access April 12, 2016.

(a) The path of War buildings   (b) Cultural and religious POIs

Fig. 4. Mobile application running in the park, with different path.

The particular case selected for this work encompasses a various Cultural Heritage, including Romans relics, as well as buildings dated the Second World War. By categorizing all the POIs, we have given the possibility to follow specified trajectories among the park. Some screen shots of the application running are shown Figs. 4 and 5.

4.2   Edge-Based AR

The recognition of contours (edge feature detection) is the second tracking technology used for the presented application. This tracking technique is particularly suitable to augment:

- a previously defined solid 3D object from any view angle on a non-planar environment;
- different objects independently of their texture;
- the scene to obtain the scale of the environment;
- objects in an unpredictable environment where motions and changing lighting conditions make image matching difficult.

(a) Route guidance labels   (b) App close to the POI

Fig. 5. Mobile application running in the park, in way finding mode.

To obtain this function, the following steps have been implemented into the application. First of all we have built the 3D model of an historical building within the park and preloaded it into the system as a tracking object. In this case an ancient barrack, as shown in Fig. 6a. Within the app, the edge detection process has been implemented with Canny algorithm [6], running once with the device's camera is enabled. An example of the edges extracted from camera frame is showed in Fig. 6b.

The 3D model is managed by the Layar SDK, allowing the matching between the edges of the image from the camera and the edges of the 3D model, managed in wireframe with hidden line mode. Once the user has reached a specified POI, for instance, is closer to it by a given distance (e.g. less than 50 m) and the cultural object is in the line of sight, the navigation switches into edge-tracking mode allowing the visitor to display more detailed information. The initialization starts with predefined views from several locations in the environment, according to an initial pose, setted up by default, that specifies a rough initial estimation of the camera position and orientation to the target object. In order to avoid visual occlusions, the tracking 3D object has been developed to appear in *Silhouette* mode (Fig. 7a).

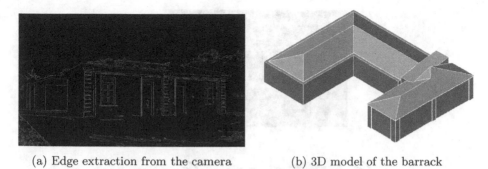

(a) Edge extraction from the camera   (b) 3D model of the barrack

Fig. 6. Steps for the implementation of the edge extraction from the real scene.

(a) App close to the POI   (b) Images superimposed to the building

Fig. 7. Mobile application running with edge tracking enabled near the POI.

In this specific case, since the building access is forbidden to the public, the application allows the visitors to virtually explore the interiors with its related pictures (Fig. 7b).

5   Results and Discussion

The application has been validated by several tests realized both in laboratory, to optimize the content retrieval, and in the real environment. During the outdoor testing sessions, we observed that the application retrieved and displayed the labels in real time; labels and contents were responsive and integral with the device's movements. The a priori definition of a categorization for the POIs resulted a winning solution for the personalization of the path. Users found this feature very useful to perform an experience tailored according to their interest. In this light, the enrichment of metadata to deep the knowledge of the user is useful but very time consuming; AR browsers should be developed using semantic web technologies [17]. For our experiment, we have used an iPad 2 and a Samsung S3. Whenever the GNSS service was available, accuracy ranked between 5 m up to 10 m, depending on the vegetation canopy. By the way, the accuracy for the overlaying of the digital contents is strictly dependent on the

Fig. 8. Hypothesis of a possible use of wireless sensor network in the park.

current accuracy of consumer grade GNSS receiver. However, working as a path-finder, this accuracy can be considered satisfactory to guide the users towards the POIs. Even if location-based services demonstrated to be an effective solution to improve way finding, especially in wide areas such as archaeological sites, the use of edge-based tracking within the same application ensures an improved knowledge of the items scattered among the trails. The possibility of switching to the edge tracking whenever the user gets near the POI implies two main advantages:

- edge feature detection works regardless the lighting conditions, ensuring the registration of digital contents;
- 3D edges models are small, allowing the possibility of being remotely stored and retrieved also with the use of 3G/4G connection.

The target building, chosen for the test, is approximately $30\,\text{m} \times 30\,\text{m}$ large and is composed of simple geometry. The tracking system resulted very responsive, showing quickly the augmented contents. To evaluate the usability we have tested the application with different subjects, allowing us to draw useful feedback for further improvements. One impediment is represented by the initial pose of the 3D object, chosen in advance. With this set up, the user have to move along the building until he find the corresponding pose. Besides, the user-test conducted for this case highlighted other issues that need further investigations, caused by the intuitiveness of the tracking system. In fact, whilst in location-based mode labels appears automatically on the user screen, in edge-tracking mode the users have to catch the correct camera pose in order to trigger the augmented contents.

This task did not result usable for the users and could represent an impediment in terms of fruition for the user.

6   Future Work and Conclusion

In this paper, an interactive route guidance through augmented reality is presented. Location-based services guide the tourist towards the main attraction of Cardeto park. The database containing the POIs have been enriched with metadata, in order to categorize the various cultural goods, spread in the park. Thanks to the addition of edge-based tracking in the same application, the user can experience an enriched visit when arrives in proximity of buildings or archaeological findings. The recuperation of urban parks means, first of all, persuading people to visit them; by providing users with digital tools, making their visit more interesting, funny and simple, this objective should be pursued. With our solution tourists can discover more easily the space, visiting also what is invisible. The merging of location and edge tracking represents a rapid and affordable solution to be developed, also because the simplicity of the architecture make it easer to be constantly updated by the public administrations. In the future we are planning to use Cardeto park like our open air laboratory, making it a sensible space with new sensors like Beacons (see Fig. 8). The advantage of disseminating the park with an active network of beacons is twofold: on one hand, by using beacon's localization system it will be possible to reduce the error arising from GNSS receiver. The Wireless Sensor Network in fact can be exploited to localize smartphones inside it. On the other, in case of lack of GNSS signal, beacon's position can be used to provide users with push and notification services, enriching the experience. In this direction, we are working on the AR visualization of labels, getting the position from beacons' position instead of from the GSNN one.

In this way, we envisage to create a pervasive environment [14], [18] where contextual information are automatically provided to the users with proximity technology, but with a more precise localization with wireless sensor networks.

Acknowledgements. This research has been carried out within the Cyberparks project COST Action TU 1306, fostering knowledge about the relationship between Information and Communication Technologies and Public Spaces supported by strategies to improve their use and attractiveness (http://cyberparks-project.eu). The authors would like also to thank Rosanna Petrilli Fonte for her efforts during the development of the presented application.

References

1. Banterle, F., Cardillo, F.A., Malomo, L.: LecceAR: an augmented reality app for cultural heritage. ERCIM News **103**, 16–17 (2015). http://vcg.isti.cnr.it/Publications/2015/BCM15

2. Chung, N., Han, H., Joun, Y.: Tourists intention to visit a destination: the role of augmented reality (ar) application for a heritage site. Comput. Hum. Behav. **50**, 588–599 (2015)
3. Clini, P., Frontoni, E., Quattrini, R., Pierdicca, R.: Augmented reality experience: from high-resolution acquisition to real time augmented contents. Adv. Multimedia **2014**, 18 (2014)
4. Clini, P., Quattrini, R., Frontoni, E., Pierdicca, R., Nespeca, R.: Real/not real: pseudo-holography and augmented reality applications for cultural heritage. In: Handbook of Research on Emerging Technologies for Cultural Heritage (2015, in press)
5. Deliyiannis, I., Papaioannou, G.: Augmented reality for archaeological environments on mobile devices: a novel open framework. Mediterr. Archaeol. Archaeometry **14**(4), 1–10 (2014)
6. Ding, L., Goshtasby, A.: On the canny edge detector. Pattern Recogn. **34**(3), 721–725 (2001)
7. Etxeberria, A.I., Asensio, M., Vicent, N., Cuenca, J.M.: Mobile devices: a tool for tourism and learning at archaeological sites. Int. J. Web Based Communities **8**(1), 57–72 (2012)
8. Forte, M.: Cyber-Archaeology. Archaeopress, Oxford (2010)
9. Garau, C., Ilardi, E.: The non-places meet the places: virtualtours on smartphones for the enhancement of cultural heritage. J. Urban Technol. **21**(1), 79–91 (2014)
10. Jung, T., Chung, N., Leue, M.C.: The determinants of recommendations to use augmented reality technologies: the case of a Korean theme park. Tourism Manage. **49**, 75–86 (2015)
11. Kounavis, C.D., Kasimati, A.E., Zamani, E.D.: Enhancing the tourism experience through mobile augmented reality: challenges and prospects. Int. J. Eng. Bus. Manage. **4**(10), 1–6 (2012)
12. Petit, A., Marchand, E., Kanani, K.: Augmenting markerless complex 3D objects by combining geometrical and color edge information. In: 2013 IEEE International Symposium on Mixed and Augmented Reality (ISMAR), pp. 287–288. IEEE (2013)
13. Pierdicca, R., Frontoni, E., Zingaretti, P., Malinverni, E.S., Colosi, F., Orazi, R.: Making Visible the invisible. augmented reality visualization for 3D reconstructions of archaeological sites. In: De Paolis, L.T., Mongelli, A. (eds.) AVR 2015. LNCS, vol. 9254, pp. 25–37. Springer, Heidelberg (2015)
14. Pierdicca, R., Liciotti, D., Contigiani, M., Frontoni, E., Mancini, A., Zingaretti, P.: Low cost embedded system for increasing retail environment intelligence. In: 2015 IEEE International Conference on Multimedia & Expo Workshops (ICMEW), pp. 1–6. IEEE (2015)
15. Pierdicca, R., Malinverni, E.S., Clini, P., Mancini, A., Bozzi, C.A., Nespeca, R.: Development of a GIS environment for archaeological multipurpose applications: the Fano historic centre. In: XIII International Forum Le Vie dei Mercanti, pp. 588–597. IEEE Computer Society (2015)
16. Reitmayr, G., Drummond, T.: Going out: robust model-based tracking for outdoor augmented reality. In: Proceedings of the 5th IEEE and ACM International Symposium on Mixed and Augmented Reality, pp. 109–118. IEEE Computer Society (2006)
17. Ruta, M., Scioscia, F., De Filippis, D., Ieva, S., Binetti, M., Di Sciascio, E.: A semantic-enhanced augmented reality tool for openstreetmap POI discovery. Transp. Res. Procedia **3**, 479–488 (2014)

18. Sturari, M., Liciotti, D., Pierdicca, R., Frontoni, E., Mancini, A., Contigiani, M., Zingaretti, P.: Robust and affordable retail customer profiling by vision and radio beacon sensor fusion. Pattern Recogn. Lett. (2016)
19. Tatzgern, M., Grasset, R., Veas, E., Kalkofen, D., Seichter, H., Schmalstieg, D.: Exploring real world points of interest: design and evaluation of object-centric exploration techniques for augmented reality. Pervasive Mob. Comput. **18**, 55–70 (2015)
20. Dieck, M.C.T., Jung, T.: A theoretical model of mobile augmented reality acceptance in urban heritage tourism. Curr. Issues Tourism **18**, 1–21 (2015)
21. Vecchio, P., Mele, F., De Paolis, L.T., Epicoco, I., Mancini, M., Aloisio, G.: Cloud computing and augmented reality for cultural heritage. In: De Paolis, L.T., Mongelli, A. (eds.) AVR 2015. LNCS, vol. 9254, pp. 51–60. Springer, Heidelberg (2015)
22. Yovcheva, Z., Buhalis, D., Gatzidis, C.: Overview of smartphone augmented reality applications for tourism. e-review of tourism research (ertr) **10**(2), 63–66 (2012)
23. Yovcheva, Z., Buhalis, D., Gatzidis, C., van Elzakker, C.P.: Empirical evaluation of smartphone augmented reality browsers in an urban tourism destination context. Int. J. Mob. Hum. Comput. Interact. (IJMHCI) **6**(2), 10–31 (2014)
24. Zendjebil, I., Ababsa, F.E., Didier, J.Y., Vairon, J., Frauciel, L., Hachet, M., Guitton, P., Delmont, R.: Outdoor augmented reality: state of the art and issues. In: 10th ACM/IEEE Virtual Reality International Conference (VRIC 2008), pp. 177–187 (2008)

Augmenting Smart Objects for Cultural Heritage: A Usability Experiment

Marco Romano[1](✉), Paloma Díaz[1], Aedo Ignacio[1],
and Pierpaolo D'Agostino[2]

[1] Information Technology Department, Universidad Carlos III de Madrid,
Madrid, Spain
{mromano, pdp}@inf.uc3m.es, aedo@ia.uc3m.es
[2] Department of Civil, Architectural and Environmental Engineering,
University of Naples Federico II, Naples, Italy
pierpaolo.dagostino@unina.it

Abstract. In recent years the explosive growth of smartphones and the evolution of mobile communication networks have certainly revolutionized the way how people communicate and access information. This growing adoption of technology creates also some challenges. It is struggling to teach people who has had an increased exposure to technology. Cultural heritage organizations deal with this issue endlessly and look to the new technologies as an opportunity to transform and enhance the exhibition experience for matching the interest of the newest visitors. In this paper we focus on the augmented reality (AR) technologies and the role that they play to connect visitors to the modern exhibitions. Moreover, we define for the first time the concept of *Augmenting Smart Object* (ASO) that arises from the study of the state of the art of the AR systems applied to the cultural context and from our direct experience in a participatory design aimed at developing and evaluating an AR system for a museum exhibition.

Keywords: Augmented reality · Mobile devices · Participatory design · System usability

1 Introduction

Modern technologies are progressively becoming sewn into our daily lives. Small computational devices are integrated into common objects that people use to perform normal tasks or during leisure activities. This is more evident in *digital natives*, people born in the modern digital era who are used to touch and speak with their interactive devices to play, learn, and communicate or even to build their own smart and programmable toys with easy to use technologies like littleBits[1].

This growing adoption of technology creates also some challenges. As Prensky explains in [1], it is struggling to teach people who has had an increased exposure to technology. They not only will have developed an habit to use technology to look for information and to interact with others, but also they might have developed different

---

[1] http://littlebits.cc/.

© Springer International Publishing Switzerland 2016
L.T. De Paolis and A. Mongelli (Eds.): AVR 2016, Part II, LNCS 9769, pp. 186–204, 2016.
DOI: 10.1007/978-3-319-40651-0_15

ways of learning [2] and in fact most of them are experiential learners [3], and with a capacity for multi-tasking.

In the domain of cultural heritage (CH so forth) there is a growing interest in making the cultural sites "enjoyable" to this new kind of users. As stated by Hein in [22] museums are perceiving themselves more as experience providers than as object exhibitors. In order to make such experiences more satisfying for visitors, exhibitions need to link the personal motives and values of visitors with the knowledge exhibited [4]. There are some examples of CH sites enhanced with digital technology, and particularly with augmented (AR) and virtual reality (VR) [5, 6]. For instance, the *Museo Archeologico Virtuale*[2] of the ancient city of Ercolano (Italia) does not exhibit real objects but allows visitors to interact with digital reproductions generated through holograms. In the nineteenth-century palace of *S. Teodoro*[3] in Naples, the curators enrich the visits using virtual and augmented reality to recall ancient events and settings. By means of the Augmented Reality, curators recreated rooms of the temple of *Hatshepsut* in Deir-el-Bahari, of the *Calatrava* castle and of other ancient buildings.

However, to pursue the original goal, improving the experience of visitors, integrating technology per se shouldn't be the main design driven force. As discussed in [7], technology should be conceived as a mediator to improve the visitor's experience not as a tool that diverts the attention from the cultural object or site to the technical device. The experience has to be attractive and enjoyable from the users' point of view but it also has to meet the educational goals underlying most cultural heritage sites. Csikszentmihalyi and Hermanson [26] identify two main factors that improve the visitor's engagement: *situational interest*, that happens when they are pushed to face challenging or intriguing situations; and *personal interest* that appears when the exhibition links with enduring visitor values and motives. The role that virtual and augmented reality technologies can play to promote situational interest is to deploy content and support an interaction that might generate stronger links with visitors. For example, authors of [25] explore the use of an augmented object to take profit from the social nature of people to improve the user experience.

In this context, we introduce the *Augmenting Smart Objects* (ASOs) concept as a way to support engaging experiences that combine both experiential and pedagogical value. An ASO is a nonintrusive and interactive device allowing users to access and interact with AR content in different CH contexts with a view to creating personal links between visitors and the exhibit. Following a participatory design approach, field research and interviews with experts were conducted to understand the features an ASO should exhibit. This knowledge informed the design of a prototype of ASO whose usability was evaluated with users who found the ASO as a way to experiment a more personal experience to interact with each object in the exhibit.

The rest of the paper is organized as follows: Sect. 2 presents the state of the art of the AR systems for CH sites. Section 3 describes the participatory process for designing an instance of the ASO and its usability evaluation. Section 4 formalizes the lessons learned during the whole design process. Finally, in Sect. 5 some conclusions are drawn.

---

[2] www.museomav.it.

[3] www.palazzosanteodoroexperience.com.

2 Related Work

The use of AR systems in CH sites are not a particularly recent practice. Back in 1999, Brogni et al. [15] discussed the growing interest and the technological limits of this kind of systems and tried to envision their future based on some kind of wearable or mobile devices. Nowadays, despite the expectations raised by devices supporting AR, such as large see-through screens or holograms, the most common solutions in CH sites are mobile devices, such as phones, tablets and AR glasses. These technologies are generally technically feasible and affordable, and, when the system is conveniently designed on the users' necessities, can offer a more personal and rewarding user experience.

Some examples are given by Vanoni et al. [16] and from the Casa Batlló[4] (Spain). In the first case, a tablet allows visitors to select different layers of virtual content to add to the exhibited pictures of the *Salone dei Cinquecento* in Florence's *Palazzo Vecchio*. In the second case visitors looking through a smartphone and using earphones can experience a virtual and augmented visit of *Casa Batlló*. However, although mobile devices are easy to use, in [21] authors highlight that similar systems act as a distraction during the visit and the attention is transferred from the environment to the technology. Also for such reason AR designers are looking to other technologies such as AR or VR glasses.

An example is given by the "Dreams of Dalí"[5] project. The project is hosted in the museum, sited in St. Petersburg, in Florida. The VR glasses allow visitors to experience for a while the immersion in one of the a Dalí's masterpieces. The company Guidgo[6] in 2014 developed a AR guide for museums exploiting the Google Glass[7]. The device guides the visitors and add extra information to the exhibit. A significant experience about AR application is given by ARtSENSE [14]. It is a European project which aims to create mobile museum guides based on AR applications. The ARtSENSE interface is based on AR glasses and other wearable devices used to allow visitors to interact with virtual objects. Similar projects are ARCHEOGUIDE [13] and LifePlus, [12]. Differently by ARtSENSE, the AR glasses are used to augment archaeological sites. Also in this case visitors have to use other wearable devices to use the system. In [29], researchers present a system aimed at supporting tourists in the city of Naples during their cultural visits. The system is based on AR glasses, hand recognition and head movements detection. Differently by the previous projects, the users have to wear only the AR glasses integrating several needed components and carry a mini pc. However, preliminary results describe the interaction uncomfortable and difficult.

The designs of AR systems generally share some common characteristics and limitations. First of all, they try to be didactic and recreational offering multimedia content to support visitors in understanding the exhibit. Their aim is to be helpful by assisting users during the whole time spent at the site (i.e. suggesting itineraries). Moreover, they require a continuous attention and they lack an adequate study of the interaction. Indeed, in order to recognize the objects to augment, visitors often have to explore the CH site using the

---

[4] www.casabatllo.es/en/visit/videoguide.

[5] thedali.org/dreams-of-dali.

[6] www.guidigo.com/glass.

[7] www.google.com/glass/start.

provided device and have to stop and carefully stare at the exhibited items. In other cases, they are required to wear uncomfortable devices during the whole visit or in some concrete points and they may need some external helps to use them.

In [19], the authors notice that AR designers chiefly focus on visual augmentations and disregarding other visitors' necessities. Pedersen remarks in [18] that "*human users needed to be treated as centers, immersed in AR interfaces rather than as viewers, seeing interfaces or graphical overlays*". In [20], the authors present a list of AR system requirements for CH sites. In particular, they highlight the necessities to have a full interactive, recreational and didactic AR system. Moreover, the system must focus on aspects that help users relax during the visit in order to enjoy the CH experience.

Van der Vaart and Damala in [17] try to deal with these issues through the design of an AR loupe. Such device is a smart object, that is a common object integrating sensors to understand and react to the environment [28]. In this specific case, the loupe integrates an iPhone to exploit its screen and sensors. The goal is to provide a more appropriate device for a museum context, to exploit the loupe affordances and make the interaction more intuitive. The loupe is able to recognize the exhibited objects and to add any multimedia content. The visitors have to stare at the exhibited objects through the loupe to see the content. Different functionalities can be selected by moving, tilting or shaking the device. Even if the loupe tries to address some of the mentioned issues, after an experimental study, the researchers recognize that the task to look for an object to augment may easily distract visitors especially the youngest one. More in general, some testers declared to focus more on playing with the device rather than the same exhibit.

These researches highlight there is still a need to understand how to integrate useful, usable and enjoyable technology in the museum in a way that does not divert the attention to the technological devices [7] and makes it possible to provide a more satisfying experience. A participatory design approach like the one described in this paper could help to understand better how to design these technological interventions balancing the goals of the CH professionals with the traits, motivations, values, and expectations of current visitors.

3   Participatory Design: Understanding the Requirements of Cultural Heritage Professionals

With a view to understand how to design experiences with the CH site, we adopted a participatory approach where stakeholders were involved in the elicitation and analysis of the requirements of potential technological devices. During this process, interviews and field work was conducted. In particular, we conducted three interviews: one with the director of the archaeological site of the Villa de Fuente Alamo in Cordoba (Spain); a second with an archaeological practitioner working as a guide at the ruins of ancient Stabia near Naples (Italy) and as a children archaeological teacher; and, a third interview with the technological manager of the S. Teodoro Palace in Naples (Italy). Moreover, we spent time in the sites where they work to observe activities and visitors. We discussed with our interviewees the kind of visitors they usually work with, the way they interact with them, and the main difficulties they can have when trying to connect with them. Moreover, we also explore their confidence on the role of technology, and their willingness to use it in their work and in their daily life.

We obtained similar answers from the first two interviewees. The average age of "spontaneous" visitors is between 30–50 years and most visitors are women. Moreover, it is common to work with groups of school field trips. Spontaneous visitors generally show an initial interest for history and the ruins but after a certain time they get mentally tired. Pupils are more distracted and do not pay specific attention to the context. The guides try to deal with attention issues using some techniques based on a continuous interaction with visitors and trying to involve them in some recreational activities. Three examples used to get the attention of visitors through recreational activities include: (a) having actors playing the roles of the ancient dwellers of the city or recreating famous or mundane events; (b) proposing experiential activities such as having children excavating fake ruins to discover objects or (c) inviting visitors to touch and play with replicas of ancient objects found in the that archaeological site.

Apart from the attention issue, interviewers also highlighted another interesting point they have to deal with: the way to make visitors understand the different eras of the archaeological site. For instance, the director of Villa Fuente explained that some ancient ruins belong to Pre-Roman era, the thermal baths to the Roman, the Villa to a second Roman era while the cemetery was from the Arab period. The differences between periods that might seem obvious for experts are quite difficult to perceive by visitors but they make up an important fact to understand the site.

When asked about their confidence with modern technologies and their willingness to integrate them in their work they also provided similar answers. They use on daily basis devices for their personal life and to organize their work activities. For example, during the visits they use sometimes smartphones and tablets to write down notes, communicate with colleagues, take pictures and show pictures also to the same visitors. On the one hand, our interviewees do not consider themselves distrustful towards the introduction of some kinds of technological supports for their work, but on the other, they were afraid that the technology could be intrusive and could grab the attention of the visitors and divert it from the real goal: understand and appreciate the CH site. As one of the interviewers put it *"we are a small site in a non rich area, so we need people from the community liking and needing us. They have first to appreciate the value of this site and to perceive why we are valuable for the region"*. When asked which kind of objects can be considered not intrusive, portable and respectful of the context small thinks like coins, lamps, pictures, shrines, or ancient bricks, were suggested.

The last interview gave us a different point of view. In the S. Teodoro Palace, visitors are led not by a human guide but by a digital guide speaking through some totems strategically located in the different rooms. The visit is enriched by the usage of VR helmets that allow to recreate ancient events and sets of the palace. The kind of visitors is really varied. It is common to have visitors of any age and any gender. Most of the visitors come fascinated by the idea of experimenting a new kind of visit. All the technologies are installed in strategic points and require the users' attention just there. This is to allow visitors to explore the rooms without to focus continuously to the technology. However, as the technical manager of *S.Teodoro* Palace confirms: *"If on the one hand there is a necessity to improve the visits using digital content, on the other, there is a real risk to completely draw the attention on it"*.

3.1   Augmenting Smart Objects

We capitalized the knowledge gained from the fieldwork and interviews in the form of scenarios of working practices, from which we could start our brainstorming activities to envision ways to integrate technology in CH sites. Scenarios are a well known technique in design that we will use to illustrate alternative solutions [24]. In particular we introduce the concept of Augmenting Smart Object (ASOs henceforth), which are nonintrusive objects that can be naturally integrated in the physical context and that combine the ludic component with the didactic one. With that purpose an ASO is usually an existing physical object that is somehow related with the goal of the CH site. Moreover, the affordances of its physical shape [23] can be exploited to provide an easier and quicker interaction. The ASO is also a portable and interactive device aimed at providing users with AR to improve their visit without grabbing the spotlight: they can be used only in specific locations set by the administrator of the archaeological site. In the next paragraphs we describe two scenarios of use of ASOs.

Scenario 1 – Augmented Guided Visit. In this scenario the guide leads a group of visitors through the ruins of an ancient Greek-Roman colony. (S)he carries an ASO in form of a Roman lamp and uses it when (s)he wants to make people see the different eras of the site. Connecting the ASO to one of the totems distributed in the ancient city (see Fig. 1), an augmented reality system is started. A large see-through screen integrated into the totems superimposes on the reality some virtual objects recreating the ancient coast line. By changing the orientation of the ASO on the base, screen displays how the quarter looked like in the Roman era. In this case, the AR system is controlled by the expert guides, so the communication with the visitors is still managed by them.

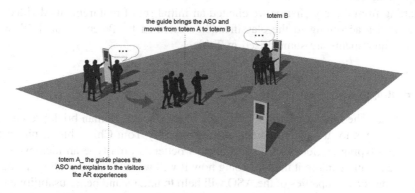

Fig. 1. A guide leads visitors through a CH site and uses an ASO to improve the explanations

Scenario 2 – Augmented Personal Visit. Visitors of the ruins of a Roman city enter the archaeological park and are provided at the entrance with an ASO in the form of an ancient Roman brick that has an integrated display. Visitors receive a brief explanation about how to use an ASO in the same way they do with a common audio guide. Then, they are encouraged to explore the site and pay attention to the bases allocated in strategic places. When a visitor puts the ASO on a base, the system recognizes the position and the orientation view, the display gets alive and shows through augmented reality the recreation of a target building. Moreover, the visitor can rotate the object and put it again on the base. The scene changes and the screen will show the recreation of that building in a different historical era. Moreover, visitors can enter well-preserved rooms where they can admire remains of ancient mosaics (Fig. 2).

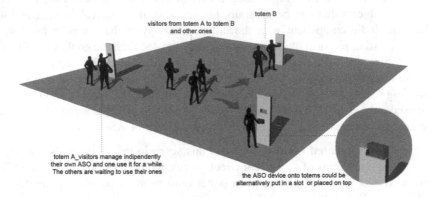

Fig. 2. Visitors exploring a CH site using an ASO

Besides an ASO's base there are coins' reproductions of different eras. After leaning the brick, they can pick a coin a put it in front of the ASO. It recognizes the exact coin and shows the reconstruction of the mosaic and the decoration of the corresponding era.

Starting from these scenarios we elicited an initial set of requirements divided into five categories according to the classification described by Preece et al. [10]. More relevant requirements are summarised in Table 1.

3.2   Prototype

In order to test the initial findings, a prototype of the ancient Roman brick presented in the second scenario. It was built since as suggested by Tom Chi in his inspiring talk "Rapid Prototyping at Google X"[8], it is always better to prototype an idea even with limited means and explore it than guessing how it will work. Also recreating the actual shape and physical properties of the ASO will help to understand better usability issues, following an experience prototyping approach [27]. Therefore, we built the brick in a fast and chip way using components that can be far from the final product but that can be combined quickly in order to have an immediate feedback.

To make the brick, we put together a Samsung Galaxy S3 running Android 4.2, an Arduino 1, a NFC reader, a tiny metal cable and a simple cardboard box. Some objects were put inside to make the brick heavy convincing.

---

[8] goo.gl/PXpLbF.

Table 1. ASO requirements

Requirements	Rationale
Functional requirements	
The system provides visitors with AR functionalities based on image recognition and localization	Augmented reality allows visitors to access to digital content without loosing the reality. AR techniques should be implemented taking into account different settings (i.e. indoor, outdoor). In the scenarios the ASOs use outdoor a technique based on recognition and indoor an image recognition technique
Different ways to interact should be implemented based on the specific affordance of the ASO and its base	The used devices have specific shapes suggesting how to interact with them. For example, in the second scenario the ASO is in a form of a brick and its base entails the usage position and the view orientation. Moreover, visitors can explore different AR experiences by changing the vertical rotation of the brick
Environmental and contextual requirements	
In CH sites some explicit areas or spots will be signalled to make users aware that can use the ASO	The AR system does not require a continuous users' attention in order to allow visitors to focus mainly on the exhibit. In the scenarios specific bases are placed to allow them to exploit the AR just when it is really needed
The environment set can be crowed	Groups of people can be small as just two or large as 20. In the first scenario the visitors are a numerous group of people led by a touristic guide while in the second some visitors explore individually the site
The visit can be outdoor and/or indoor	An archaeological site as an exhibit can have both outdoor and indoor area. Our scenarios are set in an outdoor archaeological park but some indoor areas are present (i.e. rooms of a temple)
Users may receive training before using the ASO	Exactly as it happens with audio guide, in the second scenario operators briefly explain the way to use the ASO. This is particularly useful for people not familiar with the used technology
The technological devices can be integrated in portable and contextual objects	The interviewees stated that during a visit reproductions of small ancient objects are often present to stimulate the visitors interest. The ASOs can be integrated in objects related with the CH site. In the first scenario, a lamp used to activate the AR system is carried by the touristic guide. In the second, an ASO in form of roman brick is given to each visitor by a CH operator at the entrance

(Continued)

Table 1. (*Continued*)

Requirements	Rationale
Data requirements	
The system must be able to manage different media: image, video, holograms, audio, 3D models …	The digital content that can be superimposed to the reality is heterogeneous. As reported in the *related work* there are AR systems for CH sites providing users with a plethora of media: from simple text to full-immersion 3D experiences
Data must be accurate and updated frequently	As shown in the scenarios, an ASO can recreate digitally different eras of abuilding. To make such recreation realistic it is necessary to be accurate in positioning the virtual elements on the ruins and in giving the right dimensions
User profiles	
CH guides and curators are willing to use some technological devices as far as they are not invasive	All of these requirements come from the interviews conducted with experts and the filed study
Most of the users is familiar with smartphones. The grand part of the youngest users is familiar with AR and VR technologies	
The range of the instruction level varies between primary school to postgraduates	
Most of the current users are in the range of 30 to 50 and 10–16 years	
Most visitors are occasional users	
Usability requirements	
The user interface should be effective: it should provide a simple management of users mistakes	Visitors should focus only into the CH experience without caring about the technology. Therefore, it is paramount to reduce the number of possible unintentional user mistakes
The ASO should be easy to use and should require little training effort	As we learnt from the interviews, users do not visit the same CH site frequently and do not have the opportunity to learn a complex system. In the second scenario, CH operators give only a brief explanation of the ASO and let visitors to experiment it
The object must support mobility.	As described by the scenarios, the visitors walk to explore the site and interact with the ASO standing and moving from a base to another one. Therefore, mobility is an important component to consider in the interaction design

Fig. 3. The early prototype of an ASO

Then, we build a support base with another box and a NFC label. Figure 3 shows the final result.

The mobile phone results really useful because integrates several elements, such as camera, GPS, movement sensors, gyroscope, permanent internet connection all elements necessary to build the system.

The mobile phone is used to control the ASO and to realize the augmented reality. Arduino is programmed to link the NFC reader to the phone. Finally, the metal cable is simply an extension of the NFC antenna and allows to read an NFC label nearby its bobbin (Fig. 4).

From the software point of view, we developed a real versatile mobile application. It can manage different augmented reality techniques based on image recognition or positioning. It is based on the AR framework Wikitude[9] that allows to easily manage videos, images and sounds and Vuforia[10] combined with Unity[11] that better manages 3D objects and animations. In this way, we are ready to provide a plethora of AR experiences. The assembled box looks like a lifeless object but when it is placed on a NFC label, a triggered event activates the screen and the mobile application selects the AR experience associated to that label. In this way, it is possible to associate different AR techniques and behaviours to each NFC label.

Two interaction modality were implemented: (1) Rotation movements, (2) item recognition.

---

[9] www.wikitude.com.

[10] developer.vuforia.com.

[11] unity3d.com.

Fig. 4. The Roman brick hardware scheme

Rotation Movements. Users can select a different AR experience by rotating the box and placing it again on the base. For example, let's suppose we are in front of an ancient Greek-Roman temple. We place our box on the base and we see through the screen how the temple appears set in the Greek period. We roll the box rightward making the scene change to the Roman period. By rolling it again leftward we go back to the previous scene. Removing the box from the base for a couple of seconds will make it apparently lifeless again. Figure 5 shows how the cardboard box works.

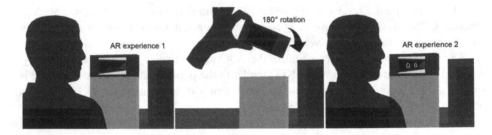

Fig. 5. Interaction based on rotation movements

Item Recognition. Users locate the ASO on the base, then, in order to select the experience, they put in front of the camera a coin to be recognized. To each coin a different AR experience is connected. Figure 6 shows a user experimenting this kind of interaction.

In the next section we report a usability evaluation and user experience linked to the usage of the prototype.

3.3 Evaluation

A usability pilot study was carried out to understand the potential of the ASO prototype. The goal of the study was to evaluate the quality of the interaction in terms of ease to use and user satisfaction. Ten users were asked to use and evaluate the brick. The group is formed by IT students and researchers, all of them have at least an idea of

Fig. 6. Interaction based on item recognition

what an AR system is. This kind of background is typical for *digital native* users and moreover we want the testers focus on the whole experience rather than the techno-logical newness. To evaluate the potential effectiveness and usefulness of the appli-cation, a "think-aloud" technique [8] was used. The "think-aloud" technique allows the observer to explore possible usability problems and to detect them in the precise moment they arise. Moreover, users were photographed and recorded by a video camera to allow the research team to review the experiment.

We asked the users to perform a specific task with the current prototype and discuss any possible suggestion to improve it. We focused on two aspects of the interface:

1. The usability: we checked whether the layout is effective to guide users in accomplishing their tasks. The interface must not confuse users or make them feel awkward.
2. The capability to navigate the different AR experiences: we needed to determine the best way to structure the navigation in order to avoid users getting lost during the interaction.

3.3.1 Participants Profile

The users were asked to fill out a questionnaire about their profile and their experience with CH sites. They had to answer and give a motivation to questions like how many times they go to a CH site in a year; if they were satisfied about the experience they are provided; what they need to improve their visit experience. Table 2 reports some of the answers to the questionnaire.

Mainly the users age is between 25–35 and just three can be consider expert of AR. Based on the questionnaire answers we score with 3 an expert user, with 2 an advanced user, with 1 a user with basic knowledge, and 0 those without any knowledge about such technology. The majority of our users (6) visit a museum or an archaeological place just one time a year. They do not feel attracted to visit CH sites of their own city but usually visit when travelling. Anyway all the testers, even those who visit frequently a museum, are never full satisfied of their visit. The main reasons they exposed were:

(1) Users feel the necessity to access to more information in order to understand art works or ancient and far places. They feel their background is usually not enough to have a rewarding experience with the exhibition. They also consider that the

Table 2. User profile questionnaire

ID	Age	Expert (min 0–max 3)	Visit frequency	Satisfied with current experiences (min 0–max 3)
1	25–35	2	Monthly	1
2	18–25	1	Annually	2
3	36–50	1	Annually	1
4	25–35	1	Annually	2
5	25–35	1	Monthly	1
6	25–35	3	Annually	1
7	25–35	3	Annually	2
8	25–35	1	Annually	2
9	25–35	1	Weekly	2
10	36–50	3	Monthly	1

information provided to them should be personalized on the basis of their own characteristics (i.e. language, cultural background, interests)

(2) Often the visit consists only in looking the exhibition and they would prefer to touch objects and have a more interactive experience.

(3) They cultural aspects are important for them but they will not spend some hours of their free time just to learn. They would like more fun activities to make the visit more enjoyable.

3.3.2 The Tasks

During the first part of the study, users received a short presentation about the prototype and were introduced to a scenario: a visit to an exhibition of ancient objects. Then they were left free to touch and get used to the prototype. This part lasted around 10 min.

After that, participants were left free to explore the exhibition and to use the ASO. During the visit they were asked to "think aloud". At the end of the activity they were asked to fill out a SUS questionnaire [9]. The SUS questionnaire is a reliable, low-cost usability scale suitable for an initial assessment of a system. Introduced in 1986, it is still broadly used in early usability experiments like the one reported in this paper. Indeed, the SUS questionnaire is considered reliable with large samples of users and also with very small ones [11].

In addition to the questionnaire, the observer interviewed them on some aspects he noticed during the visit. This part of the session took around 10–15 min.

3.3.3 The Exhibition

We simulated an archaeological exhibition with replicas of ancient objects set in a big room prepared for the experiment. Each object represents a different culture connected to the Spanish history including a small bronze board showing a high-relief of Minerva, roman coins, a pre-Columbian rainstick from Peru, a military hat of the 1900s and a completely virtual 3D sculpture representing a stone lion. Figure 7 shows participants interacting with the objects of the exhibition through the ASO.

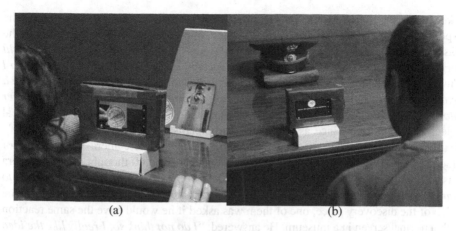

Fig. 7. Users interacting with an ASO during the simulated exhibition

Each object has one or more AR experiences associated to it. To access to each experience, participants had to interact with the ASO. In some cases, they had to rotate the ASO as shown in Fig. 5. For example, the rainstick has three experiences; the first experience is the reproduction of its sound; by rotating the ASO shows some evocative images of musicians in traditional costumes; by rotating again a short video shows the discovery location. In an other case, the users have to put a coin in front of the camera in order to select the experience. Figure 7(a) shows a tester using the coins. Anyway, anytime the ASO is positioned on a base, it gives hints on the kind of interaction in form of a splash screen, as shown in Fig. 7(b), and icons placed on the display borders.

3.3.4 Results

According to the SUS data, participants were satisfied with the experience (see Table 3) The score system in the SUS survey ranges from 0 to 100 points. There are 10 question items, SUS scales all values from 0 to 4. Odd-numbered items are scored by subtracting one from the user response. For example, if a user scores an item with five, the SUS score will be 4. Even-numbered items are calculated by subtracting the user response from 5. For example, if the user scores an item with 1, the SUS score will be 4. The final score of the SUS system ranges between 0 and 100. Therefore, it is necessary to multiply the average of the users' scores by 2.5. For example, an average score of 40 multiplied by 2.5 gives 100.

In [11] a threshold of 69 is considered valid to demonstrate the usability of a system. In our case the average score given by the users is 83.5 which is above the threshold so the ASO could be considered usable. Moreover, items 4 and 10 provide some insights also about the learnability dimension. The testers assigned to item 4 an average score of 3.2 on 4 and to item 10 a 3.3 on 4. Also in this case the learnability perception is pretty high. It is worth to remember that participants were introduced to the ASO by a researcher in the same way a museum operator would introduce an audio guide device to the visitors.

Since the SUS system is not diagnostic and can just measure the usability perception, we observed users during the experiment and, after they filled the questionnaire, we asked them for more specific information. Most of them expressed they valued the experience for a variety of reasons. For example, one of them compared the ASO to the classic museum audio guide: "*I like to visit museums and often I do not have the right background to understand a kind of art or a specific historic object. For such reason I always use an audio guide when it is available. I see that using a AR system I can have a better experience than an audio guide because I can access to a quicker and easier information*". Most of them liked the idea of watching video animations with the real object as background, since as one of the participants said "*This is really evocative*". A user watching a video showing a stream captured by a camera in the ruins of Machu-Picchu (where the rainstick was supposed to be found) thought that the camera was truly alive: "*It's like having an open window to the external world, I feel linked to that place through this object*". Since all the participants were interested in watching the video of the discovery place, one of them was asked if he would have the same reaction with a normal screen in a museum. He answered: "*I do not think so, I really like the idea to hold this object and see through it, I feel it as something more personal*".

All the users stated that they might be encouraged to go to more exhibitions if they could experiment an AR system. "*I go to a museum or to an archeological site just when I travel. I would go to visit the museums of my city if they would give me something new like this*". Other users suggested that the content of the ASO could be updated with a certain frequency. This would encourage them to go back to the exhibit to explore new things.

Five users considered the ASO bases as a limitation since they would use the ASO while walking whenever they want. However, this is exactly what the CH curators want to avoid: *the risk of technology grabbing the spotlight*.

Finally, participants were invited to provide suggestions. Three basic issues were raised:

(1) A more accurate choice of the interface icons. The icons are used to suggest to the users the way to use the ASO and the number of experiences they can access. Such icons made confused some users for a while. Moreover, the testers would appreciate to have some hints directly placed on the top of the ASO's base.
(2) The ASO should include an on-demand tutorial to make visitors feel more confident at the beginning of the visit even without a first explanation.
(3) Participants would like to interact with some of the virtual objects.

4 Lessons Learnt

In this section we give some considerations about designing of an ASO based on the state of the art of AR for CH sites, our cooperation with different CH practitioners and the experience gained during the design of the discussed artifact.

First of all, an ASO should be designed to be nonintrusive and to blend into the context. This is because an ASO is an external tool that can move the visitors' focus on itself. For such reason the designers should consider technologies that can be easily camouflaged into the context. Also specific areas should be strategically predisposed to use such technologies. In this way, the ASOs require the users' attention just there.

Table 3. SUS average score

SUS item	Average score
1. I think that I would like to use this system frequently	3.3
2. I found the system unnecessarily complex	3.5
3. I thought the system was easy to use	3.3
4. I think that I would need the support of a technical person to be able to use this system	3.2
5. I found the various functions in this system were well integrated	3.1
6. I thought there was too much inconsistency in this system	3.3
7. I would imagine that most people would learn to use this system very quickly	3.7
8. I found the system very cumbersome to use	3.5
9. I felt very confident using the system	3.2
10. I needed to learn a lot of things before I could get going with this system	3.3
Total score = 33,4	
SUS Score = 2,5 *33.4 = 83.5	

Moreover, the device should be selected to be comfortable. Wearable technologies should be avoided when bulky and heavy. Another factor to take in mind is that people usually visit a CH site as a group and interact with each other. For such reason, the selected technology should not be a barrier between visitors. Exploiting intensely headphones or requiring users to continuously look through a screen can completely alienate them.

Furthermore, the ASO is aimed at creating personal links between visitors and the exhibit. This experience is possible by exploiting individual devices that can be independently used without any external helps. From a practical point of view, the devices should be affordable for all kinds of CH organizations. Small CH organizations often cannot afford expensive technologies. A good choice is to exploit common smartphones.

To design the visit experience, we have to take in consideration some characteristics. The AR system has to be attractive and enjoyable to foment people to visit a CH site and to give more interest to the exhibit content. Indeed, the new CH visitors are in habit to access to information in new technological ways and it is important to match their inclination. Another aspect to carefully consider is that that the ASO is a didactic device. Visitors should not confuse it with a game. On the other side, we learnt that the system must provide for some recreational activities. Indeed, during long visits, people can lose interest and attention. Recreational activities can be helpful to avoid attention decreases.

Finally, particularly attention must be given to the interaction design of the ASO. Visitors are not just passive users who visualize overlapped images. They must be considered as the centre of the AR system and they can fully interact with it. Moreover, the interaction should be intuitive for each kind of users. The visitors, indeed, are likely *casual users* and should be able to use the device without a long learning process. This can be possible also exploiting the affordance of the ASO's size and shape. The ASO behaviour should be context adaptable, providing different modalities of interactions as well as different kinds of media to match users' needs of the moment. For example, there are situations in which time visitors need to be supported in imagining a reconstruction through a digital reproduction, a specific era through an animation or a far land through sounds, colours or streaming videos. For such reason the kind of media must be selected painstakingly in collaboration with specific experts to achieve the desired goal.

5 Conclusions

In this paper we introduced the definition of ASO as a physical object designed to provide augmented reality experiences to the visitors of cultural heritage sites. The goal of an ASO is to enhance the visitors experience and generate more interest towards CH sites without moving the user focus on the technological device. As part of the study we have developed an instance of the ASO in form of an ancient brick. We followed a participatory design approach to develop an early prototype involving real CH practitioners. Then, we carried out a usability study with potential stakeholders to find potential issues and get first users opinions. On the basis of these evaluation and the experience gained along the entire research process, we have pointed out some findings that we discussed in forms of *lessons learnt*. The lessons can be exploited by AR designers to develop their own instance of an ASO.

In the next future, we plan to effectively integrate an ASO within a real archeological site. In this way, we aim at reaching a wider users base and extracting more quantitative and qualitative data to confirm the preliminary findings and understanding the real feasibility of the application of an ASO in CH site.

Finally, we want to improve the ASO prototype working in very close contact with CH practitioners to prepare more useful content and to develop new functionalities.

Acknowledgement. This work is supported by the project CREAx grant funded by the Spanish Ministry of Economy and Competitiveness (TIN2014-56534-R).

References

1. Prensky, M.: Digital Natives. Digital Immigrants. MCB University Press, Bradford (2001)
2. Bennett, S., Maton, K., Kervin, L.: The 'digital natives' debate: a critical review of the evidence. Br. J. Educ. Technol. **39**(5), 775–786 (2008)
3. Kolb, A.Y., Kolb, D.A.: Experiential learning theory. In: Norbert, M. (ed.) Encyclopedia of the Sciences of Learning, pp. 1215–1219. Springer, New York (2012)
4. Dindler, C., Iversen, O.S., Motivation in the museum - mediating between everyday engagement and cultural heritage. In: Workshop Engaging Artifacts in Cultural Heritage, The Nordes Conference, Oslo, Norway, August 2009
5. Haugstvedt, A.C., Krogstie, J.: Mobile augmented reality for cultural heritage: a technology acceptance study. In: 2012 IEEE International Symposium on Mixed and Augmented Reality (ISMAR), Atlanta, GA, pp. 247–255 (2012)

6. Ardito, C., Costabile, M.F., Lanzilotti, R.: Enhancing user experience while gaming in archaeological parks with cellular phones. In: Proceedings of the 8th International Conference on Interaction Design and Children, 3–5 June 2009, Como, Italy (2009)
7. Pierroux, P., et al.: MUSTEL: framing the design of technology-enhanced learning activities for museum visitors. In: International Cultural Heritage Informatics Meeting - ICHIM 2007: Proceedings, Archives and Museum Informatics (2007)
8. Lewis, C.H.: Using the "Thinking Aloud" method in cognitive interface design. Technical report, IBM, RC-9265 (1982)
9. Brooke, J.: SUS - a quick and dirty usability scale. Usability Eval. Ind. **189**(194), 4–7 (1996)
10. Preece, J., Sharp, H., Rogers, Y.: Interaction Design: Beyond Human-Computer Interaction. Wiley, Hoboken (2015)
11. Sauro, J.: A Practical Guide to the System Usability Scale: Background, Benchmarks, and Best Practices. Measuring Usability LLC, Denver (2011)
12. LifePlus. lifeplus.miralab.unige.ch/html/home.htm. Accessed 7 Apr 2016
13. ARCHEOGUIDE. cordis.europa.eu/projects/rcn/60831_en.html. Accessed 7 Apr 2016
14. ArtSense. www.artsense.eu/project-overview/. Accessed 7 Apr 2016
15. Brogni, B.A., Avizzano, C.A., Evangelista, C., Bergamasco, M.: Technological approach for cultural heritage: augmented reality. In: 8th IEEE International Workshop on Robot and Human Interaction, 1999, RO-MAN 1999, Pisa, pp. 206–212 (1999)
16. Vanoni, D., Seracini, M., Kuester, F.: ARtifact: tablet-based augmented reality for interactive analysis of cultural artifacts. In: 2012 IEEE International Symposium on Multimedia (ISM), Irvine, CA, pp. 44–49 (2012)
17. van der Vaart, M., Damala A.: Through the loupe: visitor engagement with a primarily text-based handheld AR application. In: Conference: Digital Heritage International Congress 2015, At Granada (2015)
18. Pedersen, I.: Radiating centers: augmented reality and human- centric designs. In: IEEE International Symposium on Mixed and Augmented Reality (ISMAR), Orlando, Florida, 19–23 October 2009
19. Damala, A., Stojanovic, N.: Tailoring the Adaptive Augmented Reality (A2R) museum visit: identifying cultural heritage professionals' motivations and needs. In: 2012 IEEE International Symposium on Mixed and Augmented Reality (ISMAR-AMH), Atlanta, GA, USA, pp. 71–80 (2012)
20. Zaibon, S.B., Pendit, U.C., Abu Bakar, J.A.: User requirements on mobile AR for cultural heritage site towards enjoyable informal learning. In: 2015 Asia Pacific Conference on Multimedia and Broadcasting (APMediaCast), Kuta, pp. 1–7 (2015)
21. Brancati, N., Caggianese, G., Pietro, G.D., Frucci, M., Gallo, L., Neroni, P.: Usability evaluation of a wearable augmented reality system for the enjoyment of the cultural heritage. In: 2015 11th International Conference on Signal-Image Technology and Internet-Based Systems (SITIS), Bangkok, Thailand, pp. 768–774 (2015)
22. Hein, H.S.: The Museum in Transition: A Philosophical Perspective. Smithsonian Institution, Washington, DC (2014)
23. Gibson, J.J.: The Ecological Approach to Visual Perception. Houghton Mifflin, Boston (1979)
24. Bødker, S.: Scenarios in user-centred design—setting the stage for reflection and action. Interact. Comput. **13**(1), 61–75 (2000)
25. Diaz, P., Bellucci, A., Aedo, I.: Enabling social interaction in the museum through the social display environment. Digit. Herit. **2015**, 345–348 (2007)
26. Csikszentmihalyi, M., Hermanson, K.: Intrinsic motivation in museums: Why does one want to learn? In: Falk, J.H., Dierking, L.D. (eds.) Public Institutions for Personal Learning, pp. 67–77. American Association of Museums, Washington, DC (1995)

27. Buchenau, M., Suri, J.F.: Experience prototyping. In: 3rd Conference on Designing Interactive Systems: Processes, Practices, Methods, and Techniques, pp. 424–433. ACM (2000)
28. Kortuem, G., Kawsar, F., Sundramoorthy, V., Fitton, D.: Smart objects as building blocks for the Internet of things. IEEE Internet Comput. **14**(1), 44–51 (2010)
29. Caggianese, G., Neroni, P., Gallo, L.: Natural interaction and wearable augmented reality for the enjoyment of the cultural heritage in outdoor conditions. In: De Paolis, L.T., Mongelli, A. (eds.) AVR 2014. LNCS, vol. 8853, pp. 267–282. Springer, Heidelberg (2014)

Santo Stefano in Soleto (Lecce, Italy): The Presentation of Heterogeneous Data Using Hybrid Platform

Francesco Gabellone[1]([⊠]), Ivan Ferrari[1], Francesco Giuri[1],
Paola Durante[2], and Sofia Giammarruco[2]

[1] CNR - IBAM (Istituto per i Beni Archeologici e Monumentali del Consiglio
Nazionale delle Ricerche), Via prov.le Monteroni, 73100 Lecce, Italy
{f.gabellone,itlab.giuri}@ibam.cnr.it
[2] In-Cul.Tu.Re Project, Lecce, Italy
itlab.ferrari@ibam.cnr.it, paola.durante15@gmail.com,
sofiagiamm@gmail.com

Abstract. The paper illustrates the results of the research carried out by PON
In-Cul.Tu.Re. Project (INnovation in CULture, TUrism and REstoration) on the
church of Santo Stefano in Soleto (Lecce, Italy). A multidisciplinary study has
been carried out in order to increase the knowledge of the church, through
non-invasive diagnostic tests, and to monitor the state of conservation of the
building. An Augmented Reality virtual tour has been created through the use of
Information and Communications Technologies in order to enhance the church
knowledge and make it more accessible to the public.

Keywords: Virtual archaeology · Hybrid platform · 3D modelling · App ·
Medieval church

1 Introduction

The paper illustrates the results of the research carried out by In-Cul.Tu.Re. Project
(INnovation in CULture, TUrism and REstoration) on the Church of Santo Stefano in
Soleto (Lecce, Italy).

The In-Cul.Tu.Re. Project, winner of the competition announcement Smart Cities
and Communities and Social Innovation (d.d. 84/Ric 02/03/2012), was founded by
Miur (Italian Minister of University and Scientific Research).

The activities of the Project took place for the last three years 2012-2015 in Grecìa
Salentina, an area that comprises twelve municipalities in the province of Lecce (the
Union of Grecìa Salentina), and have been supported by Ibam-Cnr Institute of Lecce,
the Politecnico of Torino "Non Destructive Diagnostic Laboratory", the Mario Boella
High Institute of Torino and CRESCo cooperative. During the course of In-Cul.Tu.Re.,
twelve cases of study have been identified in line with three main aims: to apply
non-destructive and non-invasive diagnostic tests for knowledge and conservation of
cultural heritage; to study energy efficiency of historic buildings; to develop Information and Communication Technologies for enhancement of cultural heritage.

L.T. De Paolis and A. Mongelli (Eds.): AVR 2016, Part II, LNCS 9769, pp. 205–216, 2016.
DOI: 10.1007/978-3-319-40651-0_16

The results are available on-line and could be downloaded through the www.inculture. eu web platform, an open-data solution having GIS (geographical and information system).

One of the cases of study of In-Cul.Tu.Re. was the Church of S. Stefano in Soleto (see Fig. 1).

Fig. 1. The Church of S. Stefano in Soleto, Lecce, Italy (Ph. by P.Colaiocco for In-Cul.Tu.Re., 2014)

A multidisciplinary study has been carried out in order to increase the knowledge of the Church, through non-invasive diagnostic tests, and to monitor the state of conservation of the building, with the aim to prevent decay problems after latest restoration realized in 2012 by ex-Soprintendenza Beni Storici, Artistici ed Etnoantropologici of the region of Puglia. Moreover, an Augmented Reality virtual tour has been created through the use of Information and Communications Technologies in order to enhance the Church and make it more accessible to the public.

The Church of S. Stefano, with its ornamental and iconographic scheme, represents one of the most significant examples of late Gothic painting in the region of Puglia. It is situated in the historical centre of Soleto, an important Greek Byzantine cultural and religious site from XIII to XVI century. The Church was consecrated to S. Stefano and S.Sofia and probably built before 1385 by Raimondello del Balzo Orsini, who was one of the most important feudatories of the Naples kingdom. A sequence of pictorial cycles covers completely the walls of the building. The iconographic scheme is coherent with a homogeneous project, but the executive phases are different and separated.

The bibliographic research and the study of archives allowed to create the iconographic interpretation diagrams, in which the different theories about pictorial cycles of the Church are detailed (see Fig. 2).

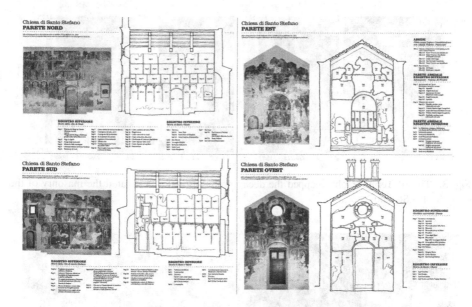

Fig. 2. The iconographic interpretation diagrams.

Non-invasive diagnostic tests were carried out in order to monitor the conservation conditions, to prevent decay problems (through IR Termography) and to characterize the pigments employed in mural paintings (through Portable Micro X-Ray Fluorescence Analysis).

Passive IR Termography, carried out by the Politecnico of Torino "Non Destructive Diagnostic Laboratory", was useful to map the degradation phenomena, to investigate the masonry and the historical stratification of the building. The researchers planned three surveys in a year, in different seasons (Spring 2013, Autumn 2013, Late Summer), hours (early afternoon, evening and midday) and climatic conditions (sunny, after rains).

They investigated the presence of rising damp and infiltrations, responsible for the past partial paintings loss. The first survey revealed the presence of thermal anomaly induced by rising damp that wasn't confirmed by next surveys (see Fig. 3).

In addition to this, it has also been possible to study the weaving of the masonry, identifying some walled up windows and the juxtaposition of different materials attributed to the several restoration works done over the time.

Thanks to an investigation carried out by Ibam-Cnr Institute of Lecce, the portable Micro X-Ray Fluorescence technique (see Fig. 4), it has been possible to extend the pigment characterization also to the western wall and to the upper parts of the northern and southern partitions, whose pictorial cycles had never been analysed by any

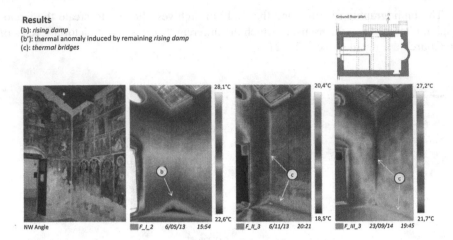

Results
(b): *rising damp*
(b'): thermal anomaly induced by remaining *rising damp*
(c): *thermal bridges*

Fig. 3. The IR Termography mapped the decay problems and investigated the masonry of the Church of S.Stefano.

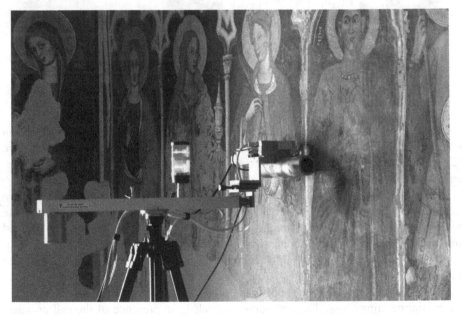

Fig. 4. The portable Micro X-Ray Fluorescence testing. (Color figure online)

diagnostic programs realized before the restoration. The pigments and the possible blends used for the main colour fields (blue, red, yellow, green, white, black and fleshy pink) have been found in nearly 70 measuring points.

The results identified pigments usually employed in frescos such as red and yellow ochre, green earth but also pigments less common in this technique such as cinnabar, azurite, etc. The study need to be improved by the use of diagnostic tests complementary to Micro-XRF.

Moreover, an Augmented Reality virtual tour has been created through the use of Information and Communications Technologies in order to enhance the Church and make it more accessible to the public.

To develop the platform of AR virtual tour for both mobile and remote devices, Ibam-Cnr IT-Lab researchers first realized the Church 3D model employing laser scanning relief, digital photogrammetry and high resolution paintings mapping. The 3D model was exploited as a support for information about paintings iconographic analysis and techniques, virtual restoration and for the results of the latest diagnostic surveys. This useful tool for the Church protection and conservation allows an interactive, immediate and efficient tour and approaches in an easy way the general public to topics which are often for experts only (Fig. 5).

Fig. 5. Screenshot of some available contents.

2 An Hybrid Platform

The virtual archaeology aims to give to the public the results of interpretation for monuments and artwork whose appearance has been damaged or compromised, a goal pursued through a systematic study, which must be traceable in its evolution and possibly must be transparent and intelligible. In this study, all the information gained in the different disciplines of archaeological and historical research converge in a "knowledge model" that can be identified as a "synthesis" of the collected data. As often happens, the reconstructive study or the digital presentation of an ancient monument is strongly affected by information gaps, such as the misspelling of the sources, the wrong translation or worse by subjective interpretations that can drastically affect the final result, leading to reconstructions and interpretations many time very different from each other. The main objective that we intend to always pursue, therefore, is the development of reconstructive studies through a strict philological path, highlighting the results achieved with the whole path from which the proposed reconstruction starts. All data collected are generally available individually on specific publications, in scientific paper form, generally too complex and detailed for the visitor who wishes to start a journey of knowledge on that cultural object. Starting from this premises, in the In-Cul.Tu.Re. project we have been developed digital output intended to be used from smartphones, focused on logics of efficient on-site use ad on-site experience, through the use of technologies mainly based on Augmented Reality (AR). These technologies allow the creation of an overlap between the actual experience and virtual information elements (media information, geo-data, analytical data, historical, archaeometric, etc.) In an environment where the media elements that "increase" the information on the reality can be added and viewed via devices, such as the latest generation of mobile phones (Fig. 6).

Fig. 6. User experience on iPad device. In evidence the different point of view.

As known, there are different approaches to use AR technologies. The most classic way provides a simple superposition of information directly over the object displayed on portable device. In recent graphics libraries implementations, you can add a simplified three-dimensional models that help the understanding of archaeological structures, or contexts of cultural and tourist interest, directly over the real site. The use of these libraries, however, is strongly influenced by the computational limitations on different devices, effectively compromising the enjoyment on many poorly performing equipments. Another possible limitation concerns the realism of the represented scenes, which for the reasons described above, do not allow to observe the complex 3D objects with its realistic textures. A solution called 3DHOP recently experienced by ISTI CNR of Pisa in collaboration with our laboratory (CNR IBAM ITLab), developed only for iOS, has allowed to represent with high quality rendering of the Hypogeum Palmieri in Lecce, but with a navigation only on fixed path (rails). One solution to this limit is given by an AR hybrid mode, where ultra-realistic three-dimensional reconstructions are mixed in spherical high resolution VR panoramas. In this process special attention is given to lighting the scene and to different set-up that re-creates the same lighting conditions of the actual site, to produce a convincing result perfectly superimposed on the real site. This process allows to view several monuments in their original context, but also to enjoy a better and efficient management of the reconstructions even in complex environmental conditions. A emblematic case, unfortunately very common, is represented by the reconstructions where the adoption of a simplified 3D model, without shadows, radiosity and low-resolution textures would result in a poor integration and a qualitatively acceptable results. Regarding the church of Santo Stefano in Soleto we have been used technologies that could be called semi-AR, where the basis of the navigation is a three-dimensional model in which are "hooked" heterogeneous contents, not simply the usual photographic restitution of the status quo. The utility of this approach has elements of interest because, through a panorama based on a 3D model, you can explore the church from unusual perspectives, very difficult to reproduce in reality. Another useful element is the easy overlapping of scenes where the same model is represented with different or modified textures, or even with architectural elements added or subtracted to the original model (Fig. 7).

Fig. 7. 3D model of church.

In general this technique is useful for the effective control of environmental impact, since its "direct" vision from a real point of view, allows to easily evaluate any volumetric disproportions, to control the actual spatial contribution and its relationship to the whole. Certainly the use of easy and portable technologies, like spherical VR panoramas based on 3D scenes, are an effective solution for small architectural spaces such as St. Stefano church. The use of a 3D model explorable in real time would not add significant functionality, but, on the contrary, it would increase the complexity of the platform, thus decreasing the usability. The architectural space, based on a single nave, is very simple and small, consequently two or three points of view cover all the space (Fig. 8).

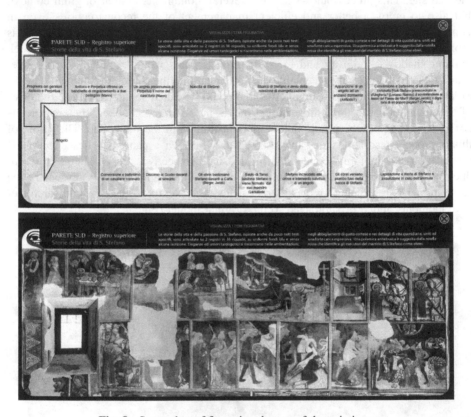

Fig. 8. Screenshot of figurative themes of the paintings.

3   Multiple Contents Accessible from the Platform

The contents accessible from the platform concern mainly the figurative themes of the paintings, but the most original aspect is definitely related to read the archaeometric data within the virtual environment. Many scientific information, from IR, XRF and microscope observations, can be certainly defined as out of "range of visible" and need suitable tools for their correct interpretation and visualization. These data are generally available within specialist technical reports and are not published for the general user, the so called "general public". For this reason has been developed the idea to place these information within a virtual platform able to make "visible the invisible", to look beyond the surface of the object, to reveal the presence of cavities, hidden object, to observe the behavior of materials under the temperature variation, highlighting cracks or plaster detachments, or to emphasize and display various types of deterioration (Fig. 9).

Fig. 9. Spherical panoramas with IR analysis (left) perfectly matched over visible colors. (Color figure online)

With the creation of a three-dimensional model, used for the generation of spherical panoramas, it was possible to obtain a perfect projection of the textures generated from the IR analysis on the inner walls of the church. This approach has solved the problems arising from the resolution of the single IR frame and lens distortion of images captured in different measurement campaigns and on different points of view.

The result is a reading, in a fading transition, of the visible color, with the possibility of comparison between the two different stages (Real-IR). An application conceived on this way immediately transfer scientific and technical information to users not prepared to read archaeometric data. We propose a "branched" reading, in which it is consulted only what you really matters. This visiting system combines the historical and humanistic knowledge with the technical and scientific disciplines: the object, as values container, is analyzed in its mineralogical, petrographic, chemical and physical components, but also in its historical and formal features related with the ancient context. The virtual space accelerates and enhances cognitive performance. It is capable of generating extremely effective learning processes, easy to use and understand. These systems improves understanding of cultural works and take advantage of the interdisciplinary contributions from several researchers, who in different ways contribute to trace the historical, artistic and archaeometrical values (Fig. 10).

The technology is an important tool, especially to represent a complex and diachronic vision of the monument. It allows to elaborate articulated script on multi-platform languages, such as JavaScript, which provide advanced solutions, but require adequate skills in programming. Despite this, the creativity and the ability to

Fig. 10. a-b: IR and XRF analysis accessible on demand.

solve problems suggest some interesting answers, such as the representation of the phases before and after the restoration of some paintings present on the walls of the church. The solution used is based on a open jQuery library. The result implemented in this enjoyment platform has allowed to obtain an interactive comparison that returns in an even more "transparent" way the restoration work. It makes the user aware of the great work of figurative recovery, that the purely conservative operation would seem overlook. The main output of the project is an HTML5 application compatible with PC and smartphone, with gyroscope function enabled on-site. This architecture allows future developments with significant enrichment of all types of information necessary to the understanding of the monument features and its transformations over the time (Figs. 11 and 12).

Fig. 11. Example of digital restoration of paintings. (thanks to Maida Leo, Fine Arts academy of Lecce)

Fig. 12. Synoptic view of church

References

1. Gabellone, F.: Integrated technologies for museum communication and interactive apps in the PON DiCet project. In: De Paolis, L.T., Mongelli, A. (eds.) AVR 2015. LNCS, vol. 9254, pp. 3–16. Springer, Heidelberg (2015)
2. Malomo, L., Banterle, F., Pingi, P., Gabellone, F., Scopigno, R.: VirtualTour: a system for exploring cultural heritage sites in an immersive way. In: Proceeding of 2015 Digital Heritage International Congress, vol. 1, pp. 309–312, September 2015
3. Berger, M., Jacob, A.: La Chiesa di S. Stefano a Soleto, Argo Editrice
4. Zacchino, V., Berger, M.: Paesi e figure del vecchio Salento, vol. secondo. Congedo editore, Galatina (1980)

5. Ortese, S.: Pittura tardogotica nel Salento, Galatina (2014)
6. Ortese, S.: Sequenza dei lavori in Santo Stefano a Soleto. In: Dal giglio all'orso: i principi D'Angiò e Orsini del Balzo nel Salento, A. Cassiano, B. Vetere, Galatina (Lecce) (2006)
7. Potenziani, M., Callieri, M., Dellepiane, M., Corsini, M., Ponchio, F., Scopigno, R.: Computers & Graphics, vol. 52, pp. 129–141, November 2015. ISSN: 0097-8493

Automatic Analysis of Eye-Tracking Data for Augmented Reality Applications: A Prospective Outlook

Simona Naspetti[1], Roberto Pierdicca[2(✉)], Serena Mandolesi[1], Marina Paolanti[2], Emanuele Frontoni[2], and Raffaele Zanoli[3]

[1] Department of Materials, Environmental Sciences and Urban Planning, Università Politecnica delle Marche, Via Brecce Bianche 12, 60131 Ancona, Italy
{naspetti,mandolesi}@agrecon.univpm.it
[2] Department of Information Engineering, Università Politecnica delle Marche, Via Brecce Bianche 12, 60131 Ancona, Italy
{r.pierdicca,m.paolanti}@pm.univpm.it, e.frontoni@univpm.it
[3] Department of Agricultural, Food and Environmental Sciences, Università Politecnica delle Marche, Via Brecce Bianche 12, 60131 Ancona, Italy
zanoli@agrecon.univpm.it

Abstract. Eye-tracking technology is becoming easier and cheaper to use, resulting in its increasing application to numerous fields of research. Recent years have seen rapid developments in this area. In light of the foregoing, in the context of Cultural Heritage (CH), the definition of a modern approach to understand how individuals perceive art is challenging. Despite the art perception is highly subjective and variable according to knowledge and experience, more recently, several scientific study and enterprises started to quantify how subjects observe art by the application of the eye-tracking technology. The aim of this study was to understand the visual behaviour of subjects looking at paintings, using eye-tracking technology, in order to define a protocol for optimizing an existing Augmented Reality (AR) application that allows the visualization of digital contents through a display. The stimuli used are three famous paintings preserved at the National Gallery of Marche (Urbino, Marche Region, Italy). We applied eye-tracking to have a deeper understanding of people visual activities in front of these paintings and to analyse how digital contents eventually influence their behaviour. The description of the applied procedure and the preliminary results are presented.

Keywords: Augmented Reality · Museums · Eye-tracking · Behavioural analysis · Mobile

1 Introduction

Eye-tracking is a technique used to determine gaze direction of eyes and also the sequence in which the eyes are moved at a given time. It is very useful for researchers, who try to understand movements of the eyes while a person is

© Springer International Publishing Switzerland 2016
L.T. De Paolis and A. Mongelli (Eds.): AVR 2016, Part II, LNCS 9769, pp. 217–230, 2016.
DOI: 10.1007/978-3-319-40651-0_17

involved in different activities. During the years, several techniques were developed for measuring eye-movements and these usually involve the use of a device commonly known as an eye-tracker. It generally consists of a camera and associated electronic components to produce data representing gaze positions (or "gaze data"). This gaze data can be used to determine where the individual is looking, which can be described in terms of fixations (a steady gaze for a predetermined period of time) and saccades (movement of the gaze between two points).

The relation between eye-movements and internal brain processes (thinking, cognition, etc.) is known for a long time. For this reason, eye gaze data have been used in many fields such as neurology, ophthalmology, psychology, and related areas to study oculomotor characteristics and abnormalities, and their relation to mental states and cognition. There are some applications, still confined to controlled environment, for research in advertising and marketing, as well as in human factors engineering to evaluate web sites and computer interfaces.

This paper is concerned with the usability of eye-tracking for a better understanding of a work of art. In fact, design and implementation of digital experiences cannot be separated from the core component of the system: humans. This is true for almost every domain, even more when we talk about museums. The comprehension of visitor behaviour during their visit can provide needful data for improving the museum exhibition [24].

This might positively affect visitor experience, hence museum appeal. A modern approach to the fruition of art is actually based on a wide and targeted use of technologies [1]. For this reason, a growing number of museums is adopting digital tools as integral part of the exhibition, providing users with new instruments to study in deep art [9,17].

One of these cutting edge technologies is Augmented Reality (AR). It allows the visualization of digital contents through a display, with the same point of view of the user, by superimposing virtual objects on the real scene. It also permits the visualization of virtual objects (e.g. 3D models, audio, text, images) avoiding the use of artefacts (i.e. QR code) to retrieve contents, in addition to an automatic and interactive visualization of Points of Interest (POIs).

In this study, we describe an experiment that used eye-tracking techniques to define a criteria for the selection of focal points for AR applications, for a better understanding of human behaviour. The main contribution of this paper is to provide useful information, analysing the movement of the eyes, in order to define the baseline towards a total User Centered Design for AR applications, forecasting the display of art contents, based on masterpiece features, technological constrains and user typology. The number of AR applications is significantly increasing, also for Digital Cultural Heritage (DCH) purposes. The reason of this increment is manifold; first of all, AR is simple to use and intuitive. Technology is mature and, up to now, there are several available tools for a cross-platform development. Markerless tracking systems (predominantly based on image matching algorithms) are robust and stable, even when lighting conditions are not optimal. Besides, thanks to the diffusion of smartphones and tablets with high computational capabilities, adoptions of such applications are more widespread. In a form of artwork, markerless AR permits the visualization of virtual objects (e.g. 3D models, audio, text, images) avoiding the use of artefacts (i.e. QR code) to retrieve contents. It works in addition to an automatic and interactive visualization of Points of Interest (POIs). Several researches show the advantages of Mobile AR (MAR) in conveying CH contents [11]. In [18] for example, an application to enhance the experience of visitors in a real case museum scenario was presented. An interactive touchscreen for a detailed visualization of the painting provides the user with a brushstroke-level visualization. The mobile applications are available in the app stores. They offer the Museum customers the possibility to deepen their knowledge of paintings like the "The Ideal City" presented in this paper, with a handy tool. Thanks to the Augmented Reality section, users can frame the artwork and interact with superimposed contents that are a continuum between the painting and the users point of view. Markerless AR is well established, but the following research questions, that triggered this work, have not been completely addressed: (i) which is the best criteria for the selection of contents? (ii) can we identify the user characteristics to personalize contents according to her background? and (iii) is it possible to analyse the most observed areas of the painting, to define attention points for AR applications? Previous work [3] delivered an optimized AR solution, finalized thanks to a classical user test and survey. This first stage allowed to define highlights and weak points of the application, towards the final solution, already published, mainly based on users suggestions. In an attempt to answer the questions mentioned above and given the results of our previous research, we used the eye-tracking to define a criteria for the selection of focal points for AR applications. The preliminary results showed that the proposed methodology for the definition of AR contents, displayed as POIs in artwork applications, is promising. The main objective is to define the baseline towards a total User Centered Design for AR applications, forecasting the display of art contents, based on masterpiece features, technological constraints and user typology.

The paper is organized as follows: Sect. 2 is an overview of the existing approaches in the context of eye-tracking; Sect. 3 gives details on the proposed method for this problem, that is still the core of our work; final section (Sect. 4) describes the results and a discussion over the potentials of this system, followed by conclusions and our future works in this direction (Sect. 6).

2   Related Works

Eye-movements are the expression of the relation between what is observed and its relevance to the interest of viewer and they are an important index of selection. It is well-known that the process of seeing is not simply the reproduction in our brain of external stimuli, but the result of more sensory part connected to individuals' own internal representation [14,20,23]. Several factors contribute to eye resolution: the density of photoreceptors in the retina, the nature of the neural connections between them, and the contrast of the stimulus. The use of eye-trackers allow to record the movements of the eyes. Recent advancements have made them smaller, less inexpensive and invasive. In [5] are used for human computer interaction and they can be mounted directly on the user's head or can be positioned in the work environment. In last applications, eye-trackers are used to select objects on the screen or in a virtual environment, to provide attentional information of a user.

In relation to art the contribution of eye-tracking is quite recent.

For example, in [10] the authors describe statistical regularities in artwork that appear related to low-level processing strategies in human vision, especially for the processing of natural scenes and the variations in these statistics.

In [20] the pattern of fixations of subjects looking at figurative and abstract paintings from different artists and at modified versions is described and several aspects of these art pieces were changed with digital manipulations. The authors found that people look at art depending on the subjects' interests and their artistic appreciation.

Another paper in which are used eye-tracking technique is [16] with the aim to investigate the influence of bottom-up and top-down processes on visual behaviour of subjects, while they observe representational paintings.

The analysis of the exploratory pattern of viewer and selection of salient visual aspects can optimize AR application.

AR was recognised as an emerging technology [12], and the diffusion of smart-phones and tablets with high computational capabilities made it look like easer to have a more widespread adoption of such applications. Recently, the focus of the evaluation on AR application has developed [6]. The first AR software is ARToolKit [13] for putting contents in overlay with the use of the video tracking and a virtual camera in the same point of view of the observer. The AR mobile applications are ARAC Maps [8] (for archeological content) and AR-TagBrowse [7] (for tagging and browsing virtual 3D objects).

A new concept of Adaptive Augmented Reality (A^2R), employed within the context of the creation of an AR guide for the museum visit is proposed in [4]. The main goal is to provide a augmented, unique, museum visiting experience, and to monitor the physiological reactions of the museum visitor. It has an important tool for better understanding the impact on human cognition of learning environments, such as museum and gallery.

3   Methods

3.1   Participants

Forty Italian students and employees at Università Politecnica delle Marche took part in the study. All participants were young adults between the ages of 18 and 56 ($meanage = 27.9$ $S.D. = 7.8$), equally distributed across gender and had normal vision. An additional group of 12 students was recruited for the pre-testing.

3.2   Procedure

The survey included two steps. During the first step, the visual behaviour of subjects using eye-tracking was analysed, in the second step respondents were asked to complete a questionnaire regarding interest and attitudes towards art.

Eye-Tracking. A Tobii Eye-Tracker X2-60 and the Imotions®Attention Tool software (vers. 5.7) were used to record the eye-tracking data. All measurements were performed in a quiet room and under standard illumination conditions. Each participant was seated 60 cm from the eye-tracker and monitor. The digital versions of the paintings were showed in a 23″ monitor, at a resolution of 1920×1080 pixels, preserving the original aspect ratio. Participants were informed that their eye-movements were recorded. The eye-movement indicators, on which the analysis is based, are fixations and saccades. Fixations are eye pauses over a particular of interest averaging about 300 ms. Saccades are rapid eye-movements between fixations. Each trial started with a 9-point calibration pattern. After calibration of the eye-tracker, the study started with an experimental task (Task 1). The first slide included instructions for Task 1 and participants were free to read and proceed to the next slide. Three famous paintings, all preserved at the National Gallery of Marche (Urbino, Marche Region, Italy), were shown in a randomised order: "The Ideal City" (Unknown author 1480–1490), the "Portrait of a Gentlewoman" (Raffaello 1507) and the "Flagellation" (Piero della Francesca 1463–1464) (Fig. 1).

During the exposure, the proportions of each painting were preserved. Participants were asked to look freely at the pictures presented. Since previous literature results on view durations varied a lot, the exposure time of the stimuli was determined during a pre-test. Twelve students, at Università Politecnica delle Marche, with no particular knowledge of art, were asked to observe a faithful reproduction of the picture "The Ideal City" as if they were at the museum. For this test we used the Eye-Glasses mobile eye-tracker. The average time of observation registered was 64 s. Based on pre-test results, each painting was shown to the participants to the main study for maximum 1 min. The pre-test that we performed was also useful to compare the outcomes between using digital image and using the real-size artwork. In fact, even if looking at the real painting would better simulate the real conditions, we noticed the following issues: due to the head movements of the testers and the low resolution of the glasses, we could not achieve a satisfactory precision to properly identify the areas of interest. Consequently, the test was carried out using the digital version of the artworks. After the three pictures sequence, respondents were asked to look again at "The Ideal City" picture (Task 2). This time, six details of the painting were framed in red in the picture, as visible in Fig. 2.

The six-framed details were defined according to the existing AR application for this painting. They include some architectural details that experts considered relevant in this painting: the doves, the vanishing point; the capitals; the landscape in the background; the floor and the geometry that characterize the whole painting.

(a) "The Ideal City" unknown author (1460-1480)

(b) "Portrait of a Gentlewoman"
Raffaello (1507)

(c) "Flagellation" Piero della Francesca
(1463-1464)

Fig. 1. Paintings used for the test.

Fig. 2. "The Ideal City" painting (Task 2) (Color figure online)

Survey. An on-line survey followed the previous tasks. Participants were asked to focus again on "The Ideal City" painting and to rank the six particulars from the most interesting to the least interesting. Then, a set of twenty items was selected to measure participants' interest in art (Table 1). Subjects were asked to express their level of agreement with a 5 Point Likert scale (from "Strongly

Table 1. Interest-in-art scale. R means "reversed scale"

N	Sentences
1	Whenever I see a poster related to art I check it out
2	I read culture and art pages of newspapers
3	I don't like talking about art with my friends (R)
4	I am interested in a branch of art unprofessionally
5	I am not interested in painting exhibition (R)
6	I could stare a long time at a beautiful painting
7	I have a strong appreciation for great architecture
8	I think that individuals who deal with art are more creative
9	I don't like reading book promotions of newspaper supplements
10	We talk and make discussions about art events in my family
11	I believe that I should spare for some money artistic activities
12	When I see a beautiful photograph, I want to obtain information about it
13	I don't like following artistic events on internet (R)
14	I think that art is necessary for individual development
15	I watch carefully when there is news on TV about art
16	I don't like buying books about art (R)
17	I'm passionate about art
18	I like decoring the walls of my room with nice artwork
19	I like making researches about artists and their works on internet
20	I like going to exhibitions with friends experts of art

Disagree" to "Strongly Agree"). This interest-in-art scale included items adapted from three existent scales (by [2,15]). Six questions were added to assess participants' art experience [2]. Socio-demographic questions (gender, age, level of instruction) concluded the survey.

4 Results

Data collected were extracted using the IMotions® Attention Tool software and analysed using STATA vers. 13. IMotions® provides different metrics for each Area Of Interest (AOI): the *TTFF-F* and the *Time spent-F*. The *TTFF-F* represents the time to first fixation or in other words, it identifies which areas of interest the participants at first sight saw; while the Time spent-F provides the time spent in a specific AOI. In general, a short time value of *TTFF-F* indicates that the participant's fixation for that particular AOI started immediately as the image appeared on the screen; while a high time value of *TTFF-F* shows that the fixation achieved late or not started. The *TTFF-F* value is equal to the entire exposure time of the image when the fixation not started.

Fig. 3. Heat map of "The Ideal City" with free-screening (Color figure online)

Figure 3 shows the heat map, for all 40 participants, when they were asked to observe the painting as they were at the museum, according to Task 1. In this figure, the red colour in the central part of the painting shows that this is the most attracting area. Participants' eyes formed a "vertical line" in the middle of the painting where is the Baptistery is located. This vertical line equally divides the painting into two parts. The heat map shows that, in the central area the number of fixations, during the "free-screening", was larger (1398 fixations) than in the rest of the painting (Fig. 3). The *TTFF-F* in this area is 0.5 s, meaning that, as the picture appeared on the screen, participants looked in the middle at first and persistently look in it for quite a long time. The Time spent-F was higher (11.00 s), as compared to other areas. The heat map, when looking at the *TTFF-F* values, also indicate that once participants have looked in the central part of the painting, they move their attention to the nearest areas. The subjects' saccade pattern is defined in Fig. 3 by the sequence of the numbers from 1 to 7. The number of fixations and the Time spent-F decreases from the centre to the external areas of the painting. While, the *TTFF-F* increases from the centre to the external sides of the painting. Subjects were initially attracted by zone number 2 (*TTFF-F* = 6.5 s, *Time spent-F* = 6.1 s and 763 fixations) and, then by zone number 3 (*TTFF-F* = 7.7 s, *Time spent-F* = 7.2 s and 846 fixations), both very close to the dominant area. The more external areas, including the zones 4, 5, 6 and 7, are characterized by a small number of fixations (zone 4: 63 fixations, zone 5: 92 fixations, zone 6: 44 fixations, zone 7: 53 fixations). In order to deepen the investigation, we relate the analysis of AOIs during the free screening (Task 1) with the results of Task 2, when we asked to observe the painting with the 6-framed details of the AR application. In Table 2, relevant data for each AOI as obtained in Task 1 and Task 2 are reported.

Table 2. The six AOIs metrics for Task 1 and Task 2

Metrics	Task 1					
AOI	1	2	3	4	5	6
TTFF (sec)	1.2	6.5	7.7	8.3	10.4	14.3
Time Spent (sec)	6.3	6.8	6.3	2.7	2.9	1.8
Ratio	40/40	40/40	40/40	40/40	40/40	37/40
Revisitors	40/40	40/40	39/30	40/40	36/40	37/37
Fixations	780	843	742	426	441	291
AOI	Task 2					
AOI	1	2	3	4	5	6
TTFF (sec)	3.0	3.5	9.7	16.1	9.0	12.8
Time spent (sec)	7.3	9.1	6.7	5.9	5.2	4.7
Ratio	40/40	40/40	40/40	40/40	40/40	40/40
Revisitors	40/40	40/40	40/40	40/40	39/40	39/40
Fixations	901	1072	847	801	734	617

Results reported in Table 2, show that AOI number 2 collected the highest
number of fixations for both tasks. In this AOI, participants also spent the
majority of time. The number of fixations for AOI 2 is significantly higher respect
to AOIs number 4, 5 and 6 ($p < 0.001$). Results for all the other AOIs, for the two
tasks, differed. During the free screening phase (Task 1) participants essentially
focussed their attention on the central areas of the painting, where they spent
most of the time. During Task 2, when obliged to follow the instructions and to
look at the six red rectangular (Fig. 4), participants show a higher number of
fixations but more balanced among the AOI.

Fig. 4. Heat map of "The Ideal City" with 6 areas of interest (Color figure online)

Results indicate that the attention of participants was higher during Task 2. Both the number of fixations and the time spent increased for each AOI. The number of fixations is significantly higher for all AOI (AOI 1 $p < 0.05$, AOI 2, AOI 3, AOI 4, AOI 5 and AOI 6 $p < 0.001$). Participants spent more time inside each AOI: the increase of time spent is significantly higher for AOI 2 ($p < 0.05$), AOI 4, AOI 5 and AOI 6 ($p < 0.001$). Participants' visual route changed when they were asked to follow the instructions (Task 2). In other words, during the free vision of the painting (Task 1) the heat map shows a wider and opened discover of the painting, later, when the view includes the 6 framed details (Task 2), participants only explored the six framed zone. Comparing the two heat maps, the vertical line in the central part of the free-vision disappears during Task 2 and the time spent on the painting is more distributed across the six-framed particulars. The presence of a vertical line means that, according to the respondents, there are other attractive areas that should be included in the AR application. Two areas of interest generated a high number of fixations: the window above the central door of the Baptistery (337 fixations) and the cross of the Baptistery (136 fixations). It is important to note that the area around the cross of the Baptistery, although it was not immediately watched (TTFF-F = 28.8 s), especially attracted the attention of participants eyes (since the number of fixations was relatively high). The temporal order of AOI (TTFF) also differed in the two tasks. On the other hand, the marginal zones are less interesting for respondents who essentially focussed on the details in the central vertical line and those on areas closed to that. This analysis reduces the areas of interest to 5 zones, all around the Baptistery: the central door, the window and the cross all on the Baptistery, plus AOI 2 and AOI 3 (see Fig. 3 for AOI codes).

5   Discussion

In this study we used eye-tracking to investigate subjects viewing pattern behaviours in AR applied to a single painting ("The Ideal city"). The preliminary results confirm some of the previous findings on art viewing behaviour investigated with eye-tracking. We found that, participants attention fall on the centre of gaze of the painting [20]. In the lack of a human figure, the Baptistery area acts as an attractor [16]. In this area the number of fixations, during both free-screening and with 6-framed areas, was significantly larger than in all the other areas of the painting. The eye-movements vary between free vision and when participants are asked to follow a task, as in [21]. People visual patterns changed as function of the task requirements by focussing their eyes on the 6- framed AR regions, in place of a global searching strategy in the free screening. Furthermore, the task influenced the temporal order of the view.

Experimental tests, depicted in Figs. 3 and 4 demonstrate that our eye-tracking system provides useful input information to design a personalised user experience in AR applications. For these reasons, considering the heat map of Fig. 3, we divided the painting in six equal areas (Fig. 5).

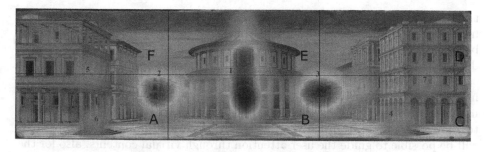

Fig. 5. Heat-maps of paths. Darker colours represent the areas with higher fixation time. (Color figure online)

At a first stage, we analysed all eyes-tracks, calculating a posteriori probabilities for eye presence in an "area of interest" and for transitions between adjacent areas (see Fig. 6).

This representation is a model of the attention scheme that can be incorporated in the AR applications to have a transition probability or to guide the user on a novel AR interaction scheme. Nodes represent "area of interest" with presence probability, darker colours indicated high probabilities. Links represent passages between adjacent areas with transition probability. For example, node B has the higher presence probability of 30 %, while link A–B has the higher

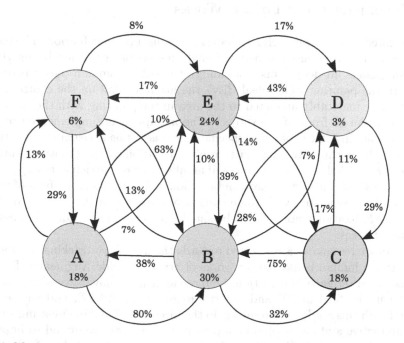

Fig. 6. Markov chain with a posteriori probabilities of a model of the attention scheme over the painting.

transition probability of 80 %. These probabilities can be used to analyse movement trends in front of painting and comparing them with a priori expected behaviour, they can provide insights to improve our application with multimedia content.

The proposed solution opens up new outcomes and possibilities, especially to improve the design and user experience of AR applications. First of all, by knowing in advance the visitors behaviour when looking at a painting, it is possible to know where their attention was focused. In this way, thanks to AR functions, will be possible to guide the user attention through virtual contents, also for the areas with less interest. The use of a visual sensing approach, besides, permits to recognize predefined patterns, based on the gaze tracking of the visitor. This represents a useful tool that allows the museum managers to know which are the details a visitor is interested in. The second important contribution will be the possibility to customize the contents according to the user typology. The adapted content, with predefined visitors' profiles, can make the experience exciting and rewarding, promoting a more tailored learning. By monitoring the interest and engagement of the visitors the organization of multimedia exhibition would be strongly improved. Finally, this methodology represents a reliable way to perform a real User-Centered Design (UC) informed approach, as well as to identify the system requirements, using an interdisciplinary approach that places the CH professionals at the center of the design process.

6   Conclusions and Future Works

We presented a novel approach for analysing AR usability evaluation. The use of eye-tracking has a potential measure of analysing people attitudes during visual processing offers an deeper understanding of possible common patterns of fixations. In the painting "The Ideal City" the attention fall on the central area, subjects were inevitably attracted to the area in the painting with the most relevant particular in front of the subject. The manipulation implemented by the researcher (adding AR squares in specific areas) acted as a visual cue, partially modifying the natural common pattern of exploration of the painting. Further analyses are needed to investigate possible influences of participants experience and interest in art on viewing pattern behaviours. Additionally analysis of physiological data, associated with some statistical analysis on the main indicators (gaze, *TTFF*, fixations, etc.) should be should be performed to identify possible dynamic patterns.

Our future researches are directed towards the use of eye-tracking techniques to investigate human behaviour for works of art, to provide Augmented Reality to users based on gaze information. Our research work have several researches going on in the filed of AR and Smart Environments [19,22], and the results obtained with this study are promising in the direction of making museum spaces more interactive and aware of human presence. Moreover, we intend to improve our eye-tracking system. We will conduct a user evaluation for identify the type of person observe painting: "expert" of art or "non-expert". For this purpose we will use machine learning techniques and many classifiers will be tested and compared, to investigate the application's adaptability to the visitor, based on the user profile and on the anticipation of the users' interest. It is well known that one of the most common problems when dealing with the development of marker based AR applications is the display of different contents at different locations at the same time. By sensing the "user awareness" to the system, for instance allowing the application to know what area the user is interested in at the moment with the aid of gaze tracking devices, contents will be provided in a more reliable and proper way.

Acknowledgements. We thank our colleagues Ramona Quattrini and Paolo Clini from DICEA Department who provided expertise and materials that greatly assisted the research. We also thank Jacopo Di Girolamo for help in eye-tracking data collection.

References

1. Cameron, F., Kenderdine, S.: Theorizing Digital Cultural Heritage: A Critical Discourse (Media in Transition). The MIT Press, Cambridge (2007)
2. Chatterjee, A., Widick, P., Sternschein, R., Smith, W.B., Bromberger, B.: The assessment of art attributes. Empir. Stud. Arts **28**(2), 207–222 (2010)
3. Clini, P., Frontoni, E., Quattrini, R., Pierdicca, R.: Augmented reality experience: from high-resolution acquisition to real time augmented contents. Adv. Multimed. **2014**, 18 (2014)
4. Damala, A., Stojanovic, N.: Tailoring the adaptive augmented reality (A2R) museum visit: identifying cultural heritage professionals' motivations and needs. In: 2012 IEEE International Symposium on Mixed and Augmented Reality (ISMAR-AMH), pp. 71–80. IEEE (2012)
5. Duchowski, A.T.: Acuity-matching resolution degradation through wavelet coefficient scaling. IEEE Trans. Image Process. **9**(8), 1437–1440 (2000)
6. Dünser, A., Hornecker, E.: Lessons from an ar book study. In: Proceedings of the 1st International Conference on Tangible and Embedded Interaction, pp. 179–182. ACM (2007)
7. Eftaxopoulos, E., Vasilakis, A., Fudos, I.: AR-TagBrowse: annotating and browsing 3D objects on mobile devices. In: Eurographics (Posters), pp. 5–6 (2014)
8. Eggert, D., Hücker, D., Paelke, V.: Augmented reality visualization of archeological data. In: Buchroithner, M., Prechtel, N., Burghardt, D. (eds.) Cartography from Pole to Pole, pp. 203–216. Springer, Heidelberg (2014)
9. Eghbal-Azar, K., Merkt, M., Bahnmueller, J., Schwan, S.: Use of digital guides in museum galleries: determinants of information selection. Comput. Hum. Behav. **57**, 133–142 (2016)
10. Graham, D.J., Redies, C.: Statistical regularities in art: relations with visual coding and perception. Vis. Res. **50**(16), 1503–1509 (2010)
11. Haugstvedt, A.-C., Krogstie, J.: Mobile augmented reality for cultural heritage: a technology acceptance study. In: ISMAR, pp. 247–255 (2012)
12. Julier, S., Bishop, G.: Guest editors' introduction: tracking: how hard can it be? IEEE Comput. Graph. Appl. **6**, 22–23 (2002)

13. Kato, H., Billinghurst, M.: Marker tracking and hmd calibration for a video-based augmented reality conferencing system. In: 2nd IEEE and ACM International Workshop on Augmented Reality, 1999, (IWAR 1999), Proceedings, pp. 85–94. IEEE (1999)
14. Logothetis, N.K.: Intracortical recordings and fmri: an attempt to study operational modules and networks simultaneously. Neuroimage 62(2), 962–969 (2012)
15. Lundy, D.E., Schenkel, M.B., Akrie, T.N., Walker, A.M.: How important is beauty to you? the development of the desire for aesthetics scale. Empir. Stud. Arts 28(1), 73–92 (2010)
16. Massaro, D., Savazzi, F., Di Dio, C., Freedberg, D., Gallese, V., Gilli, G., Marchetti, A.: When art moves the eyes: a behavioral and eye-tracking study. PloS One 7(5), e37285 (2012)
17. Pescarin, S., Wallergird, M., Hupperetz, W., Pagano, A., Ray, C.: Archeovirtual 2011: an evaluation approach to virtual museums. In: 2012 18th International Conference on Virtual Systems and Multimedia (VSMM), pp. 25–32. IEEE (2012)
18. Pierdicca, R., Frontoni, E., Zingaretti, P., Sturari, M., Clini, P., Quattrini, R.: Advanced interaction with paintings by augmented reality and high resolution visualization: a real case exhibition. In: De Paolis, L.T., Mongelli, A. (eds.) AVR 2015. LNCS, vol. 9254, pp. 38–50. Springer, Heidelberg (2015)
19. Pierdicca, R., Liciotti, D., Contigiani, M., Frontoni, E., Mancini, A., Zingaretti, P.: Low cost embedded system for increasing retail environment intelligence. In: 2015 IEEE International Conference on Multimedia and Expo Workshops (ICMEW), pp. 1–6. IEEE (2015)
20. Quiroga, R.Q., Pedreira, C.: How do we see art: an eye-tracker study. Front. Hum. Neurosci. 5, 98 (2011)
21. Rothkopf, C.A., Ballard, D.H., Hayhoe, M.M.: Task and context determine where you look. J. Vis. 7(14), 16–16 (2007)
22. Sturari, M., Liciotti, D., Pierdicca, R., Frontoni, E., Mancini, A., Contigiani, M., Zingaretti, P.: Robust and affordable retail customer profiling by vision and radio beacon sensor fusion. Pattern Recogn. Lett. (2016, in press)
23. Tang, H., Kreiman, G.: Face recognition: vision and emotions beyond the bubble. Curr. Biol. 21(21), R888–R890 (2011)
24. Yoshimura, Y., Girardin, F., Carrascal, J.P., Ratti, C., Blat, J.: New tools for studying visitor behaviours in museums: a case study at the louvre. In: Information and Communication Technologies in Tourism 2012, Proceedings of the International Conference Helsingborg (ENTER 2012), pp. 391–402 (2012)

Immersive Learning Environment for Visual Arts

Leith K.Y. Chan[1]([⊠]), Kit Sum Geran Yuen[2], and Henry Y.K. Lau[1]

[1] Department of Industrial and Manufacturing Systems Engineering,
The University of Hong Kong, Hong Kong, China
{lkychan, hyklau}@hku.hk
[2] HKSKH Bishop Hall Secondary School, Hong Kong, China
kitsumyuen@yahoo.com.hk

Abstract. In this paper, we describe the design and implementation of the Immersive Learning Environment for Visual Arts (ILEVA), which is a system that employs virtual reality technology that allows novice users to immerse into their own artworks and experience the virtual space interactively, thus providing a whole new perspective of creating and experiencing art forms to the users. This paper describes the design and architecture of ILEVA and presents a case study with a group of high school students studying in Visual Arts. The result of the work, user responses and evaluation will be discussed .

Keywords: Virtual reality · Human factors · Visual art · Education

1 Introduction

In the last couple decades, computer graphics technology has demonstrated its potential in the Visual Arts domain and been widely used in different applications such as digital art, graphics design and film making. Virtual Reality (VR), despite of its long history and promising potential, has relatively limited applications. Primarily due to the system complexity and difficulty in content development, VR applications are often restrained in some high end domains such as aerospace and automobile industry.

However, in recent years, the cost of major VR components such as 3D projectors and motion tracking systems has reduced dramatically. In addition, the advancement of software technology also greatly enhances the user friendliness of authoring tools. All of these trends help to democratize the deployment of VR technology to the general public.

In this paper, we describe the design and implementation of the Immersive Learning Environment for Visual Arts (ILEVA), which is a low cost Virtual Reality (VR) system that immerses the users into a virtual environment. With the help of this system, a workshop of integrating the traditional Visual Arts elements with the cutting edge visualization technology has been conducted for a group of secondary school students. Feedback from users and evaluation will also be presented.

© Springer International Publishing Switzerland 2016
L.T. De Paolis and A. Mongelli (Eds.): AVR 2016, Part II, LNCS 9769, pp. 231–240, 2016.
DOI: 10.1007/978-3-319-40651-0_18

2   Background

2.1   Visual Arts Education

The essence of art education is to cultivate virtues, such as caring, respect, in-depth reflection, self-discipline, striving for excellent, perseverance, meaningful worldview and the pursue for aesthetics. It is through personal experience, observation, participation, project and reflection that students are able to achieve such virtues. Students need to learn through systematic and thematic study in order to be able to understand and manipulate aesthetic expressions, coding systems, and visual structures presented by visual languages and visual forms. They can then make use of visual images to convey their personal feelings and thoughts as well as appreciate and judge the significance and value of various artistic pursuits and artifacts. Students can develop their artistic potential and values and establish global and diversified views towards the world and a variety of cultures [1].

2.2   Virtual Reality System

The Cave Automatic Virtual Environment (CAVE) is one of the most famous VR systems and is originally developed by the Electronic Visualization Laboratory (EVL) at the University of Illinois at Chicago. It produces 3-dimensional stereo effect by displaying in alternating succession the left and right eye views of the scene as rendered from the viewer's perspective [2]. These views are then seen by the viewers through a pair of LCD shutter glasses whose lenses open and close at high frequency in synchronization with the left and right eye views that are projected via cathode-ray projectors onto the translucent walls and floor acted as screens. In addition to 3D stereoscopic vision, motion parallax, the apparent displacement of objects when you move, e.g., objects closer to your eyes move faster than objects that are far away, is another very important cue to perceive objects in 3D space. In the immersive virtual reality system, it is at least, if not more, important than stereoscopic vision, especially for the 3D objects closed to the user. For example, if a user looks at a piece of virtual furniture in a CAVE, the user should be able to move around and examine the furniture from different angles. This system should be able to produce the image from the correct perspective corresponding to the relative position of the user and the virtual furniture. Because of this motion parallax cue, the user has the faked perception that the furniture exists at the same 3D space as the user. In order to achieve this motion parallax cue, the system has to know the position and orientation of the user's head in real time and this information has to be provided by a motion tracking system. As a result, the system allows the user to be immersed into the virtual environment and interact with the virtual entities realistically.

Since the CAVE system provides a highly versatile platform for 3-D visualizing complex concepts and systems, it has been deployed to explore new statistical graphics applications [3], simulate complex molecular dynamics and interactions between atomic particles [4], virtual exploration and analysis of archaeological site [5], perform assembly planning [6], and for collaborative product design and development [7].

2.3   When Visual Arts Meet VR

As sponsored by the Quality Education Fund, the Visual Arts department of SKH Bishop Hall Secondary School in Hong Kong launched the "Embrace Your Life" Creative Art Education Project. One of the highlights is the collaboration workshop of 'Walking into Virtual Reality'.

In order to broaden students' artistic view and to know the relations between digital technology and art, the Visual Arts department of the school collaborated with the Department of Industrial and Manufacturing Systems Engineering (IMSE), The University of Hong Kong. In phase one, Form 4 art class students created a series of projects, such as comics, sketches, 2D designs based on the theme "Self Growth" under teacher's guidance. After a 60-h digital certificate course, students learnt to use the SketchUp 3D modeling software [8] and designed a unique 3D art gallery which displayed their artworks of the year. In phase two, students work was integrated with ILEVA, a virtual reality system at IMSE. When students were working in this 1:1 virtual art gallery, they explored the virtual space with their 3D glasses. Students visited each corner of their own galleries and they can examine and walk through the art pieces. Meanwhile, the students experience the virtual space in the VR system and understand the combination of digital technology and Art today.

In fact, the workshop of 'Walking into Virtual Reality' is a pioneer attempt in the local secondary school education, both the teacher and the student gain new concepts and experiences through the interdisciplinary learning activity.

3   Design and Implementation

3.1   Design Concept

Despite the desirable features and performance of the CAVE system, the high cost and somehow fixed configuration are key barriers for the deployment and ownership. In this respect, the major advantages of the ILEVA are its low cost design, high performance and versatility in content authoring and visualization. The ILEVA is similar to the EVL CAVE system [2] that consists of three 3 m by 2.5 m projection walls and a 3 m by 3 m screen as the floor projection screen (Fig. 1). With the use of 3D stereoscopic digital projectors and shutter glasses, a high performance active stereoscopic projection system is obtained.

In order to archive immersive effect, the user's movement is fully tracked by an optical tracking system in both configurations of ILEVA. The tracking information is sent to the computer so that it can calculate and render the perspective correct image corresponding to the user's position in real time. Combining with the 3D stereoscopic projectors, the user is completely immersed in the virtual environment.

Instead of using a cluster of network PCs, all projectors are driven by a single powerful workstation. The advantage will be discussed in the section of imple mentation.

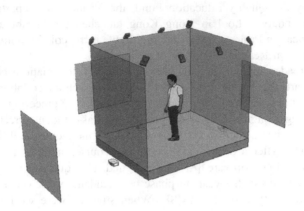

Fig. 1. ILEVA

3.2   System Implementation

Inside the ILEVA, the front, left and right walls are rear projected by three active 3D stereo projectors running at 120 Hz with XGA (1024 × 768) resolution. The advantage of rear projection is to avoid shadow casting problem. The floor image is from the projectors mounted at the top of the system. The 3D stereoscopic images from surround projection walls fill the entire field of view of the user's eyes.

For user position tracking, we use the NaturalPoint OptiTrack tracking system. This tracking system uses retro-reflective marker technology to track targets with the infrared light source that is built into individual cameras. In our setting, there are 8 infrared cameras mounted at the ceiling to provide a range of coverage of about 4 m by 3 m. As illustrated in Fig. 2, each of the devices (3D goggle and handheld controller) is attached with three markers. Each of three reflective markers defines a tracker and is continuously tracked by the optical tracking system. By analyzing the images obtained by the cameras at different angles, the tracking system is able to recognize and calculate the 3D position and orientation of the user and the controller.

Totally there are two computers used in this system. The first computer is a part of the optical tracking system and is connected to the infrared cameras. It is responsible for the calculation of the trackers' positions and orientations by analyzing information streaming from the cameras. The result is then broadcasted to the network in real time. Another computer, named the Image Generator (IG), is the core of the whole system as it is responsible for creating the virtual 3D environment. Unlike using a cluster of PCs in a traditional CAVE-like system, we only use a single computer to render all images of the virtual world. By having all of the rendering happening in a single machine, we can get rid of the overhead and limitation of event synchronization in other similar systems. Moreover, it eliminates the complexity of handling synchronization in the content development. The IG receives the input from the user and the tracking system, calculates the interactions in the virtual world, and then renders 2 channels of 3D

Fig. 2. The 3D goggle and gamepad controller with retro-reflective markers

stereoscopic images to the projectors in real time. As the performance of the whole system is greatly affected by the IG, we use a workstation class computer with a fast CPU and high performance graphics processor.

Apart from the hardware graphics performance, one the most critical factors is the software rendering engine. Not only it determines the performance of the rendering process and the quality of the final rendered images, it also affects the effectiveness and efficiency of the application development. Unity [9], as the most popular cross-platform game engine with more than 4.5 million registered developers in year 2015, is an obvious choice for us. However, although it supports many different platforms such as PCs, handheld device and tablets, it restricts itself within the traditional user interface of screen, mouse, keyboard and touch based input. Unity has no support for VR system such as 3D stereoscopic rendering, asymmetric camera and interface to motion tracking system. This drawback has limited its application in a VR system. Not until recently, a middleware named MiddleVR [10] emerged in the market and it provides support for VR systems. MiddleVR is a generic immersive virtual reality plugin and handles different aspects of VR component such as stereoscopy, interaction devices with motion tracking and clustering. One of its most unique features is the introduction of hardware abstraction. The hardware specification such as the number of projection screens, motion tracking system and the type of user interface, is abstracted in a configuration file. When running an application with a different hardware platform, a new configuration file is the only change required with the corresponding hardware setting. This has huge benefit to the software development process because the same application binary can be used in a different VR system without modification of pro-gramming codes or recompiling. In fact, our applications can be deployed to other completely different VR systems such as the AVIE [11] with 360° curve screens running with a cluster of computers.

3.3 Content Authoring

Since the target is a group of students studying Visual Arts at a local secondary school, we would not expect they have any skill of 3D modeling or programming. Instead, a 60 h course of 3D modeling is provided to the students. We choose to use the Trimble SketchUp software primary because of its ease of use. Moreover, SketchUp has a huge library of ready-to-use 3D models shared among the users. In the course, the students learn the basic 3D modeling concept and technique. At the end of the course, they are asked to prepare a personal exhibition to display all of their previous artworks such as paintings and sketches. They need to design and build an art gallery for the exhibition. Some examples are shown in Fig. 3. After all of the 3D models of their personal galleries are ready, they will be imported into Unity in order to be displayed at the ILEVA. As learning Unity is beyond of the scope of the exercise, an experienced Unity developer handles the importing process for them. A simple navigation control has also added to the final applications. After all of the virtual galleries have been deployed to the system, all students are invited to the university and experience their own virtual galleries with ILEVA. As all of the students have never use any VR system before, a brief introduction and demonstration is provided for them to familiarize with the system and learn the basic navigation control. Afterward, each student spends some time to explore his own virtual gallery, then they have to present their artwork to the rest of the class. Each student has approximately 15 min using the ILEVA (Fig. 4).

Fig. 3. 3D model of art galleries created by student

Fig. 4. Students experiencing their own virtual art galleries at ILEVA

4 Discussion and Conclusion

4.1 Preliminary Evaluation

After the workshop, we have prepared questionnaires to collect feedback and response from the students. There are totally 11 male students with age between 16–17 years old participated in the exercise and 10 questionnaires are collected. The result is list in Table 1.

The majority of result is favorable towards the use of a virtual reality system in undertaking the project. For content creation, students only agree marginally that SketchUp is an easy tool to use for building up their own 3D gallery model (Question 1-2). This reflects that building 3D model is a challenging task for them. As they are first time learners of the 3D modelling software, this finding is understandable. On the other hand, the experience in ILEVA is more positive. They enjoyed the workshop and this experience stimulates their interests in Visual Arts creation (Question 8-9). Moreover, the system also enables them to understand their own artwork in more depth and facilitate their reflection (Question 10). Some students have commented it is the most satisfying and meaningful moment as they 'walked' into their own art gallery, which is something beyond their imagination. Although students think that ILEVA is a better tool for presentation than traditional media (Question 11), as audiences, they tend to agree in a lesser extent that ILEVA provides a better means to understand other student's presentation. This is probably due to the fact that the immersive VR system is optimized for a single user. In fact, only the user with the head tracking device has the

Table 1. Summary of the result from questionnaires

	Q	Question	Average	Standard deviation
Content authoring	1	SketchUp: Easy to use	3.6	0.5
	2	SketchUp: Easy to integrate previous artwork and build a 3D virtual gallery	3.1	0.6
System performance and User interface	3	Effect of Immersiveness. You feel inside the real gallery	4.2	0.9
	4	Enough moving space	4.0	0.9
	5	Gamepad is easy to use	4.0	0.8
	6	3D glasses is comfortable	3.2	1.1
	7	Felling seasick or discomfort in orientation	2.4	1.6
Effectiveness in visual arts education	8	I enjoy the workshop	4.5	0.5
	9	The experience at ILEVA stimulates my interest in Visual Art creation	4.5	0.5
	10	The experience at ILEVA helps me to understand my artwork and facilitate my reflection	3.8	1
	11	Compared to ordinary computer and traditional media, presenting at ILEVA is more effective in expressing my artwork	3.7	1.2
	12	Compared to ordinary computer and traditional media, I can understand other students' artwork more effectively when I watch their presentation at ILEVA	3.3	0.9

1 = strongly disagree, 2 = Disagree, 3 = Neither agree/nor disagree 4 = Agree, 5 = Strongly agree

immersive feeling, as all projected images are rendered from his perspective. Other users, who look at the images from other perspectives often felt disoriented and confused as the images do not match with their positions and movements.

4.2   Advantages and Limitations

From the evaluation, it is clear that ILEVA helps students to explore the art form in a new dimension. Although their creations only exist inside a computer, the VR system provides a platform so that they can enter their artwork and explore the creation. The level of realism is so overwhelming that a student has expressed that being able to walk into his own gallery is one of the happiest things in his life. All of their hard work of building 3D models suddenly becomes worthwhile and meaningful. In fact, being able to walk into a creation helps students look into the artwork from a whole new perspective and hence getting new inspiration. This inspiration helps them to examine, understand and rediscover the meaning of their own works.

However, the evaluation also reveals that IELVA may not be an outstanding presentation tool as we have thought. As the whole system is optimized to serve a single user, the audiences, who receive the distorted images, may feel confused when looking from outside. In this case, traditional way of presentation with a single large projector may be a preferable choice.

4.3 Conclusion

This paper presents an immersive learning environment for visual arts and its actual deployment in visual art education for high school students. With the overwhelming response from the participants in the visual art creation workshop co-organized by SKH Bishop Hall Secondary School and The University of Hong Kong, the technology of Virtual Reality is starting to unfold its true potential in the world of Visual Art Education. Feedback from students suggested that ILEVA transforms the teaching and learning process of visual art education by allowing students to 'enter' their art creation and to explore the work in different dimensions. Furthermore, ILEVA provides an effective platform for students to experiment and develop new inspiration with significant saving in cost and time.

Acknowledgements. Our thanks to the Quality Education Fund from the Education Bureau of the Hong Kong SAR Government for partly funding the workshop.

References

1. Visual Arts Curriculum Guide (2003). http://www.edb.gov.hk/attachment/en/curriculum-development/kla/arts-edu/references/va_guide_p1_s3_e.pdf. Accessed 29 Jan 2014
2. Cruz-Neira, C., Sandin, D.J., DeFanti, T.A., Kenyon, R.V., Hart, J.C.: The CAVE: audio visual experience automatic virtual environment. Commun. ACM **35**(6), 64–72 (1992)
3. Jürgen, S., Dianne, C., Bradley, D.K., Carolina, C.-N.: Dynamic Statistical Graphics in the CAVE Virtual Reality Environment (1996)
4. Disz, T., Papka, M., Pellegrino, M., Stevens, R., Taylor, V.: Virtual reality visualization of parallel molecular dynamics simulation. In: Proceedings 1995 Simulation Multiconference Symposium, pp. 483–487 (1995)
5. Vote, E., Acevedo, D., Laidlaw, D., Joukowsky, M.: Discovering petra: archaeological analysis in VR. IEEE Comput. Graph. Appl. **22**(5), 38–50 (2002)
6. Ye, N., Banerjee, P., Banerjee, A., Dech, F.: A comparative study of assembly planning in traditional and virtual environments. IEEE Trans. Syst. Man, Cybern. Part C: Appl. Rev. **29** (4), 546–555 (1999)
7. Bochenek, G.M., Ragusa, J.M.: Virtual collaborative design environments: a review, issues, some research, and the future. In: Proceedings of the Management of Engineering and Technology, PICMET 2001, vol. 722, pp. 726–735 (2001)
8. SketchUp (2016). http://www.sketchup.com/. Accessed 10 Feb 2016
9. Unity (2016). http://unity3d.com/. Accessed 10 Feb 2016

10. MiddleVR (2016). http://www.middlevr.com. Accessed 10 Feb 2016
11. McGinity, M., Shaw, J., Kuchelmeister, V., Hardjono, A., Favero, D.D.: AVIE: a versatile multi-user stereo 360 interactive VR theatre. In: Proceedings of the 2007 Workshop on Emerging Displays Technologies: Images and Beyond: The Future of Displays and Interacton, vol. 2. ACM (2007)

Development of a HMD for Virtual Acoustics. Application in a World Heritage (UNESCO) Building from the Valencian Civil Gothic

Sebastián Mirasol-Menacho[1], Ana Planells-Pérez[2], Arturo Barba-Sevillano[2], Jaume Segura-Garcia[1(✉)], Máximo Cobos-Serrano[1], and Alicia Giménez-Pérez[2]

[1] Dpt Informàtica, ETSE, Universitat de València, Avda Universitat s/n, 46100 Valencia, Spain
semime@alumni.uv.es, {jsegura,macose2}@uv.es
[2] Dpt Física Aplicada, UPV, Camí de Vera s/n, 46020 Valencia, Spain
anaplape@upvnet.upv.es, agimenez@fis.upv.es
http://www.uv.es/etse/
http://www.upv.es/

Abstract. The aim of this paper is to show the development of an immersive application in a historic visual and acoustic space. The "Llotja de la Seda" ("Silk Exchange Building") is a late Valencian Gothic style civil building in Valencia (Spain), built between 1482 and 1548. The UNESCO considered it as a World Heritage Site in 1996 since "the site is of outstanding universal value as it is a wholly exceptional example of a secular building in late Gothic style, which illustrates the power and wealth of one of the great Mediterranean mercantile cities".

In this on-going work, we have joined the development of a specific Head Mount Display for our application, in combination with a HRTF rendering system, and the virtual reality and acoustic modelling of this building. The acoustical calibration of the model was made using 25 impulse response measurements according to ISO3382. The Llotja's reverberation time at mid-frequencies is 3.1 s, with a volume of 12,100 m^3. From this model we are developing applications for dynamic representation mixing voice and music.

Keywords: Virtual reality · Virtual acoustics · Acoustical archaeology · Head mount display

1 Introduction

The aim of virtual archaeological reconstructions is to recover ancient buildings or even recreate previous stages of actual ones and submerge the user in a free moving space inside or around buildings that have been lost or modified over time. This modality of virtual reality allows the user to enjoy a sensory experience, not just seeing how the building was in different ages, but also "taste" the sound in the environment.

© Springer International Publishing Switzerland 2016
L.T. De Paolis and A. Mongelli (Eds.): AVR 2016, Part II, LNCS 9769, pp. 241–250, 2016.
DOI: 10.1007/978-3-319-40651-0_19

The "Llotja de la Seda" is one of the most emblematic buildings of Valencia. It was built in the 15th century and it is considered the most brilliant exponent of the European civil gothic architecture. Nonetheless, it became a UNESCO World Heritage Site in 1996.

It was built as headquarters of the silk commerce, as there met together traders and sellers. Its conception as a temple shows the importance of the silk industry which was the main economic activity of the city.

The building has a rectangular plan and it consists of several volumes: the "Sala de Contratación", the "Pabellón del Consulado", the tower and the garden. This study is focused on the acoustics of the "Sala de Contratación" also known as "Columnario" which is the largest space and the main body of the building.

This room is divided in three longitudinal naves and five transversal ones, all of them covered by ribbed vaults which lay on 24 twisted columns. All elements are made of stone as well as the doors and windows' ornamentation but originally, vaults were painted simulating a sky full of stars between the palm trees represented by the nerves. Figure 1 shows the current state of the vaults. In this room was installed the "Taula de Canvis i Dipòsits" (Table of changes and deposits) which was the first municipal bank institution. Its function was the coin change and valuable object deposit, and it gained recognition for its money solvency and the magnitude of its operations. Even though the room was built for speech, music was also introduced during the 19th century as historical documents reflect that parties and dances were usually held in the "Columnario" [1].

In this paper we will show the design and the performance of a head mount device that has been designed to render visually and acoustically VR/VA models and which will allow visiting different buildings. In particular, we have used this device with a model of the Valencian's Silk Exchange (Llotja de la Seda), a Mediterranean Gothic building of the 15th century. We will discuss the components of the head movement detection system and the display and the virtual acoustic features of the building.

Fig. 1. Columns and vaults in the "Columnario".

2   Head Mount Display

The head mount display is divided in two parts, the display and the head movement detection system. First is the display itself, composed by a 5.6 in. LCD screen, the screen controller and two aspherical five augment lenses. Head movement is detected through a MEMS sensor with a gyroscope and an accelerometer (MPU-6000) or in addition to them a magnetometer (MPU-9025). The use of them will be discussed further in this paper.

2.1   Display

Since the display is going to be used in architectonic virtualizations, it had to have a high resolution and pixel density, so as to present the user with a very sharp image. We opted for a high definition LCD with a high pixel density. Figure 2 shows the configuration of the screen for the HMD.

Screen. The selected screen has a resolution of 1280 × 800 pixels (16:10 ratio) with a density of 270 pixels per square inch, that means that each eye receives a 640 × 800 (4:5 ratio) pixel image. It has the capability of displaying 262,144 colors and has a very compact design, to reduce the amount of weight of the device.

The screen is connected via an LVDS cable to a controller board containing adjustment buttons (such as menu access and movement), a power connection and a HDMI input connection.

Lenses. In order to achieve a 3D visual effect, the image displayed has a barrel distortion. The effect is similar to a fisheye lense, wich makes the image take an hemispherical view, this also increases the angle of view.

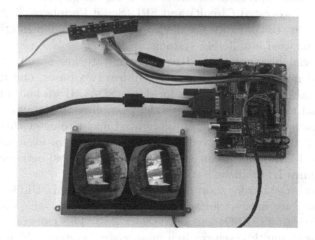

Fig. 2. LCD screen with controller.

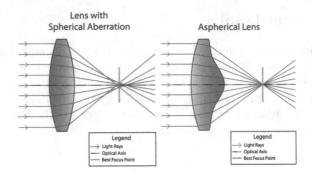

Fig. 3. Spherical aberration correction of a normal lens (left) and an aspherical lens (right). (Color figure online)

Once the image has been distorted, an aspherical lens provides a pin-cushion effect that corrects the spherical aberration given to the image (shown in Fig. 3). It also has 5x magnification, to bring the screen closer to the user's eye and fill all the filed of view.

2.2   Head Movement Detector

The head movement detection system is composed by a microcontroller and a sensor. The main goal is to achieve a high sample rate and a low latency. We want to achieve a sensor sample rate of at least 1 KHz to avoid user dizziness and provide lifelike movement sensation.

Microcontroller and Communication. For a test base we are working with a PSoC which has an Intel 8051 microcontroller. First of all, we wanted to see what communications protocol is more suitable for our goal since both IMU work with I^2C (Inter-Integrated Circuit) and SPI (Serial Peripheral Interface). This SoC also allows us to configure the device as a HID (Human Interface Device) so that it can be used in different systems.

I^2C is a serial bus mostly used to communicate low speed peripherals to processors and microcontrollers, it only requires two buses, one for the clock (SCL) and another bidirectional one for data (SDA). If we had an MPU-6000 and an external magnetometer we have the possibility to set up a master-slave system, but having an IMU with an integrated magnetometer this will not be necessary. Its standard clock speed goes up to 100 KHz or even faster at High Speed mode (3.4 MHz), but it can lead to certain delays (ηs) between transferred bytes and requires I/O buffers.

SPI is also a serial bus for short distance communications. Unlike I^2C it works with a four wire bus: master clock signal (SCK), master to salve signal (MOSI), slave to master signal (MISO) and slave select (SS). This can come handy if we were to work with multiple sensors in a master-slave system, which again, is not the case. SPI is full duplex, unlike I^2C which means it can go over 10 Mbps.

Having available both protocols on each IMU, we will conduct sample rate and throughput test to see which one is more appropriate, considering speed, low noise and reliability.

Sensors. We have tested the system with two different sensors, the MPU-6000 and the MPU-9250 (shown in Fig. 4). The difference between the two is that the MPU-9250 has, in addition to the accelerometer and gyroscope that the MPU-6000 offers, a magnetometer.

Fig. 4. MPU-6000 (left) and MPU-9250 (right).

MEMS sensors like the MPU-6000 are known to have an x-axis zeroing drift with usage. To correct this drift we explored two different approaches. One is using the MPU-6000 with different filters such as a Kalman or a complementary filter. An alternative is to use a MPU-9250 with a magnetometer to be used as a spatial reference to locate a reference at all times.

Different test are to be done to find the best user experience, and evaluate if the filter ensures an easy solution to the drift problem. If the filter adds a high computational cost to the microcontroller and slows the sample rate output to the computer, we would go for the MPU-9250 and let the computer software deal with the drift correction.

2.3 Design

The device has been 3D printed, and designed to weight the least possible. It will also let lens distance adjustment, so that users with different eyesight conditions can use it. We have also taken to consideration the fact that users may have different pupillary distance, and will provide an adjustment system for this.

Figure 5 show the main device (head mounted display) which is composed by the lenses, screen, structure, and the bands that hold it on the head. The screen controller will be installed in a different enclosure that will sit on the desk.

3 Model and Simulation

In this part of the work, we aim to obtain an immersive experience including visual and acoustical perception, so we can see and hear the room as realistically as possible. This work has been developed in several stages.

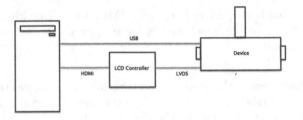

Fig. 5. Connection diagram.

It started with the 'in-situ' measurement of the acoustic parameters of the room which served as reference to calibrate the room for the acoustic simulation. Simultaneously, visual modelling was also developed.

Measurements were taken according to standard ISO3382 [2,3] and the validated protocol. It is noteworthy to mention that the number of positions measured was oversampled in order to obtain more reliable results and detailed information of the room's acoustic behavior. We measured 24 points of the room whose distribution is shown in Fig. 6.

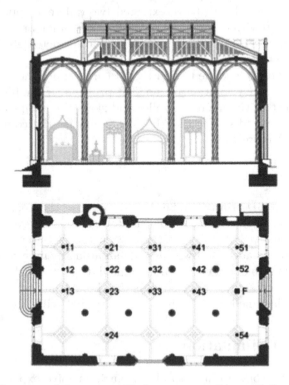

Fig. 6. Plan and section of the room with the source position and the points measured.

The room impulse responses (RIRs) are obtained at each reception point using sine sweep signals, running from 16 to 20,000 Hz, which are generated and analysed by the WinMLS 2004 software [4] via the professional sound card VX Pocket v2 from Digigram. This generated signal feeds the INTER-M 1000 amplifier for its subsequent reproduction by the omnidirectional source AVM dodecahedral DO12 01-dB Stell loudspeaker, placed at 1.50 m from the floor and on the stage.

Several microphones are used to obtain the different parameters: G.R.A.S. Type 40 AK $\frac{1}{2}$-in. and its corresponding supply source G.R.A.S. 12AA, and G.R.A.S Type 26AK pre-amplifiers are used.

Given the complexity geometry of the room and the opposite characteristics required for the visual and acoustical simulations, we decided to build two separate models. Figure 7 shows an interior view of both models. They were built up from the existing architectural plans. The number of polygons used for the visual model is 18262 and for the acoustic model is 3875.

The visual model should be as detailed as possible to give a realistic perception. After modelling the structure the model was texturized by assigning textures previously created from photographs taken in the room and post-processed. These confer the room a realistic look and recreate details that could not be modeled geometrically. Finally illumination was added to the scene to obtain the desired effect. The final result is shown in Fig. 8.

Fig. 7. Models used for the visual and acoustical simulations.

In order to get a valid acoustic simulation the geometric model used must fulfill certain requirements. For this reason modeling must follow some consideration such as include only the inner and accessible surfaces, to be concerned

Fig. 8. Texturized model.

about the normal orientation which must point inside, define accurately vertex and edges to prevent openings and avoid modeling details which can be emulated by diffusion adjustment.

The model has been calibrated adjusting absorption and diffusion coefficients from the RT30 average values and according to the criteria of not having differences of more than 1JND (Just Noticeable Difference) between simulated and measured values. Figure 9 presents the average results for RT30 calibration at each frequency.

3.1 Auralization

We calculated the impulsive response of the room (RIR) in the selected positions in the calibrated model, to do the subjective study. By convolving the impulsive response with an anecoic signal, we obtained the different auralizations of the room.

One of the main difficulties in auralization is to have anechoic recordings [5]. There have been few attempts to use synthetic signals as source signals in auralizations [6]. As far as we know there has not been a thorough attempt in the literature to use commercial products for music editing or commercial text-to-speech software to produce source signals for auralizations.

We used Finale Notepad 2012 (free distribution), which includes high quality built-in software instrument sounds, to produce separate instrument recordings. For voice sources we used TextAloud with AT&T Natural VoicesTM. TextAloud supports changing voices within an article. This feature allowed us to produce separate voice recordings with different voices. Using both programs, we have separate signals that we used as source signals.

Auralizations were computed according to the following procedure:

- Single auralization with one source. Receiver points to the source at center of stage. Source signal was a four channel mixture.
- Mixed auralizations with four sources. Receiver points to the center of stage. In each source, a separate channel of music composition or play scene was

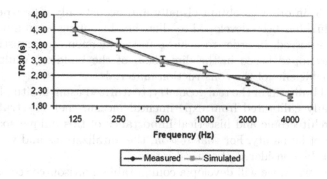

Fig. 9. RT30 calibration. (Color figure online)

used. Using ODEON [7] mixer, four channels of auralizations were combined in a stereo file.

The auralization of music with a receiver in movement has been done by computing the impulse responses in different points. The musical auralization was done by using the CATT-Walker tool in order to obtain the auralization. The auralization sequenced several IRs in the walk through the room and an excerpt of an aria from the opera Don Giovanni by W.A. Mozart was used as anechoic recording [9].

4   VA/VR Navigation Tool

For the implementation of the virtual reality/acoustic navigation tool, we have used Unity Pro 5. The graphical model used has been imported directly from the texturized model.

The audio rendering tool has been integrated into the navigation tool by using a modeled version of the CIPIC HRTF database [10]. This tool allows to render the audio directional information coming from the HMD by convolving the auralized audio source with the HRIRs in real-time. The auralized audio is transmitted by using a Bluetooth 4.0 transmitter connected to the PC, to a pair of wireless headphones.

For this prototype, the auralized audio source has been located within the environment as a single source, but in future development a multisource scenario will be considered.

5   Conclusions and Future Work

The device is intended to work with any simulator or game that allows head movement independently of the body. On this particular paper, the setup is focused in virtual archeology/architecture to provide the user a sensorial experience of the 15th century building. The architectural model has been integrated in Unity Pro 5, in order to obtain visually and acoustically a first-person navigator. A module has been developed to allow head tracking as an input to select HRTFs. As discussed, in order to achieve full immersion, an acoustic model is also being developed based in the dimension of the building, vaults, and the absorption coefficients of the construction materials.

The model built out of the real geometry, texturized using in situ photographs and acoustically calibrated from experimental measurements is truly valuable due to the architectonic and historical importance of this unique space considered heritage of humanity. For that reason, the auralizations and visualizations developed can be considered of general interest.

As a future work, we will develop a configurable multisource scenario including an auralizator tool. In this way, the model will use an anechoic audio source and the impulse response of the location of the room considered.

Acknowledgements. Authors would like to thank professor Julio Martos and Pedro Martinez for his help and advices. This study has been partially supported by the Spanish Ministry of Economy and Innovation and FEDER funds in the research project with refs BIA2012-36896 and TEC2012-37945-C02-02.

References

1. Blanco, M.R.: La lonja de Valencia y su entorno monumental: origen y desarrollo constructivo, evolución de sus estructuras, sinopsis de las intervenciones más relevantes, siglos XV al XX. Doctoral thesis. UPV (1999)
2. ISO3382-1, Acoustics. Measurement of room acoustic parameters. Part1: Performance spaces (2009)
3. ISO3382-2, Acoustics. Measurement of room acoustic parameters. Part2: Reverberation time in ordinary rooms (2008)
4. M.S. Developments. http://www.winmls.com. Accessed 13 Dec 2015
5. Vorländer, M.: Auralization: Fundamentals of Acoustics, Modelling, Simulation, Algorithms and Acoustic Virtual Reality. Springer-Verlag, Berlin (2008)
6. Savioja, L., Huopaniemi, J., Lokki, T., Väänäen, R.: Creating interactive virtual acoustic environments. JAES **47**(9), 675–705 (1999)
7. Christensen, C.L.: Odeon Room Acoustics Program, Version 10.1, User Manual, Industrial, Auditorium and Combined Editions, Odeon A/S, Lyngby, Denmark (2009)
8. Dalënback, D.I.: CATT. Acoustics. http://www.catt.se/. Accessed 13 Dec 2015
9. http://goo.gl/3aNLAe. Accessed 13 Dec 2015
10. CIPIC HRTF Database. http://interface.cipic.ucdavis.edu/sound/hrtf.html. Accessed 13 Dec 2015

Enabling Touchless Interfaces for Mobile Platform: State of the Art and Future Trends

Simone Marcutti$^{(\boxtimes)}$ and Gianni Viardo Vercelli

Department of Informatics, Bioengineering,
Robotics and Systems Engineering, University of Genova, Genoa, Italy
simone.marcutti@edu.unige.it,
gianni.vercelli@unige.it

Abstract. In this work, we discuss the existing methods to implement and use a touchless gesture-based interaction on mobile platforms such as smartphones and tablets, specifically for situations where you cannot have a direct interaction with devices. The purpose of this work is to investigate the actual solutions and establish the most convenient way to enable these interactions on mobile devices with minimally-invasive procedures. The paper is organized in three parts: a survey of the current technological possibilities; a description of trials made to know advantages and limitations of the existing solutions; a final discussion concerning the evolution of the natural user interface on mobile platforms in the next few years.

Keywords: NUI · Natural user interface · HCI · Human Computer Interaction · Mobile · Computer vision · Internet of Things

1 Introduction

Natural user interfaces (NUI) paradigm is the evolution of the concept of user-interface intended as the method of the human to interact with machines and comes historically after the previous CLI (command line interface) and GUI (Graphic User Interface).

These kind of interfaces rely on different types of control that can impart commands and actions to the machine through input such as touch, eye-tracking, voice, gesture and movement [1].

In the last years, a plenty of devices, libraries and applications dedicated to create experiences has been developed, that enable users to interact with digital artifacts using these kind of controls.

We assume here that the starting point of this revolution could be fixed in the year 2010 with the launch on the market of the Microsoft Kinect that has got a lot of success establishing also a Guinness World Record as "the fastest selling gaming peripheral"[1] in the history.

In this decade a lot of interest began to emerge from the community of developers around this type of peripherals and technology, and the natural consequence of this trend was an increase of the efforts from the hardware manufactures in order to constantly improve the stability and the features of their products.

---

[1] http://www.guinnessworldrecords.com/world-records/fastest-selling-gaming-peripheral/.

© Springer International Publishing Switzerland 2016
L.T. De Paolis and A. Mongelli (Eds.): AVR 2016, Part II, LNCS 9769, pp. 251–260, 2016.
DOI: 10.1007/978-3-319-40651-0_20

All these efforts produced several interesting applications developed in different fields, but they were restricted to a use through desktop environments with a classic monitor and a traditional computer [2].

The past years were also characterized by the proliferation of smartphone and tablet in everyday life: currently people use mobile devices to interact with the world and to improve working performances and capabilities [3].

The rise of the possibilities offered by these devices has led new possible applications in different contexts, but at the same time opens also new issues related to the interaction with devices. We refer specifically to situation where your hands are engaged with other operations or there are some conditions (e.g. dirty hands) that prevent the direct contact with the surface of the screen like surgery environments [4, 5].

These key points are at the base of the considerations that led us to investigate how could be possible to enable touchless interaction the previously mentioned platforms and what could be the trends in the future.

2 Related Work

Over the last years of research in touchless interactions and NUI was produced a lot of interesting works related to the key concept of naturalness and intuitiveness of these kind of interaction with computers. Norman [6] clearly emphasized the usefulness of "not-natural" NUI, noting that gesture-based approaches will lead to a more holistic human interaction of people with technologies. O'Hara et al. [7] considered the narrative factors as relevant keys to deal with the success of "natural" an "intuitive" approaches. Karam and Schraefel [8] deeply reviewed 40 years of literature on gesture-based interaction, to pose the question of how researchers claim about the key role of gestures in advanced HCI.

These efforts produced the result that NUI has started to be considered not only a visionary future solution to interact with computer, but a real and available possibility.

The consequence of this consciousness is the production of research and works with the aim to identify possible scenarios that could benefits from the use of this kind of interactions and interfaces.

3 Identification of Possible Approaches

In this section, we would like to illustrate the possible approaches that already exists in NUI world and that are suitable to create touchless interactions together with our considerations about their implementation on mobile devices.

It is important to say that for our analysis and interactions with mobile devices, one of the key points is the identification of solutions which use hands gesture recognition without the imposition of particular constraint.

We focused only on hand-based solution because we would like to explore the feasibility of a system that can control and manipulate contents using simple and basic gesture.

3.1 Computer Vision

Computer vision approaches to NUI derives from lots of past experiments, which enabled the creation of interactions with computers through a large use of algorithms based on the principles of the images processing.

In the past, computer vision was widely used for medical and security purposes but over the years it has evolved becoming a new way to create applications even for fields like marketing and entertainment [9].

In fact, the use of frameworks belonging to computer vision makes possible the creation of applications, which use shape and colors of objects to enable different types of interactions with the computers.

With the current computing power available on the market the main implementation of computer vision approaches to NUI does not have any specific requirements, it only needs a camera that capture images like infrared or RGB and a peripheral that elaborates the frames coming from the input stream [10].

The reason why we analyze the computer vision approach to NUI concerns the possibility to take advantage by the presence of a camera on a general device. In this way, it could be possible to implement computer vision algorithms to enable touchless interaction on mobile platforms [11].

3.2 Depth Sensor Camera

In this subsection, we evaluate solutions enabling the use of touchless interactions based on a technology that is the core of device like Microsoft Kinect and Leap Motion.

The previously mentioned devices use a combination of infrared and depth sensor that allows the tracking of movements of individuals, hands, fingers and objects in three dimensions [12].

To use their features, it is necessary that each device is connected through USB to a computer that satisfies specific hardware requirements, and this is straightforward on PCSs but not directly replicable with current smartphones and tablets. For this reason, it is easy to understand that these devices are not useful for this purpose.

During our research, focused on finding an alternative available on the market to the system described above, we found that Intel RealSense[2] seems to be the only alternative to our purpose. It consists on a platform that enables, among others cool features, the implementation of gesture-based interaction through a 3D embedded camera.

Unlike Leap Motion or Kinect, with Intel RealSense technology the device that acquire data is the same that use them. They are not separated and doesn't require any particular implementation to manage event e communication.

However, now this technology is not so widely spread to consider it as a standard or a real opportunity for the scopes.

---

[2] http://www.intel.it/content/www/it/it/architecture-and-technology/realsense-overview.html.

3.3   Wearable Devices

A third possible approach considered to enable touch-less interactions is based on the world of wearable devices and this kind of solutions includes equipment like data-gloves. Although this approach has many benefits, the fact to wear something impose an important constrain that can obstruct the right execution of task in real life and furthermore is a solution that could be expensive to implement.

For these reason and for the assumption made in the introduction of this section we didn't considered it a good alternative for a simple interaction with mobile devices.

4   Prototype System and Application

In this section, we introduce our work to better understand and explore benefits and limits of the current available touchless solutions for common mobile platforms after the analysis of the possible existing approaches.

As a starting point, we decided to build a demo of a mobile application with the aim to enable the use of the basic "swipe" gesture in the four directions: top, down, left, right. We implemented the application using iOS devices as target for our deployment but following the principles related to cross-platform development.

4.1   Investigation and Development

Since we noted that depth sensors technology is not widely available for mobile applications, we decided to implement an application using the computer vision approach.

First, we defined the framework that can help us to embed image processing inside an iOS mobile application, so that it can be replicated on Android devices. For these reasons, we tested (Fig. 1) and considered OPENCV the best choice for our purposes [13].

Fig. 1. Testing OPENCV framework on iPhone 4s

In fact, the OPENCV library has a version of SDK available even for iOS and Android platforms. Moreover, a lot of documentations and a forum with a large community of developers are available online; this means that it is easy to find best practices, feedback and suggestions[3].

According to the principles of the cross-platform development, we decided to develop the UI and the main logic of the application with Apache Cordova, an open-source mobile development framework that allows the use of standard web technologies. Such technologies (HTML, CSS, JavaScript) are world-wide standard to build applications without using the different native development language, except if you want to develop your own plugin interface between native and WebView components.

At this point, we included the OPENCV component developing a custom plugin in order to enable gesture's detection feature.

The realization of this algorithm can be achieved with OPENCV through two different techniques.

The first technique makes use of a component called "Cascade Classifier" that can recognize an object in the frame, starting from an XML representation; whereas the second one called "Skin Color Detection" works directly on the frame operating on the RGB values of the pixels (Fig. 2).

Fig. 2. Testing algorithm with a filter control

We prefer to use the second way because it is faster implemented and it can give us more control over the variables and the parameters acting in the algorithm. Furthermore, the first method requires a very strong representation of the object and this can be achieved only through a supervised process to create the XML values. Lastly, this method is more expensive, in terms of resource consuming, than the "skin color detection", with a higher possibility to cause crashes on devices.

---

[3] OPENCV official website, http://www.opencv.org.

The implementation and the customization of the "Skin Color Detection" method allowed us to create an algorithm based on the following flow:

1. Frame input from camera (f);
2. Extraction of RGB values of f_n pixels;
3. Comparison between values of f_n and f_{n-1};
4. Determination of the amount of pixels changed;
5. Analysis of the changed pixels to understand if they can trigger a gesture;
6. Determination of gesture direction (up, down, left, right);
7. Transfer information to the main logic

The just described flow can be activated and stopped through two functions accessible from the JavaScript layer of the applications, thanks to the plugin structure of the Apache Cordova frameworks.

In this way, the application logic can be easily shared between different versions of devices and platforms, modifying only the layer of the plugin with the native language to edit the flow that open, analyze and close the stream from the camera.

The result we obtained from this type of approach is the recognition of the four basic swipe gesture (i.e. up, down, left, right) and it can be used in applications, which requires to operate without direct contact of the finger on the device.

The application mentioned above gives us a good feedback about the possibilities to use touchless interactions on mobile device. For this reason, we consider it a good starting point for some future developments.; even if it is necessary to increase the types and numbers of recognized gestures through revisions and improvements of the detection algorithm.

4.2   A Novel Approach: Natural User Interface Over Internet of Things

While working on computer vision based approach we discovered that although it has some benefits related to his rapid implementation, it has also limits in terms of performances and quality.

In fact, the algorithm described in the previous section relies directly on the quality of the video captured by the device's camera which is an important variable for the precision of the detection of each gesture.

In particular, algorithm's performances are related to the fact that logical operations can consume a lot of resources to analyze the stream if they are not well implemented, with the possibility to cause a crash of the application on the device.

The quality issue emerged because the detection of the pixel's change can be affected by external factors such as environment's light and color. These limits led us to search and identify a possible alternative which enables touchless interaction without being affected by factor.

To by-pass these limits, we developed a low-cost device (Fig. 3) based on combination of hardware and software that enable the detection of gesture events and their transmission to smartphones and tablets using the Internet of Things paradigm [14].

Fig. 3. HW components assembled

We built this device using the following components:

- Raspberry Pi 2 Model B, single-board computer Linux based[4];
- Hover, a little sensor able to detects hand movements in the air[5];
- RGB led, to give feedback about events;
- USB Wireless N 802.11 N Nano Dongle (WiFi Adapter), to enable the communication;
- 3D printed box, as enclosure;
- Node.js, platform used for the creation of the server and the management of devices, events and data;
- Socket.io, Node.js module that enables real-time bidirectional event-based communication;
- hostapd and dnsmasq, Linux modules useful to create a custom wireless network;

The combination of the last two components gave us the possibility to create a custom network and assign a fixed IP address to the device, making it a node identifiable and accessible through HTTP.

This possibility enabled the exchange of http request/response and events with the Node.js server which runs on the Raspberry PI, manages data produced by the Hover sensor and controls the state of RGB led.

The implementations of all these features is possible by the presence of 40 GPIO pins on the Raspberry PI and by the modular nature of the Node.js framework: The first aspect is important because it improves the possibilities offered by Raspberry PI, giving it the chance to have connections with other things; whereas The second aspect allows the use and the development of modules to implement various features.

In particular we used:

- Express, for the creation of a web server;
- Socket.io, for the communication through socket between client and server;
- Hover, made by ourselves to manage the connection between Raspberry PI and Hover sensor trough the GPIO pins;
- pi-fast-gpio, used for the management of the RGB's state in PWM mode;

---

[4] https://www.raspberrypi.org/.

[5] http://www.hoverlabs.co/.

All operations described above allowed us to create an intermediate between the users and the final application, which enables touchless interaction with the aim of being space-saving, robust and plug and play.

This new approach is a good alternative to embedded solutions and gives the possibility to have touchless interactions in situations in which users need to use their hands for actions that obstacle the direct interaction with smartphone e tablets.

Due to its standalone nature this kind of device can be placed inside different environments acting as a sort of remote control for situation where user and content are distant.

4.3   Use Case Demonstration

To evaluate the functioning and the behavior of the two systems, we developed a proof of concept applications where user have to browse the steps that compose a recipe.

Environments such as kitchen are ideal to test the solutions developed because in these spaces are present a lot of conditions that can be resolved using touchless interactions.

We refer to problems related to aspects like cleaning and ergonomics which can interfere or extend the number of actions necessary for the right execution of tasks.

Traditionally, users that would like to follow a recipe have to use their hands and fingers directly on paper and screen in order to go over the steps.

The main difference between the two implemented methods is that in the first solution, mobile devices works at the same time as input manager and monitor, while in the second one they act only as monitor controlled by the sensor mounted on our device.

During our evaluation we seen in users a sort of social acceptance in using this unfamiliar way to get information about the steps that they need to accomplish, and at the same time we collected some interesting feedback and request about features implemented.

Table 1. Comparison between approaches

	Computer vision	Depth sensor
PROS	Rapid implementation	Reliability and precision
CONS	Performances	Expensive, intrusive
Use on mobile	Embedded	Usually not available
Technology	OPENCV	INTEL REALSENSE

5   Conclusion and Future Directions

This work started with the goal to describe how touchless interaction could be enabled on smart mobile devices that were not specifically designed for this functionality and with the aim to be low-cost and minimally-invasive.

We made a comparison between two different approaches traditionally used for the development of different type of interaction related to Natural User Interfaces.

Our point of view is summarized in Table 1. In particular, we analyzed computer vision approaches and depth sensors methods used with mobile devices, underlining their advantages and disadvantages.

In our opinion, at the moment, the most convenient and quickly way to enable touchless interaction is to use, or develop by own, a framework that use a computer vision based solution. This consideration is based on two indicators:

- Cost
- Ergonomy

The first principle is linked to the idea that touchless interaction doesn't have to impose any additional cost to the application's user, except for the device itself.

The second one is related to the idea that touchless interactions should be integrated and embedded in the devices in order to facilitate its usage and avoid the presence of external equipment which imposes a constraint to the users in terms of space and transportability.

Using the same indicators we developed a novel solution IOT based, as an alternative to computer vision based approach and that can be used for a lot of purpose, not only related to the interaction with mobile devices.

In the near future, the market trends of NUI seems to be oriented towards these solutions where devices like Kinect or Leap Motion will act as embedded systems with enough computing power inside to work in a standalone way as IP nodes [15].

However, this assumption is strictly related to future improvements in terms of hardware performances and miniaturization.

In this way NUI devices can be accessed and configured through several type of connections and easily integrated in applications or ecosystem.

In the future we also think that there will be a growth of mobile devices with embedded touchless interactions which will result in an enhancement of tailored functionalities for different kind of users.

Our assumptions are supported by the actions of the big manufactures which are playing on the market with some acquisition and development. Apple, for example, recently acquired PrimeSense, an Israeli 3D sensing company famous for the development of the core technology at the base of Microsoft Kinect, while Samsung started to enable touchless interactions on some devices with the use of the RGB and Gesture Sensor - APDS-9960[6].

At the moment we are still investigating the role and possibilities of Natural User Interface in the field of the Human Computer Interaction and our aim is to identify their possible evolutions, improvements and applications in relation to a wide range of areas like Virtual Reality, and Immersive environments.

---

[6] https://www.sparkfun.com/products/12787.

References

1. Wigdor, D., Wixon, D.: Brave NUI World: Designing Natural User Interfaces for Touch and Gesture. Morgan Kaufmann, Burlington (2011)
2. Zhang, Z.: Microsoft kinect sensor and its effect. IEEE Multimedia **19**(2), 4–10 (2012)
3. Lucero, A., Jones, M., Jokela, T., Robinson, S.: Mobile collocated interactions: taking an offline break together. Interactions **20**, 2 (2013)
4. O'Hara, K., Gonzalez, G., Sellen, A., Penney, G., Varnavas, A., Mentis, H., Criminisi, A., Corish, R., Rouncefield, M., Dastur, N., Carrell, T.: Touchless interaction in surgery. Commun. ACM **57**, 1 (2014)
5. Sivaramakrishnan, K.R., Raja, G.K., Kumar, C.G.: A touchless interface for interventional radiology procedures. In: 2015 International Conference on Automation, Cognitive Science, Optics, Micro Electro-Mechanical System, and Information Technology (ICACOMIT), Bandung, Indonesia (2015)
6. Norman, D.: Natural user interfaces are not natural. Interactions **17**(3), 6–10 (2010)
7. O'Hara, K., Harper, R., Mentis, H., Sellen, A., Taylor, A.: On the naturalness of touchless: putting the "interaction" back into NUI. ACM Trans. Comput.-Hum. Interact. **20**(1), 5 (2013)
8. Karam, M., Schraefel, M.C.: A taxonomy of gestures in human computer interaction. Technical report, ECSTR-IAM05-009 Electronics and Computer Science, University of Southampton (2005)
9. Gavrila, D.M.: The visual analysis of human movement: a survey. Comput. Vis. Image Underst. **73**(1), 82–98 (1999)
10. Rautaray, S.S., Agrawal, A.: Vision based hand gesture recognition for human computer interaction: a survey. Artif. Intell. Rev. **43**, 1–54 (2012)
11. Lv, Z., Halawani, A., Lal Khan, M.S., Réhman, S., Li, H.: Finger in air: touch-less interaction on smartphone. In: Proceedings of the 12th International Conference on Mobile and Ubiquitous Multimedia (MUM 2013), ACM, New York, NY, USA, Article 16 (2013)
12. Liu X., Fujimura K.: Hand gesture recognition using depth data. In: 2004 Proceedings of Sixth IEEE International Conference on Automatic Face And Gesture Recognition, pp. 529–534 (2004)
13. Bradski, G., Kaehler, A.: Learning OpenCV: Computer Vision with the OpenCV Library. O'Reilly Media Inc., Sebastopol (2008)
14. Atzori, L., Iera, A., Morabito, G.: The Internet of Things: a survey. Comput. Netw. **54**(15), 2787–2805 (2010). 1389-1286
15. Kortuem, G., Kawsar, F., Sundramoorthy, V., Fitton, D.: Smart objects as building blocks for the Internet of Things. IEEE Internet Comput. **14**(1), 44–51 (2010)

3D Reconstruction as a Service – Applications in Virtual Cultural Heritage

Octavian-Mihai Machidon[✉], Cristian-Cezar Postelnicu, and Florin-Stelian Girbacia

Transylvania University of Brasov, 500036 Brasov, Romania
{octavian.machidon, cristian-cezar.postelnicu, garbacia}@unitbv.ro

Abstract. As Virtual Reality (VR) expands its application range in various domains, one area that benefits more and more from VR implementation is cultural heritage. This synergy has created a new research subject: virtual cultural heritage, with specific challenges and with the key issue being to reconstruct the 3D virtual model of a real cultural artefact or item. We propose that by transcending the classic 3D reconstruction instruments to online services available remotely these newly appeared challenges can be properly addressed and the 3D reconstruction process will gain in accessibility and availability for a wider range of scientists, researchers and users. This paper presents an original implementation of such 3D reconstruction services that create virtual models based on data obtained from a 3D scanning system operating on the laser striping principle. This solution is intended to be used for digital preservation efforts of the cultural artefacts from the Brasov history museum by creating a digital archive with their 3D virtual models.

Keywords: Virtual reality · Service-oriented architectures · 3D reconstruction · Virtual cultural heritage

1 Introduction

Virtual reality has expanded its application range in various domains, one of these being the field of cultural heritage. The emerged virtual cultural heritage is a VR-based technology that creates virtual representations of archaeological artefacts, buildings, monuments and other cultural items with the goals of raising their availability to the general public, easy sharing between research parties, preservation etc. [1].

Another important application is the creation of a mixed reality environment where virtual 3D artefacts co-exist and interact with real ones, thus enhancing the visitor's experience at a cultural heritage site. Last but not least, the synergy between virtual reality and cultural heritage has the potential to enhance the teaching of history/archeology courses by offering students a more "hands-on" perspective and thus helping them in better understanding certain events in history or other elements that would be more abstract without a viewable model.

In the development of virtual cultural heritage, the key step is the 3D modelling of cultural artefacts. This process extends from 3D data acquisition to the 3D reconstruction of the artefact's virtual model.

© Springer International Publishing Switzerland 2016
L.T. De Paolis and A. Mongelli (Eds.): AVR 2016, Part II, LNCS 9769, pp. 261–268, 2016.
DOI: 10.1007/978-3-319-40651-0_21

Achieving a 3D digitization of cultural heritage artifacts either stored in museums or at archeological sites offers many advantages such as [2]:

- Digital preservation of the cultural artefacts by creating a digital archive that would represent an invaluable asset in preventing permanent loss of these items due to accidents or natural disasters.
- Creating educational resources for history and culture [3].
- Increasing the public availability and access to cultural artefacts by providing digital replicas in on-line museums and exhibits.
- Using the reconstructed 3D models for documentation and analysis. In the case of on-site acquired models, this would allow more researchers and historians to be offered faster access to the newly discovered item, and enables visualization from viewpoints inaccessible in the real world.
- Creating physical replicas based on the 3D model of a cultural heritage item – this allows interacting with objects without risking any damage. Also, this has potential applications in other fields like the film industry.

Furthermore, recent research efforts are targeting the development of large online 3D digital libraries (like the Europeana project) by a massive digitization and annotation of 3D artifacts in museums and exhibits. Leveraging the Web's infrastructure for the creation and storing of digital 3D cultural heritage artifacts brings another important asset with regard to sharing these items, since the web and mobile devices are the ideal platforms for such a dissemination [4].

2   3D Acquisition

One major issue is the workflow going from 3D data acquisition to the 3D virtual model reproduction. In the cultural heritage field, this flow implies the use of several technologies linked together, each with its own resources and specific problems, that must also take into account the particularities of this domain.

Dealing with archaeological object, any direct physical contact is obviously forbidden. Thus, the 3D shape acquisition process in this case is based on non-contact methods relying on light, leading to the use of one of the following technologies: laser scanners, structured light devices, photogrammetry, and so on.

Given the interdisciplinary approach that is used in the field of cultural heritage (involving engineers, historians, archaeologists, etc.), a special care needs to be taken when processing the data sets provided by the shape acquisition tools (clouds of points, images, etc.), as data format, accessibility and availability, and computing and storing resources become very important challenges [5].

3   3D Reconstruction

3.1   Stand-Alone Solutions

One method of processing 3D acquired data to generate a 3D model is by using stand-alone software tools, like PhotoScan or MeshLab. Usually, such applications operate with 3D data like calibrated or un-calibrated images, or point clouds, and offer a variety of options for editing, converting, and rendering the 3D meshes.

This approach however needs dedicated computers/software tools with a certain level of complexity and thus restricts the access only to specialized users – 3D engineers. Also, it makes the entire flow much slower, especially in the case where a mobile 3D scanner is used on-site for data acquisition, and so the two processes: acquisition and reconstruction are two separate tasks, performed with a considerable time delay one from another.

3.2 Service-Oriented Approach

The downsides mentioned above and the recent advances in the field of web and mobile technologies and services have led to the development of 3D reconstruction services, available online on the Web [6].

Developing new solutions and technologies for the integration of various heterogeneous components in distributed systems is made easy with the newly emerged service-oriented paradigm. This represents the most recent innovation in the creation of middleware technologies intended to provide the infrastructure needed for large-scale Internet applications while solving the problem of inter-operability.

Thus, the service-oriented approach is the ideal solution for a "seamless" integration of a variety of software and hardware technologies by providing the flexible middleware needed for granting a high degree of inter-operability. This is all possible due to the standards and protocols that are the building blocks of SOA, and which enable the unified, service-based access to different types of computing resources, abstracting away their specific particularities [7].

A particular form of service-oriented distributed system is cloud computing, the next evolutionary stage of the Internet, which delivers various types of distributed resources to clients as services [8]. The cloud computing infrastructure brings on several assets like cost reduction, limiting the need of licensing new software tools and increased flexibility of business processes.

By applying the service-oriented paradigm to 3D reconstruction solutions two main key elements are achieved: raising the accessibility of such solutions by becoming online-available services, and abstracting away part of their complexity, thus enabling a remote 3D reconstruction fast and without much specific knowledge.

Most of these 3D reconstruction services are free, and can be used by both inexperienced users and researchers. The financial aspect can be very important in areas such as cultural heritage – especially archeology – where project budgets or specifications may not allow developing or installing dedicated tools for 3D reconstruction.

4   Implementation

Our implementation deals with developing and integrating 3D reconstruction services to support a FPGA-based 3D acquisition platform.

The 3D scanning system is based on the laser striping principle for acquiring the object's 3D surface information. This information is used by the 3D model reconstruction process, which is remotely available online, "as a Service". A web interface has been implemented that creates an abstraction level masking away the complexity of the process, and also improving performance and granting an easy sharing infrastructure. An overview of our system is shown in Fig. 1.

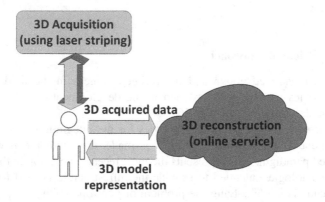

Fig. 1. Overview of the 3D model acquisition and reconstruction system.

Being a custom implementation, the system involves low-level data protocols and complex processes sequentially executed for acquiring and transferring the 3D data. If the 3D reconstruction were to be handled manually, using stand-alone solutions, the complexity of the entire flow would have been higher, with increased execution times, thus lowering the efficiency and attractiveness of the 3D acquisition system.

Thus, we have considered applying a service-oriented approach intended to abstract away the flow's complexity and offer users a friendly, fast and efficient web interface for the 3D model reconstruction.

This service-based approach was chosen especially for improving the system's usability and portability – the scanning system is being separated from the 3D reconstruction software, now available remotely online, on a "Software-as-a-Service" cloud computing model. Not only that these services can be accessed from any location (which extends the application range of the hardware acquisition system) but also they benefit from their execution on dedicated computing servers, which increase their processing speed.

4.1   System Architecture

The service-oriented integration of the workflow (depicted in Fig. 2) is based on three key elements:

1. The web interface enabling the I/O data transfer between the user and the actual web service handling the 3D reconstruction task. This interface was developed using the

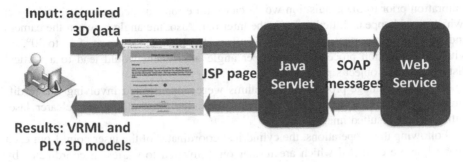

Fig. 2. Web service-based integration of the work flow

JSP (Java Server Pages) technology. JSPs were chosen since they represent a solution for generating dynamic web content, by combining HTML, XML and embedded Java code, actions and commands [9].

2. A Java servlet implemented for extending the Web application's functionality. Java servlets, key components of server-side Java development, help extend and customize Java web or application servers by improving flexibility and usability [10]. In our case, the Java servlet acts as an intermediary component (or layer) between the JSP interface and the Web server, being responsible with processing HTTP messages to/from the JSP pages and handling the SOAP-based communication with the Web service.

3. The actual Web service – a Java implementation running on a Glassfish 4.0 Server instance. On this service we implemented a method responsible with the creation and configuration of the local working environment on the server, and with running the 3D reconstruction flow.

Dealing with a large number of images, the Web service's method operates in a "buffered" technique that improves the overall processing speed. This has been accomplished by processing each pair of images (with/without laser line) as it is received, having the point coordinates extracted and stored in the database while the other images are being transferred and processed.

4.2   Functionality

The workflow basically takes as input the data uploaded by the user (e.g. scanned images) and by running the 3D reconstruction software it generates a VRML 3D model of the object and a PLY (Polygon File Format) – the 3D model obtained from point clouds. These files are then sent back to the JSP Web interface and thus made available for the user download.

The 3D reconstruction flow has been automated using Perl scripts. Its first stage consists of running the image processing software – developed in C using OpenCv 2.1 libraries [11]. For providing correct results, this stage requires two synchronization mechanisms, respectively calibration and angle adjustment. These are mandatory for a correct translation from cylindrical to Cartesian coordinates. Lacking a proper calibration prior to 3D acquisition would cause an erroneous perspective of the object (which would appear shifted towards the interior). Also, the angle between the camera and the laser is important, and for best results it should be in the range of 15 to 20°. As with the calibration process, an improper angle adjustment would lead to a vertical distortion of the object's perspective.

Further on, image processing algorithms were implemented involving image difference, median filters (for noise removal) and edge thresholding (for clearer laser outline in the resulted image).

Following these operations, the cylindrical coordinates of the laser point from each image line are extracted which are further on converted to Cartesian coordinates by applying mathematical formulae. These points are used by the application to create two databases needed for 3D model reconstruction [12]: a Cartesian coordinates' enumeration – used for 3D modeling based on point clouds using MeshLab and a VRML mesh file.

The mesh file is generated automatically by using a Poisson Surface Reconstruction algorithm. In order for the entire flow to be automated and thus be invoked by the Web service method, the processing tasks performed with MeshLab have been automated by using mlx filter scripts and meshlabserver batch scripts in the command line. In Fig. 3 is presented an example of an artefact 3D reconstruction using the proposed framework.

Fig. 3. Example of an artefact 3D reconstruction using the proposed framework

4.3   Validation and Applications

The main target and objective for this research is providing a flexible and efficient solution for the digital preservation of cultural artefacts from the various museums and other cultural institutions.

Our partner is the Brasov history museum, which contains a permanent exhibition of more than 3000 cultural objects from different historical periods: middle Paleolithic, Iron Age, objects belonging to the roman settlers in the area, and naturally a lot of items dating from the Middle Ages and modern history. These cultural heritage possessions are of great importance, being included in the Romanian national Thesaurus of cultural heritage.

Consequently, there is a great interest in extending the methods of preservation and increasing the public availability of the artefacts. The solution described in this paper aims at contributing to accomplishing these goals by creating the virtual 3D models of the real cultural artefacts. Ultimately, the target is to be able to group these virtual resources into repositories of an online museum.

We are currently working on applying the service-oriented 3D reconstruction framework for the digitization of the cultural artefacts from the above-mentioned history museum. Several trials are currently underway for validating, testing and improving the system, making it a viable solution with a high degree of mobility and reliability for fast, on-site digitization of artefacts. An example of a 3D reconstructed artefact using this platform is shown in Fig. 3.

5 Conclusions

We described in this paper a model of implementing 3D reconstruction web services that enable the generation of 3D models based on data acquired using laser-striping based scanning solutions.

The 3D model reconstruction process is available "as a service", thus offering a high degree of portability to the 3D acquisition process. As shown, this approach gains in flexibility and scalability over the traditional 3D scanning solutions, which makes it an ideal candidate for applications in the field of virtual cultural heritage, where artefact digitization and web availability of the 3D models are very important issues.

Also, there is a considerable speed-up of the reconstruction process since the image processing and the elaboration of the 3D model are being executed online on high-performance computing machines. Thus, there is no need for managing a local machine for such a task, which also leads to another strongpoint of our proposed implementation: ease of use.

Compared to the traditional setup, where one or several software tools needed to be installed and managed on a local machine – with all the implications: constant updates of the software or hardware, this novel approach offers the users a standard, easy to use web interface that abstracts away the complexity of such tasks.

This paper also brings notable benefits in the academic field and also with regard to the research in virtual heritage applications. Dealing with the possibility to enhance the digitization and web-availability of the cultural artefacts and items, the approach presented in this work leverages service-oriented architectures and Web services as viable building blocks needed to transcend the 3D reconstruction process from locally managed tools to online available services on a cloud computing model.

This leads not only to an improved and generalized access to such resources, available online, but also to a widening of the potential user categories (due to its ease of use), from specialized 3D software engineers, to archeologists, historians and other researchers without specialized knowledge. This is a key factor in the cultural heritage field, as one of its main characteristics is the interdisciplinary work that it implies, and the synergy between various branches of science.

Last but not least, we are focusing on using the online 3D reconstruction Web services to help the ongoing preservation efforts from the Brasov history museum by creating virtual 3D models of the artefacts and ultimately including these models in an online museum.

Acknowledgments. This paper is supported by European Union's Horizon 2020 Research and Innovation Programme under grant agreement No. 692103, project EHERITAGE (Expanding the Research and Innovation Capacity in Cultural Heritage Virtual Reality Applications).

References

1. Stone, R., Ojika, T.: Virtual heritage: what next? IEEE MultiMedia **7**(2), 73–74 (2000). doi:10.1109/93.848434
2. Santos, P., Serna, S.P., Stork, A., Fellner, D.: The Potential of 3D internet in the cultural heritage domain. In: Ioannides, M., Quak, E. (eds.) 3D Research Challenges. LNCS, vol. 8355, pp. 1–17. Springer, Heidelberg (2014)
3. El-Hakim, S., Beraldin, J.A., Picard, M., Godin, G.: Detailed 3D reconstruction of large-scale heritage sites with integrated techniques. IEEE Comput. Graph. Appl. **24**(3), 21–29 (2004). doi:10.1109/MCG.2004.1318815
4. Di Benedetto, M., Ponchio, F., Malomo, L., Callieri, M., Dellepiane, M., Cignoni, P., Scopigno, R.: Web and mobile visualization for cultural heritage. In: Ioannides, M., Quak, E. (eds.) 3D Research Challenges. LNCS, vol. 8355, pp. 18–35. Springer, Heidelberg (2014)
5. Callet, P.: 3D reconstruction from 3D cultural heritage models. In: Ioannides, M., Quak, E. (eds.) 3D Research Challenges. LNCS, vol. 8355, pp. 135–142. Springer, Heidelberg (2014)
6. Rasztovits, S., Dorninger, P.: Comparison of 3D reconstruction services and terrestrial laser scanning for cultural heritage documentation. ISPRS-Int. Arch. Photogrammetry Remote Sens. Spat. Inf. Sci. **1**(2), 513–518 (2013)
7. Hansen, M.D.: SOA Using Java Web Services. Pearson Education, Upper Saddle River (2007)
8. Vecchio, P., Mele, F., De Paolis, L.T., Epicoco, I., Mancini, M., Aloisio, G.: Cloud computing and augmented reality for cultural heritage. In: De Paolis, L.T., Mongelli, A. (eds.) AVR 2015. LNCS, vol. 9254, pp. 51–60. Springer, Heidelberg (2015)
9. Perry, B.: Java Servlet and JSP Cookbook. O'Reilly Media Inc., Upper Saddle River (2004)
10. Hunter, J., Crawford, W.: Java Servlet Programming. O'Reilly Media Inc., Upper Saddle River (2001)
11. Bradski, G., Kaehler, A.: Learning OpenCV: Computer Vision with the OpenCV Library. O'Reilly Media Inc., Upper Saddle River (2008)
12. Whitaker, R.T.: A level-set approach to 3D reconstruction from range data. Int. J. Comput. Vis. **29**(3), 203–231 (1998). doi:10.1023/A:1008036829907

Digital Reconstruction of Darul Aman Palace Based on Images and Implementation into Virtual Reality Environment

Mohammad Fadly Syahputra[✉], Joko Ali Permady,
and Muhammad Anggia Muchtar

Information Technology, University of North Sumatera, Medan, Indonesia
{nca.fadly,anggi.muchtar}@usu.ac.id,
jokoalipermady@students.usu.ac.id

Abstract. Darul Aman Palace is one of Langkat Sultanate palaces in Tanjung Pura. This palace had been destroyed when 'social revolution' occurred in the East Sumatera in 1946. Digital reconstruction is required in order to preserve the history. In this research, Virtual Reality has been utilised to give the user different experience when exploring the historic site digitally. Reconstruction is made based on collection of old images, which are taken before the revolution, using single-based image modelling. Thereafter, the 3D model of Darul Aman Palace is embedded into Virtual Reality (VR) environment integrated with Head-Mounted Display device in order to improve its immersive graphic. As the result, the reconstruction process permits a Virtual Tour that provides different experience for its user when exploring the reconstructed palace, especially to study the history that is almost extinct.

Keywords: Darul Aman Palace · Digital reconstruction · Virtual reality · Virtual Tour

1 Introduction

The Darul Aman Palace in the city center of Tanjung Pura has been destroyed during the social revolution in 1946 [1]. Nowadays, the site where the palace ever built has no sign of ruined palace. As the palace has historical value of East Sumatera Malay, hence the reconstruction is required to preserve the history knowledge of East Sumatera Malay.

Based on the historical evidence, Langkat Sultanate had two palaces i.e. Darul Aman and Darussalam. Darul Aman had unique malay architecture, and Darussalam had mixed architecture from Mughal, European and Malay building structures as shown in Fig. 1.

The digital research of historical relics has been developed and currently focus on the area of archaeological studies and computer application [2]. Therefore, digital reconstruction technique allows historians to preserve the historical site without build it physically. It is expected that a 3D model of Darul Aman Palace combined with the Virtual Reality, leads to a model that can provide exciting experiences to users. Virtual

© Springer International Publishing Switzerland 2016
L.T. De Paolis and A. Mongelli (Eds.): AVR 2016, Part II, LNCS 9769, pp. 269–279, 2016.
DOI: 10.1007/978-3-319-40651-0_22

(a)   (b)

Fig. 1. Darul Aman (a) and Darussalam Palace (b)

Reality allows user to feel that he or she is indeed in the ruined historic site. Past studies regarding virtual reality have been done due to its benefit to the historians and commercial industries. Scagliarini et al. had reconstructed Pompeii city destroyed by Mt. Vesuvius eruption in AD 79 [3]. They applied techniques such as 3D modelling technique based on stereo photo-pairs, virtual display technique based on Cave Automatic Virtual Environment (better known by the acronym CAVE), exploration technique based on virtual animation, and scene interaction control technique based on Virtual Reality Modelling Language (VRML) nodes.

Bruno et al. [4] presented some guidelines for development of a VR system for digital archaeological exhibition. The work illustrates a complete methodology to create a virtual exhibition system based on realistic high-quality 3D model. Calabria that built between 18th and 9th BC was the subject of his study. Using a low cost multimedia stereoscopic system called MNEME (from the Ancient Greek 'memory'), which allows user to interact in easy way.

Furthermore Syahputra et al. [5] has reconstructed Darussalam Palace using Image-Based Modelling and Game Engine as the Virtual Environment. However this last study had not implemented Full-Immersive Virtual Reality yet. Therefore, in this research, we use Virtual Reality (VR) environment and has been integrated with Head-Mounted Display device in order to improve its immersive graphic.

2   Methodology

The methodology of this study consists of several phases, i.e. data collecting, 3D modelling and virtual reality environment. It is shown in the Fig. 2.

2.1   Data Collection

The first stage in this research is data collection. In this study, we use three types of data, i.e. photos of palace that include architectural from both exterior and interior, information from sultanate family and field observation.

Images collection can determine the layout of the palace to be designed in 3D modelling. In Fig. 3, it can be seen some photos that have been made as references in order to make the 3D model of the palace.

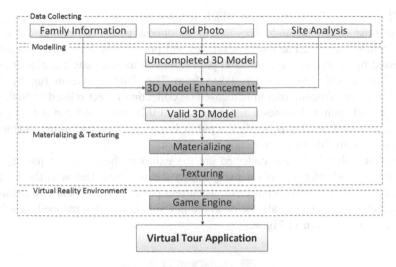

Fig. 2. Methodology

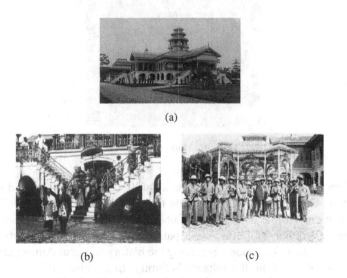

Fig. 3. The photos of palace from perspective

The result of data collection is shown in Table 1.

Table 1. Data source

No.	Data source	Photo found
1.	*The Koninklijk Instituut voor Taal-, Land- en Volkenkunde*	103
2.	*The Tropenmuseum (Museum of the Tropics)*	64
3.	*The ETH-Bibliothek*	8

KITLV is a research institution which focuses on acquiring and collecting data from the time of Netherlands invasion in Indonesia which is around 1851. This institution has data's such as journals, articles and photos which is open data that can be accessed by everyone, we found 103 photos related to Sultanate Langkat from this source. Our second data source is taken from The Tropenmuseum run by Royal Tropical Institute. Tropenmuseum is focused on collecting object related to Netherland invasion's land such as Indonesia and others, from this source we can get 64 photos. The last source is The ETH-Bibliothek, a public library focused on culture, science and engineering. From this source we collect 8 photos.

The photos that had been collected are the exterior photos of the palace, while interior photos and information's is really hard to be acquired. Below is the photos of Sultanate palace from aerial perspective, its current position of the palace in the area of Tanjung Pura City, and it can also be observed in Langkat regional mapped drew by the Netherlands. It is shown in Fig. 4.

Fig. 4. Map of Tanjung

The information acquired from sultanate's family consist of photos and stories from their ancestors. Current sultan's father (here they call him as "Raja Muda") is the last generation that entered the palace, at his father's time the social revolution is happen, resulting the destruction of Darul Aman palace. We can reach informations directly from Raja Muda, the information's regarding the history of Darul Aman palace, and we also get the old photos from the sultanate's family. In addition, other data sources are obtained from field observations and by interviewing the sultanate family. From field observations, we acquire the spacious of Darul Aman Palace complex and some left-over debris as shown in Fig. 5.

2.2 3D Modelling

The available information is limited therefore it is quite difficult to determine the layout, size and spacious of the palace accurately. In determining the size of the palace, the calculation is based on estimates of the scale and the actual size of an object in the photo of palace. The method used in this 3D modeling process is image-based

(a)   (b)

Fig. 5. Some of debris of Darul Aman Palace beside people housing.

modeling (IBM) using Blender 3D modeling software version 2.76 and using a calculation based on photo. This has been shown in Fig. 6.

Fig. 6. Palace size calculation process

Denoted x is as the height of people who were given a blue box in the image, and y is as building height 1st floor by the green box on the image. Then, the scale comparison between x and y obtained from image processing software with value of 1:2,35. According to the used scale, then y = 2,35x. The height of person in the photo is assumed 170 cm, therefore one can obtains the value of y as below.

$$y = 2,35(x) = 2,35(170) = 399,5 \text{ cm}$$

From the calculation above, one can obtain the high of palace for each floor with value of 399,5 cm or rounded up to 4 m high. Utilising the floor height then one can easily calculate other parts of the palace based on the photos. As a result this approach can generate a full layout design of the palace. From layout design of the palace, the 3D model can be produced as shown in Fig. 7.

Fig. 7. Darul Aman Palace in 3D model form

There are three basic primitives or fundamental ways to create a 3D shape: points, curves, and polygons. Points are the simplest primitive; a 3D shape can be composed of a large amount of points to cover the whole 3D surface, where each point can be represented by a 3D vertex. A more practical and compact way of representing 3D shapes is using curves, which can be approximated by lines or points. Curves are used to describe complex 3D surfaces [6].

In this research several techniques were used for 3D modelling:

1. Polygonal Modelling

Polygonal Modelling is the most common 3D modelling technique. A model defines as polygon called mesh. Polygon have size, shape and position so that the polygon forming surface [7]. The advantage of polygonal modelling is simple process on computer for display and manipulate the object. Flexible shape and has a resolution mesh which vary according to application. Polygonal modeling is used to generate low poly objects with low resolution.

2. NURBS Modelling

NURBS (Non-Uniform Rational B-Splines) is 3D modelling technique using curves. NURBS has became standard in 3D modelling object especially, to create objects with curved shapes that have a high level of complexity. This technique is different than the Polygonal.

In NURBS, an object consisting curves. Transformation curves will effect the shape of the object. NURBS is the most popular method because NURBS curve can be formed only by three point. NURBS have control point (CV) make it easier to control the curves. One point of CV can control one area [8].

As the process in measuring the size of the palace is based on assumption of old photos, then the design of the palace can be build. Most of the palace's photos are exterior photos, thus in order to do interior modelling of the palace, we took the model from other related palaces which still connected to Darul Aman Palace, such as Deli Sultanate Palace and Siak Sultanate Palace.

2.3 3D Model Enhancement

In the 3D modelling of an object, counting vertices and face on the object is not an efficient method as accurate modelling requires plenty of vertices to produce a smooth surface. However vertices reduction is useful for rendering process, making the object become low poly and simplify the UV mapping on the object.

This is not usually used on meshes which have been created by modeling carefully and economically where all vertices and faces are necessary to correctly define the shape. But if the mesh is the result of complex modeling, sculpting or applied sub-surface modifiers, the Decimate modifier can be used to reduce the polygon count for a performance increase, or simply remove unnecessary vertices and edges.

The Decimate modifier is a quick and easy way of reducing the polygon count of a mesh. However, using modifier decimate will change face position.

2.4 Materializing and Texturing

3D model of the palace should be given appropriate materials and textures. The common material at that time was metal, stone, wood and roof. Material contains parameters to determine how light interacts with the surface of the model, so the material is able to provide the level of staining that has quite good gradation and can be arranged as desired. The results from the addition of material can be seen in Fig. 8.

Fig. 8. Materialized 3D model

Virtual reality is running on a real-time rendering so it requires texture to give a real impression of the model we want to built. Texture which contains bitmap data is added to the material. In other words, the provision will only change the surface texture of a model without being affected by light as if the paint attached to the object. The feature that we can use here to improve the texture quality is using UV mapping. With UV mapping, we can tell the software to place textures at an exact location. When we create a UV map, the computer has all the instructions to place the textures where the artist wants on a face.

UV texturing permits polygons that make up a 3D object to be painted with color from an image. The image is called a UV texture map, but it's just an ordinary image [9]. The UV mapping process involves assigning pixels in the image to surface mappings on the polygon [10]. UV is the alternative to XY. It only maps into a texture space rather than into the geometric space of the object. However the rendering computation using the UV texture coordinates can determine the painting process of the three-dimensional surfaces.

In a few decades, innovations in rendering and texture mapping techniques may generate realistic images such as height mapping, bump mapping, normal mapping and displacement mapping. In this study, the mapping technique used is the normal mapping.

Normal mapping is a technique used for faking the lighting of bumps and dents. It is used to add details without using more polygons. A common use of this technique is to greatly enhance the appearance and details of a low poly model. Low poly object has a few vertex. In Fig. 9, we can see the result of texturing process into the models that have been added to the previous material.

Fig. 9. Texturized 3D model

2.5 Virtual Reality Environment

Virtual environment is built to support 3D objects that has been established earlier. When first developing virtual reality, modeling process until virtual environment is built using a VRML (virtual reality modeling language) which is quite native. However in this time, there are many development methods of VR to do, one of them using the game engine (GE) platform application development.

The virtual environment is a holistic entity of the landscape that has been designed as desired. The landscape itself is made using the existing terrain features on Unity3D and refers to the map of Tanjung Pura as in Fig. 10a. The results of the modeling of virtual environments can be seen in Fig. 10b adapted with data from field observations.

(a)   (b)

Fig. 10. Tanjung Pura Terrain

3D object that was made before then applied with terrain of the palace as shown in Fig. 11.

Fig. 11. Terrain of the palace

3 Result and Discussion

Fundamentally, Virtual Tour for non-immersive mode and full-immersive mode are not different, but only have a little different in player that is used. The visible effect to the user only bias on sight, where OVR Player for HMD device adjusts the display settings to make the display more comfortable to be seen by user. Virtual Tour display can be seen in Fig. 12.

(a)   (b)

(c)   (d)

Fig. 12. Photo and its 3D model result

As for the interior parts of the palace with minimal reference were taken from the combination of Malay palace in Eastern Sumatra region, as shown in Fig. 13.

(a)   (b)

Fig. 13. Interior of Darul Aman Palace

4   Conclusion

Based on the previous discussion and evaluation, it can be concluded as follows:

1. The application has been demonstrated to be able to represent Darul Aman Palace in digital reconstruction. The result of the reconstruction process follows the stages of 3D modeling based on Precision Match and Qualitative Test methods
2. An application of Virtual Tour provide a different experience for its users, especially in the study of history. However, the application requires hardware with high specifications, especially memory and graphic cards in order to get maximum experience.

3. Limited resources of informations and datas of Darul Aman Palace makes the researchers quite difficult in modelling the palace, so the accuracy of objects created were less than optimal, especially in term of the palace's interior.
4. The level of emissivity on applications built in presenting the virtual reality experience is quite limited. Complex aspects of engineering and high specifications of hardware are needed in order to create a virtual world with optimal immersive graphic (closer to reality).

References

1. Ramadhan, F.: Revolusi Sosial di Kesultanan Langkat Pada Tahun 1946 (2015). http://eprints.uny.ac.id/17777/1/Skripsi%20Full%2010407141001%20Fitra%20Ramadhan.swf. 10 Oct 2015
2. Duan, X., Gu, B., Shi, C.: Virtual exploration application of cultural heritage for Anyang Yinxu. In: Second Workshop on Digital Media and its Application in Museum and Cultural Heritage, pp. 237–240. Anyang (2007)
3. Scagliriani, D., Coralini, A., Vecchietti, E., Cinotti, T.S., Roffia, L., Galasso, S., Malavasi, M., Pigozzi, M., Romagnoli, E., Sforza, F.: Exciting understanding in Pompeii through on-site parallel interaction with dual time virtual models. In: Proceedings of the 2001 Conference on Virtual Reality, Archeology, and Cultural Heritage, pp. 83–90. ACM (2001)
4. Bruno, F., Bruno, S., Sensi, G.D., Luchi, M.L., Mancuso, S., Muzzupappa, M.: From 3D reconstruction to virtual reality: a complete methodology for digital archaeological exhibition. J. Cult. Herit. 11(1), 42–49 (2009). Rende
5. Syahputra, F.M., Siregar, B., Purnamawati, S.: Aplikasi Virtual Tour Istana Darussalam menggunakan Teknologi Virtual Reality. In: Proceddings of SENARAI USU, pp. 249–253. Medan (2014)
6. Gutiérrez, M.A., Vexo, F., Thalmann, D.: Stepping into Virtual Reality. Springer, London (2008)
7. Kisworo, T., Wicaksono, A.: Simulasi Kecelakaan Kereta Api dengan Menggunakan Teknik Polygonal Modelling. Thesis, STMIK Amikom Yogyakarta (2011)
8. Flemming, B.: 3D Modelling and Surfacing. Morgan Kaufmann, Burlington (1999)
9. Mullen, T.: Mastering Blender, 1st edn. Wiley Publishing, Indianapolis (2009)
10. Murdock, K.L.: 3Ds Max 2009 Bible, 1st edn. Wiley Publishing, Indianapolis (2008)

An Augmented Reality Guide
for Religious Museum

Luca Greci[✉]

Istituto di Tecnologie Industriali e Automazione (ITIA),
Consiglio Nazionale delle Ricerche (CNR), Milan, Italy
luca.greci@itia.cnr.it

Abstract. This paper describes the design and implementation of an augmented reality (AR) guide for religious museum. The aim of this study is to provide to the museums a new guide tool that allows the users to understand the complex meanings of the religious artwork in an intuitive and user-friendly way. The tool has also the intent to facilitate the born of an intercultural dialogue between visitors with different backgrounds and creeds. In our design, the artworks are used as natural markers, using the camera of a portable device (smartphone or tablet), the system recognizes the artwork and superimposes it multimedia materials, 3D models and interactive/sharing sections. The App will run on the user's device, reducing the hardware-related costs. Moreover, the guide remains available, for the users, even after the visit is finished and can be used outside the museum by framing the museum's book.

Keywords: Augmented reality · Virtual reality · Computer vision · Man-machine interaction · Multimedia · Museums

1 Introduction

The evolution of the web from phase 1.0 to phase 2.0 has generated a new kind of users, called 2.0, with different needs respect to the "normal users". The new users are not simply information consumer, they want to create, communicate, collaborate and share contents in a simple and interactive way. The launch on the market of new devices (smartphone and tablet) and technologies (ADSL, Wi-Fi, 3G, LTE), capable to reduce the geographical distance, the economic and social differences, as well as the release of platform to create digital and virtual contents allows the content's developer to satisfy the needs of the users 2.0 [1].

With the help of the Augmented reality (AR) technology (e.g. adding computer vision and object recognition), the information about the surrounding real world of the user becomes interactive and digitally modifiable. Artificial information about the environment and its objects can be overlaid on the real world [2, 3]. The superimposed objects provide to the user the way to interact with the artworks. In this way, the users have control on issues that they want to deepen moving the experience from a uni-directional flow of information to a customized experience.

Similarly the cultural sector, in particular the museums, is considering different possibilities for using these new resources to transform the visitor experience from a contemplative fruition to an interactive and contributory visit (Participatory Museum) [4].

© Springer International Publishing Switzerland 2016
L.T. De Paolis and A. Mongelli (Eds.): AVR 2016, Part II, LNCS 9769, pp. 280–289, 2016.
DOI: 10.1007/978-3-319-40651-0_23

The religious museum, in this years characterized by globalization and migration, has to face with the challenge to explain, by the use of their collections, religious faith and practice to people with different background and creeds [5]. Enabling an intercultural dialogue seems to be the way to deal with discussion of religion, among religions and through religion. To facilitate intercultural dialogue is necessary to help foreigners' visitors to understand the meaning of the artworks like actors, gestures, objects and faith so that they can make a comparison with their creed and background. The use of multimedia contents can improve the understanding of the museum's collection and engage the visitors in going in depth respect to the artwork they are looking at.

By using AR is possible to transform the linear model of a museum visit into a customized activity with multiple pathways for the visitor to experience contents, religious museums can provide new paradigm of interactions and can establish and support an intercultural dialogues.

The use of the social network like Twitter, Facebook or similar, inside the application, and the development of an in-depth section linking artifacts with similar meanings, but coming from different religions, will favorite the born of a virtual place where users can exchange opinions and let comments about their museum visit enabling an intercultural dialogue [6].

The aim of this work is to describe the development of an AR interactive guide system for religious artworks with the intent to generate an intercultural dialogue.

2 Related Works

Ronald Azuma published the first survey on AR in 1997 [7] describing the characteristics of AR systems and its limits. In 1999, with the release of ARtoolKit to the open source community, the AR has become available and usable on any OS platform and has begun to spread outside the scientific community. In the recent years three main aspects have favored the growth and diffusion of AR applications on the market:

1. The born and development of portable devices (tablet and smartphone) with high computational performance, low encumbrance and high camera resolution.
2. The step forward done by the computer vision technique in the object tracking field in terms of performance [8]
3. The release on the market of multi-platform engine like Unity3D, Aurasma and Wikitude [9–11] for the software and content development and visualization.

Computer vision offers different techniques for object tracking: positioning, marker and markerless [12]. Figure 1 shows the use of the positioning technique for AR tours at archaeological sites: by retrieving the user position and orientation by GPS and compass, the application superimpose an augmented 3D temple to live video on the display [13]. This solution is suitable for outdoor AR application. Figure 2a shows an AR experiment called Variable Museum [14]. It uses a marker based augmented reality system to add virtual pieces to the empty gallery space. Another example of marker based AR environment is the Museum of Stolen Art (MoSA) (Fig. 2b) in Hertogenbosh (NL): "The exhibition emphasizes the feeling of loss by showing empty canvases in frames, which only come to life when visitors look at them through their smartphone or tablet" [15]. In both the examples, the use of the markers do not modify the outfit of the exhibition because the markers are the exhibition. In many other cases this kind of markers are discouraged because can alter the work done by fitters.

Fig. 1. Positioning technique for augmented reality application for tours at archaeological sites and subsequent augmented 3D temple reconstruction.

Fig. 2. Markers based augmented reality art installation: (a) variable museum, (b) museum of stolen Art.

The markerless technique tracks objects in reality without special marker. In these cases, object tracking depends on natural features. The object tracking is obtained using pre-existing image as the target to be detected to display the virtual objects [16]. In Fig. 3 is shown an example of AR markerless system to add multimedia information to artworks or fossil record made for the American Museum of natural History by Ori

Fig. 3. Markerless augmented reality demo for American Museum of natural history.

Inbar and Snowball VFX. The dinosaur skeleton is used as natural marker and once it is framed the multimedia content are added to the user's device.

The choice of the computer vision technique is context depending. A wrong choice, about the computer vision technique, can negatively influence both the perception of the exhibition and the interaction between the users and the application. Moreover, the multimedia content and the interaction mode play an important role for a good user's experience. Therefore, in this work, it has been paid particular attention to the choice of the computer vision technique and on the choice of the multimedia and the interaction with them.

3 Case Study

The application has been developed for the Museo Diocesano of Milan[1], inside the MeLa project[2]. The artworks chosen by the museum to be augmented inside the application was five paintings describing miracles, more or less known, related to the sacrament of the Eucharist, located in the Hall of the Arch of SS. Sacramento. The choice of these painting has been driven by the nature of their contents rich of sacred instruments useful to create links with the other rooms of the museum where are exposed sacred jewels, chalices and other objects used during the religious rituals. Each painting is full of different meanings provided by the use of religious symbols, people and gestures. They are barely clear or invisible for the most of the people.

By using AR the App can highlight with a graphic sign the hidden aspects providing to the user the tools to understand the paintings and generate curiosity about the ritual and, if possible, comparison with his/her religion. Moreover the app will collect and share the user's comments so to create a sort of social network where exchange idea and comments between the users with the intent to enhance the intercultural dialogue.

Figure 4 shows the architecture of the application and the user's interaction with it after the AR recognition of the painting.

4 Design and Implementation

The chapter describes the system's architecture and its implementation. The app has been designed taking into account different aspects:

- Costs of the hardware: in order to minimize the costs adoption, the application will run on user's device avoiding the purchasing cost to be charged to the museum. The solution developed will be scalable depending on the device performance.
- User friendliness: the system needs to be easy and intuitive to use, with simple interface, short instructions and natural gesture for the interaction.

---

[1] http://www.museodiocesano.it/.

[2] MeLa* European Museums in an age of migrations is a four-year Research Project funded by the European Commission (FP7).

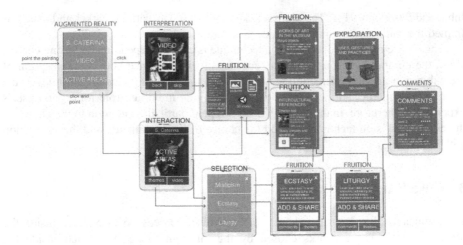

Fig. 4. Architecture of the contents and usage flow

- Multimedia content: describing religious contents is a complex task. By using videos the App can easily shows the meaning of the ritual expressed on the canvas highlighting and explaining some specific aspects of the painting. Images and texts provide both artistic and historical information of the elements represented and intercultural links with the museum's artworks. By zooming, moving, or rotating 3D models provide the user the chance to explore objects that are not inside the museum.
- Low visual impact in the real exhibition: critical aspects for the introduction of new technologies inside the museums is the visual impact they could have on the outfitting. The use of natural markers for the objects tracking reset to zero the visual impact.

The App has been developed using Unity3D and Vuforia. Unity3D is a game engine multi-platform that provides a set of tools to create adaptable user interface, import and visualize 3D models and multimedia.

Vuforia is a computer vision library developed by Qualcomm. The library can be easily integrated in Unity3D and provides the methods to generate the AR contents. By using Vuforia, Unity3D can associate the augmented contents (3D models, video, text and interactive sections) to natural markers, which in our case are represented by canvas/paintings.

The contents are stored in a local XML database. Editing the XML, the content's creator, can add or remove images and texts, enable or disable interactive sections and add new markers. Each natural marker is associated with specific contents that become visible to the users when a natural marker in the real world is framed by the device's camera. The users can interact with the augmented contents by touch and gestures. This is a description of how the App worked: after a registration phase, which allows to identify the user in the comment's section, a screen appears explaining how to use the App (Fig. 5).

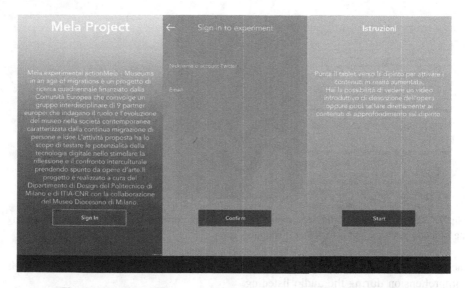

Fig. 5. Sign in and instructions steps needed to access to AR contents

Clicking on the "Start" button enables the recognition of the painting. Framing the paintings, the user can access at two different AR content's categories: Watch and Listen and Active Areas (Fig. 6).

In the Watch and Listen section, a video explaining the meaning of the paintings is shown to the users (Fig. 7). The actors, gestures and objects used to describe the

Fig. 6. When a marker is recognized two section are shown to the users: watch and listen and active areas

Fig. 7. The video explains the sacrament of the Eucharist portrayed in the painting highlighting the objects, gestures and actors that distinguish it.

sacrament of the Eucharist are highlighted with the intent to facilitate the visitor's comprehension during the audio listening.

The format of the videos is mp4 and they are embedded in the app. Each video have the same aspect ratio of the painting, depending on the device it will be superimposed to the real pictures or will played in full screen.

In the Active Areas (Fig. 8), the users will find the same objects, gestures and actors highlighted in the Watch and Listen section.

The Active Areas allows the user to deepen the contents of the paintings by using an interactive graphical user interface (GUI). A pop menu and a toolbar composes the GUI. The pop menu is positioned at the bottom of the screen while the toolbar at the right of the screen. Three buttons representing the elements that the user can inspect of the paintings (actors, gestures and objects), compose the toolbar. The active element of the toolbar enables the application to superimpose a set of virtual buttons to the real painting. The virtual buttons are positioned in correspondence of the elements with additional content (Fig. 6 on the right). Touching a virtual button, the users access the screen with the description concerning the selected object. Depending on the selection made, different choices are available on the pop menu: in-depth, museum's objects, intercultural link, 3D models and comments.

- The museum's objects: describes the objects and suggests to the users where they can find objects similar inside the museum.
- The intercultural link: shows how this objects or rituals are used in different religious context given that the meaning of rituals or sacred objects represented in the painting maybe hard to understand for people with different backgrounds and/or beliefs.
- 3D models: this selection is active only when the museum's objects section cannot gives a link to a museum's room because the object is not present in the museum's collection. By this selection, the application loads and shows on the screen a 3D model of the objects. Using gestures, the user can inspect the 3D model.
- Comments: this is the only section always available in the pop menu. It acts as a collector of information where user can exchange impressions and opinions about

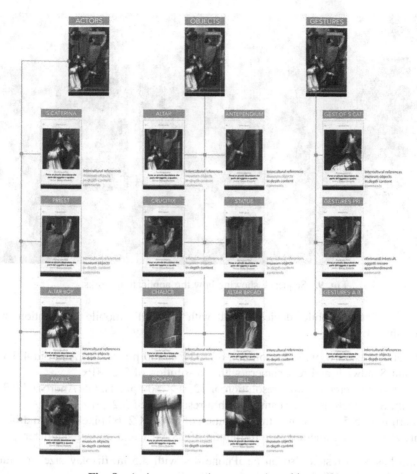

Fig. 8. Active area section: content's architecture

the application and the content provided, with the intent of enabling an intercultural dialogue. The information collected will be used to enrich the contents of the various sections and improve the application.

The data storage of the personal data and user contributions is based on a MySQL database located on a web server. The software module for the data exchange between the application and the database has been developed using the scripting language PHP.

5   Conclusion and Further Development

One of the main goal of this project is to have the application running on the user's device. Since the market offers many different devices with different processors, OS, screen resolution and dimension the application has been tested on four different device with different characteristics.

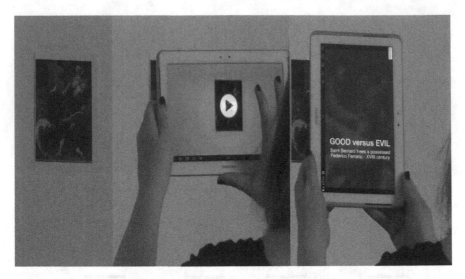

Fig. 9. Sequence showing how the application works.

Three of the mobile devices used with the AR mobile application were Android-based:

1. Tablet 7-in. screen, with a resolution of 1024 × 600 pixels, OS Android 4.0.3 Ice Cream Sandwich and rear camera with a resolution of 3.2 MPx.
2. Tablet 10-in. screen, with a resolution of 1280 × 800 pixels, OS Android 4.0.3 Ice Cream Sandwich and rear camera with a resolution of 3.2 MPx.
3. Smartphone 5.5-in. screen with a resolution of 1440 × 2560 pixels, OS Android 4.4 KitKat and rear camera with a resolution of 13 MPx and optical stabilizer.

The app has been tested also on an iPhone 4 s with 3.5-in. display size, resolution 640 × 960 pixels, iOS 5.0 and rear camera 8 MP.

The application has shown to be scalable, all the devices shown the AR contents with the proper proportions. The different OS have not generated runtime error. As easily predictable, better rear cameras and high screen resolutions offered a best visualization and the highest performing processors made the application usage more fluid. An interaction problem has been notice with the 3.5-in. display size because of the smaller size of the virtual buttons.

Another aspect to be taken into account to have the application running on the user's device is the installation of the App on the device. When the application will be adopted by the museums, it will be put on the PlayStore or AppleStore. Unfortunately, the.apk or IPA is 92 MB, because all the contents (video, 3D models, images and texts) are embedded in the application; therefore, not all the user would be available to download the App because of the excessive consumption of their internet traffic.

The next release of the application will use the cloud to store and share the contents. In this way, the users will download only the contents of their interest reducing the internet traffic consumption. The adoption by the museums of an efficient and free Wi-Fi can improve the use of this application.

As expected, the choice of natural markers for object tracking allows the user to use the application also outside the museum; by framing the pictures of a painting (Fig. 6), on any kind of support such as the museum's book or a web image, the augmented contents will become available and usable (Fig. 9).

The papers has described the design and implementation of an AR guidance for religious museum, running on mobile devices, and the improvements expected in order to help its adoption by the museums.

References

1. Bonacini, E.: Il museo partecipativo sul web:forme di partecipazione dell'utente alla produzione culturale e alla creazione di valore culturale. Il capitale culturale, pp. 93–125 (2012). ISSN 2039-2362 (online). http://www.unimc.it/riviste/cap-cult
2. Chen, B.X.: If You're Not Seeing Data, You're Not Seeing, Wired, 25 August 2009
3. Maxwell, K.: Augmented Reality. http://www.macmillandictionary.com/buzzword/entries/augmented-reality.html
4. Simon, N.: The participatory museum. http://www.participatorymuseum.org/read
5. Paine, C.: Religious Objects in Museums: Private and Public Duties. Bloomsbury, London (2013)
6. Russo, A., Watkins, J., Kelly, L., Chan, S.: How will social media affect museum communication? In: Proceedings Nordic Digital Excellence in Museums (NODEM), Oslo, Norway (2006)
7. Azuma, R.: A survey of augmented reality. Presence: Teleoperators Virtual Environ. 6, 355–385 (1997)
8. Daniel, W., Tobias, L., Dieter, S.: Robust and unobtrusive marker tracking on mobile phones, mixed and augmented reality. In: 7th IEEE/ACM International Symposium on ISMAR 2008, pp. 121–124, 15–18 September 2008
9. Unity3D. https://unity3d.com/
10. Aurasma. https://www.aurasma.com/
11. Wikitude. http://www.wikitude.com/
12. Young-geun, K., Won-jung, K.: Implementation of augmented reality system for smartphone advertisements. Int. J. Multimedia Ubiquit. Eng. 9(2), 385–392 (2014)
13. Vlahakis, V., Ioannidis, N., Karigiannis, J., Tsotros, M., Gounaris, M., Stricker, D., Gleue, T., Daehne, P., Almeida, L.: Archeoguide: an augmented reality guide for archaeological sites. IEEE Comput. Graph. Appl. 22(5), 52–60 (2002)
14. Bell, J.: The Variable Museum (2011). http://novomancy.org/john/abridged/content/variable_museum.html
15. MoSa.   http://thecreatorsproject.vice.com/blog/this-museum-displays-stolen-artworks-in-augmented-reality
16. Waruwu, A.F., Bayupati, P.A., Putra, K.G.D.: Augmented reality mobile application of Balinese Hindu temples: DewataAR. Int. J. Comput. Netw. Inf. Secur. 7(2), 59–66 (2015)

Human-Computer Interaction

Developing Touch-Less Interfaces to Interact with 3D Contents in Public Exhibitions

Andrea Sanna[1]([✉]), Fabrizio Lamberti[1], Federica Bazzano[1], and Luigi Maggio[2]

[1] Dipartimento di Automatica e Informatica, Politecnico di Torino,
c.so Duca degli Abruzzi 24, 10129 Torino, Italy
{andrea.sanna,fabrizio.lamberti,federica.bazzano}@polito.it
[2] Cluster Reply, Via Cardinal Massaia 83, 10147 Torino, Italy
l.maggio@reply.it

Abstract. Interacting with 3D contents is a challenging task and the implementation of natural and effective interfaces is usually demanded to computer programmers. On the other hand, exhibit designers would greatly take advantage of graphic tools able to completely hide technical details and code programming. This paper presents a graphic editor where interface designers can intuitively link objects, gestures and actions together, without needing computer science skills. Tests show the advantages of the proposed solution both for experts and beginners; moreover, a real example concerning the exhibit of the digital Nefertiti's bust within a holographic case controlled by hand gestures has been implemented.

Keywords: Interactive displays · Interactive exhibits · Museum visitors · Visitor engagement

1 Introduction

Computer graphics, virtual and augmented reality and, more in general, digital contents are massively used to enhance the user experience in exhibitions. For instance, museums often take advantage of digital technologies to provide visitors 3D reconstructions and background information. Static contents have been soon replaced by interactive solutions, which allow users to inspect and better understand displayed data. On the other hand, interactive contents need more sophisticated and natural interfaces. Interaction is always a complex task and Natural User Interfaces (NUIs) allow also non-expert users to immediately benefit of new interaction paradigms.

The widespread of affordable touch and touch-less devices provide researchers new stimuli to design more intuitive and natural interfaces. Digital contents can be easily controlled by voice, hand/body gestures and gaze. Unfortunately, establishing the relationship between content behavior and interface is still a challenging task, which can be performed only by technicians. Let us assume for instance to reconstruct, by a 3D scanner, a CAD model of an ancient artifact;

© Springer International Publishing Switzerland 2016
L.T. De Paolis and A. Mongelli (Eds.): AVR 2016, Part II, LNCS 9769, pp. 293–303, 2016.
DOI: 10.1007/978-3-319-40651-0_24

the reconstruction can be displayed by a stereoscopic or holographic display and we want to link a hand gesture with the rotation of the model. This task can be accomplished only by a computer programmer, whereas this activity should be performed preferably by exhibit designers. To tackle this challenge, a graphic editor able to provide an intuitive environment to associate hand gestures/poses to interactive digital contents actions, thus defining the interface logic, is proposed. Actions and events can be linked together without writing code. The Leap Motion has been used as input device, a holographic case as display and the Blender' Game Engine as the real-time interaction environment. Results clearly show benefits of the editor as non-expert people are now able to develop their own interfaces and programmers can considerably reduce implementation times.

The paper is organized as follows: Sect. 2 presents the state of the art, whereas Sect. 3 describes the editor and some quantitative results. Section 4 shows how the proposed solution can be used to implement the interactive NUI used to control the digital Nefertiti's bust within a holographic case.

2   Background

Computer graphics, virtual and augmented reality, holographic displays and so on have been proved to enhance the user experience in exhibition [1], which is also deeply related to interaction capabilities exhibit systems can provide [2]. The Exhibition Design [3] is the discipline in charge to create communicative environments in 3D spaces and it is deeply based on new technologies, thus taking also advantage of new and natural interaction forms. The MAV (Museo Archeologico Virtuale, Italy, which presents details of Herculaneum and Pompeii before the eruption of the Vesuvius 79 AD), the Llandudno Museum (Wales, where a prehistoric artifact is shown by a hologram), the Museum Lab (France, born by a collaboration between the Louvre museum and the Dai Nippon Printing, presented several installations based on tangible user interfaces, projections, gestural interfaces and so on to enable visitors to interact with digital contents), The Torino's Egyptian Museum, Italy (the augmented reality is used to enhance the user experience and the interaction with contents) and the Museum of Libya (where the Touchwindow technology, a thin interactive foils able to turn any glass surface into a touch screen, is used to interact with projections) are just a few examples of exhibition design by advanced digital technologies. The way we interact with computers, and more in general with interactive systems, is a complex and wide research area, usually labeled as Human Computer Interaction (HCI); it involves both technical areas (e.g. computer programming, operating systems, computer graphics) as well as social and human disciplines (e.g. cognitive sciences, ergonomics, psychology). Recent technological advances helped researchers and scientists to think new interaction paradigms [4]; when the screen-keyboard-mouse paradigm is scarcely usable (e.g. for exhibit) several alternative interfaces have been proposed. Analyzing interfaces for exhibit from the "input point of view", it is noticeable as almost all modes have been used.

Of course, the choice of the interface is strongly dependent on the target hardware. For instance, mobile devices such as smartphones and tablets can be used to guide users in a virtual tour of museums [5]. Furthermore, information can be easily shared, thus allowing visitors, digital contents and museums to be part of a sort of community. Visitors are used to use personal devices, therefore a training phase is not necessary and the interaction is immediate and intuitive. Touch-based interfaces are one of the most widespread solutions, even if it is not always natural to interact with 3D contents using a 2D input space [2]. Touchless interfaces can overcome the above mentioned constraint, thus expanding user interaction; gestures and poses can be now tracked by affordable devices: the Microsoft Kinect is used in [6], whereas the Leap Motion is used in [7]. Speech is one of the most intuitive way to input a command and it is diffusely used to design 3D user interfaces [8]; although speech-based interfaces can be affected by robustness problems in very noisy environments, tour assistants are sometimes used to support visitors by providing the so called Question-Answer (QA) modality [9]. Based on the premise that prolonged visual fixation is an indication of a viewer's interest, a gaze tracking-based interface has been proposed in [10] to support visitors in artwork exploration.

The same analysis from "the output/display point of view" reveals as mobile devices [11] provide an affordable and immediate solution, but they often require users to download and install an app, thus needing a network connection. Displays, large screens and kiosks assume a key role when images, text and videos have to be presented [12,13]. Augmented reality technologies are often used to overlap computer generated assets to real artifacts [14,15]. On the other hand, stereo displays, holograms and augmented holograms are the dominant solutions when 3D contents have to be displayed [16,17]. The user experience is greatly enhanced when interaction is added to 3D contents [18], but a key issues to be tackled [19]: the reduction of costs and times needed to develop interactive contents. A possible solution has been presented in [20], where the Dart programming language [21] is used to quickly integrate the Leap Motion and a touch screen in the user interface.

From the point of view of the real-time visualization engine, the BGE has been already used by other cultural heritage applications such as [22,23]. The BGE proved to be a flexible and intuitive solution for developing real-time cultural heritage applications and with respect other solutions such as X3DOM and OSG3WEB allows users to create interactive 3D worlds without any programming skills [24].

The approach proposed in this paper extends BGE's features and, always using a paradigm based on graphic bricks, the proposed solution allows users to link together gestures, actions and objects into a graphic environment, thus enabling non-expert people to create the logic of their own interfaces.

3   The Editor

The proposed editor aims to minimize the workload due to the inclusion of new interaction devices in the design of interactive interface. Without loss of generality, the Leap Motion controller has been selected as input device, but the same methodology described in this Section could be extended to other sensors. Interactive contents are displayed by holograms; the selected holographic case is based on the well-known Pepper's ghost effect to display images rendered into different viewports of a "hidden" monitor. A glass shaped like a pyramid (each face is bended of 45° with respect to a projecting monitor) provides users the illusion of (possibly 3D) objects floating within the case. A Leap Motion has been placed in front of the glass pyramid (see Fig. 6) to allow a user to interact with projected contents. The developed application has been named Leap Embedder. The relationship between objects/scenes and action is the interface logic. The Blender Game Engine (BGE) has been selected as real-time environment to run interactive applications. The BGE allows users to define the logic of an interactive application by an editor (the Logic Editor) [25] where three basic elements can be linked together: sensors, controllers and actuators. Objects can exchange messages and modify property values, which act as local variables. Even if this approach considerably simplifies the logic definition with respect a direct code writing, a non-expert user is not able to cope with the complexity of a real application logic.

The Leap Embedder provides interface designers a graphic editor where four type of nodes can be inserted and linked together:

- object nodes: each element can be an object node, therefore meshes can be object nodes as well as lights, cameras and so on. Object nodes can be related to an user interaction. A special object node (global object) also exists; it is used to add behaviors to be implemented in each level of the application (e.g. a gesture to be used to return at the start scene), as well as an object can be designed as pointer (e.g. a virtual hand);
- gesture nodes: represents different "gestural patterns" usable to interact with objects such as circle, swipe, key tap, and so on. Some gesture nodes can be further characterized; for instance, the clockwise or counterclockwise rotation can be selected for the gesture circle. A Python script running in BGE reads JASON-formatted messages from the websocket server of the Leap Motion. The script parses and processes JASON messages in order to identify hand gestures/poses; when a gesture/pose is recognized, a message corresponding the gesture/pose is posted in the BGE message pipeline;
- actuators nodes: this kind of node maps directly onto BGE's actuators (e.g. motion, action, visibility, sound, property, message, scene etc.);
- wait for nodes: this kind of node allows an object to wait for an event triggered by another object; an event can be a message sent either from another object or from the script mentioned above.

The Leap Embedder starts loading a library where all assets (objects, animations, sounds, videos, lights, and on) are available; we use Blender also as modeling and animation tool. Asset generation does not need any programming skill. An interface designer can now organize the interface in levels/scenes (a level must be designated as the "start scene") by selecting elements from the whole list of assets to be considered for each level. An asset can be selected for an

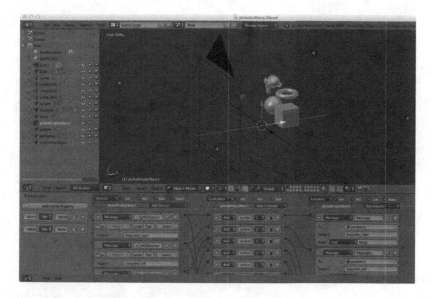

Fig. 1. The scene considered for tests. A part of the application logic in the BGE's Logic Editor is displayed at the bottom.

arbitrary number of levels; when levels have been defined, the user can set the interaction both for each object and level transitions. When the interface logic has been completed, the editor exports a XML file describing assets, interactions and level transitions. The XML is loaded in Blender by an ad-hoc add-on, which automatically loads the XML and translates it in an implementation by sensors, controllers and actuators for the BGE (see bottom part of Fig. 1). In order to test the proposed editor, a very simple application has been considered (see Fig. 1). There are six objects: two small cubes, a torus, a bigger cube, a sphere and a monkey head (Suzanne). People selected for tests were asked for designing an interactive application fulfilling the following requirements:

1. scene 1 (the start scene): a tap gesture over Suzanne has to trigger a level transition toward the scene 2;
2. scene 2: a tap gesture over the biggest cube has to trigger a level transition toward the scene 0;
3. a circle gesture has to trigger a return to the start scene independently of the current level;
4. scene 1: a tap over the torus has to trigger a Suzanne's animation (an available asset) named SuzanneAction, which is 60 frames long;
5. a swipe toward right over the sphere has to trigger a sound (another available asset);
6. users are also asked for designating the smallest cube as the pointer object.

Figure 2 shows how three different levels/scenes can be created by using the editor. Some objects (e.g. the object sphere) appear in every level, whereas Suzanne appears only in the initial scene.

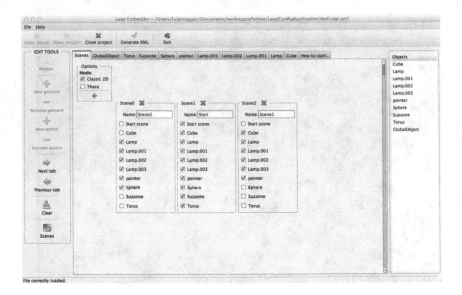

Fig. 2. Three levels/scenes have to be generated.

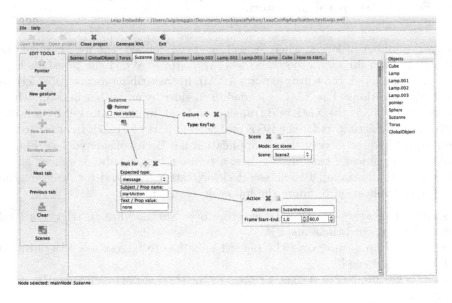

Fig. 3. The behavior of the object Suzanne is depicted.

Figure 3 shows blocks needed to implement the logic for the object node Suzanne. The object is connected to a wait for node and when receives a message StartAction the pre-recorded animation SuzanneAction is played for 60 frames. Moreover, Suzanne is sensitive to the pointer object; when it is over Suzanne and a tap gesture is detected a level transition toward Scene 2 is triggered.

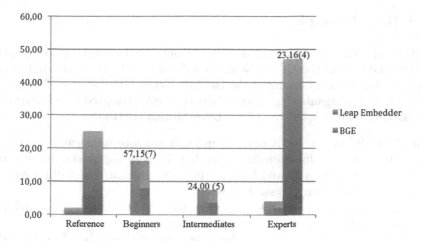

Fig. 4. Average completion times in minutes for the three user categories with respect the reference. Numbers over the bars indicate standard deviations, whereas the number of users for category is between brackets. (Color figure online)

It is important to outline how the direct implementation in the Logic Editor of this last feature needs an ad-hoc sensor to detect the position of the cursor with respect objects. The implementation of the application directly in the Blender Logic Editor needs 85 elements (31 sensors, 29 controllers and 25 actuators); on the other hand, 10 nodes are necessary by using the proposed Leap Embedder editor.   Three different user categories have been selected for tests by an interview. Users without, or with a poor, previous knowledge of Blender have been classified beginner (7 people), users with good skills in modeling and animating with Blender have been categorized intermediate (5 people) and people with also a prior knowledge of the BGE were assigned to the expert category (4 people). A developer of the proposed editor was the reference.

Each tester has been individually trained to use both of the Leap Embedder editor and the BGE's logic editor; 15 min have been devoted for each editor, basically to explain usage philosophy (expert testers have been trained only in the proposed editor). Figure 4 shows obtained results: the graph lists times in minutes needed to implement (without errors) the interface logic. Red bars refer to interfaces obtained by directly working in the Logic Editor, whereas blue bars denote average times obtained by using the proposed editor. Numbers over the bars represent standard deviations.

Beginner and intermediate testers are not able to complete the task without the proposed editor. These two user categories represent non-experts (such as exhibit designers), which are enabled by our solution to create their own interactive contents.

4   A Real Example

A real example has been also implemented; it concerns the exhibit of an Egyptian artifacts: the bust of the Queen Nefertiti wife of the Pharaoh Akhenaten (the real object has been exhibiting at the Berlin's Neues Museum since 2009).

The project is organized in different scenes/levels presented by a holographic case enabling content interaction by a Leap Motion controller:

1. the start (default) scene: it presents users gestures to be performed in order to activate a set of functionalities (see Fig. 5): pointing, selection, next text page, previous text page and back to the section menu. The section menu is presented by selecting the start "button";
2. the menu scene: it allows the user to select among three different scenes/sections;
3. scene 1: it shows the 3D bust of the Queen Nefertiti rotating. In this section it is possible to select four sub-sections focusing on some details (see Fig. 6): the collar, the eyes, the mouth and the head covering;
4. scene 2: it presents the story of the artifact by a certain number of textual information organized by consecutive pages (a text page is modeled as a textured plane);
5. scene 3: it shows a video of the real artifact (a video is an animated texture mapped onto a plane).

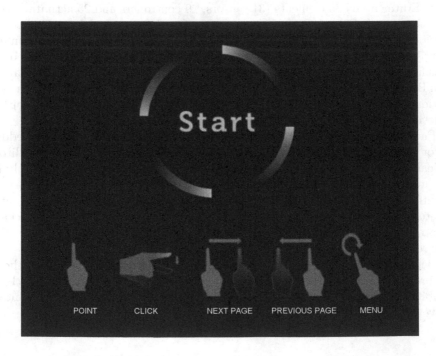

Fig. 5. The default scene: possible gestures are depicted.

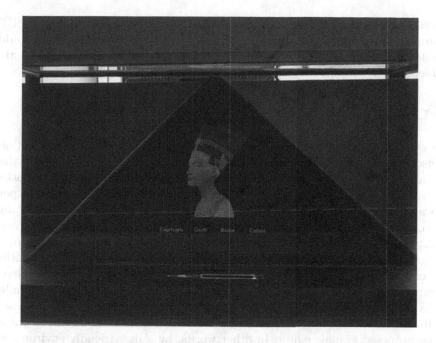

Fig. 6. Scene 1 is shown: four options can be selected to learn more about four details of the Queen Nefertiti's bust.

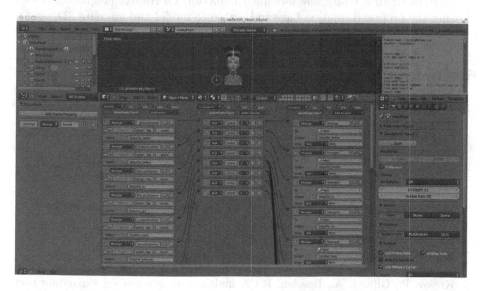

Fig. 7. A part of the logic automatically implemented by the Blender add-on related to the pointer object.

Each object/scene has been related to an action activated by a well define gesture; for instance, the circle gesture brings back to the default scene or an object selection triggers an animation activated by an ad-hoc message sent in the BGE. Figure 7 shows a part of the logic automatically implemented by the Blender add-on related to the pointer object, where received and sent messages are clearly visible.

5   Conclusion

The widespread of new affordable devices able to support natural interactions opens new and intriguing scenarios. The exhibition design is a discipline that can take a lot of advantage of more intuitive and robust interfaces. On the other hand, if new devices aim to provide end users friendliness and usability, expert software developers have to be involved in the implementation of interactive digital content. The proposed work overcomes this constraint, thus allowing non-expert people to easily embed interaction devices (such as the Leap Motion) in the design interface process. People without any prior knowledge in code writing can relate objects and scenes to actions activated by gestures. In the considered scenario, a hologram is controlled by hand gestures in order to navigate multimedia contents. The choice of the Leap Motion as an interaction/input device is not limitative and other devices such as the Microsoft Kinect could be integrated in the proposed graphic editor. In other words, by a user-friendly environment users can link elements of a scene to functionalities offered by an interaction device in order to activate a well-defined behavior. Of course, people interested in using the proposed solution have to be able to model and animate 3D assets, but these are skills usually well known to designers.

References

1. Kajinami, T., Hayashi, O., Nurami, T., Tanikawa, T., Hirose, M.: Digital display case: museum exhibition system to convey background information about exhibits. In: Proceedings of the 16th International Conference on Virtual Systems and Multimedia (VSMM 2010), pp. 230–233 (2010)
2. Hachet, M., de la Rivire, J.-B., Laviole, J., Cohé, A., Cursan, S.: Touch-based interfaces for interacting with 3D content in public exhibitions. IEEE Comput. Graphics Appl. **33**(2), 80–85 (2013)
3. Dernie, D.: Exhibition Design. W.W. Norton & Company, New York (2006)
4. Wilson, A., Benko, H.: Interacting above and beyond the display. IEEE Comput. Graphics Appl. **34**(3), 20–21 (2014)
5. Hakvoort, G.: The immersive museum. In: Proceedings of the 2013 ACM International Conference on Interactive Tabletops and Surfaces, pp. 463–468. ACM (2013)
6. Krejov, P., Gilbert, A., Bowden, R.: A multitouchless interface: expanding user interaction. IEEE Comput. Graphics Appl. **34**(3), 40–48 (2014)
7. Adikharla, V.K., Woźniak, P., Teather, R.J.: HoloLeap: towards efficient 3D object manipulation on light field displays. In: Proceedings of the 2nd ACM Symposium on Spatial User Interaction (SUI 2014), pp. 158–158 (2014)
8. Bowman, A.D., Kruijff, E., LaViola, J.J., Poupyrev, I.: An introduction to 3-D user interface design. Presence Teleoperators Virtual Environ. **10**(1), 96–108 (2001)

9. Toshniwal, S., Sharma, P., Srivastava, S., Sehgal, R.: USHER: an intelligent tour companion. In: Proceedings of the 20th International Conference on Intelligent User Interfaces Companion (IUI Companion 2015), pp. 81–84 (2015)
10. Milekic, S.: The more you look the more you get: intention-based interface using gaze-tracking. In: Trant, J. (Des.) Museums and the Web 2002: Selected Papers from an International Conference on Archives and Museum Informatics, pp. 1–27 (2002)
11. Paravati, G., Sanna, A., Lamberti, F., Ciminiera, L.: An open and scalable architecture for delivering 3D shared visualization services to heterogeneous devices. Concurrency Comput. Pract. Exper. **23**(11), 1179–1195 (2011)
12. Lo, W.Y., Tsai, Y.P., Chen, C.W., Hung, Y.P.: Stereoscopic kiosk for virtual museum. In: Proceedings of International Computer Symposium (2004)
13. Giuseppe, G., Patern'o, F., Spano, L.: Cicero designer: an environment for end-user development of multi-device museum guides. In: Pipek, V., Rosson, M.B., de Ruyter, B., Wulf, V. (eds.) IS-EUD 2009. LNCS, vol. 5435, pp. 265–274. Springer, Heidelberg (2009)
14. Avizzano, C.A., Evangelista, C., Bergamasco, M.: Technological approach for cultural heritage: augmented reality. In: Proceedings of the 8th IEEE International Workshop on Robot and Human Interaction (RO-MAN 1999), pp. 206–212 (1999)
15. Celozzi, C., Paravati, G., Sanna, A., Lamberti, F.: A 6-DOF ARTag-based tracking system. IEEE Trans. Consum. Electron. **56**(1), 203–210 (2010)
16. Bimber, O., Rasker, R.: Spatial Augmented Reality Merging Real and Virtual Worlds. A.K. Peters Wellesley, Massachusetts (2005)
17. Kim, M., Wohn, K.: Spatial AR hologram: a new exhibition system combining augmented reality technology with conventional holographic display. In: Museums and the Web Asia (MWA 2014) (2014)
18. Bimber, O., Zeidler, T., Grundhoefer, A., Wetzstein, G., Moehring, M.: Interacting with augmented holograms. In: Proceedings of SPIE, Practical Holography XIX: Materials and Applications, vol. 5742, pp. 41–54. Springer (2005)
19. Petridis, P., Pletinckx, D., Mania, K., White, M.: The EPOCH multimodal interface for interacting with digital heritage artefacts. In: Zha, H., Pan, Z., Thwaites, H., Addison, A.C., Forte, M. (eds.) VSMM 2006. LNCS, vol. 4270, pp. 408–417. Springer, Heidelberg (2006)
20. McMullen, T.H., Hawick, K.A.: Meaningful touch and gestural interactions with simulations interfacing via the dart programming language. In: Proceedings of the International Conference on Modeling, Simulation and Visualization Methods (MSV 2014) (2014)
21. Bracha, G.: The Dart Programming Language. Pearson Education, Upper Saddle River (2015)
22. Herrmann, H., Pastorelli, E.: Virtual reality visualizationfor photogrammetric 3D reconstructions of cultural heritage. In: Paolis, L.T., Mongelli, A. (eds.) AVR 2014. LNCS, vol. 8853, pp. 283–295. Springer, Heidelberg (2014)
23. Bustillo, A., Alaguero, M., Miguel, I., Saiz, J.M., Iglesias, L.S.: A flexible platform for the creation of 3D semi-immersive environments to teach cultural heritage. Digit. Appl. Archaeol. Cult. Herit. **2**(4), 248–259 (2015)
24. Baglivo, A., Delli Ponti, F., De Luca, D., Guidazzoli, A., Liguori, M.C., Fanini, B.: X3D/X3DOM, blender game engine and OSG4WEB: open source visualisation for cultural heritage environments. In: Digital Heritage International Congress (DigitalHeritage), Marseille, pp. 711–718 (2013)
25. Bacone, V.K.: Blender Game Engine: Beginner's Guide. Packt Publishing, Birmingham (2012)

A User Study on Touch Interaction for User-Perspective Rendering in Hand-Held Video See-Through Augmented Reality

Ali Samini[✉] and Karljohan Lundin Palmerius

Department of Science and Technology, Linköping University, Linköping, Sweden
{ali.samini,karljohan.lundin.palmerius}@liu.se

Abstract. This paper presents a user study on touch interaction with hand-held Video See-through Augmented Reality (V-AR). In particular, the commonly used Device Perspective Rendering (DPR) is compared with User Perspective Rendering (UPR) with respect to both performance and user experience and preferences. We present two user study tests designed to mimic the tasks that are used in various AR applications.

Looking for an object and selecting when it's found, is one of the most used tasks in AR software. Our first test focuses on comparing UPR and DPR in a simple find and selection task. Manipulating the pose of a virtual object is another commonly used task in AR. The second test focuses on multi-touch interaction for 6 DoF object pose manipulation through UPR and DPR.

Keywords: User perspective rendering · Augmented reality · Touch interaction · Video see-through

1 Introduction

Augmented Reality (AR) is the use of computer graphics to add augmentations to a view of the world. Hand-held AR is one of the AR displays that is often used due to low production costs and ease of use [1,2]. In hand-held AR a camera placed on the back side of a hand-held device is used to capture a view of the real world. Computer graphics are then added as augmentations to the captured view and rendered on the screen of the hand-held device. This is often called Video see-through Augmented Reality (V-AR). Hand-held AR is used for various purposes such as education [3], collaborative design [4], outdoor and indoor navigation [5,6], games [7,8], and etc.

Two perspective views are used for hand-held AR: The commonly used *Device Perspective Rendering* (DPR) and *User Perspective Rendering* (UPR). In DPR the view created on the screen is same as the view of the back-side camera. UPR creates a view that changes dynamically based on the relative position and orientation of the user's view and the screen. The latter makes the V-AR system

© Springer International Publishing Switzerland 2016
L.T. De Paolis and A. Mongelli (Eds.): AVR 2016, Part II, LNCS 9769, pp. 304–317, 2016.
DOI: 10.1007/978-3-319-40651-0_25

a window to the real world that is co-registered with the world based on the view of the user.

In this study we present comparison between two perspectives of hand-held AR. Our tests are designed similar to common hand-held AR tasks using touch interaction.

A common task among different AR applications is that the user looks for a virtual object by moving the hand-held device and selects the object when visible on the screen. This object selection task is used for various purposes in AR applications [9,10]. The focus of our first test is on the differences in the performance of find and selection tasks using DPR and UPR. We seek to find which perspective is faster and which is more natural and intuitive to perform find and selection tasks.

The touch interaction is an important part of the hand-held V-AR where the user interacts with the 3D virtual world using the 2D touch screen of the hand-held device. In various AR applications multi-touch gestures are used to move or rotate a virtual object [4,11]. Our second test investigates the effect of the AR perspectives on such touch-based object transform manipulation in V-AR. The results will show which of UPR or DPR is better to be used for such applications.

2 Related Work

Most V-AR applications use DPR, however, there are few approaches towards UPR V-AR. Yoshida et al. [12] for example, developed ARScope. Their method uses a head mounted projector to project on an opaque hand-held device, the world footage from a camera that also is mounted on the head. They create the homography based on feature points of the images from that camera and one that is mounted on the opaque device. This homography is then used to create UPR. Hill et al. [13] used the front and back-side camera of a hand-held device to create a homography-based UPR. Their method however assumes a scene that is parallel to the screen with a single depth. Tomioka et al. [14] presented a UPR V-AR that is based on homography using two cameras on a hand-held device. Samini and Palmerius [15,16] created a geometry based UPR using Virtual Reality concepts and external motion tracking system.

There are some studies comparing UPR and DPR in hand-held V-AR. Steinicke et al. [17] performed two psychophysical experiments on thirteen computer graphics experts to identify the optimal geometric field of view (the angle at the peak of the view frustum pyramid) for rendering and determining perspective distortion of virtual scenes and objects. The test subjects compared a real view to two renderings (with different geometric fields of view) of a physical scene and identified which rendering matched the real-world view more accurately. Their results show that the virtual scenes with a perspective projection that use the same geometric field of view (FOV) as the FOV of the screen, are perceived as most realistic representation by subjects. It also states that there is up to 20 % difference between the geometric FOV and the Screen FOV. This user study is not on V-AR UPR since there is no V-AR nor tracking and it is not done on a hand-held device. However, it shows the better perception of a user view frustum that is the same or very near to the virtual camera's.

Baricevic et al. [18] presented a user study to evaluate the benefits of UPR over DPR on a hand-held device. They did a selection and a search test using a UPR simulator. Their results indicate that using UPR view for the selection test has significantly better performance time and also a small significant benefit in terms of path distance. From a qualitative point of view users preferred UPR for selection tasks while DPR were preferred for search tasks. Their study was done using simulation of a UPR. They used a head mounted display (HMD) to render the virtual world and a wand to input user interaction which is potentially very different from real V-AR and touch interaction.

Tomioka et al. [14] did a pilot test based on two experiments that evaluate the visibility of finding the correspondences between the displayed image on screen and the real world and a third experiment on the visibility in virtual object pose recognition. They recruited eleven male subjects for two first experiments and the results indicate that the average task completion times of UPR was shorter than DPR. They state that the subjects were confused because of the jitters while using UPR thus the score may increase if the jitter is reduced. The authors also recruited nine subjects for the third experiment. Their result indicates that the approximated UPR improved the subject's ability to recognize the object pose. Also here the authors state that the results could be better without jitters and latency in the experiment. Using homography for tracking leads to registration inaccuracy that is caused by the detection and pose estimation errors. Accurate 3D pose estimation using homography is still an open problem. It is dependent on variables like the camera focus, the geometry, and the light condition of the scene. It also dictates high cost calculations to the system that may reduce the frame rate on a hand-held device.

We believe that while previous work have addressed the benefits of the different AR displays in some specific tasks, there is need for a test study designed based on touch interaction and tasks that are commonly used in hand-held AR applications.

3   Used Methods

For the presented study we used geometry based UPR to create a view from the user's perspective and compare it with camera's view (DPR). To let the subjects interact with the system we used multi-touch interaction on the screen of a hand-held device.

3.1   Geometry Based User Perspective Rendering

The 3D geometry-based UPR method that is used in this study was first introduced in [15] and later described in details, along with a registration method, in [16]. The method uses principles from Virtual Reality to create a view that matches the user's.perspective. A tablet device is used as the video see-through and the processing unit. The tracked poses of the tablet screen and user's head are used to create a dynamic frustum that is continuously updated. A camera placed on the back side of the tablet device is used to capture the real world. The extrinsics and intrinsics of the camera are used to create a virtual image plane that is placed in the virtual frustum. The camera's video feed is placed on this virtual image plane and is rendered with the virtual augmentations on the screen of the device. The method allows for both on-board camera-based tracking and external tracking. In our experiments we have used external tracking.

3.2 Multi-Touch Interaction

In our study, touch screen of a hand-held device is used to interact with the virtual world. Multi-touch gestures are used to select, rotate, and translate virtual objects. The first finger selects the object and moves it along the X and Y axis (panning). Using a second finger object can be both; translated along the Z axis by pinching and rotated around the same axis by swivelling. Adding a third finger allows to rotate the object around its X and Y axis (parallel to the X and Y axis of the screen) by panning.

4   User Study

Two user experiments where designed to investigate the benefits of hand-held AR perspectives in two various tasks. Fourteen test subjects (four females and ten males), age 21–37 took these tests. The test subjects were all university students. None of the subjects had any physical disabilities or eye condition that would effect the test.

4.1 Pre-test Procedure

In a pre-test questionnaire the subjects were asked to assess their level of familiarity with hand-held devices and Augmented Reality on a scale of 1–5. For the familiarity with hand-held devices 78.6 % answered 4 or 5. For familiarity with AR 50 % answered 4 or 5. Figure 1 shows the results of the latter questions.

Each subject had a pre-test learning session about the system and used methods. To prevent the familiarity effect, we had longer sessions for the people less familiar with the system, based on their pre-test questionnaire result. We made sure that all the participants where at the same level of familiarity with the system and used methods before starting the tests. The subjects also were trained how to perform each test. Latter training included performing the test for a few times as practice. The length of the training varied for each subject and took between five to ten minutes for each test. To increase the fairness each test only started when the subject was confident that they completely learnt how to perform the test.

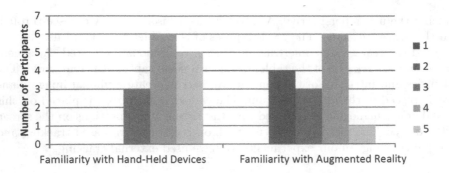

Fig. 1. Results from the pre-test questionnaire. The subjects were asked to assess their level of familiarity with hand-held devices and Augmented Reality on a scale of 1–5. (Color figure online)

The order of the conditions was balanced between the subjects to minimize the impact of learning effects. The start order in each test was balanced to minimize this effect. To have the same physical experience test subjects wore the tracking goggles for both DPR and UPR although it was only used in UPR. To find out the opinion of the subjects about the experiment they were asked to fill a *post-test questionnaire* after each test. Each participant was awarded a lunch coupon as a thank you for their time and effort.

4.2 Test Environment and Prototype

The tests were performed within an area of two square meters which was covered by a PhaseSpace optical motion tracking system for 6 DoF real time tracking. An off-the-shelf Microsoft Surface Pro 3 tablet PC was used as the central processing and video see-through rendering unit. The live video feed was captured using the tablet's back-side camera with Full HD resolution. The tablet was attached to a 3D printed frame along with the illuminative markers. A pair of safety goggles attached with the illuminative markers was used for head tracking (Fig. 2).

VRPN [19] is used to communication with the PhaseSpace motion tracking system. The software is developed using the C++ programming language and OpenGL. OpenCV is used for camera capture, calibration, and image undistortion. SDL [20] is used to access input devices and graphic hardware via OpenGL.

4.3 Find-and-Select Test

The first test was designed to investigate which of UPR or DPR is beneficial for the find-and-select tasks, where a virtual object (visible only on screen) is searched for in a real environment and selected when found. Baricevic et al. [18] indicated that in their study UPR was significantly faster for selection tasks and DPR was preferred for search tasks by the users. Here we want to investigate which perspective is better for a coupled search and select task. We believe

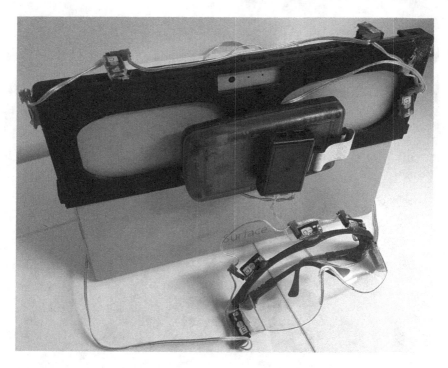

Fig. 2. The system prototype: Back side of the tablet computer with the 3D printed frame attached to it. The frame holds the illuminative markers and the LED unit driver that also is the power source for the LED markers. The safety goggles attached with illuminative markers that also is connected to the unit driver.

selection can be faster in UPR because the object will be rendered with its actual size and placement in the user's view direction. Finding an object can be faster in DPR due to the wider field of view (FOV) that makes it easier to find the object with less movement of the device (camera). Both perspectives had their benefits and drawbacks for the designed test so we hypothesized that either can be faster to complete the task.

Method. Each test participant had to find and select thirty virtual spheres to complete the test. The test subjects stood in the center of the test environment and used the tablet device to perform the task. Four printed paper signs were placed in the test area which showed the pre-defined appearance positions of the spheres. The virtual spheres appeared one by one randomly on one of the signs. The subjects did the test once with DPR and once with UPR while the task completion time was recorded by the system. The order of starting the test using DPR or UPR was balanced to minimize the learning effect. Figure 3 shows a test participant performing the test.

Fig. 3. The find-and-select test: Finding and selecting thirty virtual Spheres in one of the four pre-defined positions in 3D space in relation to the physical signs placed in the test environment.

Quantitative Results. The results from find-and-select test can be seen in Table 1 and Fig. 4. Our hypothesis was that the test task may be completed faster in either of UPR or DPR. We used significance level of 0.05. Paired two-tail t-test $t(14) = 2.77$, $p = 0.016$ ($p < 0.05$), stated statistical significance between find-and-select test time using DPR and UPR.

In general ten test subjects did the test faster in DPR and the Mean total time of job completion was 11.96 s faster using DPR. We can conclude that subjects did the find-and-select task significantly faster using DPR.

Table 1. Paired samples statistics for UPR and DPR in the find-and-select test. The mean is the task completion time for all (N) users in seconds.

	Mean	N	Variance
DPR	106.42	14	776.04
UPR	118.38	14	954.28

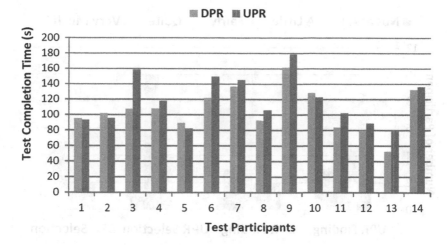

Fig. 4. Results from find-and-select Test: The completion time for each user for both DPR and UPR. Measured time is in seconds and is the addition of find and select time of thirty virtual balls separately for each perspective. (Color figure online)

Post-test Questionnaire. The goal of the post-test questionnaire was to capture the feeling of the subjects about the test. We asked how natural and intuitive each perspective felt to perform the finding and the selection parts of task separately. We categorized the answers to "not at all", "a little", "fairly", "quite", and "very much". To understand the similarities, the test subject could vote for both methods to be as good or bad. As is shown in Fig. 5, four people felt UPR, six DPR, and four both to be "quite" or "very much" natural and intuitive to find a virtual object in 3D space. Nine subjects found UPR, three DPR, and two both to be "quite" or "very much" natural and intuitive for selecting a virtual object on the screen of the hand-held device.

4.4 Multi-touch Pose Manipulation Test

The second test was designed to investigate if using either of AR perspectives benefits the applications that include rigid transformation of a virtual object in 3D space with the use of the touch interaction. The rigid transformation of a 3D virtual object consists of both translation and rotation. In the test multi-finger touch is used to translate and rotate the virtual object in relation to real world, as described in Sect. 3.2. We investigated if either of UPR or DPR is faster or more natural and intuitive to move a virtual object using multi-touch on the tablet device. We believe that UPR creates a more realistic and aligned view, and therefore better perception of perspective, distance and position of the virtual objects placed in the real environment. We thus hypothesized that test subjects will perform the pose manipulation test better using UPR.

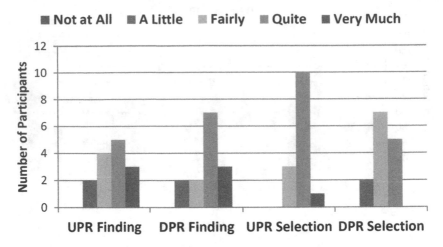

Fig. 5. The post-test questionnaire results from the find-and-select test. The subjects were asked how natural and intuitive they felt to find and select virtual objects using UPR and DPR. (Color figure online)

Fig. 6. Multi-Touch pose manipulation Test: Moving the virtual model of a coffee mug from a start point to an end point and aligning its orientation with a real coffee mug placed at the end point. The multi-touch interaction is used for the pose manipulation of the virtual object.

Method. A coffee mug was placed on a meter high stand in the test environment. A virtual model of the mug was placed randomly oriented on the floor about 2 m away from the real object. To complete the test each participant had to move the virtual model to the same place as the real one and align its orientation. The touch screen of the tablet device was used to manipulate the virtual object. To avoid the effect of searching time for the objects, the start and end points were marked with physical target signs in the real environment. The time of the test completion were recorded by the system. Each test participant performed the test four times using UPR and four times DPR. The order of starting the test with either of the perspectives was balanced between the subjects. Figure 6 shows a test participant aligning the virtual mug with the real one performing the test.

Quantitative Results. Table 2 and Fig. 7 show the results from the multi-touch pose manipulation test. Our hypothesis was that the subjects will have better performance using UPR. Paired one-tail t-test $t(14) = 0.57$, $p = 0.29$ ($p > 0.05$), indicated no significant difference between DPR and UPR performing the pose manipulation test. The paired two tail test $p = 0.58$ ($p > 0.05$) also agreed with the latter result.

Post-test Questionnaire. The post-test questionnaire explored what the subjects felt during the test. We categorized the answers to "not at all", "a little", "fairly", "quite", and "very much". The test subjects could vote the same for both methods in case that they had the same feeling.

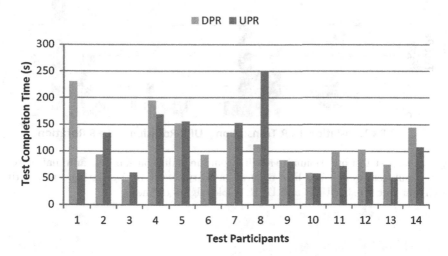

Fig. 7. Results from the multi-touch pose manipulation test: The completion time for each user for both DPR and UPR. Measurement time is in seconds and is the time to move the virtual coffee mug from the start to the end point and align it with the real mug four times separately for each perspective. (Color figure online)

Table 2. Paired samples statistics for UPR and DPR in the multi-touch pose manipulation test. The mean is the task completion time for all (N) users in seconds.

	Mean	N	Variance
DPR	115.79	14	2612.61
UPR	106.11	14	3435.99

First the subjects were asked if either of the perspectives felt natural and intuitive for moving the virtual object in 3D space. Six people found UPR, two DPR and six both to be "quite" or "very much" natural and intuitive to move the virtual object during the test (Fig. 8).

Then we asked how natural and intuitive the subjects felt using each perspective for rotating the virtual object during the test. Five people found UPR, two DPR, and seven both perspectives to be "quite" or "very much" natural and intuitive to change orientation of the virtual object during the test. The post-test questionnaire results are shown in Fig. 8.

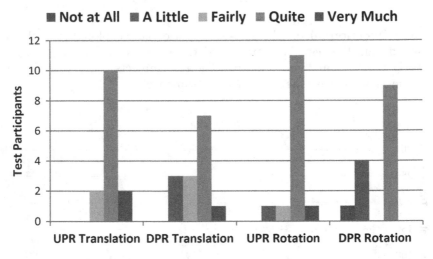

Fig. 8. The post-test questionnaire results from the multi-touch pose manipulation test. The test subjects were asked how natural and intuitive were translating and rotating the virtual object using UPR and DPR. (Color figure online)

5 Discussion

For the design of the presented tests we considered the fundamental functionality that are shared among the AR applications for multiple purposes. The first test focused on a task that coupled finding and selection using a tablet device. The virtual objects were found and selected in the real environment in correspondence with physical cues. In our opinion both perspectives had their benefits for the test. DPR could be beneficial for finding due to its larger FOV that made it easier to find an object with less movement of the device. UPR could benefit the selection because the object was rendered on the user's view direction so the user could point the device towards the object and select it in his view direction. Fourteen subjects performed the test. The results yield a significant difference in favour of DPR. The test subjects stated that the wider view of DPR on the screen made it easier to find the object. They also expressed that selection was easier and more intuitive with the user's perspective instead of the camera's perspective. But over all they did the task significantly better using UPR.

The second test investigated if any of the perspectives is beneficial for user interaction with the virtual objects. The subjects had to use the touch screen of the tablet to transform a virtual object and align it with a real object of the same shape. We believe UPR creates a more correct perspective that leads to better understanding of the depth and the size of the virtual and real objects and the environment. Therefore Our hypothesis was that UPR would benefit the test. Fourteen subjects took the test. Although more subjects found UPR more natural and intuitive to perform the test, the results showed no significance between two perspectives for the test. The insignificant result can be because the misalignment using DPR is mostly between what is rendered on the screen and the real world that can be seen around the screen. The on screen render of the real and virtual world is aligned in both perspectives. The test is performed in a small environment and with near objects. Here the user mostly looks at the screen and not the world visible around it and thus the task is not effected by DPR misalignment.

6   Conclusion

In this paper we presented the results from a user study on differences of DPR and UPR, based on common AR application tasks. The study illustrates an experimentation in real condition in contrary to the work of Baricevic et al. [18] that is performed in a simulated environment.

The results from the search and select showed a statistical significant difference using DPR compared to UPR. That might be explained by the wider field of view in DPR compared to UPR. Generally the subjects found UPR more natural to select and DPR to find a virtual object. The multi-touch manipulation test did not show statistical significant difference between two perspectives. That might be explained by the near manipulation that made DPR misalignment less harmful. However, subjects preferred UPR to perform the test. On the other hand DPR requires less tracking and is easier to implement that may make it a better technique for many applications.

References

1. Van Krevelen, D.W.F., Poelman, R.: A survey of augmented reality technologies, applications and limitations. Int. J. Virtual Reality **9**(2), 1 (2010)
2. Wagner, D., Schmalstieg, D.: First steps towards handheld augmented reality. IEEE (2003)
3. Liu, T.Y., Tan, T.H., Chu, Y.L.: 2d barcode and augmented reality supported english learning system. In: 6th IEEE/ACIS International Conference on Computer and Information Science, 2007. ICIS 2007, pp. 5–10, July 2007
4. Rekimoto, J.: Transvision: a hand-held augmented reality system for collaborative design (1996)
5. Dunser, A., Billinghurst, M., Wen, J., Lehtinen, V., Nurminen, A.: Technical section: exploring the use of handheld ar for outdoor navigation. Comput. Graph **36**(8), 1084–1095 (2012)
6. Mulloni, A., Seichter, H., Schmalstieg, D.: Handheld augmented reality indoor navigation with activity-based instructions. In: Proceedings of the 13th International Conference on Human Computer Interaction with Mobile Devices and Services, MobileHCI 2011, New York, NY, USA, pp. 211–220. ACM (2011)
7. Squire, K.D., Jan, M.: Mad city mystery: developing scientific argumentation skills with a place-based augmented reality game on handheld computers. J. Sci. Edu. Technol. **16**(1), 5–29 (2007)
8. Huynh, D.-N.T., Raveendran, K., Xu, Y., Spreen, K., MacIntyre, B.: Art of defense: a collaborative handheld augmented reality board game. In: Proceedings of the ACM SIGGRAPH Symposium on Video Games, Sandbox 2009, New York, NY, USA, pp. 135–142. ACM (2009)
9. Mossel, A., Venditti, B., Kaufmann, H.: Drillsample: precise selection in dense handheld augmented reality environments. In: Proceedings of the Virtual Reality International Conference: Laval Virtual, p. 10. ACM (2013)
10. Wagner, D., Pintaric, T., Ledermann, F., Schmalstieg, D.: Towards massively multi-user augmented reality on handheld devices. In: Gellersen, H.-W., Want, R., Schmidt, A. (eds.) PERVASIVE 2005. LNCS, vol. 3468, pp. 208–219. Springer, Heidelberg (2005)
11. Jung, J., Hong, J., Park, S., Yang, H.S.: Smartphone as an augmented reality authoring tool via multi-touch based 3D interaction method. In: Proceedings of the 11th ACM SIGGRAPH International Conference on Virtual-Reality Continuum and Its Applications in Industry, VRCAI 2012, New York, NY, USA, pp. 17–20. ACM (2012)
12. Yoshida, T., Kuroki, S., Nii, H., Kawakami, N., Tachi, S.: ARscope. In: ACM SIGGRAPH 2008 New Tech Demos, SIGGRAPH 2008, New York, NY, USA, p. 4:1. ACM (2008)
13. Hill, A., Schiefer, J., Wilson, J., Davidson, B., Gandy, M., MacIntyre, B.: Virtual transparency: introducing parallax view into video see-through AR. In: 2013 IEEE International Symposium on Mixed and Augmented Reality (ISMAR), pp. 239–240 (2011)
14. Tomioka, M., Ikeda, S., Sato, K.: Approximated user-perspective rendering in tablet-based augmented reality. In: 2013 IEEE International Symposium on Mixed and Augmented Reality (ISMAR), pp. 21–28, October 2013
15. Samini, A., Palmerius, K.L.: A perspective geometry approach to user-perspective rendering in hand-held video see-through augmented reality. In: Proceedings of the 20th ACM Symposium on Virtual Reality Software and Technology, VRST 2014, New York, NY, USA, pp. 207–208. ACM (2014)

16. Samini, A., Palmerius, K.L.: Device registration for 3D geometry-based user-perspective rendering in hand-held video see-through augmented reality. In: De Paolis, L.T., Mongelli, A. (eds.) AVR 2015. LNCS, vol. 9254, pp. 151–167. Springer, Switzerland (2015)
17. Steinicke, F., Bruder, G., Kuhl, S.: Realistic perspective projections for virtual objects, environments. ACM Trans. Graph. **30**(5), 112:1–112:10 (2011)
18. Baricevic, D., Lee, C., Turk, M., Hollerer, T., Bowman, D.A.: A hand-held AR magic lens with user-perspective rendering. In: 2012 IEEE International Symposium on Mixed and Augmented Reality (ISMAR), pp. 197–206, November 2012
19. Taylor, R.M., II, Hudson, T.C., Seeger, A., Weber, H., Juliano, J., Helser, A.T.: VRPN: a device-independent, network-transparent VR peripheral system. In: Proceedings of the ACM Symposium on Virtual Reality Software and Technology, VRST 2001, New York, NY, USA, pp. 55–61. ACM (2001)
20. SDL: Simple directmedia layer. http://www.libsdl.org/

An Investigation of Leap Motion Based 3D Manipulation Techniques for Use in Egocentric Viewpoint

Giuseppe Caggianese$^{(\boxtimes)}$, Luigi Gallo, and Pietro Neroni

Institute for High Performance Computing and Networking,
National Research Council of Italy (ICAR-CNR), Naples, Italy
{giuseppe.caggianese,luigi.gallo,pietro.neroni}@na.icar.cnr.it

Abstract. In this paper we investigate suitable 3D manipulation techniques for a new generation of depth trackers exploitable in ego-vision for an immersive virtual environment. After presenting the specific configuration and hardware used, the paper focuses on an investigation into the advantages and disadvantages of the various techniques in order to choose the one most suitable for the manipulation of an object in an immersive virtual environment. We have faced the problem of canonical manipulation which includes, besides the selection, the positioning and rotation. Two different approaches are described allowing respectively a direct or constrained manipulation of the virtual object. Our aim is to evaluate the perceived usability of the two proposed manipulation techniques in the specific configuration and for this reason qualitative data have been gathered using the System Usability Scale questionnaire. The results show a different level of difficulty perceived by the testers between the two canonical manipulation techniques and a general preference for techniques that prove to be less tiring.

Keywords: 3D manipulation · Ego-vision · Leap Motion · Immersive virtual environments · Questionnaire evaluation

1 Introduction

In recent years, both Virtual (VR) and Augmented Reality (AR) have received increasing attention from the research community thanks to the rapid spread of low cost head-mounted displays (HMDs) and VR headset kits, such as Google Cardboard [1], with which the user can use her/his smartphone to dive into an immersive virtual environment (VE). These new low cost devices have been opening up new opportunities with the result that they have started to be profitably used in many different application areas, such as entertainment, marketing, education, training and tourism. The main factor behind the success of these devices is their extreme portability that allows users to immerse themselves in a virtual environment anywhere, and at any time without having to wear cumbersome equipment.

L.T. De Paolis and A. Mongelli (Eds.): AVR 2016, Part II, LNCS 9769, pp. 318–330, 2016.
DOI: 10.1007/978-3-319-40651-0_26

The main characteristic of immersive VEs is that users engaged in an immersive experience cannot see anything of the real world around them. This leads to a generic issue in immersive VEs that is related to the interaction modalities with which the users can interact with the virtual object in the surrounding environment. The common input devices such as the keyboard, mouse, joystick or touch surface prove to be no longer suitable for these applications because their result to be completely invisible to the user while wearing the VR headset. Moreover, the extreme portability of the actual headset adds a further constraint in the design of the human-machine interfaces related to the necessity of preserving the user's mobility and comfort.

An interesting possibility arises from the fact that the new sensing devices have become small enough to be worn together with the VR headset. Such devices mounted in front of the VR headset allow the system to track the user's actions by exploiting egocentric vision. The benefits of this solution are twofold: the user can interact with the VE by using her/his hands without the need to manipulate any specific physical device that will result invisible to the user; and her/his hands tracked by the sensor can be reproduced in the VE improving the sense of presence perceived by the user and at the same time softening the aforementioned interaction limitations.

Fig. 1. The hardware components used for the design and evaluation including the interactive VR headset worn by a user.

Nowadays, while considerable progress has been made in terms of interacting with virtual objects, from the best of our knowledge, much more can be achieved in terms of improving and/or facilitating interaction for immersive VEs exploiting sensors with an egocentric viewpoint. Immersed users need to interact and manipulate virtual objects naturally by using interaction techniques which are easy to learn and to memorize, and which improve performances without any physical or mental discomfort.

In this paper, we deal with mid-air freehand interaction techniques supported by 3D spatial gesture input in a situation in which the sensor is positioned in ego-vision. As we will see in the discussion, this solution presents advantages and disadvantages and not all the interaction techniques presents in the literature prove to be suitable for this particular configuration. The paper presents a preliminary investigation into the most widely accepted interaction techniques applicable to an hardware configuration including a low cost VR headset together with a small wearable sensors usable in ego-vision. Finally, our attention has been focused on a specific sensor, the Leap Motion Controller since this proves to be one of the lightest and best performing devices available off-the-shelf.

The rest of the paper is structured as follows. In Sect. 2, we review related work in the design of 3D manipulation techniques for VEs. In Sect. 3 we describe the chosen hardware and the specific configuration while Sect. 4, presents our investigation into suitable 3D manipulation techniques, resulting in the definition of two possible approaches. Afterward, Sect. 5 focuses on the qualitative evaluation test performed, also including a discussion of the experimental results. Finally, in Sect. 6, we present our conclusions.

2   Related Work

Manipulation is a fundamental task in VR which allows users to interact with an object or multiple objects in the VE. According to [5,10] manipulation can be divided into three sub tasks: selection, positioning and rotation.

Selection is the task of selecting a target or a group of targets within a VE: it includes distance to target, direction to target, target size, selection count and target occlusion. In [17] four techniques are designed for the selection of a group of object in a VE. The authors distinguished between serial selection, which concerns selecting only one object at a time, and parallel selection, where a group of objects can be selected. They conclude that parallel selection can be far more effective than serial techniques as the number of target objects increases. When the selection becomes more demanding due to object occlusion in a cluttered environment, disambiguation techniques may be needed [15].

Positioning concerns the task of changing the position of a specific object within the world by translating it along the X, Y and Z axes, whereas the rotation task allows the user to rotate the target object. A complete taxonomy of manipulation techniques is provided in [5]. In [20] manipulation techniques are divided into exocentric and egocentric techniques. In exocentric techniques, the user interacts with the virtual environment in a third person view: a classical example is World in Miniature technique [24], where the user interacts with a miniature model of the environment. In egocentric interaction, the users are within the virtual environment and interact with it in the first person. The most common egocentric technique is the virtual hand [4] where the users can interact with virtual objects by touching and picking them up with a virtual representation of their virtual hand. This type of technique is considered isomorphic [6] because the manipulation is defined by a geometrical one-to-one relationship between the motion in the real world and the motion in the virtual environment. The main problem with issue of these techniques is that the physical arm is confined to a small space around the users body, making it impossible to interact with distant virtual objects. To deal with this limitation, hybrid techniques have been designed, such as HOMER [4] that combine direct manipulation (the virtual hand) and indirect manipulation (the ray-casting technique [19]).

Recently, range sensors like Microsoft Kinect, which use infra-red lights and cameras to determine the 3D position and pose of the entire body without the need to hold a device or wear a data glove, have encouraged researchers to develop free-hand gestural interfaces. In [9] a gestural interface is presented for an interactive exploration of medical images. Since the user interface is touch-free and does not require complex calibration steps, it is suitable for use in operating rooms, where non-sterilizable devices cannot be used. In the same way, mid-air object manipulation techniques are designed to interact with a large display from a distance: in [23], using the Kinect sensor, a handle bar metaphor is proposed as an effective visual control metaphor between the user's hand gestures and the corresponding virtual object manipulation operations; while in [18] a vision-based gesture interaction is developed which exploits scalable computing techniques to accelerate the frame image processing. Finally, gesture-based interfaces are considered also to interact with the volumetric display [12]. In [22] GestureVR is described, a gesture recognition system which allows a single hand object manipulation by tracking the thumb and index finger in real-time.

3   System Hardware Configuration

In the investigation of a suitable 3D User Interface (3DUI) for an immersive VE, we have considered a specific hardware configuration in which the user wears both the headset and the tracker sensor (see Fig. 1). In this configuration both the physical movements of the head and hand can be mapped to some interaction commands. The head movements are tracked by using a magnetometer and a gyroscope embedded in the smartphone used as a display for the VR headset while a fine segmentation and tracking of the hands is achieved by using a depth sensing device integrated with the headset. The hardware configuration chosen for this experimentation includes the Durovis Dive 5 as the headset that, combined with a 4.95 in. smartphone and a pair of lenses, allows a field of view (FOV) of about 90°. The sensor used to track the user's hands is the Leap Motion [2], probably one of the lightest off-the-shelf sensors (45 g), which allows a robust hand segmentation even in gloves or with cluttered backgrounds.

This device tracks mid-air user gestures with a degree of accuracy that allows the tracking of individual fingers in the hand. Leap Motion works by using two infrared cameras arranged so that their field of view intersects and three infrared red IR light-emitting diodes (LEDs) positioned to be alternated with the cameras. The Leap Motion sensor provides a horizontal FOV of 135° while a vertical FOV of 120°, and a maximum operating distance of 0.60 m (see Fig. 2).

4   Egocentric 3D Manipulation Techniques

In this paper we aim to investigate the most suitable manipulation techniques for the specific configuration described in the previous section. For 3D manipulation we have considered all the approaches which allows you to manipulate an object while preserving its original shape (spatial rigid object manipulation).

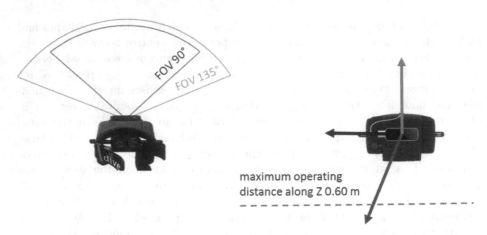

Fig. 2. On the left, the differences between the horizontal FOVs respectively in green of the Leap Motion and in blue of the user's point of view using the VR headset. On the right, the coordinated reference system of the Leap Motion and the maximum operating distance of 0.60 m (Color figure online).

First, in our analysis, we have to consider the possible interactions allowed to the user from the specific configuration. In the situation described the user can interact with the VE and the virtual objects mainly in two modalities. The first modality exploits her/his head movements tracked with the inertial sensors of the smartphone and uses them to control the user's view point. This interaction represents a main interaction in an immersive VE because, thanks to the fact that the user is allowed to perform the natural action of looking around, it drastically improves the user's sense of presence. With the second interaction modality, the user is allowed to use her/his hands: the system maps their movements to a set of interaction techniques used to accomplish the manipulation task on the virtual objects in the scene. While the first modality proves to be intuitively connected to the manipulation of the first person view point, choosing a specific interaction technique for the second modality is not an easy task. There are a wide range of methods and approaches to interact with 3D content in a virtual space [6]. Since this work focuses on an investigation into the most suitable freehand mid-air interaction gestures with an egocentric viewpoint we will discuss in detail the advantages and disadvantages of the proposed configuration in order to define a set of possible interactions suitable for this particular context.

Among the advantages of a 3D manipulation in this configuration there is the low cost of the hardware used, which has already been discussed, and the possibility of exploiting free-hand interaction that allows the user to move freely without being constrained by physical devices or wires. Despite the user proving to be blind in the sense that she/he is immersed in a VE, in this configuration she/he is always aware about the sensor position. Moreover, when the ego-centric position of the sensor is joined to a virtual representation of the user's hand projected into the VE, the user has the full control of the interaction, being able

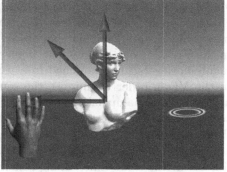

Fig. 3. 3D Positioning. On the left, with the direct manipulation, the user after the selection controls 3 DOFs simultaneously to change the object position in the VE. On the right, with the constrained manipulation, the user after the selection is allowed to change the object position by acting on the related widgets. The red place-holder in the background indicates the required object position in the task (Color figure online)

to decide when to interact by simply moving her/his hand in the FOV of the sensor. In this context, also the incoming and the outgoing of the user's hand from the sensor FOV can be used as a voluntary interaction exploitable in a 3D User Interface (3DUI). The main advantage of this configuration is the way in which the user interacts. In fact the user has to place her/his hands at eye level in front of the sensor, performing an interaction modality that corresponds to the natural way that humans behave when they need to directly manipulate an object. In such a case, the human usually first centers the object in her/his FOV and than starts to manipulate the object by introducing also her/his hand into the VE. At this time a coordination between the view and the hand movement is performed in order to complete the task. However, this configuration presents also some disadvantages in terms of the design of a valid 3DUI. The sensor placed in egocentric vision shares the view point position with the user's gaze direction. In fact, each time the user moves her/his head, the view point of the tracking sensor rotates accordingly. This aspect causes a series of unintentional user interactions that happen each time the user rotates her/his head having is hand still in the FOV of the sensor. Indeed, these movements are usually wrongly translated by the system into a spatial movement of the hand. Moreover, despite the fact that in a real direct object manipulation both the hand and object are in the FOV of the user we have to consider that humans rarely perform the manipulation with mid-air gestures. The large muscle group involved in a mid-air interaction does not represent an advantage for both interaction precision [26] and user comfort which aims to avoid the *Gorilla arm* effect [3]. In fact, the user by keeping her/his hand at eyes level for a long time can easily feel tired and progressively lose accuracy in the interaction.

With this said, in order to investigate the most suitable interaction techniques for this particular configuration we followed both the main design guidelines described in Bowman et al. [6] and the main characteristics of the chosen system. Fist, we considered the task of performing, aiming to allow the user to select and manipulate an object changing both its position and rotation in the VE. Moreover, being in an immersive VE, we aimed to exploit egocentric manipulation techniques joined to a virtual representation of the user's hands in the VE in order to improve the sense of presence of the user. In order to apply the best manipulation techniques, it is important to match the interaction techniques to the sensor device properties. Therefore, Leap Motion being a 6 degrees of freedom (DOF) devices, it become possible to exploit both integrated and separated manipulation techniques. We decided not to manipulate all the 6 DOF at the same time adding constraints to generic 3D manipulation techniques in order to help the user to be more efficient and precise [21]. Finally, given the limited FOV of the sensor, especially in the allowed distance interaction, we decided to reduce the limitation of the real interaction by adopting non-isomorphic techniques [14]. In fact, isomorphic approaches would not be able to map the limited movements executed by the user in her/his motor space in a virtual space indefinitely greater.

After these considerations we designed two different manipulation techniques for the specific configuration and then evaluated them in a qualitative user study. We decided to differentiate them based on the allowed interaction modality: direct for the first technique and constrained for the second one. In the first case the user was allowed to directly manipulate the virtual object, namely simultaneously manipulating the object across all dimensions in Euclidean space, while in the second approach the user manipulation is constrained to managing a single dimension at a time. This differentiation is performed for two tasks, the positioning and rotation of virtual objects.

Before presenting the manipulation techniques in detail, it is necessary to explain how the user is allowed to select the virtual object to manipulate. We implemented a selection technique called Wait to Click based on our previous work [7] in which the user can easily select an object by pointing at it and, in order to confirm the selection, must keep her/his index finger still on that object for a configurable number of seconds.

In the direct manipulation approach the positioning problem is performed by allowing the user after the selection to move the object in all the 3 dimensions of the virtual space by exploiting 3 DOFs tracked from the sensor. On the contrary, the positioning performed with the constrained modality allows the user to move the selected object by selecting the corresponding widget and moving the virtual object along a single axis at a time by exploiting the corresponding DOF tracked from the device. Similarly, to change the object orientation in the direct manipulation the user after the selection is able to change its orientation by rotating her/his the open hand in the Euclidean space. The constrained manipulation allows the user to choose a single angle at a time to rotate by acting on the corresponding widget. In this way the direct manipulation requires a single selection of the object while the second technique requires the user to

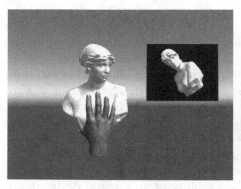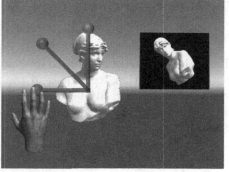

Fig. 4. 3D Rotation during the trial performed in the user study. On the left, with the direct manipulation, the user after the selection controls 3 DOFs simultaneously to change the object rotation in the VE. On the right, with the constrained manipulation, the user after the selection is allowed to change the object rotation by acting on the related widgets. In the black box, the object orientation required in the task

first select the object to manipulate and then, when the widgets are visible, to select the one desired.

For both the manipulation approaches, the user's hand movements performed in the motor space are not linearly mapped to the movements of the virtual hand in the virtual space but, instead, a filter based on the user velocity is used to map fast hand movements to a coarse-grained manipulation (corresponding to a ballistic phase) and slow hand movements to a precise interaction (corresponding to a correction phase) [11]. Moreover, we decided to implement both the interaction modalities by using the open hand in order to reduce the perceived fatigue. With the same goal, we decided that the metaphor used to deselect an object at the end of the manipulation would be removing the hand from the FOV of the sensor.

In order to face the problem of the required coordination between the head and hand movements each time the user was, with an open hand, manipulating the orientation of the virtual object the user head movements are completely filtered out. This approach was possible because, for the rotation, after the selection of the object the system automatically moves the user's view point to the correct distance from the object in order to facilitate its manipulation. In this way, the user focuses on the rotation manipulation, not feel the need of move also his view point. Obviously, this consideration proves to be not applicable for the positioning of the objects in the scene. To accomplish this task the user is always left free to move her/his view point so that a coordination between the head and hand movements is needed. Finally, each time the user ends the manipulation of the object orientation by moving her/his hand out of the sensor's FOV, the constraints applied to her/his view point are removed.

5   User Study

5.1   Goal

The object of this study was to evaluate the perceived usability of the two proposed manipulation techniques in the specific configuration. Our aim was to verify what had already been shown in previous research. In fact, in [13] it is observed that performing tasks which are perceptually integral (performable by controlling simultaneously all the allowed dimensions) with an integral device (allowing a simultaneous control of the involved DOFs) increases performance, the same rule applying to the case of separable tasks performed with a separable device. In our case we wanted to test the usability of an integral device in an immersive VE in both direct (integral) and constrained (separable) manipulation. In more detail, our goal was to test the two proposed techniques separately for the position task and rotation task.

5.2   Design

We conducted a questionnaire evaluation, in which all the subjects tested both the proposed manipulation techniques. The experiment was performed using a single VR headset and the same simulated scenario for all the users, guaranteeing the same set-up and conditions for each tester. Each subject performed four trials, one for each combination of proposed technique and task to accomplish, namely positioning and rotation. Finally, the combinations of the trials among the volunteers were counter-balanced to reduce any carry over effects.

5.3   Participants

We recruited 10 unpaid volunteers to perform the study. The participants' ages ranged from 26 to 45 years old, with an average age of 33.1. Four of the participants were female and all of them were right-handed.

5.4   Procedure

Initially, a facilitator showed, to each volunteer, a brief demonstration video to introduce the system, including its functionalities, and to demonstrate how to use the two proposed techniques. Specifically, the video was used to explain how to engage and disengage a manipulation, the head-hand coordination needed in the positioning task and the constraint applied to the user's view point during the rotation task.

Afterwards, in a practice session, designed to make the participants feel more comfortable and relaxed, the subjects were left free to familiarize themselves with the interface without any limitations using a training VE similar to the experimental one and being allowed to switch between the two proposed techniques. The practice session is aimed at improving the subject's confidence in wearing the VR headset and especially in dealing with the hand movements necessary to interact with the widgets in the constrained interaction. In this phase, the facilitator was only allowed to switch between the approaches on the participants' request.

Next, the test session started with the users receiving precise instructions from the facilitator about the tasks to perform. The simulated scenario was composed of an uncluttered environment populated by the object to manipulate. That simple scenario was chosen in order to avoid distracting the user during the manipulation. For each trial the users were required to perform a rotation or change the object position in the space. In the rotational tasks the system provided the user with a picture of the same object in the desired final position asking her/him to place the object in the same position as that of the picture (see Fig. 3). In the positioning tasks the system showed a place-holder highlighted in space in which to move the object (see Fig. 4). For both tasks a visual feedback reports to the user the conclusion of the task. Anyway, the user was left free to abandon the trial at any time.

The test session was organized with the repetition of two different and consecutive moments for each trial. In fact, each tester was allowed first to perform the trial using one of the two techniques and then, systematically, was asked to evaluate it by using a questionnaire. No time limit was imposed on the participants during the trial; each user's interaction was observed to collect all the possible impressions of her/his experience. The participants were also asked to think aloud, describing their intentions and possible difficulties. In the same way, no time limit was imposed on the completion of the proposed questionnaire. However, the users were asked to record the answer to each item as quickly as possible, rather than thinking about the questions for a long time.

To measure both the usability and the user's experience, we used five-point Likert-scale questionnaires [16] structured to fulfil all of the criteria listed by Uebersax [25]. The participants answered the questions using a scale from 1 (very low) to 5 (very high). In detail, the users were asked to complete the System Usability Scale (SUS) [8], which allows you to obtain a rapid evaluation of the techniques expressed as a single number which ranges from 0 to 100.

5.5   Results and Discussion

After the practice section almost all the subjects complained of an initial difficulty in coordinating their head and hand movements during the manipulation of the objects. However, all the users expressed a positive evaluation of the virtual hand shown in the VE, an aspect that has helped them to address better the coordination problem.

During the trial execution, the testers showed fewer difficulties performing the positioning task with both the proposed techniques. In fact, after the confidence gained with the head-hand coordination in the practice session, all the users were able to move the object in the space also controlling simultaneously 3 DOFs. Even better, after the practice session, the testers started to consider the constrained positioning too slow and sometimes even more difficult than of the direct manipulation.

On the contrary, the rotation task was considered, as expected, more complex than the positioning task. Almost all the users found extremely difficult control 3 DOFs at the same time for the rotation task expressing, consequently, a preference for the constrained rotation. In more detail, this consideration should be considered as the product of a perceived discomfort during the interaction modalities. In fact, the testers complained that the fine rotation of the virtual object performed while manipulating simultaneously 3 DOFs was extremely tiring.

Finally, the evaluation showed that the users prefer to have a full control when positioning the object in the space, when coarse-grained movements followed by fine adjustments are not perceived as strenuous. Conversely, in the rotation task, the users prefered to have a fine control restricted to a single dimension at a time. Moreover, the interaction based on the widget manipulation was considered simple to use and understand. These observations were also confirmed by the results of the SUS questionnaire whose average score ranges from 0 to 100 For the positioning manipulation, the score was 65.6 for the direct solution and 59.4 for the constrained solution. On the contrary, for the rotation, the score was 49.86 for the direct rotation and 61.34 for the constrained rotation.

6 Conclusions

The rapid development and dissemination of low cost wearable VR technologies has the potential to bring such techniques into our everyday life. However, many challenges are still present, such as the design of 3D manipulation techniques that do not force the user to wear or handle any type of device.

In this paper, we have investigated the design of two free-hand manipulation techniques for wearable VR systems in which the tracking sensor is placed in ego-vision. The two proposed techniques allow, respectively, a direct and constrained manipulation of the synthetic object, to modify both its rotation and position by using free-hand gestures. We performed a preliminary usability evaluation test, which showed that users perceive the two types of manipulation to be extremely different, preferring a direct manipulation for the positioning task and a constrained manipulation for the rotational task. However, we also noticed that these choices are guided by the tendency of the users to express a preference for interactions that do not cause any physical discomfort. In the future, our work will focus on improving the manipulation techniques in ego-vision by following the user's preferences collected in this preliminary test and then on carrying out a quantitative evaluation of these techniques with a larger group of users.

References

1. Google cardboard. https://www.google.com/get/cardboard/
2. Leap motion controller. https://www.leapmotion.com/
3. Boring, S., Jurmu, M., Butz, A.: Scroll, tilt or move it: using mobile phones to continuously control pointers on large public displays. In: Proceedings of the 21st Annual Conference of the Australian Computer-Human Interaction Special Interest Group: Design: Open 24/7, OZCHI 2009, pp. 161–168. ACM, New York (2009)

4. Bowman, D.A., Hodges, L.F.: An evaluation of techniques for grabbing and manipulating remote objects in immersive virtual environments. In: Proceedings of the 1997 Symposium on Interactive 3D Graphics, pp. 35–ff. ACM (1997)
5. Bowman, D.A., Koller, D., Hodges, L.F.: Travel in immersive virtual environments: an evaluation of viewpoint motion control techniques. In: Virtual Reality Annual International Symposium, pp. 45–52. IEEE (1997)
6. Bowman, D.A., Kruijff, E., LaViola Jr., J.J., Poupyrev, I.: 3D User Interfaces: Theory and Practice. Addison-Wesley, Boston (2004)
7. Brancati, N., Caggianese, G., Frucci, M., Gallo, L., Neroni, P.: Touchless target selection techniques for wearable augmented reality systems. In: Damiani, E., Howlett, R.J., Jain, L.C., Gallo, L., De Pietro, G. (eds.) Intelligent Interactive Multimedia Systems and Services, pp. 1–9. Springer, Cham (2015)
8. Brooke, J.: SUS: a quick and dirty usability scale. In: Jordan, P.W., Weerdmeester, B., Thomas, A., Mclelland, I.L. (eds.) Usability Evaluation in Industry. Taylor and Francis, London (1996)
9. Essmaeel, K., Gallo, L., Damiani, E., Dipanda, A., De Pietro, G.: Comparative evaluation of methods for filtering kinect depth data. Multimedia Tools Appl. **74**(17), 7331–7354 (2015)
10. Foley, J.D., Wallace, V.L., Chan, P.: The human factors of computer graphics interaction techniques. IEEE Comput. Graph. Appl. **4**(11), 13–48 (1984)
11. Gallo, L., Minutolo, A.: Design and comparative evaluation of smoothed pointing: a velocity-oriented remote pointing enhancement technique. Int. J. Hum. Comput. Stud. **70**(4), 287–300 (2012)
12. Grossman, T., Wigdor, D., Balakrishnan, R.: Multi-finger gestural interaction with 3D volumetric displays. In: Proceedings of the 17th Annual ACM Symposium on User Interface Software and Technology, pp. 61–70. ACM (2004)
13. Jacob, R.J., Sibert, L.E., McFarlane, D.C., Jr. Mullen, M.P.: Integrality and separability of input devices. ACM Trans. Comput. Hum. Interact. (TOCHI) **1**(1), 3–26 (1994)
14. Knight, J.L.: Manual control and tracking. In: Salvendy, G. (ed.) Handbook of Human Factors, pp. 182-218 (1987)
15. Kopper, R., Bacim, F., Bowman, D.A.: Rapid and accurate 3D selection by progressive refinement. In: 2011 IEEE Symposium on 3D User Interfaces (3DUI), pp. 67–74. IEEE (2011)
16. Likert, R.: A technique for the measurement of attitudes. Arch. Psychol. **22**(140), 5–55 (1932)
17. Lucas, J.F.: Design and Evaluation of 3D Multiple Object Selection Techniques, M.Sc thesis, Virginia Polytechnic Institute and State University, Blacksburg, VA (2005)
18. Luo, X., Kenyon, R.V.: Scalable vision-based gesture interaction for cluster-driven high resolution display systems. In: Virtual Reality Conference, VR 2009, pp. 231–232. IEEE (2009)
19. Mine, M., et al.: Virtual environment interaction techniques. UNC Chapel Hill Computer Science Technical report TR95-018, 507248–2 (1995)
20. Poupyrev, I., Ichikawa, T., Weghorst, S., Billinghurst, M.: Egocentric object manipulation in virtual environments: empirical evaluation of interaction techniques. In: Computer Graphics Forum, vol. 17, pp. 41–52. Wiley Online Library (1998)
21. Poupyrev, I., Ichikawa, T.: Manipulating objects in virtual worlds: Categorization and empirical evaluation of interaction techniques. J. Vis. Lang. Comput. **10**(1), 19–35 (1999)

22. Segen, J., Kumar, S.: Gesture VR: vision-based 3D hand interace for spatial inter-
    action. In: Proceedings of the Sixth ACM International Conference on Multimedia,
    pp. 455–464. ACM (1998)
23. Song, P., Goh, W.B., Hutama, W., Fu, C.W., Liu, X.: A handle bar metaphor
    for virtual object manipulation with mid-air interaction. In: Proceedings of the
    SIGCHI Conference on Human Factors in Computing Systems, pp. 1297–1306.
    ACM (2012)
24. Stoakley, R., Conway, M.J., Pausch, R.: Virtual reality on a WIM: interactive
    worlds in miniature. In: Proceedings of the SIGCHI Conference on Human Factors
    in Computing Systems, pp. 265–272. ACM Press/Addison-Wesley Publishing Co.
    (1995)
25. Ucbcrsax, J.S.: Likert scales: Dispelling the confusion. http://www.john-uebersax.
    com/stat/likert.htm
26. Zhai, S.: Human performance in six degree of freedom input control. Ph.D. thesis,
    University of Toronto (1995)

PaSt: Human Tracking and Gestures Recognition for Flexible Virtual Environments Management

Dario Di Mauro[✉], Davide Maria Calandra,
Antonio Origlia, and Francesco Cutugno

Department of Electrical Engineering and Information Technology,
University of Naples "Federico II", Naples, Italy
{dario.dimauro,davidemaria.calandra,antonio.origlia,cutugno}@unina.it

Abstract. This paper presents a CAVE-like architecture to support the
interaction for small groups of people with a leader in a multi-projection
environment in the unusual condition where a vertical depth camera
records people and their movements. In this framework, modelling people as gaussians, we localise and track people when they step into a
defined area. We compared our approach with a typical local minimum
one and our algorithm results to be faster and more accurate. Detected
leaders manage the interaction with hands. We developed a trained gesture recognition model and a rule-based one and the former approach
reports better outcomes. While the proposed virtual environment is
mainly intended as a multi-projection system, the presented architecture allows to dynamically change the area such as to integrate further
input and output devices. It can be extended up to provide support in
collaborative tasks for remotely connected groups acting in the same virtual room. The whole system has been adopted in Cultural Heritage scenarios to provide an immersive experience for art, historical contents or
virtual environments. Interviews with people participating to the experimentation phase of the OrCHeSTRA project show that the system was
well-received by the general public and that future extensions towards
collaborative environments are encouraged by the end-users.

1 Introduction

Providing an immersive experience allows users to enjoy artistic as well as virtual
environments; this is the purpose of PaSt (from the Italian "Passeggiata nella
Storia" - "History walkthrough"). Natural environments often react to people
moving inside them. Providing users with coherent reactions in artificial environments where free roaming is allowed strongly contributes to the quality of the
experience. When data sources are presented in free-roaming artificial environments, content access can be linked to the users' movements in the environment
itself. Position and behaviour, gestures in our case, can have different outcomes
depending on their combination.

L.T. De Paolis and A. Mongelli (Eds.): AVR 2016, Part II, LNCS 9769, pp. 331–347, 2016.
DOI: 10.1007/978-3-319-40651-0_27

In this paper, we explore the domain of Natural User Interfaces (henceforth NUI) [13], applied to cultural heritage. NUIs are characterised by their reduced intrusiveness with respect to wearable devices so we designed the experience without recurring to such technologies. PaSt is a modular software application, independent from the context and driven only by the naturalness of the interaction. It is currently composed of an array of projectors showing contents on the floor and on the wall, while a depth camera on the ceiling detects small groups of people and tracks their movement on the scene; one of these users will be elected to leader and her position and gestures will be interpreted as input to activate and change the contents. The high modularity of the software and its independence from the contents allowed us to apply PaSt to different contexts and with different functions: in the presented case studies we applied it, first, to the cultural context, projecting on the floor a set of historical pavings browsed using scroll-like gestures; then, we applied it to the archaeological context, providing a set of maps projected, one at time, on the floor, and allowing the leader to browse the maps with a gesture and to step inside the maps to activate the contents related to specific points; this way, we designed an exhibit illustrating the urban evolution of the inner city of Naples, during the XIX century; in a different case study, we applied it to the gastronomic context, considering people could step into a menu and see the available specialities of a virtual restaurant.

2   Related Works

PaSt comes from an explicit request: visitors had to step into the layered cultural history of their city and browse through ages just like if they were book pages. The best way to satisfy these requirements was to provide an immersive environment that granted a didactic and, at the same time, attractive experience to visitors; thus, we chose to design PaSt as a virtual floor, expressed by contents that users could change with a simple *browsing* gesture. The motivation of an interactive floor finds explanation in different branches of literature: learning, for example, especially for children, is often supported by interactive floor systems, as children sense and learn through their body [5]; movement, in fact, stimulates the sensory system, providing individual experience and knowledge of their own identity, as well as of the physical outside world. Social studies often take advantage from interactive floors: movement based playing can be relevant in developing social skills, as explained by [6,7], where authors highlight the relationship between language and body movement, and propose iGameFloor: an interactive floor technology that provides collaborative learning games for hearing impaired children. We find one of the first interactive floors for cultural heritage in the Puccini Set Designer [12], an exhibit organised with the support and collaboration of Milan's renowned opera theatre "La Scala". Among a wide range of technological solutions, authors present an "immersive cinema" consisting of a carpet of 2.5 by 3.5 m and of a vertical surface; five icons representing the sets of Puccini's Turandot are projected on the carpet and, when the visitor stops on one of them, the related contents are projected on the vertical screen.

When the user, then, points an arm toward the vertical screen, he activates the multimedia contents. The implemented metaphor considers the carpet as a computer mouse-pad, the person moving is the mouse selecting information and the vertical screen like the monitor that shows the chosen information. This system used two computers and seven synchronised software applications to implement the system: in particular, they used Macromedia Flash for the carpet and proprietary software for the vertical wall.

The concepts of *virtual floor* or *virtual wall* naturally lead towards the realisation of a CAVE-like environment such as the one presented in [3], where each projection represents a *façade* of the virtual environment. The usage of CAVE-like environments avoids eyestrain or nausea, common effects of head mounted displays (HMD) [11] and makes it possible to display actual-size objects, which is an important aspect in education, as observers can compare the size of the objects with their body, as explained in [8]. As we will see in the next sections, we preferred a CAVE-like environment over a HMD solution as the former is suitable to support a small group interacting in a defined area and the latter is limited to one person. Moreover, off-the-shelf HMD solutions, such as Oculus Rift[1], require wired connections, a strong limitation in considered scenarios. In this setup a vertical depth camera localises and tracks people. A related solution is proposed in [14], a Water-filling inference algorithm based on local minimum. This system is interesting from a model point of view, but it is very expensive in performance. At each frame the algorithm starts from a depth map and, choosing random points, it searches local minimums by adding temporary values, called "rain drops", in an area. A minimum is intended as a person if rain drops amount goes beyond a threshold. A preliminary configuration is needed to setup a set of parameters.

3   The Architecture

In the case studies considered in the framework of the OrCHeSTRA project, the virtual environment consists of a multi-projection system turning a real environment into a complex digital exhibition. The PaSt architecture is based on a multiple client-server application in which each client handles a side of the virtual environment with its multimedia contents, while the server detects and tracks the users, chooses the leader, catches the input events, and activates the specific clients. This allows the system to handle clients running on the local machine and on remote machines as well. In our case, a single PC manages the interaction as the computational load is kept at a minimum. Another advantage of the client-server architecture is that it allows us to make the system independent from the virtual environment. This way, it is possible to easily adapt PaSt to different scenarios: from a basic setting characterised by only one projection (usually the floor), to multiple facades (usually walls) composing the virtual environment. Integration with a 3D-Audio diffusion system for virtual auditory

---

[1] https://www.oculus.com/, retrieved on 30th March 2016.

scene rendering is also supported. Similarly, the system represents each possible input, such as the presence of the leader or the execution of a gesture, as generic events triggering transitions in a state-machine. Different scenarios can be defined and loaded on startup, using the XML languages described later in this Section.

In order to manage the interaction, PaSt detects users, tracks them, chooses the leader and catches the events. Moreover, it interprets the input signals, handles the output devices, and manages the virtual environment. Some of these tasks are controlled by a central unit; some run in parallel. In order to build the system, we designed a client-server multi-threaded application, organised as shown in Fig. 1.

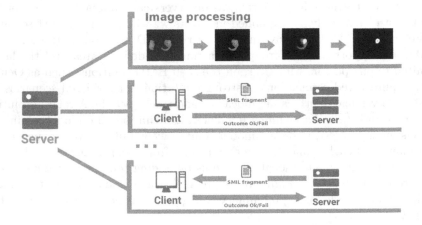

Fig. 1. Server architecture

Specifically, the server launches as much clients as defined in the configuration file and it handles two main threads: the "working thread" processes the input stream to detect users, tracks their position, chooses the leader, and interprets the input events; the "interaction thread" handles the communication with the clients: it assigns a task to each client, depending on the context. Once they have received the task to accomplish, each client processes it, and if the task requires the parallel execution of multiple contents, it creates a thread for each content. This is a very abstract approach that allows to implement different case studies using the same architecture. In our tests, we consider the leader position and four types of gesture as input sources: (i) one hand, left to right (ii) one hand, right to left (iii) two hands, zoom-in (iv) two hands, zoom-out. The input stream is acquired by means of a depth camera detecting people in semi-dark environments. This technology allows to easily separate the foreground subjects from the background. The image processing steps are implemented in openFrameworks[2]. While our tests run under OSX, the high portability of the

---

[2] http://openframeworks.cc, retrieved on 4th March 2016.

framework makes it easy to run the software under the other supported operating systems (Windows, Linux, Android...). The experimental setup is composed of a MS Kinect v1 and of a projector arranged in a *smart box* located on the ceiling of a free room to avoid interference with obstacles (for example stairways, walls, or tables). We used Kinect just as a depth camera; this sensor is very useful in a typical horizontal configuration, recurring to body recognition, but this feature is not available in the proposed setup, where the camera is on the ceiling and oriented towards the floor. Kinect v2 does not highly improve depth camera resolution, so the chosen sensor is sufficient for our purposes.

After deployment, some preliminary operations are necessary like configuring the height of the Kinect, the frame rate, and the tolerance for the gesture detection. To manage interaction, a set of documents using standard XML languages is parsed to manage interaction and select the contents. Details about this are presented in Sect. 3.4.

3.1 People Detection

In order to implement an interactive system based on gesture recognition, it is necessary to detect and track people moving in the area the MS Kinect detects. The server processes the acquired depth map, a grey-scaled image in which the higher the grey value, the higher the closeness of the point from the camera, as shown in Fig. 2(a). A noise reduction algorithm using a threshold computed on the basis of the height of the smart box, removes noise coming from the IR sensors and erases any point that is too far from the Kinect to belong to a human user. Then, it computes the minimum and maximum pixel values of the whole map and, if the difference between the values is lower than a fixed threshold, no user is detected. Otherwise, the system proceeds to isolate the users.

Taking advantage of the anatomic geometry, from a mathematical point of view a person moving in the environment can be approximated from the top with a 3D multivariate Gaussian, where the human head is usually found on the highest part of the curves. Multiple people on the floor are modelled as different Gaussians on the map. Calculating precise expression about these curves can be very expensive but, for our purposes, it is sufficient to approximate this phase in the following way:

1. a threshold action separates the upper half of the body from the legs, which are not relevant for our goals;
2. result is converted in a binary image, whose white blobs identify the users;
3. a contours detection algorithm isolates the boundaries of each blob, and returns their area and the centroid coordinates, which allow us to track the blobs on the scene.

The binary image is a mask reporting a raw description of the arrangement, because coordinates are a first approximation of the head centroids. To reduce computational load, our goals allow us to apply more detailed analysis to the leader only.

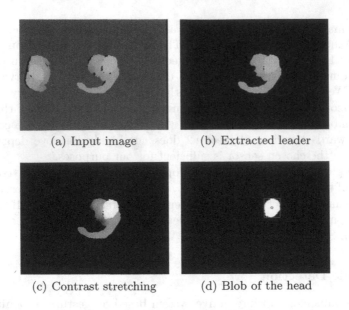

(a) Input image   (b) Extracted leader

(c) Contrast stretching   (d) Blob of the head

Fig. 2. Performed steps to extract the head position of the leader

Groups and Leadership. After obtaining rough positions for the detected people, the system tracks these points in time to follow the users and chooses a leader among them. In this implementation, the leader is the first subject who enters the scene. To implement the interaction, more accurate tracking data are needed for the leader. To do this, the following operations are applied on the leader blob, as shown in Fig. 2(b):

1. minimum and maximum pixel values of the input image are computed. Black pixels are excluded by using the previously obtained map;
2. the image contrast is stretched, as in Fig. 2(c), so that the minimum pixel value is set to zero (black) and the maximum to 255 (white). The result is a normalised frame that does not depend anymore on the camera height;
3. a threshold operation at the 85 % of the maximum value (255) is applied to isolate the head. This threshold is chosen on the basis of commonly used anatomic ratios [1];
4. blob detection is applied, as in Fig. 2(d), to find head contours and its centroid in order to keep a punctual leader position, independent from arms' variations, which may altering the centroid.

Our centroid results more accurate and stable at leader's movements than that obtained by Water-filling, due to two motivations: (i) Water-filling is a randomly initiated algorithm so the final result highly depends on starting point, and (ii) shoulders are efficiently excluded, avoiding erroneous detection to which Water-filling is subject.

In our case studies, only one user at time, the leader, can interact with PaSt. We tag the leader as the first detected user and if she leaves the detection range, her nearest neighbour is elected to leader; nevertheless different dominance strategies can be applied, as discussed in [2]. We set this limit to improve the interaction in a small space for a group of people.

3.2 Gesture Recognition

Starting from results obtained in Sect. 3.1, the system knows the leader's position and its contour. Then, both hands have to be tracked to recognise gestures. In order to detect the hands, the system calculates an ellipse fitting the contours of the leader's body. The minor axis of the ellipse follows the direction of the user; the major axis is an estimate of the distance between the shoulders. For each frame, the contour of the leader is divided in two parts following the direction of the body. This way, right and left hands are independently detected. For each part, the farthest point from the centroid is calculated; if the distance is higher than half of the shoulder distance, the corresponding point is tracked as a hand.

After one or two hands are detected, further processing is applied to correctly identify right and left hands. As shown in Fig. 3, a hand is undefined until it does not fall in a disambiguation area. If the hands are not clearly identified during the movement, the resulting gesture is not completed.

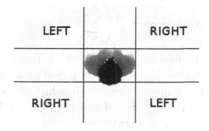

Fig. 3. Considerations on left and right hands

In order to detect performed gestures, both hands are tracked in time. We developed two different modules to recognise gestures; these are mutually exclusive and they will be compared in Sect. 5. Independently of the used module, the position of the leader does not affect the gesture results, because hands position are processed in a reference system centred on the leader. A first recognition module has a rule-based approach with empirical time and space limits. By moving the hands, angles are drawn in space. By considering the vector made by one hand with respect to the head, we have an initial vector as the hand is detected. The angle between the initial vector and iteratively observed ones is analysed: if the hand draws an adequate angle in a specified time interval, the gesture is valid; hands and their directions discern the type of gesture. Left and right hands are processed independently. Examples are in Fig. 4(a) and (b).

Once the leader triggers a new event, the server sends the related instructions to the specific client.

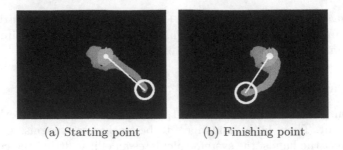

(a) Starting point   (b) Finishing point

Fig. 4. Tracked points for gestures.

3.3 Machine Learning Approach

A second version of the recognition module based on machine learning introduces the use of a specific type of Conditional Random Field (CRF) [9] for the gesture recognition step. CRFs were designed to capture inter-class relationships by maximising the conditional probability of the sequence of labels from a sequence of observations. Given a set of trained weights λ, the sequence of labels Y and the sequence of observations X, a Linear-Chain CRF estimates $P(Y|X)$ as

$$P(Y|X,\lambda) = \frac{1}{Z(X)} exp \left(\sum_{k=1}^{K} \lambda_k f_k(y_t, y_{t-1}, \mathbf{x}_t) \right) \qquad (1)$$

where $Z(X)$ is a normalisation constant, N is the number of observations and $f_k(y_t, y_{t-1}, \mathbf{x}_t)$ is either a *state feature function* or a *transition feature function*. State feature functions model the relationship between observation/label pairs. Transition feature functions model the relationship between the observations and the transitions from one state to another. Feature functions include the observations vector x_t, representing an arbitrarily extended context of observations having length W. One limit of CRFs is that they only model inter-class relationships. When the target classes are characterised by complex, not explicitly annotated, internal dynamics, it is necessary, for an automatic approach, to model these *latent* structures to obtain complete description of the annotated class. This is the typical case for gestures, where a target class is defined by, non annotated, latent dynamics (e.g. *waving hello* is composed by left-to-right and right-to-left hand movements). Latent Dynamic Conditional Random Fields (LDCRF) [10] are an extension of CRFs designed to introduce hidden variables in the model, in order to capture both kinds of dynamics and have been explicitly developed to segment and annotate gestures. Hidden states represent a sequence of unobserved variables H and define the latent conditional model

$$P(Y|X,\lambda) = \sum_{H} P(Y|H,X,\lambda)P(H|X,\lambda) \qquad (2)$$

This allows only disjoint sets of hidden states for each class label. Therefore, each label y_j has an associated set H_{y_j} of hidden states with $H_{y_i} \cap H_{y_j} = \emptyset$ for $i \neq j$, making it is possible to rewrite Eq. 2 as:

$$P(Y|X, \lambda) = \sum_{h \in H_{y_j}} P(H|X, \lambda) \tag{3}$$

The conditional probability of the hidden states given the set of observations and weights can then be formulated as for the CRF model:

$$P(H|X, \lambda) = \frac{1}{Z(X)} exp \left(\sum_{k=1}^{K} \lambda_k f_k(h_t, h_{t-1}, \mathbf{x}_t) \right) \tag{4}$$

A comparison between Linear-Chain CRFs and LDCRFs is shown in Fig. 5. LDCRFs do not provide connections between observations and labels due to the hidden variables layer. As the labels are disconnected from the observations, they are assumed to be conditionally independent.

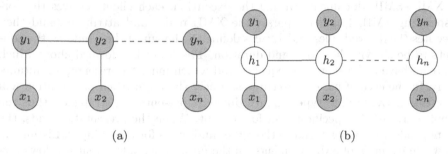

(a)   (b)

Fig. 5. A Conditional Random Field (a) compared with a Latent-Dynamic Conditional Random Field (b)

3.4   Virtual Environment

As explained earlier, in our case a virtual environment is a multi-projection system. We used XML-based standards to model the interaction: the sequence of states is represented with the SCXML (State Chart XML) standard, which is able to describe state-machines. A SCXML file includes multimedia contents, coded with SMIL (Synchronized Multimedia Integration Language); it aims at integrating and synchronising different multimedia contents to create presentations. The combination of SCXML and SMIL is a powerful instrument to model a large set of scenarios and, to change a setting just need to write a suitable XML file. We could easily vary input strategies, depending on the specific requirements; in particular, the interactions are intended as generic state transitions expressed by the triple <event, condition, action> and represented by SCXML elements, while the multimedia contents are SMIL elements describing in detail the operations linked to the SCXML states.

Listing 1.1. A snippet of SCXML-SMIL file.

```
1  <scxml initial="intro">
2   <state id="intro">
3    <datamodel>
4     <data> <!-- SMIL elements --> </data>
5    </datamodel>
6    <transition event="leaderIn" target="s1"/>
7   </state>
8   <state id="s1">
9    <datamodel>
10    <data> <!-- SMIL elements --> </data>
11   </datamodel>
12   <onentry>loadContent</onentry>
13   <transition cond="0" event="leaderInClass" target="s2"/>
14   <transition cond="1" event="leaderInClass" target="s3"/>
15  </state>
16 </scxml>
```

By loading the SCXML document, all the states in which the system will be are known; moreover, the transitions between the states are known, too. In particular, a state is represented by its ID and by the entry and exit actions that declare the behaviour about the contents. Listing 1.1 shows an example of SCXML+SMIL document. During the execution, each client receives the corresponding SMIL fragment, parses the XML nodes and attributes, and then executes the derived rules. SMIL rules define the layout of the windows, the contents to be shown, their area and duration. The client is informed about which contents have to be shown in sequence and which must be presented simultaneously. In the case of parallel executions, a new thread for each presentation will be created. Every data type requires different presentation strategies, thus the client activates the specific player for content. When the presentation ends, the client sends a stopping signal to the server and waits for a new input. Listing 1.2 shows an example of SMIL elements. In the *head* node, data about windows layout are listed; the *body* block defines the rules to simultaneously present different multimedia contents - text, video, images, and audio - in different regions of the window and for different durations. Sequential/parallel contents are possible and different strategies to synchronise them.

Listing 1.2. Example of SMIL code

```
1  <smil>
2   <head>
3    <layout>
4     <topLayout id="win1" title="floor" width="640px" height="480px">
5      <region id="full" width="100%" height="100%" fit="best-fit"/>
6      <region id="reg1" top="50%" left="60%" fit="best-fit"/>
7      <region id="reg2" top="10%" left="10%" fit="best-fit"/>
8     </topLayout>
9    </layout>
10   </head>
11   <body>
12    <par>
13     <img region="full" src="img/naples.png" dur="10s"/>
14     <text region="reg2" src="Text to show" dur="15s"/>
15     <video region="reg1" src="vid/expl.mp4" begin="2s"/>
16     <audio region="full" src="aud/expl.mp3"/>
17    </par>
18   </body>
19  </smil>
```

4   Case Studies

We designed the gestural interaction to keep the user in the middle of the action. Gestures are not intended to be just represented by hands or arms movements: the whole body is involved in the process of interaction and the semantic of an event depends on the states defined in the particular case study or in the SCXML as explained in Sect. 3.4. The user's position is therefore part of the interactive experience. The system monitors the position of users on the floor interested by the horizontal projection, can take note of the leader's movements, such as stepping into or out the scene, or of her intention to move to a different quadrant giving rise to a new action.

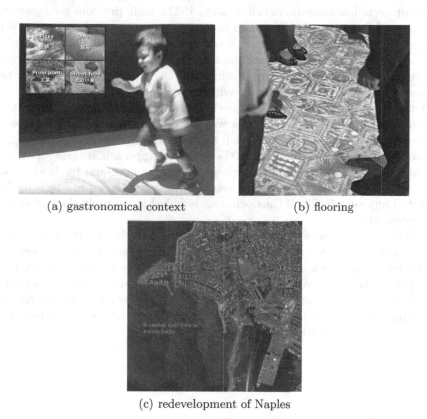

(a) gastronomical context   (b) flooring

(c) redevelopment of Naples

Fig. 6. Different applications for PaSt

In a simplified version of our system, PaSt has also been designed as a human pointing system in an application showing gastronomical products organised on a menu on the floor. In order to make the interaction as more natural as possible, the proposed approach just relies on the leader position. People stepped into the projection to explore available specialities. Figure 6(a) shows an example with the proposed menu. The next step aims at improving the experience and introduces gesture interaction with the CAVE; it allows users to manage cultural contents integrating hands movements with their position. In this view, a dedicated module recognises the gestures made by the leader by tracking her arm and hands. All these events could alter the experience. In order to make the experience concept as abstract as possible, this is represented as a sequence of states; navigation among these is driven by introduced events. Ideally, a free roaming interaction area is composed of a set of projections: a "base" on the floor, a sequence of walls, and, possibly, a projection on the ceiling. The activated projections change based on the chosen configuration: the increasing number of projected parts makes the area more and more involving for the user. In a particular state, multimedia content needs to be presented: images, texts, and video can be projected; audio sources can be played. The main problem is to select the right part of the interaction area and the exact time to play the content. With these premises, a state is represented from a piece of possible multimedia content and a set of transitions to navigate toward other states. The general concept is not strongly linked to a single application, but can be redeployed in every task proposing the navigation of either physical or conceptual maps.

A first version of PaSt has been used to browse important flooring situated in historical buildings of Naples; this was an experimental version reacting to just two gestures made by one hand: left to right and right to left, simulating the browsing gesture in two directions. In the proposed approach, images reporting a pavement of a historical period were projected on the floor and the leader could change the flooring by browsing; the proposed setup is shown in Fig. 6(b). The presented implementation of the document is linked as a simple chain, following a temporal sorting.

In a second version of PaSt, two other gestures have been introduced: zoom-in and zoom-out, made by separating or joining hands movements, respectively; in addition, a gesture was related to the position where it was performed: the same gesture G may have different meanings in positions P_1 and P_2, where P_1 and P_2 are points in the depth image. The extended set of gestures changed the pattern of interaction: zoom-in and zoom-out gave the possibility to require more or less information about an area.

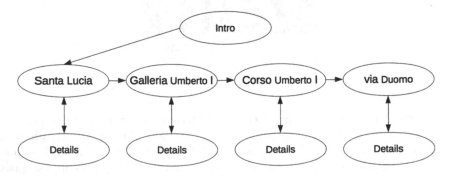

Fig. 7. The interaction pattern of PaSt applied to the redevelopment of Naples

Navigation could be represented as a layered-graph: zoom gestures navigate in depth and single-hand gestures explore the breadth of the structure. We employed this version of PaSt to explain the redevelopment of Naples at the end of XIX century: a map is projected on the floor, the leader navigates the contents following the schema in Fig. 7. An example of projected image is shown in Fig. 6(c).

In the final version of PaSt, leader tracking has been used as a source of events: leader-in, leader-out and leader-changed events have been introduced and the multi-window software architecture has been added. The representation based on the combined use of SCXML and SMIL was introduced, and the interaction pattern has a free graph structure; this version also includes the previous ones. In the framework of the OrCHeSTRA project, PaSt has been applied to show the "ten layers" of Naples: the city evolved by changing existing buildings and by extending the area of the previous one; so, many historical parts are not visible. This version of PaSt presents a map of Naples on the floor, highlighting the active areas in a selected period; the user can change the map - by the browsing gestures - or can require information about an area, by zooming in; a front projection shows multimedia contents about the selected part. Once the user is in a detailed state - by examining an area in depth - the browse gestures are used to navigate frontal contents. A leader-out event is used, for example, to restore the initial state of the interaction. In this version, the gesture recognition module is modelled with the LDCRF classifier, as explained in Sect. 3.2.

As explained in Sect. 3.4, in our experiments, we consider a virtual environment as a multi-projection system and we presented a number of case studies using either one or two sides configurations. This concept can easily be extended both from the point of view of the immersiveness degree (number of virtualised *sides*) and from the point of view of the specific application, by exploiting the portability of the system architecture. This specific characteristic allows the system to include interface systems that do not use multi-projection systems. For example, it is possible to use a client on another kind of remote device such as smart glasses, tablets, smartphones or smart TVs. It is also possible to support collaborative environments by running multiple instances of the system on remote machines. For example, two groups in different PaSt environments could interact remotely with each other in the same virtual *room*. Assuming a centralised *host* machine handling the representation of the collaborative environment, a number of client instances can synchronise with the central unit and provide feedback about the activities of the groups they are monitoring in order to let these intervene on the overall scenario. An example of this kind of CAVE-like interconnected systems is presented in [4].

5   Results

This paper presents an interaction system based on gestures and virtual reality for a small group of people. Tracking users in a defined area is the first requirement and it is not a recent issue, but we propose a computer vision algorithm that highly improve this phase, compared with approaches cited in Sect. 2, with specific attention to *Water-filling*. Our algorithm is based on a different concept, because we approximate a person with a Gaussian curve and we search its mean; details about our method are in Sect. 3.1. Table 1 summarises time of execution at different image resolutions. We used a Mac mini, Intel-i5 2.5 GHz, 4 GB RAM, MacOSX 10.10.2, openFrameworks v0.9.0, based on OpenCV 2.4. On the basis of the above considerations, PaSt is explicitly designed to be a low cost system from both the hardware and software points of view. The high-performance implemented algorithms and the modular architecture, do not necessarily require neither a single powerful station nor a physical infrastructure typically used in CAVE-like environments.

Table 1. Execution time of people detection algorithms

Image resolution	Water-filling	Proposed approach
160×120	9 ms	3 ms
320×240	47 ms	5 ms
640×480	261 ms	8 ms

Concerning the data shown in Table 1, further considerations are needed. In order to improve performances of Water-filling algorithm, we scaled the depth map and applied it to a smaller area; very high reduction of resolution yields better results, but image copy and scale operations have to be added each time. Moreover, some system parameters are strongly dependent on number of pixels: the higher the resolution, the higher the required amount of "rain drops", decreasing performance. Our approach, indeed, has a small set of thresholds and is less sensible to noise - related to flat areas and close people. Eventually, the obtained head centroid is more accurate than Water-filling result; motivations are explained in Sect. 3.1. By executing both the algorithms on the same frame, we obtained some difference among results: the former approach produces a fixed point that coincides with the real centroid; the latter system has a mean spread of $(11.95, 8.42)$ pixels for x and y, that could change in time. Variations in head centroid are dangerous to gesture recognition, because a fixed hand and a moving centroid is interpreted as a opposite situation.

A second essential part of the system proposed in this paper is gesture recognition module. The primary version relied on a rule-based approach analysing position of both hands in time; worse results have been gathered in zoom-in and zoom-out gestures. Second version was based on LDCRF: the training set has been populated by data collected by 7 people; each person has performed the four gestures 10 times at 8 fps. In order to obtain a user-independent model, the classifier has been trained and tested using leave-one-subject-out (LOSO) validation approach; resulting F-measures are 69.11 and 96.12 respectively for rule-based and trained models.

When designing these approaches, it is important to keep the users involved in the development process. PaSt has been presented during the experimentation phase of the Italian OrCHeSTRA project. During a public exhibit, 51 people tried the technologies developed in the framework of this project and provided feedback by compiling a questionnaire. In this paper, we concentrate on the evaluation users gave to two specific aspects of PaSt: the usability for the tasks at hand and the disposition of the users to participate in collaborative tasks in the same environment. Specifically, people were asked if (1) *the data presented by PaSt were correctly integrated in the application* and if (2) *they considered the proposed virtual environment suitable for collaborative tasks*. People reacted positively both to the current way for accessing data, in the cultural heritage domain, and to the possibility of using the same framework for collaborative tasks. On a scale of 1 to 5, the average value assigned to the system by the participants is 4.5. Disposition towards working together with other participants in the same environment obtained an average score of 4.2.

6   Conclusions and Future Works

In this paper we presented PaSt, a virtual reality CAVE-like architecture to support interaction for a small group of people in a multi-projection environment. In this work, we compared a gaussian-based people detection algorithm with a water-filling approach. Both systems use a vertical depth camera for tracking. We have shown that the proposed approach is faster and more precise than reference one, improving a key aspect towards extending the system to a larger area and to introduce support to higher resolution devices.

Concerning the gesture recognition phase, we tested two different approaches: a rule-based algorithm and a trained model. Each system uses the same features: the tracked positions of both hands. The former system analyses angles drawn in a given time period and considers hands directions and angles amplitude to discern the target gestures. The latter approach applies a normalisation step and is trained on the reference dataset using a LOSO approach to account for generalisation. Obtained results show that the LDCRF offers better results and is more robust with respect to tracking interruptions. Future work on this part will focus on applying geometric transforms to account for varying camera heights, which currently disrupts the recognition capabilities of the trained model. Scores obtained with the questionnaire show that the proposed interactive modality is well-received by the users, who reported that the data are well-integrated in the application. Independently of the used gesture recognition approach, gesture are not correctly identified when the leader is located on the boundaries of the detection range, as the arms could be not detected. Moreover, the leader could not be correctly detected on the boundaries, due to variations of perspective.

The final strong point of the proposed system is the designed architecture: client-server organisation with SCXML+SMIL offers a high degree of adaptation to a wide range of possible virtual environments. Given the modular design of the architecture, extending the environment corresponds to changing the number of clients at run-time to handle more sides or to introduce interfaces that are completely different from the ones considered in our case studies. Remotely connected clients can provide support for collaborative environments where multiple groups operate in the same virtual room, extending the potential applications of the proposed system. Scores obtained from the questionnaire show that people appear to be well-disposed towards exploring the environment together with other users for collaborative tasks.

Acknowledgment. This work has been funded by the European Community and the Italian Ministry of University and Research and EU under the PON Or.C.He.S.T.R.A. project.

References

1. Braus, H., Elze, C.: Anatomie des menschen: ein lehrbuch für studierende und ärzte, vol. 1. Springer, Heidelberg (1932)
2. Caso, A., Rossi, S.: Users ranking in online social networks to support pois selection in small groups. In: UMAP Workshops (2014)
3. Cruz-Neira, C., Sandin, D.J., DeFanti, T.A.: Surround-screen projection-based virtual reality: the design and implementation of the cave. In: Proceedings of the 20th Annual Conference on Computer Graphics and Interactive Techniques, SIGGRAPH 1993, pp. 135–142. ACM, New York (1993)
4. Galambos, P., Weidig, C., Baranyi, P., Aurich, J.C., Hamann, B., Kreylos, O.: Virca net: a case study for collaboration in shared virtual space. In: 2012 IEEE 3rd International Conference on Cognitive Infocommunications (CogInfoCom), pp. 273–277, December 2012
5. Gardner, H.: Frames of Mind: The Theory of Multiple Intelligences. Basic Books, New York (2011)
6. Grønbæk, K., Iversen, O.S., Kortbek, K.J., Nielsen, K.R., Aagaard, L.: Interactive floor support for kinesthetic interaction in children learning environments. In: Baranauskas, C., Abascal, J., Barbosa, S.D.J. (eds.) INTERACT 2007. LNCS, vol. 4663, pp. 361–375. Springer, Heidelberg (2007)
7. Iversen, O.S., Kortbek, K.J., Nielsen, K.R., Aagaard, L.: Stepstone: an interactive floor application for hearing impaired children with a cochlear implant. In: Proceedings of the 6th International Conference on Interaction Design and Children, pp. 117–124. ACM (2007)
8. Kenyon, R.V., Sandin, D., Smith, R.C., Pawlicki, R., Defanti, T.: Size-constancy in the cave. Presence Teleoper. Virtual Environ. **16**(2), 172–187 (2007)
9. Lafferty, J.D., McCallum, A., Pereira, F.C.N.: Conditional random fields: probabilistic models for segmenting and labeling sequence data. In: Proceedings of the ICML, pp. 282–289 (2001)
10. Morency, L.-P., Quattoni, A., Darrell, T.: Latent-dynamic discriminative models for continuous gesture recognition. In: IEEE Conference on Computer Vision and Pattern Recognition, CVPR 2007, pp. 1–8. IEEE (2007)
11. Sharples, S., Cobb, S., Moody, A., Wilson, J.R.: Virtual reality induced symptoms and effects (VRISE): comparison of head mounted display (HMD), desktop and projection display systems. Displays **29**(2), 58–69 (2008)
12. Sparacino, F.: Scenographies of the past and museums of the future: from the wunderkammer to body-driven interactive narrative spaces. In: Proceedings of the 12th Annual ACM International Conference on Multimedia, pp. 72–79. ACM (2004)

13. Wigdor, D., Wixon, D.: Brave NUI World: Designing Natural User Interfaces for Touch and Gesture. Elsevier, Amsterdam (2011)
14. Zhang, X., Yan, J., Feng, S., Lei, Z., Yi, D., Li, S.Z.: Water filling: unsupervised people counting via vertical kinect sensor. In: 2012 IEEE Ninth International Conference on Advanced Video and Signal-Based Surveillance (AVSS), pp. 215–220. IEEE (2012)

Natural Interaction with 3D Content on Mobile AR Systems Using Gesture Recognition

Victor Kyriazakos, Giorgos Nikolakis,
and Konstantinos Moustakas$^{(\boxtimes)}$

Electrical and Computer Engineering Department,
University of Patras, Patras, Greece
{kyriazakos, gniko, moustakas}@ece.upatras.gr

Abstract. We present a mobile AR interaction system where the user can naturally interact with and manipulate 3D content by recognizing discrete in-air gestures and temporal poses of a hand in front of the camera. Our system consists of established image processing, pose estimation and AR rendering steps, and a novel fingertip detection algorithm that can run real-time on off-the-shelf mobile devices with the use of an external depth camera. We also present an application prototype implemented on a tablet with a mounted IR structured-lighting depth camera.

Keywords: Natural interfaces · Augmented and mixed reality · Gesture recognition

1 Introduction

Mobile devices, such as smartphones and tablets are commonly used nowadays and play an important role in our everyday life. As a result, mobile application development is growing rapidly worldwide, including augmented reality (AR) applications and technologies for mobile devices [8]. In this paper we present an AR content manipulation scheme designed for mobile devices. Our proposed system uses gesture recognition and range sensing as an input interface for manipulation of virtual objects in a mixed reality environment.

Hand gesture recognition is one of the most natural ways to interact with an AR environment [1]. A typical gesture recognition pipeline consists of two major steps: (a) Segmenting the hand from the rest of the scene, and (b) classifying the detected pose/gesture. Various approaches are used in order to detect the hand and identify poses or gestures. A finger tracking method for interaction in augmented reality environments was presented in [2]. The use of existing depth sensors for robust hand gesture recognition is proposed in [3], while in [4] the hand is tracked during interaction with an object. A fast algorithm for automatically recognizing a set of gestures is proposed in [5]. Recently, a random forest approach was presented in [7], and an offline approach in [9], where only an RGB camera is used and was argued that depth sensor usage in mobile scenarios is prohibitive due to power consumption, heat dissipation and size. However, recent advances in depth-sensing technology have allowed the miniaturization of depth sensors, like the one used in our prototype (Sect. 5),

© Springer International Publishing Switzerland 2016
L.T. De Paolis and A. Mongelli (Eds.): AVR 2016, Part II, LNCS 9769, pp. 348–357, 2016.
DOI: 10.1007/978-3-319-40651-0_28

which also uses an internal battery for power supply, alleviating, thus, the aforementioned issues.

This paper aims to present a real-time gesture-based interaction scheme for mobile depth-capable devices. The implementation requires that the algorithms run in real-time on resource-constrained mobile processors. The following section provides an overview of the system architecture. Section 3 describes the input acquisition and depth registration pipeline. Section 4 describes the hand detection scheme including background extraction, hand detection, fingertip recognition and hand pose-gesture recognition. In Sect. 5, we provide some implementation details specific to the example application we created and provide the results of our framework. Finally in Sect. 6 we discuss the limitations of our proposed system and possible future work.

2 System Overview

The proposed system consists of 4 processing modules, a mobile device that has both front and rear cameras, and a depth sensor mounted on the device.

The 4 processing modules (Fig. 1) are:

- Input acquisition and depth registration: This processing module handles the capturing and processing of the raw input color and depth frames. It soft synchronizes the two streams and releases a registered RGB-D image as described in Sect. 3. The results are sent to the Hand Gesture recognition module.
- Hand Pose-Gesture recognition: This modules detects the hand in the scene, identifies the gesture and pose of the hand. The module is described in detail in Sect. 4.
- Interaction handler: This modules receives input from the Hand gesture recognition module and applies relative manipulations and transformations to the virtual objects in the AR scene.
- AR Rendering Engine: This module maintains the scene data and virtual objects, and collaborates with the input acquisition stage to perform marker tracking and estimate the pose of the camera.

3 Input Acquisition and Depth Registration

Most systems that employ depth-sensing, use devices capable of providing a registered and hardware-synchronized RGB-D Image (e.g. MS Kinect). In our case, the range data information is provided by an external IR structured-lighting depth sensor (Structure IO[1]) and the color data by the mobile device's internal camera. Therefore, the first processing module of our pipeline handles the synchronization and registration of the depth stream onto the color one, as well as the marker-tracking operations necessary for pose estimation and AR Rendering.

---

[1] http://structure.io/.

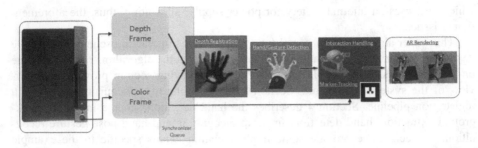

Fig. 1. The system's schematic pipeline. The two red blocks (depth registration and hand/gesture recognition) denote the computationally-heavy processing tasks of the framework, while the blue block denotes that Marker-tracking and Interaction-Handling are done in parallel to speed-up the overall processing time. (Color figure online)

3.1 Streams Synchronization

In order to preserve tracking and detection of hand gestures, it is important to keep the image pairs tightly synchronized so that the content doesn't vary in case of quick movements. To achieve this, the two capturing threads, retrieving frames asynchronously, timestamp the input frames and push them to a synchronizing queue. From there, the synchronizer checks the timestamps of the arrived frames, and publishes an RGB-D pair by choosing the temporal closest ones.

3.2 Depth to Color Registration

The most computationally-heavy task of the input acquisition module is the depth registration. This is the process of re-projecting the depth frame in order to match the color camera's characteristics and position. We assume that we have estimated the depth and color camera intrinsic matrices, denoted K_d and K_c respectively, through standard calibration procedures. Having previously undistorted the two input frames based on their estimated distortion coefficients, the depth to color registration process is reduced to the following calculation:

$$D_r(x) = PK_cT_{dc}K_d^{-1}P^{-1}D_u(x)$$

where P is the perspective division operator, T_{dc} the rigid body transformation between the depth and color camera, and D_u, D_r the unregistered and registered depth pixels of the current frame.

4 Gesture Recognition

The Gesture recognition process consists of three steps: (a) background extraction and hand detection, (b) fingertip recognition, (c) Classification of pose and/or gesture. These steps are described in the following subsections.

4.1   Background Extraction – Hand Detection

A depth-sensing camera makes background extraction relatively easy. Empirically defining a distance threshold is enough to identify objects near the camera and reject all the areas that are farther as background. Pixels that have an error value are treated as background (these pixels include the visible part of user's arm that is near the camera). Using the threshold a binary image mask is produced. A morphological opening followed by an extra dilation is then applied to the mask in order to remove small defects and holes. The steps are presented in Fig. 2.

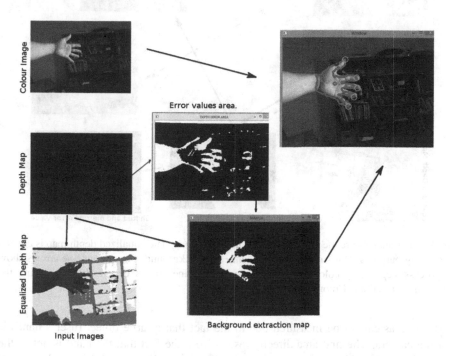

Fig. 2. Input images are the color image and the depth map. The equalized depth map is created for viewing purposes. Areas far away and error values are defined as background. In the background map it can be seen that the pinky finger is not attached to the rest of the hand. Also, some noise-induced artifacts can be seen. Post-processing the map identifies the green area as a hand and allows the detection of the fingertips. (Color figure online)

The hand of the user is near the camera and thus the area of the hand occupies the biggest part of the image. We accept as hand area the larger area in the mask that is over a threshold. Distance to other areas in the mask is measured and while it is below a threshold the areas are connected to the main hand area. This operation selects the area of the users palm and the fingers.

However this is not always the case. The device minimum measurable distance is approximately 40 cm and many users are not comfortable having their hand at that distance. When the user's hand is near the camera (i.e. camera to hand distance is less than 40 cm), the method described above cannot be used. In that case the depth map has large areas that cannot be measured including the users hand and a second method (Fig. 3) is used.

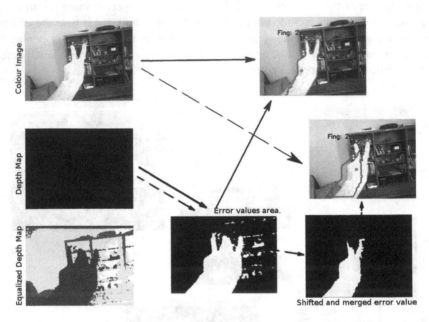

Fig. 3. Input images are the color image and the depth map. The equalized depth map is created for viewing purposes. Non-error values are defined as background. Continuous line arrows show the process steps using color selection, while dashed line arrows denote the steps using the shifted map selection. (Color figure online)

Two areas cannot be measured due to the fact that a large object (user's hand) is near the camera. The first area directly results from the fact that the hand is not in the measurable area. This creates an area with the same shape as the hand that is not measured in the depth map. The second problem is the depth "shadow" created by the hand due to the pixel shift needed to correct the IR projector-camera offset. Practically, the first area is a shifted image of the hand that appears to the left of the hand compared to the color image. The second area is a shifted and distort image on the right side. Shifting to the left is relative to the distance of the object from the camera and shifting (and distortion) to the right side depends both to the distance of the object to the camera and the distance of background objects.

To overcome this problem two different approaches are proposed. The first method assumes that the user keeps the distance of her hand in a constant distance from the camera and that the background objects do not have large distance differences. The second method assumes that colors in the image have a relatively large difference to the skin color of the hand.

In the first case the two shifted images of the hand have a constant horizontal distance. In order to estimate the hand shape we create a mask of the area the distance was not measured. Then a horizontally shifted copy of the mask is produced. Finally a bit wise and operation between the two masks returns the hand shape. This allows us to detect the hand. Actually, the result is shifted compared to the color image and shows the hand shape as seen by the infrared camera. The absolute position of the hand is not important, to identify pose or gestures so in this case we may accept as truth the position in the infrared camera input.

In the second case we assume that other objects that appear in the scene do not have similar colors to the human hand and that lighting conditions are good enough so that color camera can take clear images. In order to estimate the hand center we create a mask of the area that distance was not measured and calculate its centroid. Dilation is applied to the mask using a one line kernel so that areas on the sides of the mask are included in the accepted area. The centroid and four other points near it are selected as a base colors and used to select the hand area using color thresholds and the dilated mask. The result is a binary mask of the estimated hand area.

4.2 Fingertip Detection

Hand area detected in the previous step is used as input to detect finger tips. A k-curvature approach is used in many cases to detect fingertips. However, the fact that user's hand is near the lower measurable distance of the camera often produces noisy results. This leads k-curvature method to produce false detects.

To resolve this problem a different approach is proposed. The centroid of the detected hand is calculated, using Hu moments [6]. The centroid is then used as the center of a polar coordinate system. Every hand contour point is then transformed to this coordinate system. Calculated angles are rounded to the nearest degree. The largest calculated distance is accepted for each degree. This way an array of 360 distance values is filled. The average distance is calculated and used as a threshold to detect fingertips (Fig. 4).

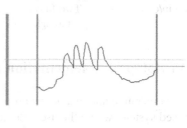

Fig. 4. The green line shows the area detected as hand. The small green circle is the hand centroid and the blue circles are the detected fingertips. The right side diagram shows the distance of the surrounding line from the centroid. 0° is on the left side. The distance is ignored and not measured for angles near the hand entry angle (in this case 350° ± 60°) (Color figure online)

Each fingertip candidate is a local maximum in the distance array that is greater than the average distance. Results include fingertips and other points. Selected points that are not fingertips are usually near the wrist of the hand.

In order to exclude these points the hand entry angle is computed. The hand entry angle is the direction from the hand centroid to a point of the arm on the edge of the image. Then fingertip candidates that have an angle difference smaller than a threshold are excluded. Fingertip candidates are also rejected when another fingertip candidate that has a greater distance value is within a few degrees.

The rest of the fingertip candidates are accepted as fingertips and counted as open fingers. In the very rare case more that more than 5 fingertips are valid only 5 of them are accepted and returned.

4.3 Pose and Gesture Recognition

The system using simple angular and distance thresholds is able to detect eight in-air hand poses and five temporal gestures, as shown in Table 1.

Table 1. The available in-air poses and gestures detected by the proposed system. All of them are programmable to be handled by the interaction handler.

Pose/Gesture	Description
Closed hand	No detected fingertips
One to five fingers opened	Number of detected fingertips
Victory sign	Index and middle fingers are open
Gun	Thumb and index fingers are open
Gestures	
Grasp	Five fingers are detected in one frame and the next frame detects a closed hand
Click	One finger detected. The finger closes and opens again through frames
Release	Five fingers detected after closed hand
Zoom in/out	Two fingers are detected with their distance decreasing (increasing) through frames

5 Prototype Implementation and Results

For demonstrative and evaluative purposes, we built an indicative application using the proposed system, where the user interacts and transforms a virtual object in a 3D scene.

5.1 System Configuration

We implemented the software prototype on a mobile configuration as seen in Fig. 5. We used the tablet Nexus 9, running Android Lollipop (5.1.0). For depth-sensing, we used the Structure IO sensor, mounted on the tablet using a custom 3D-printed bracket. The application software, and the proposed framework, are written in C/C++ and OpenGL. We tested the system by developing an example application where the user can translate-scale a virtual object on the scene by using specific gestures.

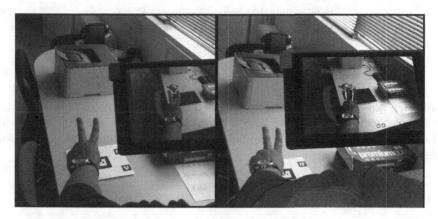

Fig. 5. Example usage of our system for the manipulation of a single virtual object. In the first frame (left) the fingers are not over the object, while in the second (right), the object is picked (and outlined) and transformed according to the user's movement.

Interaction Handler. The proposed system's Interaction Handler (see Fig. 1) consists of a programmable pipeline corresponding to the available in-air gestures that can be detected. In our experimental prototype, we used the single-finger detection to choose and highlight the selected object, the two-finger pose to translate the selected object and the Closed-Hand gesture to scale the object.

Marker-Tracking. Marker-tracking is performed asynchronously with the Interaction Handler. We use a simple rectangular multi-maker configuration to handle tracking in cases where there is occlusion by the user's hand. It is done on a later stage so that we track the marker only on frames published by the synchronizer. The reason for that, is to avoid erroneous transformations resulting from the markers transformation and not the user's hands.

5.2   Results and Performance

In order to assess the performance of the proposed system, we timed the main stages of the processing pipeline. As shown in Table 2, the proposed system performs real-time on the mobile device at an average of 11 frames per second (FPS). The bottleneck of the system is the Gesture detection stage, followed by the Depth registration and marker-tracking processes.

An exemplary usage of the framework and the developed prototype can be seen in Fig. 5. The user selects the 3D object by hovering a fingertip over it, and translates it when holding two fingers up. All transformations are calculated accurately on world

Table 2. Processing times of the proposed system on the prototype mobile configuration. Interaction handling and marker-tracking is done asynchronously in parallel, thus the time displayed is that of the slowest one (marker-tracking).

Acquisition/synchronization	<1 ms
Depth registration	18 ms
Hand/gesture detection	42 ms
Interaction handling-marker tracking	27 ms
AR rendering	4 ms
Total:	**92 ms**

coordinates, achieving thus, a close tracking of the user's hand by the virtual object. It is also noteworthy that since we have a depth-capable device, we handled real-life occlusions of the virtual objects by pre-filling the graphic's pipeline depth buffer before rendering the virtual content.

6 Conclusions

In this paper we presented an integrated system for naturally interacting with 3D content on mobile AR scenarios using in-air gestures. The proposed system uses an external depth-camera, which is self-powered, so as to not affect the device's battery life. We tackle the problems created by using external cameras, such as depth registration, and provide a complete framework for gesture recognition and handling, and AR marker-based rendering, integrated into a mobile device. We have proposed a novel scheme for real-time gesture detection, branched off to two methods corresponding to two different scenarios, (a) when the user's hand is in measurable distance, and (b) when it's not. To our best knowledge, this is the first integrated gesture-based AR manipulation system used on a depth-capable mobile device that is comprised of off-the-shelf hardware. We have qualitatively evaluated our system by developing a single-object manipulation application and showed that it performs real-time on the target device by measuring its computation times. Our future work is: (a) to provide a parallel implementation of the computationally-heavy stages, (b) to improve the capabilities and accuracy of the gesture recognition component to reduce false-positives and (c) to provide gesture-recording features to allow the addition of user-defined poses.

Acknowledgements. This work has been supported by the Greek Secretariat for Research and Technology Bilateral Collaboration Project MOMIRAS (ISR-3215).

References

1. Malik, S., McDonald, C., Roth, G.: Tracking for interactive pattern-based augmented reality. In: ISMAR 2002, pp. 117–126 (2002)
2. Dormfuller-Ulhaas, K., Schmalstieg, D.: Finger tracking for interaction in augmented environments. In: ISAR 2001, pp. 55–64 (2001)
3. Ren, Z., Yuan, J., Meng, J., Zhang, Z.: Robust part-based hand gesture recognition using Kinect sensor. Multimed. IEEE Trans. **15**(5), 1110–1120 (2013)
4. Oikonomides, I., Kyriazis, N., Argyros, A.A.: Full DOF tracking of hand interacting with an object by modelling occlusions and physical constraints. In: IEEE International Conference on Computer Vision, pp. 2088–2095 (2011)
5. Malima, A., Özgür, E., Çetin, M.: A fast algorithm for vision-based hand gesture recognition for robot control. In: IEEE Conference on Signal Processing and Communications Applications, Antalya, Turkey (2006)
6. Hu, M.: Visual pattern recognition by moment invariants. IRE Trans. Inf. Theor. **8**(2), 179–187 (1962)
7. Song, J., Sörös, G., Pece, F., Hilliges, O.: Real-time hand gesture recognition on unmodified wearable devices. In: IEEE Conference on Computer Vision and Pattern Recognition (2015)
8. Kyriazakos, V., Moustakas, K.: A user-perspective view for mobile AR systems using discrete depth segmentation. In: 2015 International Conference on Cyberworlds (CW), Visby, pp. 69–72 (2015)
9. Serra, G., Camurri, M., Baraldi, L., Benedetti, M., Cucchiara, R.: Hand segmentation for gesture recognition in EGO-vision. In: Proceedings of the 3rd ACM International Workshop on Interactive Multimedia on Mobile and Portable Devices, pp. 31–36 (2013)

Development of Innovative HMI Strategies for Eye Controlled Wheelchairs in Virtual Reality

Luca Maule, Alberto Fornaser, Malvina Leuci, Nicola Conci,
Mauro Da Lio, and Mariolino De Cecco[(✉)]

University of Trento, Trento, Italy
mariolino.dececco@unitn.it

Abstract. This paper focuses on the development of a gaze-based control strategy for semiautonomous wheelchairs. Starting from the information gathered by an eye tracker, the work aims to develop a novel paradigm of Human Computer Interaction (HCI) by means of a Virtual Reality (VR) environment, where specific motion metrics are evaluated.

Keywords: Interaction design · Virtual reality · Eye tracking

1 Introduction

Collaborative Assistive Robotics is the discipline that studies the support of automatic machines to people in the execution of many different tasks involving specific design of human machine interaction HMI. The support and the assistance of patients suffering from mobility problems such as spinal cord injuries or degenerative diseases as ALS (Amyotrophic Lateral Sclerosis), is a very relevant research branch in the field of Assistive Robotics. Of course, and in addition to the physical deficit, these kind of pathologies are often cause psychological distress. In order to alleviate the loss of mobility and the capability of interacting with the surrounding world, the market offers solutions based on motorized wheelchairs and combined with a suitable HMI. A very promising yet challenging interface is the adoption of eye tracking technologies. This kind of interaction paradigm is indeed very useful, since it can help enhancing the user mobility, consisting in a valuable support also until the last and most critical phases of the disease.

Existing solutions for gaze-based interaction often require wearing glasses [8] or electrodes for Electrooculography [7], while others are based on less invasive solutions as for example Video Oculography (VOG). However, due to the patient health conditions, it would be highly desirable to develop HMIs that are least tiring and invasive as possible. Moreover, the user needs a certain amount of time to become familiar with it [3], the designer is often required to develop customized HMIs [1] and clinicians need assistance in performing standardized wheelchair driving assessments [6].

Unfortunately, VOG, although being minimally invasive, achieves lower performances in terms of eye gaze estimation accuracy compared to more traditional interaction paradigms. This is due to the different elements and environmental conditions

© Springer International Publishing Switzerland 2016
L.T. De Paolis and A. Mongelli (Eds.): AVR 2016, Part II, LNCS 9769, pp. 358–377, 2016.
DOI: 10.1007/978-3-319-40651-0_29

that influence the system performances and cannot be fully kept under control. Among them illumination, relative motion between the user and the instrument (rotation and translation), objects in front of the eyes, physiology of the different users [4]. Another problem underlined from many authors is that the performances provided by the manufacturers seems to be neither repeatable not representative as they are obtained in ideal conditions [9].

From the considerations above it is evident the need to have an instrument able to train the user, let the designer develop optimized HMIs taking into account also the instrument accuracy, and eventually assist clinicians in performing standardized wheelchair driving assessments. In [2] the authors used VR to assess lateralized spatial attention and neglect for users hit by right hemisphere strokes, adopting a complex hardware simulator based on a treadmill. In [1] a virtual reality platform based on a game engine (Unreal EngineTM) has been chosen for training, HMI evaluation, and optimization of a so-called "natural gaze-based wheelchair driving". In our work we propose a VR-based simulation engine to develop an innovative HMI for VOG that uses, for the first time, the information on the eye tracker accuracy to achieve better performances in usability, comfort during navigation and fault tolerance to noise induced by the intrinsically low accuracy of the interface, as previously described. With respect to [2] we use one of the current state of the art game engine, UNITY, to develop our VR tool, as it is able to provide immersive and high quality 3D graphics in a much simpler and reconfigurable platform. The work of [1] is quite interesting and very close to our goals and general approach. Compared to them our contribution consists of the inclusion in the model of the eye tracker accuracy; we developed different HMI interfaces that we believe to be more "natural", and we used a more complete set of metrics to assess the user performances.

2 State of Art in Wheelchair Control for Severely Impaired Users

With reference to the availability of systems that exploit the gaze information to control and drive a wheelchair, or more in general for mobility enhancement in patients affected by severe motor disabilities, the literature presents some works carried out in the past years that have been considered as a reference and starting point for our application. The first attempts in this area can be found in [23], where the authors propose a model to drive the wheelchair using, as a driver, the information gathered by a glass-mounted camera that takes a close look on the users' eye. A rather simple yet effective method to control the wheelchair by interpreting the position of the eye was proposed more recently by [24]. The method exploits the positioning of the eye and the blinking information to extract basic commands, as moving ahead, left and right. However, due to the incapability of dealing with head motion, both systems require a head-mounted device for tracking.

It is worth noting that wearing additional equipment may result uncomfortable for the user and therefore it would be highly desirable to reduce the invasiveness of the technology. To this aim, other researches in this area [25] have proven that the task can also be solved adopting external devices. However, an eye-tracking system as the one used for their experiments is rather expensive, considerably reducing the affordability of a complete system especially by a private user. Electrooculography [26] has also been recently used as a tool to understand the users' intentions and control the wheelchair accordingly. Besides requiring the use of a wearable device, electrooculography is an efficient diagnosis tool, but also in this case it may turn out to be fatiguing, and the number of commands that can be configured is somehow limited. This is the reason why we have chosen to use an external device, similarly to previous studies [25], but adopting an affordable system that can be easily configured and customized to fit the requirements of the specific application context.

3 Motion Metrics

Driving through the view of a display implies as the first main disadvantage a strong limitation of the visible field of view. A visual interface based on a common LCD presents limitations similar to the ones associated to common diseases that cause a loss of the peripheral view (for example in hemianopia [10, 15]). Such limitations results in common behaviours as a sub-optimal road/lane positioning when driving, slow motion during manoeuvres, reversing, or through narrow gaps. The user may not detect peripheral cues and therefore may lose forewarning as well as suffering of losses in the reaction time [13].

Methodologies and guidelines for an objective and general assessment of the driving performances can be identified in literature (usually derived from known drive test, i.e. Miller Road Test [12]). In our work, the simulation environment is designed to be a dynamic framework for training and design. Therefore, the definition of suitable metrics to quantify the driving performances, the usability of the HMI, and the motion comfort is fundamental for the iterative application of corrective actions both for the HMI and the training phase [3]. A good HMI for driving is indeed the one that not only allows a proper motion, but also guarantees the safety of the user, the safety for the others and the minimum stress in the daily usage. A number of papers have been published about the problem of assessing the driving performances. These, however, differ according to the application focus. Some are more targeted at safety features (for example for the renewal of driving licenses, problem currently associated to elderlies [16, 17]), HMI usability [18, 19], or the characterization of the driving comfort for the driver and/or passengers, relying mostly on the dynamic behaviour of the vehicle [20, 22]. Therefore, in order to provide a complete and meaningful evaluation, different metrics should be considered [6, 11, 14], related to the vehicle management and comfort of the passengers, but also to the cognitive and emotive response of the subject to different stimuli. Hereafter the main categories to take into account are:

- **Vehicle Metrics**
  - **Manoeuvrability Metrics**, related to vehicle position and orientation, lane positioning, driving speed, vehicle steering angle, brake distances. These metrics are useful to assess the skill and driving capability of the user.
  - **Comfort Metrics**, related to the motion characterization, longitudinal and lateral acceleration, jerk, vibrations, smoothness [20]. Derived from standard ISO

2631-1 [21], these metrics identify under which conditions the driving results comfortable, uncomfortable, or even potentially harmful for the subject.

- **Human Metrics**
  - **Stress Metrics**, track biological parameters such as heartbeat, blood pressure, eye-positions, pupil diameter, blinks. These metrics are useful to assess the level of stress of the user in using the interface.
  - **Cognitive Metrics**, related to the locus of attention or cognitive workload of the driver, usually obtained through interaction with an examiner under different testing condition, i.e. detection of signs, time to perform a given computation, the accuracy in committing items to memory. These metrics are useful to assess the level of mental load required to use the interface and drive.
  - **Subjective Metrics**, include norms of driving performance that are difficult to assess by automated means, or do not include cognitive issues of driving workload, interactions with the domestic spaces, responses to persons, obstacles etc. Direct feedback from the subjects, useful for usability estimation.

The metrics that we implemented originate from a subset of items in the list presented above and are hereafter described:

- **Circuit:** to complete a given course. The path performed is recorded and evaluated in relation to a reference path that must be followed. Figure 1, room and space marked with A.

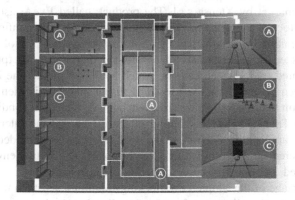

Fig. 1. UNITY virtual environment, the letters indicate the areas used for the tests

- **Comfort Assessment**: longitudinal and lateral acceleration and jerk analysis. The standard ISO 2631-1 proposes a comfort assessment based on the RMS from weighted accelerations

$$a_{RMS}(k\text{T}) = \left[\frac{1}{T} \int_0^T a_W^2(t)dt \right]^{\frac{1}{2}} \tag{1}$$

- $a_W(t)$ weighted acceleration. Horizontal (lateral and longitudinal) accelerations are weighted using a human transfer function defined in the standard;
- T, time interval for the RMS evaluation
- $a_{RMS}(kT)$ weighted RMS acceleration, function of the k-th T period
- **Manoeuvring**: to drive through a series of cones, positioned on a wide flat section of a course, as quickly as possible without touching any of them. Each cone touched or knocked over is recorded and considered as an error score. The time to complete the manoeuvring task is recorded. A manoeuvring score is calculated as the time to complete the task plus a time penalty for each error (Fig. 1B).
- **Depth perception**: to drive from a starting point to an ending reference at highest possible speed and stopping as close as possible to the reference. The reference can be either a line on the ground, that is visible direct reference, or a virtual line between two physical entities (cones or signs), namely an indirect reference. The distance between the final position of the wheelchair and the reference is recorded. Time taken to complete the task is recorded. A depth perception score is calculated as the time required to complete the task, plus a penalty score depending on the final gap (see Fig. 1C).

4   The Eye-Tracking System

For the implementation of this project we have relied on an eye-tracking solution made available on the market by Xtensa s.r.l. The product, called EyeAssist, which stems from an early prototype presented in [5], is a low-cost and highly configurable system that can be customized so as to satisfy the customer needs in terms of functionalities and application scenarios. It consists of a software driver that interprets the video information captured by the video camera, which goal is to predict the location of the point on the screen observed by the user. The visual interface is then handled by a separate application that reads the gaze stream to activate the corresponding function at the system level. Thanks to the decoupling of the driver and the interface, we have implemented our application exploiting the sole information provided by the gaze tracker. The gathered information is then used to control the virtual environment that we have developed and that will be described in the next paragraph.

The big advantage of the adopted eye-tracking solution consists in the provisioning of a solution that mostly relies on software, while limiting the hardware infrastructure to a video camera and four infrared illuminators used for calibration and pupil detection purposes. In fact, no strict constraint is imposed as far as the computer and the type of display is concerned. The power supply for the whole system (camera and lights) is guaranteed by the USB plug directly, so that no additional power source must be employed.

An overview of the eye-tracking components and the installation on the computer used for testing is shown in Fig. 2.

As can be seen, and for demonstration purposes we have adopted a regular desktop display, although, thanks to the flexibility in positioning the lights and calibration, the system can be easily tweaked to be used also in a mobile context, e.g., with a tablet.

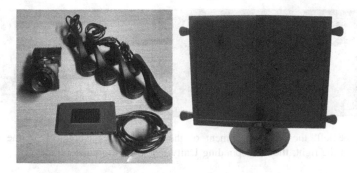

Fig. 2. The necessary hardware components (left): camera, infrared illuminators, and power distribution plug for the illuminators. A sample installation of EyeAssist (right), with details on the camera and light positioning

This turns out to be a considerably strong advantage compared to other solutions available on the market, since it allows testing the same system on different display devices, a highly desirable feature especially in the prototyping phases of the project.

To ensure maximum personalization of the platform and to make it easier to develop third-party applications on top of the existing eye-tracking driver, the interaction with the EyeAssist is possible querying a selected UDP port.

The data accessible by the user consist of the x and y coordinates of both eye pupils in the image, as seen by the camera, and the coordinates of the observed point on the screen, again for each eye. For completeness also the weighted average of the gaze combining the information of the right and left eye is also made provided. The weight is decided automatically during the calibration phase, to maximize the use of the dominant eye.

If desired, the user can decide to work with one eye only, by easily selecting the option from the configuration tool.

5   The Eye-Controlled Virtual Reality Environment

The 3D virtual scenario represents the environment of our mechatronics laboratory. It is developed starting from the 2D map, and completing the missing information using a common 3D modelling application (Fig. 3).

The HMI interaction and the wheelchair simulation was developer with UNITY 3D. The game engine permits to obtain a better realistic simulation from a graphical point of view, taking into account the collision with the wall (bouncing on collision) and the dynamics of the wheelchair.

Furthermore, the simulation takes into account the dynamics of the vehicle by means of the field "mass" applied to the rigid body component and a viscous friction. Both the kinematics and the friction models are very simplified. The kinematics of the wheelchair is a unicycle while the friction simulates the rotational friction along the wheel axis and the wheel lateral slippage. The control of the wheelchair is achieved providing a reference velocity that the object reaches imposing a maximum

Fig. 3. On the left: the 3D environment of the mechatronics laboratory in the modelling application. On the right: the corresponding Unity 3D scenario (game engine)

acceleration law (bang-bang control) to the rigid body. Each dynamical update is computed at a fixed time stamp like in a real time operating system, see Eq. (2). During each "FixedUpdate" cycle, the application estimates the variation of the linear and rotational velocity taking into account the HMI commands that provide the reference linear and angular velocities. In this way, the behaviour of the two velocities follows a common trapezoidal tread (in Fig. 11 a simulation example) characterized by a speed limit equal to the reference provided by the HMI.

$$v_k = v_{k-1} + a \cdot \Delta t_{frame}$$
$$\dot{\theta}_k = \dot{\theta}_{k-1} + \alpha \cdot \Delta t_{frame}$$
$$\tag{2}$$

- v_k is the linear velocity at k-th frame
- a is the bang-bang maximum forward acceleration
- $\dot{\theta}_k$ is the rotational velocity at k-th frame
- α is the bang-bang maximum angular acceleration
- Δt_{frame} is the time between two consequent frames

The following code is part of the script used to simulate the wheelchair velocities.

```
// Current attitude of vehicle
float delta = transform.rotation.eulerAngles.y * Mathf.PI /
180.0f;
float vxLocal =   rb.velocity.x * Mathf.Cos (-delta) +
rb.velocity.z * Mathf.Sin (-delta);

float vzLocal = - rb.velocity.x * Mathf.Sin (-delta) +
rb.velocity.z * Mathf.Cos (-delta);

vxLocal *= 0.999f; // forward viscous friction
vzLocal *= 0.850f; // lateral viscous friction
float vx = vxLocal * Mathf.Cos (-delta) - vzLocal * Mathf.Sin (-
delta);
float vz = vxLocal * Mathf.Sin (-delta) + vzLocal * Mathf.Cos (-
delta);
rb.velocity = new Vector3 (vx, 0.0f, vz);

if (Mathf.Sqrt( Mathf.Pow( rb.velocity.x, 2.0f ) + Mathf.Pow(
rb.velocity.z, 2.0f ) ) <  forwardSpeedReference ) {
   if (movementSpeed <0)
     v=-v;
   deltaSpeed = Math.Abs(movementSpeed)*v * movementAcceleration
   * Time.deltaTime;
   rb.velocity += new Vector3(deltaSpeed * Mathf.Cos (delta),
   0.0f, - deltaSpeed * Mathf.Sin (delta));
}
if ( Mathf.Abs(rb.angularVelocity.y) < angularSpeedReference) {
   deltaRotationSpeed = rotateSpeed*h * rotateAcceleration *
   Time.deltaTime;
   rb.angularVelocity += new Vector3 (0.0f, deltaRotationSpeed,
   0.0f);
}
rb.angularVelocity *= 0.94f; // angular viscous friction
```

6   Interaction Design

The HMI proposed in this article aims to minimize the stress of the patient resulting
from the intensive use of the system, and at the same time maximize his driving
performances and motion comfort. For this purpose we believe that the HMI has to be
intuitive for all the users (i.e. for youngsters and elderly) and the computed commands
must take into account the metrological performances of the eye tracker and the
physiological characteristics of the users (Fig. 4).

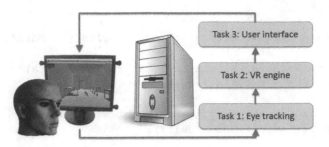

Fig. 4. Interaction block diagram

For this purpose we projected the 3D visible environment on the screen and, on the top part (1/3 of the screen), we overlapped the buttons to start and stop the simulation. This area is the one where the eye tracker is typically subject to a lower accuracy and where the ceiling and a narrow part of the walls are projected, so it has been used for general-purpose commands.

The control of the wheelchair is performed in the remaining central and bottom area. We used the VR environment to develop and optimize the two HMI strategies.

According to the first strategy, we divided the whole screen using a 3×3 grid of virtual buttons. As shown in Fig. 5 the top row and the first and third element of the bottom row are reserved for the customization of the graphical interface. The other four areas are used to perform the control of the wheelchair and, in particular, each button corresponds to a fixed set point of maximum linear and rotational speed. The information about the uncertainty gives a measure of precision of the eye tracker. The HMI strategy takes into account the uncertainty to evaluate the compatibility of the estimated point of sight on the screen with the possible commands. The values of compatibility are multiplied by the velocity set point in order to obtain two simultaneous movements, as in Eq. (3).

$$v_f = C_f \cdot V_{MAX}$$
$$\dot{\theta}_r = C_r \cdot \dot{\theta}_{MAX}$$

(3)

- v_f is the linear velocity
- C_f is the compatibility with the forward button
- V_{MAX} is the reference for the linear velocity
- $\dot{\theta}_r$ is the rotational velocity
- C_r is the compatibility with the turning right button
- $\dot{\theta}_{MAX}$ is the reference for the angular velocity

The second HMI strategy foresees a continuous variation of the two set point velocities with the aim to increase manoeuvrability, reduce jerks, and thus increase comfort. In particular, the traction speed has a trend following a rational function with two cubic polynomials (Eq. (4)):

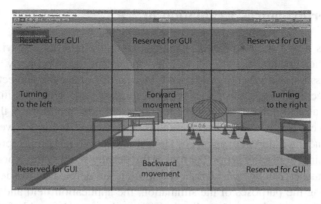

Fig. 5. HMI with 3 × 3 grid buttons. *Cf* forward and *Cr* right turning compatibilities

$$F(x) = \frac{-2.29 \cdot x^3 + 1.18 \cdot x^2 + 1.13 \cdot x - 0.017}{x^3 - 4.38 \cdot x^2 + 1.71 \cdot x + 2.22} \tag{4}$$

The parameters in Eq. (4) are obtained by fitting the function model with a set of reference 2D points (screen position vs speed) using a trust region routine.

The rotation speed follows a linear law from the value −1 rad/s on the left side of the screen to +1 rad/s on the right side, as reported in Eq. (5), where W is the screen width (Fig. 6).

$$G(x) = \begin{cases} \frac{3}{W} \cdot x + \frac{1}{2} & (\text{left side}) \\ \frac{3}{W} \cdot x - \frac{1}{2} & (\text{right side}) \end{cases} \tag{5}$$

For both control functions, we inserted a flat zone around the zero, where the wheelchair does not move. The amplitude of this area is defined to be comparable to the maximum eye tracker uncertainty. We obtain the reference speed multiplying the maximum speed by the value of the previous functions.

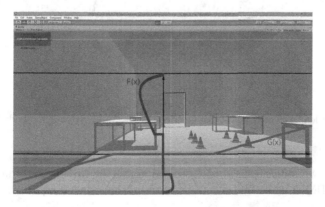

Fig. 6. Control functions for translation and rotation

7   HMI Performances Evaluation in VR

Seven subjects tested the two HMIs. Each user initially familiarized with both, performing a sufficient number of trials to fully understand and "properly" manage the driving (self-assessment given by the users). During this phase the subject can take all the time he needs to accomplish each task. In the last part of the familiarization the subject is instructed on the parameters of test that are under monitoring, the associated metrics and weighting factors. The weighting factors are multiplicative coefficients used to combine the different elements of the test into a homogeneous representation as a unique meaningful penalty score: the higher the penalty score is the worse the overall driving performance can be considered. The weights are defined by the designer of the tests considering the purposes of the simulation, the application field and the potential risk levels of the equivalent real application. The values are defined before the testing phase and kept constant for all subjects. For the sake of completeness, each factor of the penalty function is provided separately.

After the familiarization, subjects performed each test once. The data is here recorded and analysed using the metrics described in Sect. 3.

7.1   Circuit Metric

The objective of the test is to follow a given path inside an indoor environment. The main difficulty of the test is to not collide with the walls while following the reference.

All subjects reached the final position with a very limited number of collisions, all performing similar trajectories. However, the paths obtained using the HMI-2 achieved smoother trajectories compared to the ones obtained using HMI-1. In Fig. 7, the best and worst cases (lowest and highest penalty) for both the HMIs are shown.

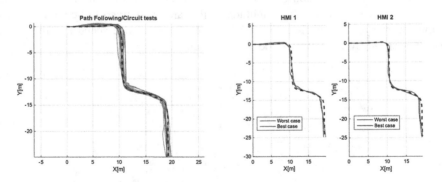

Fig. 7. On the left: executed paths. On the right: best and worst case for both HMIs. (Color figure online)

In Eq. (6) we indicate the metric used to assess the driving performances of the subjects and HMIs, while in Table 1 the result of the tests are reported.

Table 1. Circuit metric, tests results

Subject	HMI	Time [s]	RMS D [m]	Collisions	Penalty [s]
1	1	160.8	0.270	0	163.5
	2	133.4	0.195	1	137.3
2	1	139.2	0.309	0	142.3
	2	127.2	0.333	0	130.5
3	1	146.2	0.240	0	148.6
	2	133.1	0.282	1	137.9
4	1	121.6	0.397	0	125.6
	2	121.1	0.233	0	123.4
5	1	132.4	0.207	0	134.5
	2	135.7	0.235	0	138.1
6	1	149.7	0.533	0	155.0
	2	149.5	0.328	0	152.8
7	1	158.7	0.248	0	161.2
	2	140.9	0.242	0	143.3

$$P_{Ci} = Dt + D_{RMS} \cdot W_{RMS} + Hits \cdot W_{hit} \tag{6}$$

- P_{Ci} is the penalty score of the circuit test.
- Dt is the time interval from the first motion till the reaching of an imaginary line at the end of the circuit.
- D_{RMS} is the RMS distance from the reference path.
- W_{RMS} is the weighting factor for RMS distance: 1 s for 0.1 m. The value is meant to penalize those trajectories affected by a displacement bias or ones with a strong variably around the reference trajectory.
- $Hits$ corresponds to the number of collisions with the environment.
- W_{hit} is the weighting factor for collisions: 2 s for each collision. The value is the same used for the manoeuvrability metric.

Figure 8 shows the comparison between the penalty scores achieved with the two HMIs. The lower the value, the better can be considered the driving performances.

Six out of seven subjects achieved better performances (lower penalty) with HMI-2. The parameter that mostly influences such results it is the time required to complete the task: when using the HMI-1 the users are usually slower. Such operative condition is due to a limitation in performing the turns maintaining a constant frontal speed. With HMI-1, the user can control only one element per time, frontal or angular velocity; the compatibly analysis on the active areas helps the user to provide hybrid driving control in speed but still such driving interface implies a strong loss in the management of the frontal feed. We can then conclude that HMI-2 seems to provide a more agile driving experience.

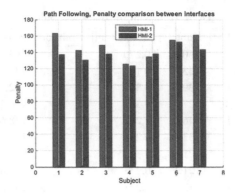

Fig. 8. Circuit test, HMIs penalties comparison (Color figure online)

7.2 Comfort Metric

The aim of this metric is to assess the level of comfort experienced by the user on the virtual wheelchair. The metric is developed according to the ISO 2631-1 guidelines and the related literature [20].

$$P_{Co} = \bar{a}_{RMS} \cdot W_{RMS} + max(a_{RMS}) \cdot W_{RMS} \tag{7}$$

- P_{Co} is the penalty score for comfort analysis.
- $\bar{a}_{RMS}$ is the mean of the RMSs accelerations (longitudinal and lateral) along the path (period for the RMS evaluation set to 2 s).
- $max(a_{RMS})$ is the maximum value of the RMSs longitudinal accelerations (frontal and lateral) along the path.
- W_{RMS} is the weighting factor for the comfort level: 0 if a_{RMS} is within the range of comfort, 2^n otherwise, where n is and index of the level of comfort (1 is "A little uncomfortable", 5 "extremely uncomfortable"). The values are set to penalize the occurrence of acceleration spikes and continuous variations of acceleration associated to an RMS value over threshold (Table 2).

In all tests the resulting acceleration, main parameter for the comfort assessment, remains under the threshold associated to the "comfortable" level (a RMS less than 0.314 m/s^2). Nevertheless, it must be underlined that the level of RMS accelerations is lower in the case of HMI-1; such result is mainly due to a more stable frontal speed when moving. With HMI-2, the continuous control law, together with the eye tracker uncertainty, causes small but continuous variations of the frontal speed, with associated frontal accelerations, resulting in a potentially less comfortable driving experience.

Table 2. Comfort metric, tests results

Subject	HMI	Mean a RMS [m/s^2]	Max a RMS [m/s^2]	Penalty[s]
1	1	0.016	0.043	0
	2	0.039	0.140	0
2	1	0.015	0.073	0
	2	0.022	0.091	0
3	1	0.012	0.052	0
	2	0.029	0.113	0
4	1	0.020	0.056	0
	2	0.021	0.089	0
5	1	0.020	0.057	0
	2	0.029	0.129	0
6	1	0.022	0.061	0
	2	0.049	0.167	0
7	1	0.015	0.044	0
	2	0.030	0.095	0

7.3 Manoeuvring Metric

The objective of this test is passing through a set of cones, starting the manoeuvre aligned with the passing direction but from both a lateral and longitudinal displacement. This test mimic a change of line manoeuvre.

In Fig. 9 the overall results are shown. The first important noticeable element is that subjects involved in the tests perform smoother motions using HMI-2.

The metric used for the assessment of the manoeuvrability is presented in Eq. (8), and Table 3 reports the data collected and the results of the metric.

$$P_M = Dt + Hits \cdot W_{hit} + |\vartheta| \cdot W_\theta \tag{8}$$

- P_M is the penalty score of the manoeuvring test.
- Dt is the time interval from the first motion till the reaching of an imaginary line at the end of the cones.
- $Hits$ corresponds to the number of cones hit in the test.
- W_{hit} is the weighting factor for hitting a cone: 2 s for each cone. The weighting factor is chosen to penalize a potentially dangerous manoeuvre due to a collision with objects or environment. The specific value of 2 s is set in order to assign a moderate penalty to the score.
- ϑ is the angle of the trajectory performed through the cones as linear segment.
- W_θ is the weighting factor for the alignment mismatch between the reference direction (defined by the cones) and ϑ: 2 s for each degree. The factor is chosen to penalize the wrong positioning during the manoeuvre. The value is equal to W_{hit} in order to give the same importance to both elements in the test.

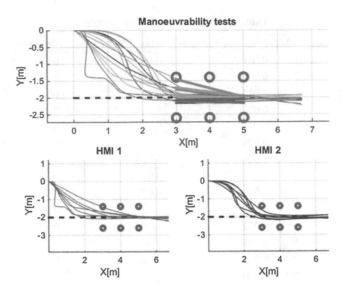

Fig. 9. Manoeuvrability tests (Color figure online)

According to the application each weighting factor value can be increased or reduced. An example could be the HMI control of a space rover, in this case the main objective is to avoid collisions with obstacles (i.e. rocks) and so W_{hit} should be increased. In the case of long vehicles the alignment with the loading station is a mandatory requirement, in those cases it would be recommendable an higher value of W_{θ}. In our case the alignment is an important parameter since the capability to reach a position in space with the desired attitude is a fundamental element for usability of the system a far as the user, in this way, minimizes the need for continuous re-alignments.

In Fig. 10 the relation between the penalty scores achieved using HMI-1 or HMI-2 are reported. The distributions underline and confirm what already stated in the circuit metric, namely that HMI-2 offers a more agile interface. When using HMI-2 the users are able to perform the task in a less amount of time.

Regarding the accuracy in manoeuvring, no explicit evidence was found to state that HMI-2 is better than HMI-1. The number of cone hits and angular driving does not highlight the presence of particular trends; in fact the accuracy seems then related more to the driving skills of the subject rather than to the HMI used.

7.4 Depth Perception Metric

In this case we aim at assessing the depth perception of the subjects when using the proposed HMIs. The test requires moving at the maximum possible speed and stopping the motion as close as possible to a transversal line placed 5 m ahead the starting position. The difficulty of the test is that the frontal view displayed on the monitor implies the visual loss of the ending line when the wheelchair approaches the line, due to the limited field of view of the virtual (and real) camera. This element forces the subjects to extrapolate the position of the line in order to estimate the relative distance and perform the stop manoeuvre at the proper time.

The metric used to assess the depth perception is the one in Eq. (9). Table 4 reports the collected data and the corresponding results.

$$P_D = Dt + |Dd| \cdot W_d + Dv \cdot W_v \tag{9}$$

- P_D is the overall score.
- Dt is the time interval from the first motion till the reaching of the target.
- Dd is the distance between the ending line and the vehicle when this one is stopped (end of the test).
- W_d is the weighting factor for the final distance: 2 s for each 0.1 m before the line, 3 s per 0.1 m after the line (the crossing of a limit it is commonly considered a worse scenario than an early stop).
- Dv is the difference between the maximum admissible speed and the one reached by the user.
- W_v is the weighting factor for the maximum speed mismatch: 0.5 s per m/s. The difference between the maximum possible speed and the one reached by the subject is a parameter also related to the time used to finish the test. This weighting factor is set to have a moderate effect on the metric since the time it is already included and the element of main interest is the distance from the reference line.

In Fig. 12 the relation between the penalty scores achieved using HMI-1 or HMI-2 are shown. The distributions are similar, not underling particular evidences or differences in performances in depth perception. None of the subjects, independently of the HMI, managed to stop closer than 10 cm from the line.

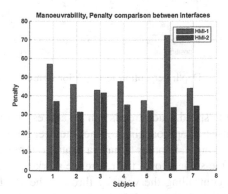

Fig. 10. Manoeuvrability tests, HMIs penalties comparison (Color figure online)

An interesting fact can however be derived from Fig. 11. The main discrepancy between the HMIs is the speed management. When using HMI-1, the subjects are able

Table 3. Manoeuvrability metric, tests results

Subject	HMI	Time [s]	Cone hits	Entry angle [rad]	Penalty [s]
1	1	40	2	−0.113	56.9
	2	28.1	1	−0.060	37.0
2	1	44.9	0	−0.011	46.1
	2	27.3	2	0.001	31.4
3	1	31.1	1	−0.087	43.1
	2	25.8	1	−0.121	41.6
4	1	29.5	2	−0.124	47.7
	2	27.1	0	−0.071	35.2
5	1	34.9	0	−0.022	37.5
	2	25.4	2	−0.023	32.0
6	1	39.1	2	−0.255	72.3
	2	29.7	0	−0.035	33.7
7	1	42.2	0	0.015	43.9
	2	26.1	2	−0.037	34.4

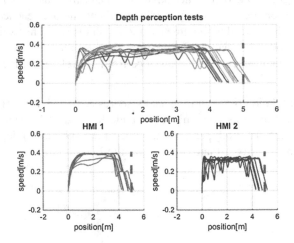

Fig. 11. Depth perception tests (Color figure online)

to maintain a more stable speed. Such trends can be addressed to the behaviour of the eyes during the motion: when approaching to line, the user tends to gaze such specific point on the display, tracking it, in order to have a spatial reference. When the line exits from the field of view, the subject loses the reference marker, and starts using the eyes in a more proper way, controlling the velocity through the HMI. This behaviour has different results in the two HMIs: in HMI-1 it has a limited influence thanks to the intrinsic filtering effect coming from the rather large dimensions of the active areas (variations of gaze inside the active square do not influence the final velocity command). In HMI-2 the variation of gaze causes a variation of the frontal speed, so the subject must continuously correct the speed.

Table 4. Depth perception metric, tests results. The maximum admissible speed was 0.4 m/s

Subject	HMI	Time [s]	Distance [m]	Max speed [m/s]	Penalty [s]
1	1	20.3	−0.787	0.373	28.2
	2	22.6	−0.439	0.361	27.0
2	1	19.7	−0.631	0.398	26.0
	2	20	−0.72	0.366	27.2
3	1	25.1	0.157	0.396	29.8
	2	24.7	0.203	0.346	30.8
4	1	23.3	−0.267	0.400	26.0
	2	22.7	−0.194	0.352	24.7
5	1	17.8	−0.28	0.400	20.6
	2	19	−0.719	0.339	26.2
6	1	22.8	−0.655	0.398	29.4
	2	21.1	−0.428	0.359	25.4
7	1	22.8	−0.138	0.347	24.2
	2	16	−0.158	0.364	17.6

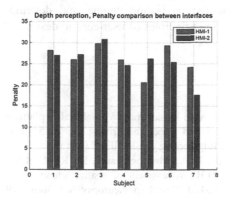

Fig. 12. Depth perception tests, HMIs penalties comparison (Color figure online)

8 Conclusions

This paper focuses on the development of optimized strategies of HMI based on eye trackers by means of a Virtual Reality (VR) environment where several motion metrics were evaluated. To this aim we developed two HMI: HMI-1 is button based; HMI 2 embeds a continuous control law. Both were tested with seven subjects.

For the circuit metrics all subjects managed to achieve the goal with a very limited number of collisions. However, the tests performed using HMI-2 achieved paths definitively smoother than the ones from HMI-1. It is possible to conclude that HMI-2 provides a more agile driving experience.

Regarding comfort, in all the tests the horizontal acceleration remains under the threshold associated to the "comfortable" level. Nevertheless, it must be underlined that the level of RMS accelerations is lower in case of HMI-1; this result is mainly due to a more stable frontal speed when moving. With HMI-2, the continuous control law, together with the eye tracker noise, causes small but continuous variations of the frontal speed leading to a potentially less comfortable driving experience.

Regarding manoeuvrability, HMI-2 offers a more agile interface, performing the same task in less time. About accuracy in manoeuvre, no explicit evidences were found to state that HMI-2 is better than HMI-1. The number of cone hits and angular displacements varies between subjects and interfaces without a specific trend; the accuracy seems then related more to the driving skills of the subject rather than to HMI used.

Regarding depth perception the distributions are similar, not underling particular differences in performances. None of the subjects, independently of the HMI, managed to stop closer than 10 cm from the line.

As an overall conclusion we can state that the HMI-1 is more suitable for precise and localized manoeuvre close to a target while HMI-2 is much better for driving till the approach.

Future work will focus on the refinement of the two interfaces with the possibility to filter the eye tracker noise in order to increase comfort for HMI 2, on the modelling of the wheelchair kinematics, on the enhancing of the depth perception and on the investigation of the driving performances from a subjective viewpoint. This should enable to further refine the navigation engine and develop a real-world robotic wheelchair that matches the principles of user-centric design.

References

1. Ktena, S.I., Abbott, W., Aldo Faisal, A.: A virtual reality platform for safe evaluation and training of natural gaze-based wheelchair driving. In: 2015 7th International IEEE/EMBS Conference on Neural Engineering (NER). IEEE (2015)
2. Buxbaum, L.J., Palermo, M.A., Mastrogiovanni, D., Read, M.S., Rosenberg-Pitonyak, E., Rizzo, A.A., Coslett, H.B.: Assessment of spatial attention and neglect with a virtual wheelchair navigation task. J. Clin. Exp. Neuropsychol. **30**(6), 650–660 (2008)
3. Cooper, R.A., et al.: Virtual reality and computer-enhanced training applied to wheeled mobility: an overview of work in Pittsburgh. Assist. Technol. **17**(2), 159–170 (2005)
4. Fornaser, A., De Cecco, M., Leuci, M., Conci, N., Daldoss, M., Maule, L., De Natale, F., Da Lio, M.: Eye trackers uncertainty analysis and modelling. XXIII Convegno Nazionale A.I. VE.LA., Perugia, 12–13 November 2015
5. Armanini, A.; Conci, N.: Eye tracking as an accessible assistive tool. In: 2010 11th International Workshop on Image Analysis for Multimedia Interactive Services (WIAMIS), pp. 1–4, 12–14 April 2010
6. Mahajan, H.P., et al.: Assessment of wheelchair driving performance in a virtual reality-based simulator. J. Spinal Cord Med. **36**(4), 322–332 (2013)
7. Champaty, B., et al.: Development of EOG based human machine interface control system for motorized wheelchair. In: 2014 Annual International Conference on Emerging Research Areas: Magnetics, Machines and Drives (AICERA/iCMMD). IEEE (2014)
8. Jain, M., Puri, S., Unishree, S.: Eyeball motion controlled wheelchair using IR sensors. World Acad. Sci. Eng. Technol. Int. J. Comput. Electr. Autom. Control Inf. Eng. **9**(4), 906–909 (2015)

9. Clemotte, A., Velasco, M., Torricelli, D., Raya, R., Ceres, R.: Accuracy and precision of the Tobii X2-30 eye-tracking under non ideal conditions. In: Proceedings of the 2nd International Congress on Neurotechnology, Electronics and Informatics, pp. 111–116 (2014)
10. Wood, J.M., Troutbeck, R.: Effect of visual impairment on driving. Hum. Factors: J. Hum. Factors Ergon. Soc. **36**(3), 476–487 (1994)
11. Wood, J.M., Troutbeck, R.: Effect of restriction of the binocular visual field on driving performance. Ophthalmic Physiol. Opt. **12**(3), 291–298 (1992)
12. Wood, J.M., Mallon, K.: Comparison of driving performance of young and old drivers (with and without visual impairment) measured during in-traffic conditions. Optom. Vis. Sci. **78** (5), 343–349 (2001)
13. Lövsund, P., Hedin, A.: Effects on driving performance of visual field defects (1986)
14. Sodhi, M., et al.: Driver Performance Evaluation: Considerations Underlying Selection and Design of Routes. Vision in Vehicles X. Elsevier Sciences Publishers, Amsterdam (2005)
15. Peli, E.: Driving with low vision: who, where, when, and why. Albert Jokobiec's Princ. Pract. Ophthalmol. **4**, 5369–5376 (2008). Elsevier
16. Bowers, A., et al.: On-road driving with moderate visual field loss. Optom. Vis. Sci. **82**(8), 657–667 (2005)
17. Odenheimer, G.L., et al.: Performance-based driving evaluation of the elderly driver: safety, reliability, and validity. J. Gerontol. **49**(4), M153–M159 (1994)
18. Carr, D., et al.: The effect of age on driving skills. J. Am. Geriatr. Soc. **40**(6), 567–573 (1992)
19. Kamaraj, D.C., et al.: Quantifying power wheelchair driving ability. In: Conference Proceedings, RESNA (2014)
20. Castellanos, J.C., Susin, A.A., Fruett, F.: Embedded sensor system and techniques to evaluate the comfort in public transportation. In: 2011 14th International IEEE Conference on Intelligent Transportation Systems (ITSC). IEEE (2011)
21. ISO 2631/1: Evaluation of human exposure to whole body vibration - Part 1: general requirements. International Organization for Standardization, Geneva, Switzerland (1985)
22. Hoberock, L.L.: A survey of longitudinal acceleration comfort studies in ground transportation vehicles. J. Dyn. Syst. Meas. Control **99**(2), 76–84 (1977)
23. Lin, C.-S., et al.: Powered wheelchair controlled by eye-tracking system. Opt. Appl. **36**(2/3), 401 (2006)
24. Gajwani, P.S., Chhabria, S.A.: Eye motion tracking for wheelchair control. Int. J. Inf. Technol. **2**(2), 185–187 (2010)
25. Wästlund, E., et al.: Evaluating gaze-driven power wheelchair with navigation support for persons with disabilities. J. Rehabil. Res. Dev. **52**(7), 815 (2015)
26. Pingali, T.R., Dubey, S., Shivaprasad, A., Varshney, A., Ravishankar, S., Pingali, G.R., Polisetty, N.K., Manjunath, N., Padmaja, K.Y.: Eye-gesture controlled intelligent wheelchair using electro-oculography. In: 2014 IEEE International Symposium on Circuits and Systems (ISCAS), pp. 2065–2068, 1–5 June 2014

An Immersive VR Experience to Learn the Craft of Printmaking

Marcello Carrozzino[1](✉), Cristian Lorenzini[1], Mihai Duguleana[2],
Chiara Evangelista[1], Raffaello Brondi[1], Franco Tecchia[1],
and Massimo Bergamasco[1]

[1] PERCRO – TECIP - Scuola Superiore Sant'Anna of Pisa,
Via Alamanni 13b, 56017 San Giuliano Terme, Pisa, Italy
{m.carrozzino, c.lorenzini, c.evangelista, r.brondi,
f.tecchia, m.bergamasco}@sssup.it
[2] Transilvania University of Braşov, 29, Eroilor Blvd., Braşov, Romania
mihai.duguleana@unitbv.ro

Abstract. This paper presents the AMICA VR system, aiming at exploiting immersive visualization paradigms enabling visitors to be physically and emotionally involved in a virtual experience conceived for the dissemination of the activities related to craftsmanship of printmaking. The developed platform aims at spreading a better knowledge about printmaking by appropriately using Interactive Digital Storytelling and Immersive Virtual Environments, exploiting their features in terms of presence, immersion, interaction and multi-modality.

Keywords: Craft · Engraving · Immersive virtual reality · RGBD camera · Augmented Virtuality · Natural interaction

1 Introduction

Today's constantly evolving technology and growing need for information has led to a proliferation of data and knowledge now available in the digital domain. From mathematics to literature, almost all categories of human knowledge are available in the information-sphere. However there remain certain types of knowledge that are difficult to digitize, store, preserve and share. Manual skills, for example, are difficult for individuals to acquire and, typically, are easily lost. The learning process of motor activities requires a constant and recurrent training almost always based on the emulation of the movements performed by an experienced craftsman. It is extremely difficult to sum up the complex and articulated experience accumulated by an artisan during an entire life of practice. It is equally difficult for a novice to understand the meaning of a gesture from a written text. Indeed, since the Industrial Revolution, entire categories of manual skill have been supplanted by industrial processes or have been lost due to illness or the declining of years of skilled artisans. Because manual learning requires a significant investment of time from both student and teacher devoted to hands-on study and practice, there are few technological means for preserving this knowledge.

Consequently, the products, skill, know how, long-term tradition and tips transmitted so far from our master experts and processes of such craftsmanship (such as

© Springer International Publishing Switzerland 2016
L.T. De Paolis and A. Mongelli (Eds.): AVR 2016, Part II, LNCS 9769, pp. 378–389, 2016.
DOI: 10.1007/978-3-319-40651-0_30

pottery, wood carving, metalsmithing, printmaking, etc.) are in jeopardy of being lost. Taken on whole this constitutes a significant loss for our heritage. Indeed, not only are these crafts an important means of artistic expression, they represent a significant aspect of humanity at large.

Artisan skills are acquired by demonstration, learned by doing [1], and sharpened by practice. Typically, the transfer modality of artisan skills is the learning-relationship between the master artisan and his/her apprentice in the artisan workshop. Watching the master at work is therefore a fundamental step in learning. At the same time, opening craft workshops to the public is the best way to stimulate the interest, promote and raise awareness on this incredibly rich world of knowledge.

The project AMICA (standing for "AMbienti virtuali Immersivi per la Comunicazione delle maestrie dell'Artigianato", i.e. Virtual Environments for the Communication of Handicraft) aims at realizing the purpose of conserving and disseminating such heritage through the use of immersive Virtual Environments (VEs). VEs are interesting instruments to create tools to communicate culture, because information is disseminated through sensory feedback and therefore easy to understand also from not skilled users. These tools might be available in dedicated locations, such as museums, or through the web [2], and use different types of metaphor, including the use of totally abstract environments which act as spatial context for information [3].

AMICA (Fig. 1) aims at exploiting immersive visualization paradigms and Natural User Interfaces (NUI) enabling visitors to be physically and emotionally involved in a virtual experience conceived for the dissemination of the activities related to artisanship. The product of the research consists of an edutainment application proposing to the users a virtual travel in an artisan workshop. The virtual tour is built around a storyboard touching the most significant steps required to produce an artistic print. As a corollary to the virtual application, a web site collecting detailed information and materials collected during the first part of the project is made available on line for a deeper understanding of the procedures shown by the VR application. The resulting platform will become an interactive educational tool showing the involved processes and the competencies needed in order to create an artistic craftwork. The project is focused on the sectors of engraving and printmaking, although it is foreseen to test the replicability of the developed metaphor also to other craft contexts like carpet-weaving. The project has been developed in partnership with 2RC, one of the most famous and renowned Art printwork centers[1], which has granted access to artists, craftsmen and students of the ongoing academic master in Techniques and Management in Editorial Printmaking Art. The director of the 2RC center and the students of the master have been trained in the theoretical aspects of Virtual Environments and have collaborated with us in the definition of the VR application storyboard, making themselves available as the protagonist of the interactive experience. The developed platform aims at spreading a better knowledge about the craftsmanship of engraving and printmaking by appropriately using Interactive Digital Storytelling and Immersive Virtual Environments, exploiting their features in terms of presence, immersion, interaction and multi-modality.

---

[1] http://www.2rcgallery.com.

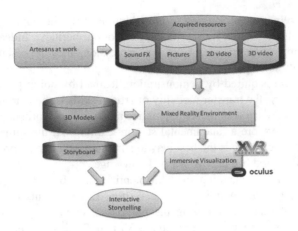

Fig. 1. Conceptual diagram of the AMICA system

2 Related Work

Safeguarding and passing over skills and intangible cultural heritage features is the subject of several experiments, as well as large research projects [4, 5]. Teaching crafts isn't very different from forming skills. Digital fabrication can be combined with craftsmanship to create new objects starting from destroyed ones [6], through 3D printed reconstruction or through 3D recording.

The easiest and more efficient way to transfer practical skills consists in observing and emulating an experienced user. This approach is a perfect expression of the constructivist theory (or better said, leaning by doing), which assumes that if active natural processes are involved in the phase of learning, the efficiency of the knowledge-transfer is much higher [7]. However, this presumes the existence of masters which can be seen here as pedagogical agents willing to train others [8]. These are sometimes hard to find due to several reasons, including the industrial advancements, the demographic shift and the lack of interest in the younger generation. Many of these disappearing crafts need to be preserved as a part of key heritage legacy, for validating possible historic hypotheses, for referencing human cultural diversity and last but not least, for educating generations to come [9].

Several research papers target this field, such as the work described in [10, 11]. Some of the most pursued crafts are those who involve subjects into using their hands (whereas the name: handicrafts). Sculpture is one of the activities which fits this area [12]. Pottery is another [13]; in this case serious games were used to ease the knowledge transfer. Painting is yet another [14]. Handicrafts are not the only crafts which have been tackled; i.e. in [15] the visitors are invited to do wedding arrangements.

Considering the availability a pedagogical agent, as in the case of our study, learning crafts from VR applications would not be possible without means of acquiring his motions. The lower invasiveness of markerless techniques makes them more suitable to capture human motion in natural environments [16].

An alternative solution consists in 3D recording as it meets the needed accuracy, efficiency, robustness and minimal setup criteria. Until a few years ago, acquiring real time data from dynamic scenes was a complex task. With the introduction of Microsoft Kinect, and the possibility of acquiring streams of RGBD data (including, therefore, depth), the burden was lifted and thus many researchers began to expand the field. A particular feature of the Kinect sensor makes it the most often used, as it offers the possibility of dividing the image in foreground and background. Kinect is already at its second generation, evolving from Structured-Light to Time-of-Flight cameras [17].

One of the most common use of 3D recording is to create avatars. In [18] an RGBD camera is mounted on top of an HMD and used to provide a visual feedback of the user's hands. In [19], researchers use simultaneously 2 Kinects to create the full view of a human operator. Similar problems encountered in this study were also discussed in a different setup, based on similar RGBD cameras [20]. When using RGB-D cameras for recognizing a human activity, one can chose among many benchmark datasets already developed, such as: UTKinect, RGBD-HuDaAct, Mivia Dataset, TJU dataset, RGBD activity dataset, and so on [21]. Each dataset has its specifics. For instance, the database RGBD-HuDaAct was created to recognize a set of human activities combining two methods: spatio-temporal interest points (STIPs) and motion history images (MHIs) [22].

In any collaborative VR scenarios, accuracy and speed are very important; as such researchers tried to achieve robust action retrieval through 3D recording and Dynamic Time Warping (DTW) [23]. Other studies focused more on balancing the descriptive power and robustness of the local 3D descriptor, obtaining better object recognition and 3D shape reconstruction and retrieval [24]. Several ideas described above were exploited in initiatives such as the FP7 BEAMING project [25].

The recent spreading of devices interfacing users with interactive applications by means of the innate human means of communication (e.g. voice and gestures), has led to the design of paradigms of natural interaction. Such paradigms, namely Natural User Interfaces (NUIs), relevantly impact both on presence and immersion in VR applications allowing users to execute even complex interactions in the VE. Shafer et al. [26] have studied how natural interaction increases feelings of spatial presence, perceived reality, and enjoyment in video games. In [27] NUIs have demonstrated to enhance user experience in Serious Games applications providing deeper level of engagement and immersion. Roupé et al. [28] used the natural interaction with the VE to ease the navigation and usage of the application. They have also observed that the participants have used their body during spatial reasoning showing that this kind of interfaces can enhance the spatial-perception.

Therefore, we argue that Immersive VEs combined with natural interaction would provide a powerful solution to develop a system to transfer practical skills. Providing in such environment detailed and realistic examples of actions to be observed, by means of 3D recorded video of skilled people executing those activities, should generate a rich experience for users. This way they will be able to start an effective interactive path of knowledge by accessing information inside a real-looking digital environment and selecting custom points of view (including the craftsman's one). Thanks to VR technologies, in fact, users will be able to subjectively experience ("with the artisan's eyes") how the artwork is created by the artisan's hands and which are the processes and the abilities needed to achieve the final result.

3 The Project

The first step of the project was to actually understand how the artisans work. We spent a period inside the 2RC workshop, watching masters and disciples at work and filming their activities (Fig. 2) with a variety of technological means: photo-cameras, "standard" video-cameras, first person action cameras, and RGBD cameras. We also made conversations and interviews with artisans in order to better focus the process of creation and to define the storytelling keypoints. We identified four main phases in the process of printmaking, namely: preparing the metal plate, engraving, colouring and printing. Each of this phase is in turn based on serial steps where artisans use different gestures and tools in order to complete the process.

Fig. 2. Visual material acquired from artisans at work

All of this resources have been used to create the virtual environment (Fig. 3) which reproduces the workshop. We made the choice not to reproduce faithfully the real environment but rather to draw inspiration from it and model a plausible place, taking advantage of the absence of constraints in the digital context and aiming at designing a pleasant and effective experience.

Fig. 3. Particulars of the reconstructed Virtual Environment

Then we had to decide how to breath live in this environment, as a craft workshop is hardly barely a place with tools and instruments but rather a space where humans act, behave and share knowledge. The classic option in Virtual Environments is to use avatars, i.e. digital 3D models of humans which are animated either via motion capture 29 or through motion synthesis. However, in case of complex actions, involving also tools of different types, this would require enormous production efforts running also the risk of misrepresenting the gestures that are the basis of the craft work; moreover, precise devices often require wearing objects that can hinder movements and, therefore, sometimes obstruct the motion they are meant to capture. We therefore decided to acquire artisans' actions and manual abilities using 3D recording by means of depth cameras (Fig. 4). We have used two different kind of devices for recording: ASUS Xtion (range from 0.8 m to 3.5 m) and Primesense Carmine 1.09 (range 0.35 m to 1.4 m). Although the libraries we have developed permit to handle multiple RGBD cameras avoiding or minimizing the known interference between multiple infrared beams [9], this operation leads to better visual results in case of live playback while, when dealing with recorded streams, achieving a good spatial and temporal synchronization between multiple sources proved to be trickier. We made the choice to show two privileged viewpoints: a frontal view of the artisan at work, acquired with the Xtion camera, and a first-person view taken with the Primesense camera from a position as close as possible to the artisan's head; this made multiple simultaneous streams non-necessary for our purposes.

Fig. 4. Example of an acquired RGBD stream

The acquired RGBD streams have been stored in the OpenNI ONI format. Having acquired streams in the real workshop, and not in a purposely set up studio, many undesired features have been recorded that must not appear in the final render. For this reason we have developed dedicated tools enabling loading, editing, processing and mixing the streams (rendered as 3D meshes, after polygonalizing [18, 29] the acquired depth maps) in a Virtual Environment, so as to achieve a particular experience of Mixed Reality, commonly referred as Augmented Virtuality (Fig. 5, left).

The storytelling elements are demanded to the master craftsman, acting as the pedagogical agent, who introduces and explains all the operations involved in printmaking, coordinating the narration with the 3D streams and/or 3D animations showing the same operations. In order to lighten the narrative, the master's tale is occasionally punctuated by questions made by the visitor (i.e. the user of the system).

Fig. 5. The resulting Augmented Virtuality environment (left). The pedagogical agent: the master craftsman (right)

Note that these questions are pre-built and are automatically asked at the right time, therefore there is no active user interaction in dialogs. The artifice we used is based on exploiting 3D audio in order to differentiate the origin of the speeches sounds, with the visitor's sound seemingly coming from the user's head. In order to have the best flexibility in the management of the narrative, and considering that the master's body motion is limited to simple "idle" movements accompanying his speech, we decided to use a CG virtual human (VH) to represent the master (Fig. 5, right) instead of an acquired 3D stream. We also developed a lip-sync module able to animate the VH mouth accordingly to his pre-recorded spoken vocals.

Interacting with the story takes place by means of a visual GUI, made up of 3D floating buttons, which enables "moving" inside the laboratory and observe a specific phase of the process, changing the point of view entering the "craftsman's eyes", selecting a specific object in order to retrieve related information.

4   The System

The system has been designed and realized on top of the XVR technology [29]. This allowed for a good flexibility in terms of support of hardware devices and ease of developing dedicated software add-ons able to expand the capabilities of the framework.

We are currently working on two different versions of the systems, using either the Oculus Rift HMD or a projection-based system (such as the X-CAVE facility at PERCRO laboratory) for visualization (Fig. 6). In the first case user interaction is achieved by using a Leap Motion camera mounted on the HMD front and in charge of retrieving motion data required to animate an avatar of the user's hands and to interact with the virtual environment. In the second case, standard equipment such as a mouse or a joypad can be used to interact with the application GUI.

Dedicated tools have been developed in order to handle the recorded RGBD streams, since existing tools lack of the features needed to opportunely post-process this kind of data. In particular the suite of developed tools allow to trim the stream (in order to select specific portions of the stored data) and to clean the video data in order

Fig. 6. The HMD experience (left); the X-CAVE experience (right)

to make it easier to seamlessly mix it with the virtual environment (Fig. 7). Cleaning operations include:

- removing the background (as extracted from the first frames of the stream, provided that none of the desired objects/actors appear in these frames),
- applying a depth threshold (in order to remove components which lie beyond a certain distance),
- applying a background mask (in order to recover selected portions of the removed background that are instead required),
- applying a stencil mask (in order to finely define portions to be removed).

Fig. 7. Results of the application of post-processing filters to RGBD streams

These two masks are in fact black and white bitmaps that can be easily manually produced starting from a selected frame extracted from the stream. The combination of all these tools allow to separate, with a good precision, the desired content of the stream from the unwanted background/noise.

The main application presents the structure of an immersive interactive storytelling experience. The flow follows a storyboard that is basically a linear sequence of actions, mapping the sequence of the steps of the printmaking process.

When the application starts, a home menu is presented to the user. From here the user can navigate to an explanatory video where it is described what he/she is going to experience and how to navigate in the VE. Otherwise the user can choose to start the virtual journey from one of the four main chapters of the printmaking process. Each main chapter is subdivided in several subchapters.

The application implements the storyboard by interpreting in real time a sequence of instructions that form the Virtual Storyboard (VS). The VS, defined in text files in order to be easily authored by any text tool, and provides the possibility of defining custom key-points that can alter the flow of the application (basically "goto" points allowing to go back and forth along the timeline). The VS allows also to specify camera animations, interactive elements, movements and dialogues. ONI streams showed in the application are also managed through the VS; it is possible to place the animated meshes reconstructed from the acquire RGBD data by specifying their position and orientation, to load/unload and show/hide each ONI stream on demand. Although the systems supports up to 16 ONI streams concurrently, in order to avoid performance issues only one stream is visible and playing at a time. For each step of the storyboard there are 2 different available ONI streams corresponding to two different viewpoints, i.e. a frontal view (as seen from a "visitor") and a first-person view (as seen from the artisan).

The artisan master's virtual human is a HALCA [30] avatar. The module managing the VH allows to move it in the world and to make him talk. In addition to executing pre-recorded animations, the VH manager also allows keeping the eye contact (i.e. the VH always looks towards the camera) and to move the VH lips coherently with the speech. The lip-sync library [31] forces the playback of "visemes" (visual correspondents of phonemes) synchronized with the timing of phonemes extracted by the audio files implementing the speech.

A VideoBox module is also present in the application. This module implements a floating and semi-transparent video screen. The video screen is moved and rotated in the environment coherently with the user position and orientation. Videos are shown in correspondence of particular moments in the storyboard in order to enhance the information given to the user by visually showing concepts and details difficult to express otherwise.

The Leap-Motion Interaction Module (LIM) allows to animate a 3D model of the user's hands and enables the natural interaction with objects in the scene and with the GUI buttons (Fig. 8). By pointing the hand towards such an active element, the action associated with that element is executed. To prevent unwanted selections, users have to point the desired object for half a second. A spinning wheel provides a visual feedback to the user to notify the ongoing action.

Fig. 8. Using the LIM to interact with the Virtual Environment (left). Watching own hands and the artisan's hands at the same time (right)

Generally, an object of the scene becomes selectable when it is introduced by the master during the storytelling. Whenever an object is selected (i.e. if the user palm is on top of the object for more than 0.5 s) it starts floating and orbiting in front of the user in order to allow a better and closer examination. At the same time, the VideoBox shows additional information and details related to the object under examination. By selecting again the object, it is put back in place.

GUI buttons are placed, coherently with what specified in the VS, as 3D elements in the Virtual Environment. Only the "Home" button is always present in the scene. By selecting it, the user can stop the journey at any time and go back to the main application menu. At the end of each sub-chapter, GUI buttons appear allowing to play again the current sub-chapter or to proceed to the next one. An additional button appears when an ONI stream is being played; this button allows to switch the viewpoint from the visitor view to the artisan's first person view and vice versa. Optionally, selectable objects can also act as GUI elements enabling triggering specific keypoints of the VS.

5   Conclusions and Future Work

The system will be demonstrated starting from May in the context of an exhibition at the Gallery of Modern and Contemporary Art (GAMC) of Viareggio, a museum hosting an important collection of printmaking artworks. Several exhibitions showing the current advancement of the system have been held in our laboratory or in other nearby facilities. In April a series of sessions to be held in Art Schools is programmed in order to test and verify the potentials of the system for education and learning. Currently two art high schools, located in Tuscany, have subscribed to the program, and other schools (including junior high schools) have expressed their interest to test the system. The programmed tests will verify the usability of the system and its effects on the transfer of knowledge and on retention. The system implements with limits advanced interaction features, such as the simulation of actually performing operations, but the hypothesis is that immersive features enabling visitors to be "physically" present in the place where certain operation take place, will activate a learning-by-seeing paradigm that should result effective for educational purposes.

We also plan to check the replicability of the developed system to other contexts in the craft sector. We have so far performed a small-scale set of RGBD acquisitions of textile artisans at work at the loom (Fig. 9), in order to demonstrate the possibility of adapting the setup methodology to different craft activities.

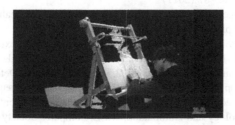

Fig. 9. ONI stream of a carpet-weaving artisan at work

The expected results at the end of the project are the demonstration of the potentials of the VR technology for educational purposes and for digital preservation, and the contribution to the adoption of novel, innovative and replicable forms to preserve, transfer, and disseminate the "invisible" heritage of manual skills leading to the realization of a craft work. This way the technology that, in time, has reduced the relevance of manual abilities, will be in the position to give them back importance and dignity.

Acknowledgements. We warmly thank 2RC Gallery for their invaluable partnership and, in particular, Valter and Simona Rossi, and their collaborators Nicola Salotti, Laura Peres, Elisa Favilli, Irene Puglisi, Elena Mantovani, Laura Fonsa. We also thank Emily Manfredi for contributing to the storytelling text. The **AMICA** project is funded by Fondazione Telecom Italia under the "Beni Invisibili" financing program. The study of the related work and the setup of the test methodology have been carried out in the context of the EU eHERITAGE project.

References

1. Schank, R.C., Berman, T.R., Macpherson, K.A.: Learning by doing. Instr. Des. Theor. Models: New Paradig. Instr. Theor. **2**, 161–181 (1999)
2. Carrozzino, M., Bruno, N., Bergamasco, M.: Designing interaction metaphors for Web3D cultural dissemination. J. Cult. Herit. **14**(2), 146–155 (2013)
3. Ruffaldi, E., Evangelista, C., Neri, V., Carrozzino, M., Bergamasco, M.: Design of information landscapes for cultural heritage content. In: Proceedings of the 3rd International Conference on Digital Interactive Media in Entertainment and Arts, pp. 113–119. ACM, September 2008
4. Skills project, CORDIS EU. http://cordis.europa.eu/project/rcn/103956_en.html
5. Carrozzino, M., et al.: AMICA - Virtual Reality as a Tool for Learning and Communicating the Craftsmanship of Engraving (2015)
6. Zoran, A., Buechley, L.: Hybrid reassemblage: an exploration of craft, digital fabrication and artifact uniqueness. Leonardo **46**(1), 4–10 (2013)
7. Driscoll, M.P., Driscoll, M.P.: Psychology of learning for instruction (2005)
8. Johnson, W.Lewis, et al.: Integrating pedagogical agents into virtual environments. Presence: Teleoperators Virtual Environ. **7**(6), 523–546 (1998)
9. Mitchenson, D.: Safeguarding intangible cultural heritage by creating meaningful transmission experiences. Int. J. Herit. Digit. Era **4**(1), 57–70 (2015)
10. Forte, M.: Virtual worlds, virtual heritage and immersive reality: the case of the Daming Palace at Xi'an, China, chap. 26 (2013)
11. Carrozzino, M., et al.: Virtually preserving the intangible heritage of artistic handicraft. J. Cult. Herit. **12**(1), 82–87 (2011)
12. Lu, P., et al.: Image-based non-photorealistic rendering for realtime virtual sculpting. Multimed. Tools Appl. **74**(21), 9697–9714 (2015)
13. Dagnino, F., et al.: Serious Games design: reflections from an experience in the field of Intangible Cultural Heritage education. In: The International Scientific Conference eLearning and Software for Education, vol. 2. "Carol I" National Defence University (2015)
14. Zhang, X.-M.: Computer simulation of the interaction on pigment and paper in virtual painting. In: Proceedings of the 2014 7th International Conference on Intelligent Computation Technology and Automation. IEEE Computer Society (2014)

15. Mäkilä, T., et al.: The Futuristic History project: recreating history with augmented reality solutions. In: Proceedings of NODEM, pp. 165–170 (2013)
16. Cheng, Z., et al.: Capturing human motion in natural environments. Procedia Manuf. 3, 3828–3835 (2015)
17. Sarbolandi, H., Lefloch, D., Kolb, A.: Kinect range sensing: structured-light versus time-of-flight Kinect. Comput. Vis. Image Underst. 139, 1–20 (2015)
18. Tecchia, F., et al.: I'm in VR!: using your own hands in a fully immersive MR system. In: Proceedings of the 20th ACM Symposium on Virtual Reality Software and Technology, pp. 73–76. ACM, November 2014
19. Chen, Y., et al.: Fast capture of personalized avatar using two Kinects. J. Manuf. Syst. 33(1), 233–240 (2014)
20. Rafighi, A., Seifi, S., Meruvia-Pastor, O.: Automatic and adaptable registration of live RGBD video streams. In: Proceedings of the 8th ACM SIGGRAPH Conference on Motion in Games. ACM (2015)
21. Zhang, J., et al.: RGB-D-Based Action Recognition Datasets: A Survey (2016). arXiv preprint arXiv:1601.05511
22. Ni, B., Wang, G., Moulin, P.: RGBD-HuDaAct: A Color-Depth Video Database for Human Daily Activity Recognition. Consumer Depth Cameras for Computer Vision, pp. 193–208. Springer, London (2013)
23. Zhao, S., et al.: Strategy for dynamic 3D depth data matching towards robust action retrieval. Neurocomputing 151, 533–543 (2015)
24. Salti, S., Tombari, F., Di Stefano, L.: SHOT: unique signatures of histograms for surface and texture description. Comput. Vis. Image Underst. 125, 251–264 (2014)
25. Normand, J.M., Spanlang, B., Tecchia, F., Carrozzino, M., Swapp, D., Slater, M.: Full body acting rehearsal in a networked virtual environment—a case study. Presence: Teleoperators Virtual Environ. 21(2), 229–243 (2012)
26. Shafer, D.M., Carbonara, C.P., Popova, L.: Spatial presence and perceived reality as predictors of motion-based video game enjoyment. Presence: Teleoperators Virtual Environ. 20(6), 591–619 (2011)
27. Brondi, R., et al.: Immersive Technologies and Natural Interaction to Improve Serious Games Engagement. Games and Learning Alliance. Springer International Publishing, Switzerland (2015)
28. Roupé, M., Bosch-Sijtsema, P., Johansson, M.: Interactive navigation interface for virtual reality using the human body. Comput. Environ. Urban Syst. 43, 42–50 (2014)
29. Tecchia, F., et al.: A flexible framework for wide spectrum VR development. Presence 19 (4), 302–312 (2010)
30. Spanlang, B.: HALCA a library for presence research. Rapport technique, Event Lab, Barcelona, Spain (2009)
31. Tanca, C.A.: Progettazione e sviluppo di un modulo software per la creazione e manipolazione di animazioni facciali realistiche in Virtual Humans conversazionali. Master Degree Thesis, University of Pisa (2015)
32. Huang, W., Alem, L., Tecchia, F.: HandsIn3D: supporting remote guidance with immersive virtual environments. In: Winckler, M. (ed.) INTERACT 2013, Part I. LNCS, vol. 8117, pp. 70–77. Springer, Heidelberg (2013)

Time-Based Nonlinear Interactive Player

YanXiang Zhang[(⊠)] and Hui Ye

Department of Communication of Science and Technology,
University of Science and Technology of China, Hefei, Anhui, China
petrel@ustc.edu.cn, yh0819@mail.ustc.edu.cn

Abstract. As a significant part of learning contents for children, natural phenomena and scientific processes could promote cognitive competence and expand their scope of knowledge. However, some of natural processes take a long time while some scientific processes happen at high-speed, making it difficult for children to observe only with their bare eye. Additionally, there is a lack of interaction and exploring interests for children to watch traditional videos. In order to help children learn long-period natural phenomena and high-speed scientific processes, a Time-based Nonlinear Interactive Player (TNIP) is designed. Children are able to control the playback direction and playback speed by moving the mouse left or right and quickly or slowly. The selecting of frame range and frames depend on the drag speed of mouse so as to make the interactive playback smooth. In the aspect of immersive experience, schema integration, real-time feedback and learning interesting, TNIP has the prominent learning advantages over other common instructional media. TNIP could promote the education of children in terms of scientific processes at a deep cognitive level.

Keywords: Time-based Nonlinear · Interactive player · Scientific processes · Long-period · High-speed

1 Introduction

There are numerous factors affecting the understanding of scientific concept by children, including the limitation of cognitive, instructional media and others [1]. As a significant part of scientific concept, scientific processes could promote cognitive competence and expand the scope of knowledge of children. However, some natural phenomena and scientific processes occur in a long-period of time or at high-speed, making it difficult for children to observe them only with their bare eye.

Traditionally, long-period or high-speed phenomena or processes could be recorded by time lapse photography or high speed photography technologies, then it will be retimed to a much slower or faster speed to play in normal digital video players.

Normally, a digital video player allows a simple control of the playback content (stop, backward, forward, elementary controls on the playback speed, and perform random temporal jumps between image frames). Children are used to watch videos with traditional digital video player. But these players are short of interaction especially they could only have fixed playback speeds. Besides, traditional video players in most cases do not provide features to retrieve specific frames. If children are interested in

L.T. De Paolis and A. Mongelli (Eds.): AVR 2016, Part II, LNCS 9769, pp. 390–399, 2016.
DOI: 10.1007/978-3-319-40651-0_31

some specific moments in the video, it is difficult to stop just at a specific frame precisely due to key frame mechanism [2] in video compression and retrieve.

Some research works such as Khronos Projector [3] allow the users to send parts of the image forward or backwards in time, this kind of interaction could bring great enjoyments and emotions to the users. But Khronos Projector focuses more on providing artistic experience than teaching children scientific concept.

Another interesting interactive video observing mode is used in Quick Time VR Object Player, which allows users to grab and rotate the object using the mouse [4]. Nevertheless, it has some shortages for children to observe the long-period or high-speed processes if it is used as an interactive player for scientific process. The object player is used to view an object from the outside and from 360 degrees angle of view. It is suitable for observing a still object with a "look around" mode but does not provide a control over time that is more interesting for observing a scientific process. And in QTVR object movie making, the camera typically moves at 10-degree increments in each direction [5], so usually there are totally 36 frames in a QTVR object, which is very limited to represent natural phenomena and scientific processes that undergo huge changes.

Motivated by these issues, the authors developed a Time-based Nonlinear Interactive Player (TNIP), which aims to go beyond the traditional forms in digital video players, giving the users exclusive temporal control to achieve an entirely new dimension to play with: by dragging mouse freely on the workspace, the contents could be played at nonlinear speed and directions which corresponds to mouse drag speed and direction (Table 1); users could have the experience of controlling the flowing speed and direction of time. By using it, children could observe and learn the long-period and high-speed scientific processes in an interactive way. They can be able to control the playback direction and playback speed of these processes by moving the mouse left or right and quickly or slowly.

During the experiment conducted to use this novel player, most of the users were excited with emotion, thus deeply impressed. Recent research in the cognitive and neurobiological sciences has shown that the relationship between cognition and emotion is more interdependent than separate [6, 7]. So, in fact users could promote their cognition effects by using TNIP to learn, as they could get higher emotion while using TNIP instead of normal digital video players.

During the implementation of this Time-based Nonlinear Interactive Player, there were some issues. For scientific processes, some of them include huge changes, which need plenty of frames to observe clearly. If the frame rate is too high in the interaction, the player will be stuck. On the basis of the problem, we design a mechanism of selecting frames to guarantee a smooth interaction. In this mechanism, the selection of frame range and frames depend on the drag speed of the mouse. With the movement of the mouse, the playback speed is presented in the interface in real time. For children, TNIP has advantages over other instructional media during their study. It remedies the observing limitation of children and improves their cognitive skills of long-period and high-speed scientific processes. We also conduct an empirical study to verify the existence of learning advantages.

Table 1. Contrast between traditional digital video players and Time-based Nonlinear interactive player

	Traditional Digital Video Players	Time-based Nonlinear Interactive Player
Playback speed	Fixed and could be 2x,4x,8x,16x…	No fixed speed, could play at any speed, playback speed is defined by mouse movement speed
Frame retrieving	Could only stop at key frames, and there are many frames between two "key" frames	Could stop at any frame accurately
Feeling of manipulation over contents	Weak	Strong
Feeling of manipulation over time	Very Weak	Strong
Interactions during playing	Weak	Strong, can't play without interaction
Immersive experience	Weak	Strong
Performance when skimming fast or slowly	Frame skip occurs, will play intermittent, not smooth	Could play very smoothly at any speed

2 System Design and Implementations

2.1 Contents for Player

Scientific phenomena play an important role in the formation of children's scientific concept. They not only lead children to understand the principles of the nature, but also develop in them logical abilities. In order to help children learn scientific phenomena better, we select both processes of natural phenomena and scientific experiments. And we classify them by the subject of physics, chemistry, biology and others.

2.2 Shooting

For long-period processes, we calculate the shooting interval by firstly estimating the total time. Then time lapse technology is used to take photos. Finally we get the image sequences. For high-speed processes, we use high-speed camera to shooting videos to capture more details. Then the videos are exported to image sequences. Because some long-time processes take a long time and include huge changes, hence plenty of frames are needed for children to observe the details. Based on many experiments, we set the final total frames of each item from 600 to 1200.

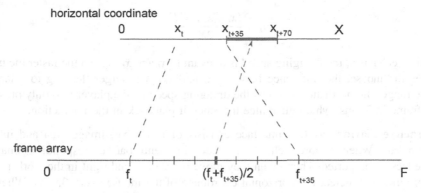

Fig. 1. The mapping relationship between horizontal coordinate and frame array, x_t and x_{t+35} determines the frame selected in the next 35 ms.

2.3 Time-Based Nonlinear Interactive Play Implementation

Frame Selection Mechanism in Real-Time Playing. Some scientific processes include huge changes, which need plenty of frames to observe clearly. But in our interactive player, if the frame rate is too high, the player will be stuck. On the basis of the problem, we design a mechanism of frame selection to guarantee smooth interaction. In this mechanism, the selecting of frame range and frames depend on the drag speed of the mouse.

We suppose the resolution of the image area in the player interface is X × Y (pixel). The playing frame rate is 35 ms per frame which is as fast as normal video's frame rate so that most of computer could play smoothly. The total number of frames of each item is F ($600 \leq F \leq 1200$).

The programs detects the mouse's horizontal coordinates every 35 ms. We suppose that the initial horizontal coordinate as x_t and the final one as x_{t+35} during the mouse's dragging in 35 ms. The horizontal coordinate is mapped to frames (Fig. 1). In the mapping relation, we suppose that f_t corresponds to x_t and f_{t+35} corresponds to x_{t+35}. The following formula could be written:

$$f_t = \frac{x_t}{X} * F, \tag{1}$$

$$f_{t+35} = \frac{x_{t+35}}{X} * F, \tag{2}$$

We select the middle frame f_i between f_t and f_{t+35} for the next frame to be presented in the next 35 ms (from $t+35$ to $t+70$),

$$f_i = \frac{1}{2}(f_t + f_{t+35}), \tag{3}$$

According to the above, we get:

$$f_i = \frac{(x_t + x_{t+35})F}{2X},$$ (4)

In this mechanism, the dragging speed is relevant to x_t and x_{t+35}. So the faster the user moves the mouse, the difference between x_t and x_{t+35} is larger, leading to a larger frame range. But no matter how fast the dragging speed is, the player will only present one frame in 35 ms, which guarantee the smooth playback in the interaction.

Interactive Playing. System interface consists of menu bar, image area and information bar. When children choose an item in menu bar, corresponding images sequences are imported. Then when they move mouse left and right in the workspace, the program will detect the horizontal coordinate of the mouse every 35 ms. When it saves the value of x_t and x_{t+35}, the frame to be presented in next 35 ms is selected according to formula (4).

And when the user moves the mouse right, the process will be shown in a normal order. When the user moves the mouse left, the process will be shown in a reverse order. Besides, the rate of change is presented in information bar. For example, when children interact with the item of 'decay of fruit', with the movement of the mouse, '+(129000 ± 372) times' will show based on the ratio of interactive play speed and physical speed of scientific processes. If the user moves the mouse in a relatively even speed, the first rate '129000' will not change, but only '372' changes so that users could catch it clearly. The flowcharts of interface events of TNIP are as Figs. 2, 3 and 4.

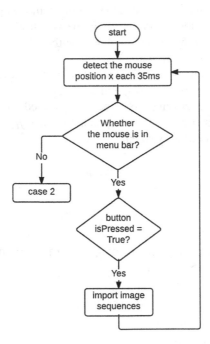

Fig. 2. Flowchart of Case 1 in interface events of TNIP

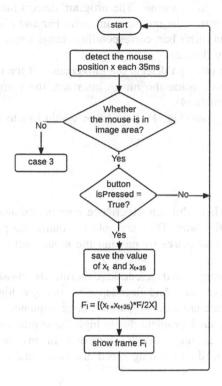

Fig. 3. Flowchart of Case 2 in interface events of TNIP

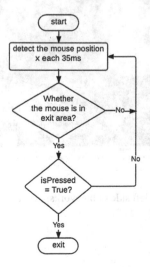

Fig. 4. Flowchart of Case 3 in interface events of TNIP

There are three cases in all events. The program detects the mouse position each 35 ms. Case 1 judge whether the mouse is in menu bar and clicks an item or not. If children click an item in menu bar, corresponding image sequences will be imported into the player for ready (Fig. 2).

Then in Case 2, the program detects the movements of the mouse (Fig. 3). When children move the mouse inside the image interface, the corresponding frame will appear according to formula (4).

Case 3 is an exiting case (Fig. 4). If children would like to exit the player, it will work.

3   Result

We develop a player to help children experience long-period and high-speed scientific processes in an interactive way. They are able to control the playback direction and playback speed of these processes by moving the mouse left or right and quickly or slowly.

Both natural phenomena and scientific experiments classified by subjects are selected as presenting contents. And time lapse technology, high-speed cameras and image processing software are used to get the image sequences.

In order to solve the stuck problem due to high frame rate, we design a mechanism of selecting frames to guarantee smooth interaction. In this mechanism, frame range and frames selected depend on the drag speed and horizontal coordinate of mouse.

Fig. 5. When the mouse is in the left side of the workspace, the first frames are presented (Fig. 5).

Fig. 6. When the mouse is in the right side of the workspace, the last frames are presented (Fig. 6).

4   Empirical Study

To verify the learning advantages of TNIP over other common instructional media towards long-period and high-speed processes, we conduct an empirical study among 200 children aging from 5 to 13 years old. These children are selected randomly from two primary schools and one junior high school.

Considering the interdependence between cognition and emotion, we set four indexes of "immersive experience", "schema integration", "real-time feedback" and "learning interesting" to describe learning effects. And a questionnaire is designed according to these indexes. Because scientific processes include natural phenomena and scientific experiments, we select as contents "decay of fruits" and "wither of flowers" for the former one and "chemical waves" and "candle burning" for the later. For other instructional media, we select print media, material object and traditional video player as control groups. Firstly we present the content of "decay of fruits", "wither of flowers", "chemical waves" and "candle burning" to children by using print media, material object, traditional video and TNIP. Then, we distribute questionnaires to 200 children. They are asked to choose which media provides them with the best effects or experience among the four indexes respectively.

After the end of the evaluation, we got back 193 effective questionnaires, answered by 105 boys and 88 girls.

From Table 2, we could know that 45.08 % of the children think TNIP builds a suitable environment for scientific process learning, because they attain immersive experience with the interaction with TNIP. For schema integration, also 45.08 % of them consider TNIP could make a connection between new knowledge and the experience before. For real-time feedback, nearly half of the children believe they could get best real-time feedback by using TNIP compared to other medium. Besides, the same contents of four media have different level of interests. 62.18 % of them think TNIP makes learning more interesting.

Table 2. Results of empirical study

Learning effects	TNIP (%)	Print media (%)	Material object (%)	Traditional video player (%)	Total (%)
Immersive experience	45.08	18.13	31.09	5.70	100
Schema integration	45.08	18.65	22.28	13.99	100
Real-time feedback	49.74	13.99	24.34	11.91	100
Learning interesting	62.18	10.36	21.24	6.22	100

The overall conclusion is that TNIP offers more learning advantages over other common instructional media in immersive experience, schema integration, real-time feedback and learning interesting. Children could get more emotion experience in these four aspects, which leads to better cognition. So TNIP leads kid to learn scientific processes at a deep cognitive level.

5 Discussion

Based on existing problems of traditional video players, we design a Time-based Nonlinear Interactive Player (TNIP) for children to observe and learn long-period and high-speed scientific processes. They could control the playback speed and playback direction by moving mouse quickly or slowly in the left or right direction. Some scientific processes include huge changes, which need plenty of frames to observe clearly. In order to solve the stuck problem due to high frame rate, we design a mechanism of frame selection to guarantee smooth interaction. In this mechanism, frame range and frames selected depend on the drag speed of the mouse. So children could interact with the player smoothly. In the aspect of immersive experience, schema integration, real-time feedback and learning interesting, TNIP has the prominent learning advantages over other common instructional media. TNIP could promote kid learning scientific processes at a deep cognitive level.

Acknowledgments. The research was sponsored by China National Key Technology Support Program project (project number: 2014BAH15F02) and Student Innovation Training Program project "Research on Teaching Advantages and Technology Realization of Interactive Nonlinear Video Player".

References

1. Weiqian, Z.: On children's mental age characteristics of science learning. Stud. Presch. Educ. **1**, 23–25 (2007)
2. Wolf, W.: Key frame selection by motion analysis. In: Proceedings of the 1996 IEEE International Conference, vol. 2, pp. 1228–1231 (1996)
3. Cassinelli, A., Ishikawa, M.: Khronos projector. In: Cox, D. (ed.) ACM SIGGRAPH 2005 Emerging technologies (SIGGRAPH 2005), Article 10. ACM, New York, NY, USA (2005)
4. Chen, M., Mountford, S.J., Sellen, A.: A study in interactive 3-D rotation using 2-D control devices. In: Proceedings of ACM SIGGRAPH Computer Graphics, vol. 22, no. 4, pp. 121–129 (1988)
5. Chen, S.E.: Quicktime VR: an image-based approach to virtual environment navigation. In: Proceedings of the 22nd Annual Conference on Computer Graphics and Interactive Techniques, pp. 29–38 (1995)
6. Pessoa, L.: On the relationship between emotion and cognition. Nat. Rev. Neurosci. **9**(2), 148–158 (2008)
7. Liu, Y., et al.: The interaction between cognition and emotion. Chin. Sci. Bull. **54**(22), 4102–4116 (2009)

Author Index

Printed in the United States
By Bookmasters